RESEARCH IN ECONOMIC HISTORY

Supplement 3 • 1984

TECHNIQUE, SPIRIT AND FORM IN THE MAKING OF THE MODERN ECONOMIES: ESSAYS IN HONOR OF WILLIAM N. PARKER

RESEARCH IN ECONOMIC HISTORY

A Research Annual

TECHNIQUE, SPIRIT AND FORM IN THE MAKING OF THE MODERN ECONOMIES: ESSAYS IN HONOR OF WILLIAM N. PARKER

Editors: GARY SAXONHOUSE
Department of Economics
University of Michigan

GAVIN WRIGHT
Department of Economics
Stanford University

SUPPLEMENT 3 • 1984

 JAI PRESS INC.

Greenwich, Connecticut   *London, England*

CONTENTS

LIST OF CONTRIBUTORS

Jeremy Atack

Department of Economics,
University of Illinois,
Urbana

Fred Bateman

School of Business,
Indiana University,
Bloomington

J. de Vries

Department of History,
University of California,
Berkeley

Barry Eichengreen

Department of Economics,
Harvard University

George Grantham

Department of Economics,
McGill University

Elizabeth Hoffman

School of Management,
Purdue University

Joel Mokyr

Department of Economics,
Northwestern University

Lon L. Peters

Portland, Oregon

Gary Saxonhouse

Department of Economics,
University of Michigan

George J. Sheridan, Jr.

Department of History,
University of Oregon,
Eugene

Ross Thomson

Department of Economics,
New School of Social
Research, New York

Gavin Wright

Department of Economics,
Stanford University

WILLIAM N. PARKER

PREFACE

Anyone who sets out to write a *Festschrift* for William N. Parker quickly learns that there are many more individuals eager and qualified to participate than one volume can possibly include. No other economic historian has so many admirers and well-wishers. Parker's graceful prose, his sharp wit and warm good humor, his uncanny ability to find order and understanding in a maze of disparate facts, his consummate skill at puncturing nonsense and pomposity—all these are well known to those who have read his articles and reviews, and all are doubly appreciated by anyone lucky enough to hear him hold forth in his characteristic role as moderator, discussant, or raconteur. Like Franklin D. Roosevelt, Parker is the sort of individual whose public appearance creates a sense of personal closeness with large numbers of readers and listeners.

The contributors to this volume are only a subset of a subset of the world's stock of Parkerphiles. Excepting coauthors Atack and Hoffman, we are all former Parker students who have carried on in the field of economic history. Our only defense against the charge of undue exclusivism is that we have something to add to the outside world's appreciation for Bill Parker, namely, that his distinctive influence has not been restricted to the channels of the written word or the conference podium, but rather spreads through an oral tradition conveyed to generations of students. Though we have, "like the sons and tenant families of a landowner, spread out from his intellectual shelter in all directions,"[1] the core of our thinking about economic history comes from Parker. In what may be unique among *Festschriften*, every essay in the volume originates in an idea, a suggestion, or a line of study begun by Parker. Our hope is that in this way we will combine to do him an honor which is well deserved, and to advance the approaches to economic history which he has long championed and with which he has imbued his students.

Our contributions have clustered in three broad areas of Parker's thought: (1)

the explicit study of organizational forms in economic history, in the belief that these forms—family farms, industrial cartels, land tenure arrangements, systems of labor management—are "created through human action," but in turn "mold and channel human action";[2] (2) quantitative measurement of growth in national income and agricultural productivity, the "harsh statistical method, against which none of the devices of an historian's rhetoric can avail";[3] and (3) the analysis of technological progress in the distinctive Parker mode. As he argues, better than any of us might try to restate it: "Technology is, like land settlement, a point where the social and material universes meet. The internal logic of its history, like that of geographic discovery, is set not only by human energy, ingenuity, enterprise, and social structure, but also by the harsh facts of nature and by the levels at which, in relation to the human mind's powers of inquiry and inspiration, nature keeps her secrets."[4]

Doubtless we have come up short. Having fallen under the influence of Parker only in combination with the specialized training programs of American history and economics departments, our essays are all industry or sector or perhaps even national studies. We have not nominated a member to imitate the broad strokes of the master's own brush, as illustrated for example in the lecture whose title we have adapted for our collection.[5] Instead, we have settled for the journeyman's task of doing specialized research while trying to be faithful to Parker's teaching. The essays make some effort to acquaint the general reader with this heritage,[6] but they will surely not adequately convey the mixture of gratitude, respect, affection, and loyalty that we all feel. Imperfect as our efforts may be, we present them to our teacher with our thanks.

Gary Saxonhouse
Gavin Wright

NOTES

1.   William N. Parker, "American Economic Growth: Its Historiography in the Twentieth Century," *Ventures*(Fall 1968): 73, with reference to the students of Frederick Jackson Turner.

2.   William N. Parker, "From Old to New to Old in Economic History," *Journal of Economic History* 31(March 1971): 13.

3.   William N. Parker, "Labor Productivity in Cotton," *Agricultural History* 53(January 1979): 235.

4.   William N. Parker, "Old Wine in New Bottles," *Journal of Economic History* 26(March 1966): 102.

5.   William N. Parker, "Technique, Spirit and Form in the Growth of Modern Industry," Sir Ellis Hunter Memorial Lecture, University of York, England, February 1973.

6.   An opportunity for more extended sampling will soon be available in a two-volume collection of Parker's essays entitled *Europe, America and the Wider World: Essays in the Economic History of Western Capitalism,* to be published by Cambridge University Press.

ACKNOWLEDGMENTS

For assistance in preparing this volume, the contributors extend thanks to Stanley Engerman, Heywood Fleisig, Richard Porter, Martha Shiells, Richard Sylla, Steven Webb, Thomas Weisskopf, and also to Sally Whelan of JAI Press Inc. Special appreciation goes to Yvonne Parker for the picture.

PART I

ORGANIZATIONAL FORMS IN ECONOMIC HISTORY

TWO FORMS OF CHEAP LABOR
IN TEXTILE HISTORY

Gary Saxonhouse and Gavin Wright

I. INTRODUCTION

In his presidential address to the Thirtieth Annual Meeting of the Economic
History Association in 1970, W. N. Parker urged a return to "the interest of the
earlier old economic historians in institutional forms," the study of "how social
organizations are created through human action and how in turn they mold and
channel human action." This advice recalls to mind the concerns of Parker's
own early work on the organizational structure of the German coal industry, in
which he found that the system functioned efficiently to channel individual
abilities and energies along productive lines, despite the absence of a conscious
plan for promoting these ends. As he put it: "An anthill, after all, can grow at a
rapid rate, but we would be hard put to find any ant more enterprising than
another."[1] (In typically Parker fashion, he proceeded to deflate his own conclusion by footnoting a study of *The Ant World,* which found that in isolation some

Technique, Spirit, and Form in the Making of the Modern Economies:
Essays in Honor of William N. Parker
Research in Economic History, Suppl. 3, pages 3–31
Copyright © 1984 by JAI Press Inc.
All rights of reproduction in any form reserved.
ISBN: 0-89232-414-7

ants were "just bone lazy" while others "beavered away at a great pace, like a dog searching for a bone.")

Taking Parker's injunction as its inspiration, this study takes up the choice between two old chestnuts of American industrial history: the *Waltham system* in which young women lived in dormitories while working in the mills for a brief period of their lives; and the *Rhode Island* or *Slater system* of company-supplied housing and employment on a family basis. Of the two great triumphs of cheap labor competitors in textiles history, Japan over Lancashire and the American South over New England, the first chose Waltham while the second followed Slater. In other major respects the two episodes are remarkably similar, offering us a rare opportunity to identify the effects of labor systems themselves. Significantly, when H. Fukuhara came to the South to study the cotton mills and report back to Japan, his interest centered overwhelmingly on matters of labor organization (job assignments, age and marital status of workers, payment on time or piece rate), rather than technology, raw materials, marketing, or finance.[2]

In the next section, we argue that the choice of labor system at an early phase of an industry's history may be interpreted as a rational economic choice, in the manner of the "new institutional history." From this beginning, however, we then argue that each system had corollary features and evolutionary tendencies which were not necessarily part of the originator's plan. Many developments which American observers attribute to inherent features of technology or industrialization are refuted by the Japanese example, and hence are more properly traced to the labor system. The contrast reveals the importance of institutional forms and the wide range of social outcomes consistent with a single technology.

II. MARKET AND FAMILY-BASED LABOR SYSTEMS

So much has been written about the early mills of Lowell and their robust young women workers that extended description is not necessary.[3] First established in the wake of the War of 1812 by a group known as the Boston Associates, mills of this type recruited young unmarried women from the farms of New England. The women were required to live in company boardinghouses and to adhere to strict rules of conduct enforced by the "housemothers." The companies sought educated workers of good character, whose commitment to mill work was distinctly temporary, perhaps three to four years on average. Though the system declined in the late antebellum period, it is rightly viewed as a notable American innovation which helped to adapt factory technology to the American setting. Idyllic accounts of these years found in the *Lowell Offering* and in the reminiscences of Lucy Larcom and Harriet H. Robinson were well known to Japanese industrial leaders of the late nineteenth century, who gave close attention to foreign examples in matters of organization as well as technology.[4]

The family labor system, which preceded and survived the Waltham system in New England, was less a product of conscious design and is more difficult to define with precision. Distinguishing features, however, were the recruitment of large families for residence in company-owned housing, combined with a more-or-less explicit stipulation that the family would provide a certain quota of workers to the factory. The designation "Rhode Island system" comes from Slater's early mills said to be modeled on the English pattern; but family-labor mills were also found in Connecticut and southern Massachusetts (hence the later references to the "Fall River system"), and elsewhere in New York, New Jersey, and Pennsylvania.[5]

Some writers have questioned whether the Rhode Island pattern should be called a "system" at all.[6] It is true that many smaller mills simply used whatever labor could be coaxed from nearby farms. But as soon as labor requirements began to outrun the local pool, those companies had to recruit at a distance and invest in housing facilities, both of which required some degree of commitment to a labor "system." Frequently, substantial investments in community infrastructure were involved, which tended to commit the labor strategy along certain lines. Slater's recruitment ads were explicitly directed toward "large, growing families," and as the Fall River superintendent of public schools commented in 1868:

> The families are large . . . and the mill owners are not willing to fill up their houses with families averaging perhaps ten members and get no more than two of all the number in the mill. The families are also, in most instances, so poor that the town would have to aid them, if the children were taken from their work.[7]

The implicit suggestion that Fall River mills set piece rates on a "family wage" basis tends to confirm Wallace's assertion (concerning Rockdale): "The factory treated the domestic family, not the individual, as the unit of production."[8] To the student of the so-called New South of the post–Civil War period, these accounts (and many others like them) have an uncannily familiar ring.

The Japanese and Southern cotton industries employed labor systems similar to the Waltham and Rhode Island systems. The contrast is most vividly illustrated by the percentage of women workers (see Table 1), which stayed above 80 for Japan while declining below 40 in the South. Young Japanese girls were recruited from the farms to live in boardinghouses and work for short periods prior to marriage (90 percent of a typical cohort having departed within three years of entry). In the South, the mill village system held sway from antebellum times until well after World War II. Each family was expected to meet a quota of workers as a precondition for obtaining housing. Can the analogy to the early New England systems give us some perspective on the divergent "cheap labor" paths?

One insight which comes quickly from the comparative approach is the difficulty of interpreting these institutional choices in consistent ideological terms. A recent book by Dwight Billings, for example, views the Southern mill village as an embodiment of "plantation paternalism," an attempt by landed classes to transfer traditional social relationships to a factory setting—a formulation in-

Table 1.   Females as Percentage
of Cotton Textile Labor Force

Japan		U.S. South		India	
1897	78.5	1880	57.6	1884	22.5
1909	83.0	1890	52.1	1894	25.9
1914	83.3	1900	46.6	1909	22.1
1920	80.0	1910	37.0	1924	21.6
1925	80.6	1920	38.2		
1930	80.6	1930	39.1	1934	18.9

Sources: G. Saxonhouse, ''Country Girls,'' p. 100; U.S.
Bureau of Labor, Report on Condition of Wom-
en and Child Wage-Earners (1910), Vol. I, p.
31; 13th Census (1910), Vol. X, p. 41; 14th
Census (1920), Vol. X, p. 186; 15th Census
(1930).

spired by what he takes to be the typical Japanese industrial pattern (in amalgamation with the ideas of W. J. Cash).[9] Setting aside a logical difficulty—antebellum plantation laborers were black, not white—this interpretation suffers from the contradiction that the same industry in Japan was utterly ''un-Japanese''! And this was so, despite the efforts of strong Japanese advocates of the family system. A 1912 book by Rieman Uno argued with vigor and cogency that a family-based system would improve employee health and morale, reduce turnover, and raise productivity.[10] His case seems so powerful, yet his crusade so unsuccessful, that one must ask what considerations he may have omitted.

A second line of explanation, discussed in the New England literature, associates the choice of labor system with capitalization and new technology. The Waltham mills were much larger, integrated spinning and weaving using the latest power-driven machinery, and paid their workers in cash rather than goods or company-store credits (as was frequently the case in Rhode Island).[11] But here again these correlations do not hold up for the latter-day cases. The Japanese mills were large by American standards, but they did not integrate spinning and weaving (as most Southern mills did). As Uno noted, the erection of boarding-houses for a homogeneous group of workers is almost surely fixed capital *saving,* especially when compared to the costs of building an entire community of houses, stores, churches, libraries, etc.[12] And as for the notion that modern textile machinery required ''older'' workers, it runs contrary to the central technological trend of the entire nineteenth century, which was toward *reduction* of the strength and experience required of operatives, adapting job content for ''a succession of learners.''[13] The ''young women'' of the Japanese mills were clearly ''children'' by modern standards.

The grain of truth in the link between scale and the dormitory system lies in the likelihood that the Lowell mills would not have been able to recruit the large number of workers needed in any other way, except at prohibitive expense. This possibility points toward a third type of explanation—conditions of labor supply. The shape of the labor supply curve is the one consideration that Uno over-looked; more recent research has shown that prevailing industrial wages in pre-war Japan were below the supply price of male farm operators, when that supply price is taken to include the costs of closing out the farm and moving an entire family from the rural village.[14] Which is to say that Japan could not have switched to the family system, despite its advantages, except at greatly increased wage levels.

What the Japanese and Waltham mills had in common was a labor pool drawing upon financially pressed family farms, but where the adult farm operator was not threatened by wholesale dispossession and eviction. Japanese farm fami-lies might lose ownership of their land, but they could still expect to continue farming their traditional acreage as tenants.[15] Similarly, the Lowell girls typ-ically came from middle-class farm-owning families in northern New England.[16] From these families, the supply price of unmarried daughters on a temporary basis was well below that of any other family members; in both cases, firms were able to attract them from long distances very early.

There was one key difference, however: Japan had a well-developed rural market in female farm labor, transactions unheard of in the United States.[17] According to a deeply rooted cultural norm, white American women did not do field work, and employment opportunities for them were so restricted one might fairly say there was ''no market'' for their labor. In the Japanese case, the supply price was market-determined; in the U.S. case, the supply price was determined on the individual farm and may often have been negative (from the family's point of view). For these reasons, a major part of the transaction in Japan was the recruitment bonus paid by the employer to the family. There may be some analogy between this bonus and the motives Lowell girls listed in traditional accounts (paying off a family mortgage, putting a brother through college), but the most recent research indicates that the majority were saving money for their own security.[18] Either way, the prevalence of goals defined *external* to the mill setting virtually required that payment be made in cash.

In the South the family system also seems to have been dictated by the character of labor supply, most strikingly in the case of William Gregg's un-sucessful effort to replicate the boardinghouse system at Graniteville in the 1840s.[19] Presumably he could have done so at a higher wage, but poor Southern families had neither security of land tenure nor well-developed wage labor mar-kets to turn to. For large landless families, the mill village offered the only way to hold the family together as an economic unit, while providing parents a return on the labor of their daughters as well as their sons. From the employer's standpoint, the supply price of the family as a package was therefore less than the

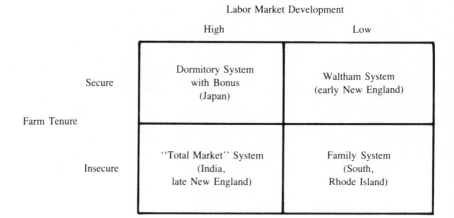

Figure 1. Origins of Textile Labor Systems

sum of the supply prices of the separate components, while at the same time the system carried the prospect of obtaining some mature labor at bargain rates. But where the household had no security against destitution, it was rational for the mill to provide family housing even where the labor of the adult members was not utilized. This was so, because of the absence of urban development in the antebellum South.[20]

The argument is summarized in stylized fashion in Figure 1. The term *labor market development* is not easy to define with precision, but in this context we refer specifically to the geographic density and variety of wage-earning opportunities, as well as the availability of employment for women. Only the combination of a labor pool cut off from agrarian ties and a well-developed array of job opportunities would lead firms to abandon the "family economy" altogether as a labor strategy. In the modern era, such developments have also been associated with an increase in wage costs and a decline in the importance of the textiles industry as a whole.

III. THE DEMOGRAPHY OF THE FAMILY SYSTEM

The preceding section considers how social organizations are created through human action; we now turn to how in turn social organizations mold and channel human action. In both Japan and the U.S. South, the industry began with a completely inexperienced labor force; in both cases, experience levels rose over time, and in the South the composition of the labor force shifted markedly toward older workers, particularly men (see Tables 2 and 3). In Japan, these changes are widely attributed to the rise of "employer paternalism," the improvements in

Table 2. Length of Service, Japanese Cotton Textile Industry

	1897	1918	1927	1936
Less than 1 year	46.2	50.3	18.3	29.5
From 1 to 2 years	23.3	18.4	19.8	20.5
From 2 to 3 years	13.3	11.1	17.2	15.4
From 3 to 4 years	7.7	9.3	11.9	14.9
From 4 to 5 years	4.7		7.9	
Total less than 5	95.2	89.1	75.1	80.3
From 5 to 10 years	4.6	7.0	17.5	11.9
Above 10 years	0.2	3.9	7.4	7.8

Source: G. Saxonhouse, "Country Girls," pp. 101, 103.

Table 3. Age–Sex Composition
Cotton Textile Labor Force,
U.S. South, Four States
(percentages of total operatives)

1880	Male	Female
Age		
10–15	13.9	14.0
16–24	16.9	29.4
25 & over	12.1	13.8
1980		
10–15	12.4	12.4
16–24	19.1	26.7
25 & over	18.6	10.8
1900		
10–15	14.1	15.7
16–24	22.2	21.1
25 & over	19.4	7.3
1920		
10–15	2.5	2.5
16–24	24.7	19.8
25 & over	36.0	14.3

Source: G. Wright, "Cheap Labor," Table III.

dormitory living conditions, and opportunities for personal development which were initiated in an effort to stabilize the work force and cut recruitment and training costs.[21] In the United States, these changes are most commonly interpreted as a decline in the relative demand for female and "child labor," resulting from the introduction of new machinery "beyond the physical and nervous capacity of women," requiring "greater physical endurance and concentration than women possess."[22]

The accumulation of experience in the South was far more rapid than in Japan, a direct reflection of the difference in labor systems. Though mill owners complained constantly about "the moving disposition of mill people,"[23] studies of payroll records show that average work experience *at particular mills* quickly surpassed Japanese levels (see Table 4). Since this measure neglects experience

Table 4. Mean Work Experience, Japanese Spinning Industry and Two North Carolina Textile Mills (years)

	Japan	Alamance Mill	Royal Cotton Mill
1891	1.15	3.37	
1892	1.42	4.44	
1893	1.53	5.01	
1894	1.64	4.98	
1895	1.78	5.38	
1896	1.93	6.34	
1897	1.72	5.95	
1898		7.29	
1899	2.16	6.82	
1900	2.37	7.03	
1901	1.83	6.70	
1902	1.98	7.94	
1903	2.75	6.57	
1904	2.98	7.75	1.11
1905	3.18	7.81	1.41
1906	3.26	9.49	1.59
1907	3.33	8.62	1.65
1908	3.23	9.02	2.00
1909	3.13	9.72	1.65
1910	2.50	9.74	1.99
1911	2.56	10.89	2.33
1912	2.44	10.28	2.67
1913	2.28		3.07
1914	2.29		3.15
1915	2.46		3.19
1916	2.49		
1917	2.53		2.81

(Continued)

Table 4. (*Continued*)

	Japan	Alamance Mill	Royal Cotton Mill
1918	2.25		3.31
1919	2.30		3.89
1920	2.69		3.79
1921	2.97		4.48
1922	2.82		4.30
1923	2.94		4.58
1924	3.03		4.42
1925	2.99		5.05
1926	2.97		4.81
1927	3.16		4.97
1928	3.42		5.30
1929	3.22		6.08
1930	3.69		
1931	3.45		
1932	3.29		
1933	3.07		
1934	2.81		
1935	2.85		

Sources: Alamance and Royal compiled from payroll samples, Alamance Company records, Southern Historical Collection, University of North Carolina; Royal
Cotton Mill records, Duke University Library. Japanese data are estimated from
cohort data, except for benchmark years. G. Saxonhouse, "Productivity
Change in Japanese Spinning," (Ph.D. dissertation, Yale University, 1971).

from other mills, it understates the aggregate accumulation. In comparative
terms the Southern employers had little to complain about. The link between
these results and the labor system is supported by evidence from Japan that
workers housed on a family basis had significantly lower turnover than the
dormitory girls.[24]

Average experience for the Japanese work force did grow, however, and this
growth played an important part in the productivity growth of the industry. In an
earlier study, Saxonhouse was able to show that the apparent impact of paternalism on these trends is illusory. If we follow particular cohorts of entering workers through time, we find no clear trend toward increasing stability: the average
entering worker continued to leave the industry within two years. The increase in
average experience for the aggregate work force occurred because the small
percentage of "stayers," the 10 percent or so who stayed on beyond three years,
gradually accumulated with the passage of time. The precise rate of accumulation, of course, depended upon the growth rate of industry employment, and
Saxonhouse was able to generate a pattern of increasing experience after 1918
from an extremely simple entry–exit function (see Table 5). The importance of

Table 5. Actual and Simulated Length
of Service, Japanese Cotton Textile
Industry (months)

	Actual	Simulated
1924	33	36.2
1927	38	38.1
1930	46	44.8
1933	37	35.4

Sources: G. Saxonhouse, "Country Girls," p. 106.

worker experience for productivity was recognized, but it was not readily subject to influence by the employers, given the other features of their labor system and the competitive environment.[25]

In the Southern case the prima facie evidence for structural change in the demand for women and child workers appears stronger. Not only did the male–female proportions reverse themselves in 40 years, but two available surveys of age at first employment for women workers seem to show a rising trend. Of women working in 1907, 60.5 percent began work at less than 14 years of age; of those working in 1922, only 30.2 percent had started that young (see Table 6, Part A). If, however, we look at a particular age cohort (25–29 years, which roughly compares entry in the early 1890s to entry 15 years later), we find no decline whatever in the fraction beginning work below age 14 (see Table 6, Part B). Far from suggesting a decline in the demand for child labor, the age-specific figures show that the median age of new hires was *lower* in the later than in the earlier years.

Buoyed by this preliminary finding, we have attempted to track the evolution of the labor force more comprehensively, using an entry–exit pattern appropriate to the family system. As Table 6 shows, most workers began as teenagers, the median age being less than 15. The data in the 1907 survey on "months since beginning work" for 15-year-olds suggest a roughly uniform distribution of beginning ages from 10 to 15, with little difference between boys and girls in this respect.[26] This is just what we would expect in a family system where decisions are being made by the family, and where the major expansion of the labor force took the form of the migration of new families to the mill villages. Above age 15, however, a marked difference emerged between males and females, reflecting the different character of family attachment: the young men could leave to take wage-paying jobs in agriculture, but the young unmarried women had no such choice. As Table 3 shows, males aged 16–24 were the "missing" demographic category in the early years, numerically only about half as prominent as females of the same age.[27] It is primarily in this category that the family system was linked to an "outside" labor market.

Table 6. Age of Women Beginning Work, Southern Cotton
Textiles, 1907 and 1922 (percentage distribution)

	1907		1922	
	%	Cum%	%	Cum%
A. All women working:				
Under 14	60.5	60.5	30.2	30.2
14 & under 16	19.9	80.4	35.2	65.4
16 & under 18	10.6	91.0	14.0	79.4
18 & under 20			6.7	86.1
20 & under 25	9.0		5.6	91.7
25 & over		100.0	8.3	100.0
B. Women aged 25–29:				
Under 14	42.9	42.9	42.2	42.2
14 & under 16	7.9	50.8	22.2	64.4
16 & under 18	11.1	61.9	11.9	76.3
18 & under 20			8.1	84.4
20 & under 25	38.1		11.9	96.3
25 & under		100.0	3.7	100.0

Sources: U.S. Bureau of Labor, *Women and Child Wage-Earners,* Vol. I, p. 234; Women's Bureau, Bulletin No. 52, pp. 144–145.

The years 16–24 were particularly crucial for young men, because those who stayed beyond age 25 or so were unlikely ever to leave the industry. Apparently, someone with no farm experience by that point, but accustomed to mill work from early childhood, had virtually no real choice thereafter. Women, on the other hand, began to drop out of mill work gradually in their 20s after marriage or perhaps after the birth of their first child. These statements emerge, however, not from independent evidence on exit rates but from the replication exercise. A qualitative summary of the entry–exit pattern is displayed in Figure 2.

The simulation proceeded in two stages. Initially, the annual labor force change for each sex was taken as predetermined, and the age-specific exit rates were adjusted by trial and error so as to replicate the age structure over time, taking 1880 as the base year. These sex-specific exit rates (which were assumed to hold for the entire period 1880–1920) were then applied to the *total* labor force change in conjunction with the assumption that exactly 50 percent of new entrants were male in all years. The resulting age–sex structure is displayed in Tables 7 and 8, in comparison with available benchmark data.[28] Despite the extreme simplification, we find that a stable behavioral structure, largely derived from the logic of family relationships over the life cycle, can account for more than 80 percent of the decline in the female share of workers between 1880 and 1920, and tracks the age structure of employment closely down to 1915! There is

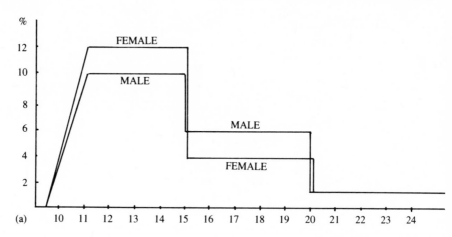

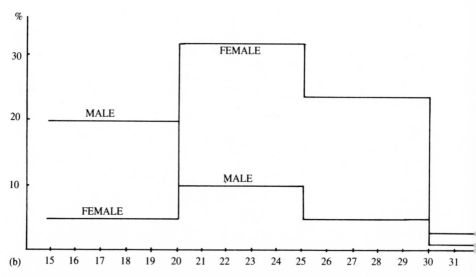

Figure 2. (a) Distribution of Age Beginning Work. (b) Rates of Departure from Textile Employment.

no question that structural change occurred after 1915 (or perhaps slightly earlier for women): despite growth in total employment, child labor virtually disappeared between 1915 and 1920. This very sudden development, however, is much more readily attributed to the Keating–Owen child labor act of 1916, and other state-level legislation, than to any deep technological imperative.[29]

We do not mean to contend that the behavior structure actually was unchanged

Table 7.   Age Distributions of Male and Female Southern
Textile Workers, 1890–1920 (actual and simulated)

		Male		Female	
		Actual	Simulated	Actual	Simulated
1890	24 & under	62.9	62.3	78.4	79.6
1900	15 & under	25.3	27.4	35.5	35.7
	16–24	39.9	37.1	47.7	47.5
	25–44	27.2	30.4	14.5	15.1
	45 & over	7.2	5.1	2.2	1.7
1907	15 & under			26.7	27.6
	16–24			52.6	53.9
	25–44			18.6	16.5
	45 & over			2.1	1.9
1910	15 & under	18.6	18.6	26.5	27.2
	16–24	22.4	20.0	35.7	37.8
	25–44	47.5	52.0	34.7	32.6
	45 & over	11.5	9.4	3.1	2.4
1915	15 & under	14.4	15.4	17.4	24.9
1920	17 & under	14.0	23.6	24.8	42.0
	18–24	28.9	19.8	36.2	34.8
	25–44	40.4	39.9	32.7	19.4
	45 & over	16.7	16.7	6.3	3.8

Sources: See Table 3 and text.

Table 8.   Sex Distribution of Southern
Textile Workers, Actual and Simulated

	Actual	Simulated
1880	57.2	57.2
1890	52.1	49.1
1900	46.6	47.1
1910	37.0	45.1
1915	35.0	42.6
1920	38.2	41.3

Sources: See Table 3 and text.

over 1880–1915. The exit pattern almost surely changed, because of fluctuations in agricultural prosperity and because the productivity of the adults who brought their families to the mills during the 1880s and 1890s was surely lower than the later generation of adults who had grown up in the mills. Doubtless, by allowing for such structural change within the period, we could replicate the facts even more closely, but since we have already strained the limits of the available data, we prefer to stop with the more modest claim that the essential outlines of labor force change—the expansion and subsequent decline of child labor, and the swing to males—were generated endogenously by the evolution of the family system, not by technology or other demand-side changes. Of course, the entire Japanese experience rebuts the idea that "modern technology" required adult male labor.

An alternative interpretation of the process just described may be found in the writings of the critics of the mill village system during the interwar period, who argued that the system was *consciously designed* to achieve this end. According to Herbert Lahne, the village was "a vehicle perfectly calculated from all angles to restrict the development of the workers into independent free-acting citizens."[30] In a chapter entitled "The South Buries Its Anglo Saxons," Frank Tannenbaum wrote that all Southerners agreed: "once a mill-worker, always a mill-worker. Not only you, but your children and children's children forever and ever."[31] Were the lives of the millworkers molded and channeled by "social organization," or was the organization designed precisely to channel them in a particular direction?

Just how far into the future the mill owners of 1880 and before were able to see, we cannot say. But the claim that the system was designed as an exploitative instrument from the beginning seems excessive on several counts. The roots of the system stretched far back into antebellum times, whereas the vigorous criticism waited until well into the twentieth century, and came mostly from non-Southerners.[32] Employers were not able to tie their workers to any one mill, and the limited array of job opportunities in the Piedmont cannot be entirely blamed on them. Despite these remarks, there is little question that mill owners did come to see quite early that the best training for future mill work was mill work itself, and that they actively sought to socialize young people into factory life. Consider, for example, the following statement made at the American Cotton Manufacturers Association in 1910:

> But if you can get them young enough—yes, I say young enough, because I know as every other cotton mill man knows in the South, who has had anything to do with these people, you must commence with them while they are young—and if you commence with them young enough you can train them to work, to acquire industrious habits, and become excellent worksmen and good citizens. If you wait until they are sixteen, eighteen, or twenty years old, it is too late, for they are already becoming atrophied in body and mind to such an extent they don't want to work, and will not work.[33]

Mill owners were not, therefore, either entirely responsible for nor entirely innocent of the rise by the 1920s of a generation of mature, predominantly male workers who had known nothing but mill life. They probably did not desire all of the consequences of this development.

IV. ASSIGNING WORKERS TO JOBS

It frequently happens that divisions of labor by sex, by age, or by race which vary widely between one economic setting and another will nonetheless be viewed by local observers as dictated by inherent human productivities or by technology. Harriet Herring, long-time student of Southern textile workers, listed as one of the advantages of the mill village the fact that "cotton mills have jobs for men and women, and in the early days for children, in about the same proportion in which they are available for work in families. . . ."[34] Such a statement reverses the implied direction of causality: because the Southern mills used the family system, they *designed* a system of jobs so as to make use of all of the labor available from the family. The contrasting cases of Japan, India, and the South show just how malleable job assignments could be under essentially similar technologies.

It is instructive to try to identify just which tasks were most readily shifted between men and women. In both countries, there were some relatively heavy, unskilled jobs that were all male, and in both cases virtually all of the technical jobs in machine maintenance were male. Ring-frame spinners were predominantly female in both cases. But many of the other semiskilled machine-tending jobs which were done by women in Japan were almost exclusively male in the South: examples include the positions of draw-frame tender, slubber tender, speeder tender, slasher tender, beamer tender, and warp-tying machine tender.[35] Differences in organization and terms make comparisons difficult, but some idea of the contrast is conveyed by Table 9, which compares the staffing of a representative Japanese firm with Fukuhara's remarkably detailed sketch of the Durham Manufacturing Company in 1902. The comparison is hampered somewhat by the fact that Japanese firms were not yet vertically integrated at that time; but when Japanese firms did move into weaving, these jobs too were done by women. In 1930, 62 percent of weavers in the South were male, while 83.3 percent of Japanese weavers were female.[36]

Other criteria for job assignments include age and experience. Table 10 displays scraps of data suggesting that an age hierarchy prevailed among the rooms, the gap between spinners and weavers stretching up to 10 years shortly after 1900.[37] The Japanese figures on median experience show much smaller differentials, with only carding matching the Southern pattern. Of course, age medians and experience medians cannot be used interchangeably, but the evidence on age

Table 9.   Male and Female Job Assignments,
Japanese Cotton Spinning Firm (June 1907)
and Durham Manufacturing Company (1902)

	Durham		Japan	
	M	F	M	F
Engine and repair section	7	0	8	0
Picking, mixing, scratching	6	0	14	6
Speeder section	27	6	11	79
Slubbing frame	4	0	0	10
Intermediate frame	5	0	0	28
Roving frame	5	6	0	30
Spinning section	41	43	15	153
Ring spinner	6	40	0	120
Finishing and bundling or preparing	12	27	33	203
Weaving	81	60	—	—
Cloth and dye sections	12	0	—	—
Total	186	136	81	441

Sources: Fukuhara, pp. 13–19.

at first employment (cited in the preceding section) suggests that most of the weavers had started out as spinners or doffers. By the 1920s, Japanese experience differentials had opened up somewhat (see Table 11), along lines roughly similar to the South; but except for the predominately male picker room, there was no more than a year's difference in median experience between any two departments.

Can we identify a general principle underlying these assignment patterns? Reflection on the institutional systems suggests that the allocational principles were actually quite different. In the Japanese case, employers confronted an elastic supply of relatively homogeneous labor at an externally established wage. The "assignment problem" approximated a textbook example of equating relative wages to relative marginal products: in practice, this meant always using cheap female labor unless the male productivity advantage was large. In the South, by contrast, firms were not buying individual units of labor but a family package. The supply price of any one type of labor was low, given that the "family wage" (the sum of the earnings of the members) was high enough to keep the family in the village. Hence the assignment problem had much more of the character of allocating a given *stock* of resources so as to maximize output, the wage structure being largely arbitrary. "Endowed," as it were, with a heterogeneous pool of workers without market-determined wage rates, the Southern firms' task was to develop rules for relating worker attributes to job requirements and to design jobs so as to find some useful work for everyone. It is

Table 10.   Age and Experience by Job

Kanegafuchi Spinning Mill, 1903 (Hyogo Mill No. 1)	Median Years Experience		
	Men	Women	Total
All occupations	1.4	1.6	1.6
Carding	0.8	1.5	1.4
Drawing and slubbing	3.0		3.0
Ring spinning	1.7	2.2	2.0
Finishers	1.9	1.5	1.6

Durham Manufacturing Co., 1902	Median Age		
	Men	Women	Total
Picking	40		40
Carding	27		27
Drawing and slubbing		24	24
Spinning (87% female)			17
Doffing (79% male)			17
Weave preparation (69% female)			27

Hyogo Mill No. 1, 1910	Mean Years Experience		
	Men	Women	Total
Mixing and scratching	3.1	2.4	2.7
Carding	2.7		2.7
Drawing and slubbing	3.1	1.5	1.6
Spinning	2.1	1.1	1.2
Finishing	3.9	1.8	2.0

Source: Sanji Mutō, Shihaininkai (unpublished), No. 783,1268; Fukuhara, pp. 13–19.

rather like the contrast between capitalist farms using wage labor and family farms (or under certain assumptions, slave plantations) allocating a given amount of land and labor.[38]

One implication of this analysis is that the degree of vertical integration in the industry, until now only a complicating factor, is associated with the difference in labor systems. The Japanese mills engaged in a carefully limited set of activities, comparing marginal value-added to marginal wage costs at every point. The Southern mills, on the other hand, tried very early to *expand* their array of productive activities to exploit the comparative advantage of the older workers in weaving, dyeing, finishing, etc.[39] (The exceptions to this pattern, the spinning mills of North Carolina, were primarily smaller establishments able to draw a predominantly young female labor force from nearby farms.) From this perspective, it is correct to associate the adoption of the automatic loom with the swing

Table 11.   Median Age and Experience by Department

U.S. South, 1922 (women)	Median Age	Median Experience[a]
All departments	25.0	8.3
Carding	30.2	11.9
Spinning	22.0	6.0
Spooling	30.1	11.8
Weaving	27.1	9.7

	Women		Men	
Japan, 1930	*Med. Age[b]*	*Med. Exp*	*Med. Age[b]*	*Med. Exp*
All departments	16.8	3.1	25.9	6.1
Picking, carding	32.5	3.6	28.5	5.8
Draw frames, etc.	18.6	3.2	25.0	5.6
Spinning	14.9	2.9	23.8	5.7
Doffing, reeling	16.9	2.8	27.2	6.6
Weave preparation	15.7	2.6	24.9	5.4
Weaving	17.8	4.0	23.7	5.2

[a]Estimated from information in Tables V and VI of source.
[b]Estimated by subtracting 1.5 from Confucian age.
Sources: Women's Bureau Bulletin No. 52; Rōdō Tōkei Jitchi Chōsa Hokokushō.

toward adult male labor; but the causation does not run from technology to labor so much as from labor supply to diffusion.[40]

A second set of implications lies in the greater importance attached in the South to occupational titles, associated with jobs assigned more-or-less explicitly on observable worker attributes such as sex, age, and race. Despite the much larger number of workers in the Japanese mills, as compared to Southern plants of comparable scale, we do not observe major differences in the proportions of the work force assigned to each of the major processes or rooms. *Within* the rooms, however, the Southern workers were often subdivided into job categories by sex, a practice not prevalent in Japan. A good example is the position of doffer, the job of removing the full bobbins from the spinning frame and replacing them with empties; in the South it was almost exclusively a boy's job. In the South in 1907, there was one doffer for every 1.67 ring spinners; but of the 522 employees of the Nakashima mill in the same year (see Table 9), not a single doffer could be found, nor any similar category suggesting a specialized assignment of that sort. Another example from the other end of the seniority spectrum is the position of loom fixer, an elite all-male category in the United States. The South in 1930 had one loom fixer for every three weavers, but the Japanese survey of the same year (which recorded 17,477 weavers) did not list "loom fixer" as a category.

It is not difficult to argue that the use of sex as a basis for job assignment is economically rational. If there are any costs of "mixing," such as white workers objecting to working with blacks, or boys and girls distracting each other, a segregated pattern will dominate mixed alternatives.[41] And if, on a statistical basis, the aptitude of girls for machine-tending exceeds that of boys, it will be more efficient to divide responsibilities and assign by sex than to assign randomly or to include both tasks under the same job. So long as the job categories are not excessively narrow or rigid, and so long as *some* "swing" occupations can accommodate surpluses or deficits elsewhere, job segregation need not involve static inefficiency.[42] Indeed, almost the entire shift in sex composition of the Southern work force occurred within the largest single job category, weaver, which was nonsegregated. At some point, however, job assignments on the basis of sex, age, or race may acquire a social or institutional character which is not readily changed when conditions alter.

V. WAGE DIFFERENTIALS AND WAGE PROFILES

A third set of implications concerns the differences in "wage structure" in the two cases. In Japan wage levels were largely determined externally to the industry, or at most externally to the firm in the case of experienced workers. In the South, only the wage rates of young adult males were directly influenced by an outside labor market, and the scope for possible variation around this numéraire (subject only to the constraint that the "family wage" exceed its supply price) was large. Rather than a wage attached to an *individual* as in Japan, wages in the Southern mills were attached to *jobs,* and occupational differentials were much more significant.

These points are illustrated in Table 12, which compares wage differentials by department and sex in the Hyogo Mill and the Durham Manufacturing Company. What is striking is the greater heterogeneity of payments at Durham. At Hyogo the male/female wage ratio was highly stable across all departments; the only rooms paying above-average wages are those with all-male workers. At Durham there really was no "sex differential" as such, the females earning more than males in two departments—this was particularly notable to Fukuhara—but room-to-room differentials were extreme for both sexes. In Japan the mills paid a premium whenever they used male labor, even in unskilled tasks. In the South, many kinds of male labor were cheap, though there also were all-male occupations which were highly paid. The contrast looks much the same in the aggregate data for 1930 (see Table 13).

From the foregoing, one might expect that the wage–experience profile would be flatter in Japan than in the South, reflecting the lesser degree of differentiation among jobs. When we compare the profiles for women workers, however, we find that the opposite is true (see Table 14). After four or five years of service,

Table 12.   Wage Differentials, Hyogo Mill No. 1 (1910)
and Durham Manufacturing Co. (1902)

	Dept. Wage Average	Male Wage Average	Female Wage Average	Male Wage / Female Wage
Mixing	1.01	1.63	1.00	1.87
Scutching	1.77	1.77	—	—
Carding	1.59	1.59	—	—
Drawing	1.03	—[a]	.98	—[a]
Intermediate frames	1.06	1.75	1.01	1.73
Spinning	.84	1.56	.80	1.96
Finishing	.97	1.67	.90	1.85
Bundling	1.79	1.88	.88	2.14
Waste	1.09	1.54	.81	1.88
Technicians	1.81	1.81	—	—
Machinery, etc.	2.49	2.49		
Total		1.74	.87	2.00

[a]Two male workers.

the Japanese women were able to increase their earnings at a much faster rate. From the information that older women were relatively more numerous in the South and received a relatively lower wage, one would conclude that the difference in profiles is strictly a female labor supply-side phenomenon, perhaps only indirectly a result of the labor system. However, the available evidence on *male* age earnings profiles (which is unfortunately extremely limited for the United States) raises doubt about such simple interpretation (see Table 15). Adult males, who by the 1920s were even more numerous than females, had a much steeper profile, less regular than the Japanese men but essentially similar. The resolution to this question lies in the *interaction* between male and female opportunities, which in turn takes us back to the different relationship between wages and occupations in the two countries.

The critical occupation is weaver, which was always paid by piece rate. The average premium for male weavers of about 10 percent shown in Tables 12 and 13 does not represent discrimination but simply a productivity advantage of males over females, on average.[43] Both male and female weavers were well paid relative to other operatives, but for women there was no further step on the ladder. Males, however, could look forward to promotion to such jobs as foreman, section hand, and loom fixer. Now if we ask whether such "vertical segregation" were based on discrimination or on differences in aptitude, the answer has to be, some of both: those who rose to the top in the rank of weaver tended to be men, but it is hard to believe that the sex differences were so great as to justify the complete exclusion of women from these positions. Nor can the policy be attributed to differences in technical education. The great majority of

Table 13. Relative Wages
by Occupation, 1930
(dept. wage/average)

	Japan	U.S. South
Picking, carding	1.21	.91[a]
Male only	1.39	.91
Female only	.82	—
Draw frames, etc.	.99	1.07[b]
Male only	1.36	1.10
Female only	.93	.95
Spinning	.88	.80
Male only	1.39	.66
Female only	.84	.80
Doffing, spooling	.95	.92
Male only	1.56	1.02
Female only	.87	.81
Weave preparation	.96	1.17[c]
Male only	1.34	1.26
Female only	.84	1.05
Weaving	.99	1.20
Male only	1.33	1.24
Female only	.95	1.14
Loom fixers	—	1.49
All male employees	1.46	1.07
All female employees	.87	.86

[a]Picker tenders, card tenders and strippers, card grinders.
[b]Draw-frame tenders, slubber tenders, speeder tenders.
[c]Warper tenders, beamer tenders, slasher tenders, draw-
ing-in.
Sources: Rōdō Tokei Jitchi Chōsa Hokokushō; 15th U.S.
Census (1930), Vol. 4, Table 11 for each state.

foremen and superintendents as of the 1920s had begun work in unskilled positions at an early age, and had little, if any, formal education.[44] Dale Newman
reports that many workers felt that loom fixer positions were passed out as
rewards for long service, most weavers of both sexes believing that they understood the operation and repair of the machinery at least as well as the "fixers."[45]

In Japan most of these considerations just did not arise. It is true that most of
the highest paid technical and managerial workers were men, and that at the most
detailed level of job categories a nominal segregation prevailed. But women so
dominated the ranks of operatives, that the slowly emerging cadre of experienced

Table 14. Women's Experience–Earnings Profile,
U.S. South (1921/22), Japan (1930)
(relative to 3–4 years of experience)

	Georgia	South Carolina	Alabama	Japan
Less than 6 months	.613	.749	.636	.678
6 months to 1 year	.740	.845	.816	.773
1–2 years	.822	.895	.838	.891
2–3 years	.870	.955	.899	.950
3–4 years	1.00	1.00	1.00	1.00
4–5 years	.854	1.00	1.06	1.06
5–10 years	1.02	1.03	1.02	1.16
10–15 years	1.15	1.16	1.21	1.25
15–20 years	1.21	1.19	1.20	1.32
More than 20 years	1.18	1.17	1.15	1.35
Median years	4.3	6.3	4.1	3.6
Percent > 10 years	27.9	34.4	25.7	4.6

Source: Womens Bureau Bulletins No. 22, 32, 34.

women were moved into jobs such as "group head," "trainer," "inspector," or "short-term reorganizer." In this way the women were able to earn more, but also to stay on the job much longer in life. In the South the markedly higher "retirement" rate for women above age 45 than men (see note 28) was surely not due to any inferiority of a physiological sort, but to the fact that men were able to move into assignments that were less physically demanding in the later years.

We have attempted an econometric test of our argument, by comparing wage-determination function for Japan and for the Royal Cotton Mill (see Table 16).

Table 15. Men's Experience–Earnings Profiles

	Alamance Mill, 1911/12	Royal Cotton Mill, 1929	Japan, 1930
Less than 6 months	{ .778 }	.896	.694
6 months to 1 year		1.14	.802
1–2 years	.878	1.00	.851
2–3 years	.913	1.06	.893
3–4 years	1.00	1.00	1.00
4–5 years	1.09	1.14	1.05
5–10 years	1.17	1.24	1.21
10–15 years	1.17	1.32	1.45
15–20 years	1.20	1.85	1.64
20–25 years	{ 1.45	{ 1.53 }	1.73
More than 25 years			1.77

Table 16. Regression Coefficients, Log Earnings Against Experience and Room Assignment (t-ratios in parenthesis)[a]

Variable	March 1913 [1]	March 1923 [2]	March 1926 [3]
A. Royal Cotton Mill: Individual Data			
Constant	1.23*** (10.0)	2.49*** (17.7)	2.54** (16.7)
Experience	.135*** (6.67)	.025*** (2.02)	.026** (2.51)
Experience squared	−.005*** (4.71)	−.000 (0.81)	−.000 (1.00)
Sex	.006	−.104	−.409***
Sex*exp	−.008 (0.21)	.015 (0.52)	.015 (0.71)
Sex*exp squared	−.000 (0.23)	−.000 (0.29)	−.000 (0.30)
Card room	.056 (.045)	−.124 (0.87)	−.259 (1.71)
Spin room	−.201* (1.70)	−.383** (3.05)	−.290* (1.98)
Engine room	.195 (0.84)	−.000 (0.00)	.365 (0.86)
Outside	.532* (2.13)	−.270 (1.07)	−.364 (1.36)
R²	.325	.164	.253
N	285	208	257
	1927	1930	1933
B. Japan: Grouped Data[b]	[4]	[5]	[6]
Constant	0.11*** (4.46)	−0.07*** (3.58)	−0.17*** (7.16)
Experience	0.07*** (13.7)	0.07*** (20.4)	0.06*** (24.9)
Experience squared	−0.001*** (7.28)	−0.001*** (10.7)	−0.001*** (19.2)
Sex	−0.29*** (11.39)	−0.31*** (15.9)	−0.60*** (26.4)
Sex*exp	0.03*** (4.21)	0.01 (1.22)	0.06*** (15.5)

(*continued*)

Table 16. (Continued)

Variable	1927 [4]	1930 [5]	1933 [6]
Sex*exp squared	-0.002*** (6.24)	-0.001*** (4.75)	-0.004*** (19.1)
Preparatory	-0.02 (0.92)	0.00 (0.29)	-0.00 (0.07)
Spin room	-0.09***	-0.07***	-0.06***
Finishing	-0.06*** (3.45)	-.01 (0.80)	-0.00 (0.21)
Packing	0.01 (0.20)	0.03 (1.03)	0.03 (0.77)
Other	0.00 (0.00)	0.03* (1.73)	0.00 (0.23)
R^2	.854	.943	.969
N	288	288	288

[a]Excluded room dummy is weaving.
[b]Weighted by $\sqrt{n}$.
 *Significant at 10 percent level
 **Significant at 5 percent level
 *** Significant at 1 percent level

The hypothesis is that wages in Japan were determined by individual attributes, such as experience and sex, whereas in the South, earnings were heavily influenced by job assignments. The results generally confirm these patterns, but differences in the character of the data in the two cases make it difficult to define statistical tests appropriately. The Japanese data are cell means for room and experience categories from surveys of over 15,000 workers in 1927, 1930, and 1933. The Royal Cotton Mill data are developed from the records of a single firm; so far as we know, however, this is the only available American data set which combines experience, earnings, and job assignment information for both men and women workers. It is obvious from Table 16 that the overall fit is much better for the Japanese regressions, but we are unable to say how much of this difference results from the use of grouped vs. individual data.

Despite this problem in comparability, however, the regressions support the larger role for job assignments at the Royal mill. Taking the room dummies as a group, we are able to detect a statistically significant effect in the Japanese data (reflecting the high statistical precision of all of the Japanese estimates). However, the contribution of these dummies to explaining the overall variance in earnings is trivial: in 1930, for example, a model with only experience and sex terms explains 93.0 percent of the variance, while the full model explains 94.3

Table 17. Contribution of Room
Dummies to Explained Variance[a]

	Royal			Japan	
	ΔR^2	$\dfrac{\Delta R^2}{R^2}$		ΔR^2	$\dfrac{\Delta R^2}{R^2}$
[1]	.050	.153	[4]	.024	.028
[2]	.057	.345	[5]	.013	.014
[3]	.019	.076	[6]	.002	.002

[a]Numbers in brackets represent the columns in Table 16.

percent. In the Royal regressions, the relative importance of the room dummies is much greater. The comparison is summarized in Table 17. In every case, the relative contribution of room dummies to explained variance is many times greater than in Japan.

VI. SOME IMPLICATIONS

We have endeavored in this paper to show something of the malleability of industrial technology in its use of various types of labor on various terms. An implication is that there is an essential indeterminateness to the social implications of industrialization, at least so far as the requirements of technology itself are concerned. At the same time we have tried to show the continuing effects of an institutional system which, having been established by human choice, then runs its own course, generating behavior which is often mistaken for entrepreneurial brilliance or perversion. In this era of international comparisons, it is instructive to learn that a 1902 Japanese visitor urged his countrymen to learn from the management practices of the Southern mills, noting particularly the high skill, diligence, and morale of the American workers, the quality of supervision, the absence of drunkenness, and the strong sense of mutual obligation between employers and employees.[46] If this seems excessive, one should also note that a Southerner who returned Fukuhara's visit viewed the Japanese mills as grim prisons, the workers attracted by misrepresentations and kept against their wills in overcrowded, unventilated barracks.[47]

While the Southern system thus had certain advantages in morale, stability, and the "spread" of production into weaving and dyeing, it is not so clear that the dynamics of the system were as favorable. As Parker wrote:

Fortunate indeed is the society in which the social structure . . . is relatively fluid, in which the number and kinds of jobs are well suited to the supply of individuals becoming available for them, and in which the structure of economic activity channels individual . . . ambitions and energies directly and efficiently into productive work.[48]

The very eagerness of the Japanese girls to leave gave the system flexibility in matters of job assignments and work organization, and the relative scarcity of males meant that the system was eager to make efficient use of those women workers who chose to stay on. In the South, by contrast, the work force came to be dominated by men who had invested their identities and career aspirations in their jobs. As a result the system made poor use of mature experienced women and may well have become top-heavy with older men by the 1930s.

These Southern mill workers were not unionized, but the mature mill village community developed strong notions of appropriate work organization and employer behavior. This kind of "moral economy" perception made drastic changes difficult. The bitter strikes over the "stretch-out" and wage cuts in the late 1920s and early 1930s, which did so much to earn the mill villages their sordid reputation, were marked by a sense of betrayal on the part of the workers at attempts to change accepted job definitions and work norms.[49] The Japanese were also faced with weak markets during the interwar period and had to accommodate to a relatively drastic abolition of night work as of 1930, but this did not stop them from a major expansion of production and exports in the midst of the worldwide Great Depression.

But it would be foolish to attribute every development in both industry histories to the labor systems alone, and this is not our intent. A full account would have to consider that the international marketing opportunities in the two cases were quite different, because the Southern industry had grown up behind a tariff wall. And after 1933 labor conditions in Southern textiles became heavily influenced by federal pressures. Our point is that the historical setting in which these events took place had been shaped by the evolution of two systems of "cheap labor" put in place many decades earlier.

NOTES

1.   "From Old to New to Old in Economic History," *Journal of Economic History* 31 (March 1971), pp. 12–13; "Entrepreneurship, Industrial Organization, and Economic Growth: A German Example," *Journal of Economic History* 14 (Fall 1954), p. 400.

2.   H. Fukuhara, *Minami beikoku bōseki jijō* (Osaka: Dainihon bōseki rengokai, 1903).

3.   The best general treatment remains Caroline F. Ware, *The Early New England Cotton Manufacture* (Boston, 1931). A significant recent study is Thomas Dublin, *Women at Work* (New York: Columbia University Press, 1979). Useful contemporary materials and descriptions may be found in Benita Eisler (ed.), *The Lowell Offering: Writings by New England Mill Women 1840–1845* (Philadelphia: Lippincott, 1977).

4.   Gary Saxonhouse, "A Tale of Japanese Technological Diffusion in the Meiji Period," *Journal of Economic History* 34 (March 1974), esp. p. 161.

5.   Ware, pp. 199 and 210–213; John R. Commons and Associates, *History of Labour in the*

United States (New York, 1918), Vol. I, pp. 173, 418, and 422. Anthony Wallace's description of Rockdale, near Philadelphia, is remarkably similar; *Rockdale: The Growth of an American Village on the Early Industrial Revolution* (New York: Knopf, 1978), pp. 36–39, 66–67, and 172.

6. Norman Ware, *The Industrial Worker 1840–60* (Boston, 1924). "The Rhode Island system . . . was not a conscious method at all, but simply a growth along English lines with the material at hand" (p. 74). See also Gary Kulick and Julia C. Bonham, *Rhode Island: An Inventory of Historic Engineering and Industrial Sites* (U.S. Dept. of the Interior, 1978), p. 8.

7. Massachusetts Senate Document 21 (1868), quoted in Edith Abbott, "Study of the Early History of Child Labor in America," *The American Journal of Sociology* 14 (July 1908), p. 29.

8. Wallace, p. 172. For an explicit analysis of the use of the family by industrial employers, see Barbara M. Tucker, "The Family and Industrial Discipline in Ante-bellum New England," *Labor History* 21 (Winter 1979/80), pp. 55–74.

9. Dwight Billings, *Planters and the Making of a "New South"* (Chapel Hill: University of North Caroline Press, 1979), esp. chs. 5–6. A good antidote to Billings is David Carlton, "Builders of a New State," in Walter J. Fraser and Winifred B. Moore (eds.), *From the Old South to the New* (Westport, Conn.: Greenwood Press, 1981).

10. Riemon Uno, *Shokkō mondai shiryō* (1912), Vol. W, pp. 90–128.

11. See particularly Howard M. Gitelman, "The Waltham System and the Coming of the Irish," *Labor History* 8 (Fall 1967), pp. 231–235; Kulick and Bonham, p. 8.

12. Uno, p. 100. See Edith Hadcock, "Labor Problems in the Rhode Island Cotton Mills 1790–1940," *Rhode Island History* 14 (July 1955), p. 88; Peter Coleman, *The Transformation of Rhode Island 1790–1860* (Providence: Brown University Press, 1963), p. 231.

13. This phrase is from Samuel Batchelder, *Introduction and Early Progress of the Cotton Manufacture in the United States* (Boston, 1863), p. 89.

14. Yukio Masui, "The Supply Price of Labor: Farm Family Workers," in Kazuchi Ohkawa, Bruce Johnston, and Hiromitsu Kaneda (eds.), *Agriculture and Economic Growth: Japan's Experience* (Princeton, N.J.: Princeton University Press, 1970).

15. One survey found that nearly 70 percent of previously landed farmers remained as tenants after losing their lands (1899–1916). Teikoku Nōkai, *Hōmpō jisakuten no sōyō* (Tokyo, 1920), p. 6.

16. Dublin, pp. 23–36.

17. A detailed wage series is reported in R. Minami, *The Turning Point in Economic Development: Japan's Experience* (Tokyo: Kinokuniya, 1973), Table 7-6, p. 148.

18. Ibid., pp. 36–41.

19. Ernest M. Lander, Jr., *The Textile Industry in Antebellum South Carolina* (Baton Rouge: LSU Press, 1969), pp. 60–61.

20. Many studies have shown the sparsity of Southern rural wage-earning opportunities well into the twentieth century. A good example is William N. Parker and D. G. Davies, "The Agricultural Adjustment to Urban Growth," in F. S. Chapin, Jr., and S. F. Weiss (eds.), *Urban Growth Dynamics* (New York: Wiley, 1962).

21. Koji Taira, *Economic Development and the Labor Market in Japan* (New York: Columbia University Press, 1970), pp. 119–127.

22. U.S. Census (1900), Vol. IX, Pt. III, p. 32; Robert W. Dunn and Jack Hardy, *Labor and Textiles* (New York, 1931), p. 91. See also Melvin T. Copeland, *The Cotton Manufacturing Industry of the United States* (Cambridge, 1912), p. 114; Jack Blicksilver, *Cotton Manufacturing in the Southeast* (Atlanta, 1959), p. 28.

23. Statement by M. Allred, Granite Falls Manufacturing Co:, in North Carolina Bureau of Labor and Printing, 18th Annual Report (1904), p. 104. Every annual report contains a sampling of these complaints in the section "Letters from Millmen."

24. Uno, p. 174.

25. This paragraph is based on Saxonhouse, "Country Girls," pp. 102–106. Analysis of the difficulty facing firms attempting to raise experience levels may be found in Saxonhouse, "A Tale of

Japanese Technological Diffusion in the Meiji Period,'' *Journal of Economic History* 24 (March 1974). The importance of worker experience in productivity growth is documented in Saxonhouse, "Productivity Change and Labor Absorption in Japanese Cotton Spinning 1891–1935,'' *Quarterly Journal of Economics* 91 (May 1977).

26.   Compiled from *Women and Child Wage-Earners,* Vol. I, Table XXIX, pp. 826–931. The distributions for 15-year-olds were as follows:

Months Since Beginning	Boys	Girls
12 and below	.080	.090
24 and below	.224	.236
36 and below	.396	.407
48 and below	.574	.568
60 and below	.735	.725

However, the sample contained 211 girls and only 174 boys. Subsequent work has led us to drop the assumption of complete uniformity between boys and girls, tilting the entry slightly toward girls at early ages.

27.   A similar pattern and explanation is found in Wallace, pp. 35–37.

28.   The entry–exit structure used in the simulation summarized in Tables 7 and 8 is as follows:

	Percentage of Yearly New Entrants by Age Class				
	10 and Under	*11–14*	*15–19*	*20–24*	*25–28*
Female	12	48	20	8	12
Male	10	40	30	8	12

	"Retirement" Rate by Age Class				
	15–19	*20–25*	*25–29*	*30–44*	*45 and Over*
Female	5	31	24	3	10
Male	20	10	5	1	1

29.   The Keating–Owen bill seems to have had lasting impact despite being overturned by the Supreme Court in 1918. See Elizabeth Davidson, *Child Labor Legislation in the Southern Textile States* (Chapel Hill, 1939), esp. Chap. XIII.

30.   *The Cotton Mill Worker* (New York, 1944), p. 63.

31.   *Darker Phases of the South* (New York, 1924), p. 43.

32.   Harriet Herring, *The Passing of the Mill Village* (Chapel Hill, 1949), p. 4. Broadus Mitchell, a Southerner who joined the critics in the 1920s, had earlier written an enthusiastic account of *The Rise of the Cotton Mills in the South* (Baltimore, 1921).

33.   Thomas R. Dawley, Jr., "Our Mountain Problem and Its Solution," in American Cotton Manufacturers Association, *Proceedings of 14th Annual Convention* (Charlotte, N.C., 1910), p. 154. We are indebted to Cathy McHugh for this reference.

34.   Herring, p. 5.

35.   The first three assignments refer to machines preparatory to spinning which gradually transform the loose cotton fibers into an increasingly yarnlike appearance, known as "roving." The latter three tasks involve machines which prepare the warp yarn for weaving.

36.   Computed from *15th U.S. Census (1930), Population Vol. 4* (Occupations), Table 11 under each state.

37.   A very similar picture for the South as a whole as of 1907 is conveyed in *Women and Child Wage-Earners,* Vol. 1, pp. 51 and 54–56, though the data are not in convenient form.

38.   The clearest analysis of slavery along these lines is Robert E. Gallman and R. V. Anderson, "Slaves as Fixed Capital," *Journal of American History* 64 (June 1977).

39.   We do not mean to overlook the well-known fact that integrated mills have a long history in the United States going back, indeed, to the earliest Waltham Mills! Our point here is that the Southern encroachment on the Northern market did not take the form of gradually exploiting "forward linkages," but for the most part involved the whole cloth-making process from the start.

40.   The more rapid diffusion of the automatic loom in the South is discussed in Irwin Feller, "The Draper Loom in New England Textiles, 1899–1914," *Journal of Economic History* 25 (December 1966), and "The Diffusion and Location of Technological Change in the American Cotton-Textile Industry, 1890–1970," *Technology and Culture* 15 (October 1974). Feller's interpretation is critically reexamined by William Mass in an unpublished paper.

41.   See particularly Kenneth Arrow, "Models of Job Discrimination," in Anthony Pascal (ed.), *Racial Discrimination in Economic Life* (Lexington, Mass.: Heath, 1972).

42.   Claudia Goldin has proposed that segregation by sex was a by-product of segregation by method of payment (time vs. piece rates), which in turn reflected the "greater expected attachment to the labor force" of males. "The Work and Wages of Single Women, 1870 to 1920," *Journal of Economic History* 40 (March 1980), p. 87. There may be some broad truth in this conception, but it is not a robust explanation for patterns of job segregation in the textile industry. Of the 16 job categories identifiable as "male" or "female" in the U.S. Bureau of Labor Statistics (BLS) survey of 1914–1920 (Bulletins Nos. 190, 239, 262, and 288), only one (spooler tender) is unambiguously "female" and "piece rate." Three predominantly male occupations were paid by the piece (not including mule spinners in the North, who were also paid by the piece). The largest female job category (ring spinner) was paid on a time basis, with rates adjusted "by the side" (i.e., according to how many spindles were assigned), and the job with the largest number of males (weaver) was always paid by the piece.

Indeed, the premise of Goldin's statement is inappropriate for Southern textiles because, from the perspective of workers beginning in their early teens, the boys were more likely to leave than girls (within 10 years or so). By paying weavers by the piece, conversely, employers gave males a chance to collect on their superior potential in that occupation, presumably encouraging some to stay on through their critical years of occupational choice.

43.   Cathy McHugh, "The Family Labor System in the Southern Cotton Textile Industry, 1880–1915" (Ph.D. dissertation, Stanford University, 1981), Chap. 2. Prior to 1902–1906, the BLS data show *no* wage differential for male over female weavers, reflecting the absence of experienced males up to that time.

44.   See the survey reported in Jennings J. Rhyne, *Some Southern Cotton Mill Workers and Their Villages* (Chapel Hill, N.C.: 1930), Chap. 14.

45.   Dale Newman, "Work and Community Life in a Southern Town," *Labor History* 19 (Spring 1978), p. 216.

46.   Fukuhara, pp. 19–20 and 128–141.

47.   W. A. Graham Clark, *Cotton Goods in Japan,* U.S. Department of Commerce, Bureau of Foreign and Domestic Commerce, Special Agents Series No. 86, 1914, pp. 198–202.

48.   Parker, "Entrepreneurship, Industrial Organization, and Economic Growth," p. 400.

49.   The strong sense of group identity among the mill workers is particularly stressed in Glenn Gilman, *Human Relations in the Industrial Southeast* (Chapel Hill, N.C.: 1956). There are many accounts of the textile strikes, but see Lahne, *Cotton Mill Worker,* Chap. 16; Thomas Typpett, *When Southern Labor Stirs* (New York, 1931).

FAMILY AND ENTERPRISE IN THE SILK SHOPS OF LYON:

THE PLACE OF LABOR IN THE DOMESTIC WEAVING ECONOMY, 1840–1870

George J. Sheridan, Jr.

I. INTRODUCTION

In 1844 Antoine Vernay, a young master silk weaver, resided in his household weaving shop in the Croix-Rousse, a silk-weaving suburb of Lyon, France, with his wife, three male "workers" (probably journeymen weavers), and one male apprentice. The Vernays had two children, both infants still in nursing outside the family living quarters. This household of largely unrelated members operated three looms for fancy silk cloth. With the same labor force, it could have set to work its two currently inactive looms, if additional orders should suddenly arrive.[1] Using its own resident labor force, in short, the household could meet

Technique, Spirit, and Form in the Making of the Modern Economies:
Essays in Honor of William N. Parker
Research in Economic History, Suppl. 3, pages 33–60
Copyright © 1984 by JAI Press Inc.
All rights of reproduction in any form reserved.
ISBN: 0-89232-414-7

demands for increased output to the limit of its loom capacity. Twenty-two years later, at the time of the 1866 census and amidst a severe depression in the urban silk trade, Antoine Vernay's household-shop had only one less loom, but its human character had changed significantly from what it had been in 1844. The household consisted entirely of family members—Vernay and his wife, three children, all of working age, and what appeared to be their 77-year-old grandmother, the mother of Madame Vernay. One child, a 23-year-old male, worked outside the household as an *employé;* another, a 17-year-old girl, was a *tailleuse* (maker of clothing). Only the 14-year-old boy, and perhaps his grandmother, both of whom were listed without occupation, were likely to have worked in the weaving shop. Thus Vernay and his wife probably operated the two active looms themselves, assisted in the auxiliary tasks of weaving by their son and by Madame Vernay's mother. The family work force sufficed, in short, for all work in the household-shop at the level of its current activity. However, the Vernays would have had to hire labor not residing in the household to operate the two inactive looms.[2] Thus, resident labor alone no longer sufficed for activating all looms. Moreover, the earnings of resident children who worked outside the household in trades other than silk weaving supplemented earnings from domestic weaving. In other words, while the co-resident household had become a more homogeneous kinship unit, its economy was more fragmented, relying more than in the past on external labor for increasing its output and on external employment for supplementing its income.

Samples of households taken from censuses for 1847 and 1866 in the same silk weavers' district, as well as contemporary reports on working and business conditions in the Lyon silk manufacture around the same period, suggest that the above example illustrates a more general trend. The data show a reduction in household size (number of residents and looms), an increase in the share of family among household residents and among workers occupying active looms, and a slightly greater dependence on nonresident labor to occupy at least some looms. These indices are summarized in Table 1.

Observations by contemporaries suggest some of the same tendencies. In the early 1870s, responses of merchant-manufacturers to an inquiry about working conditions in Lyon noted "few" household-shops "where there [were] more than one outside worker." The average number of children per household was "one or two," or "two or three" at most, in the opinion of one merchant, and "tending to decrease."[3] Households, in short, were small, and they relied on a largely family work force. One merchant also noted that "the worker called journeyman working on the loom of the master weaver is composed ⅔ of women and girls."[4] This remark highlighted an increase in the proportion of females as residents and silk workers in the household-shops, a trend also evident in the census data. This increase was due in part to "master weavers . . . having their children learn other trades" during the economic crisis of the 1860s.[5] Sons rather than daughters were more likely to be encouraged and more likely to be successful in finding outside work, and in the late 1860s and early 1870s, many sons of

Table 1.   Changes in Silk Weavers' Households[a]

	Year	
Characteristic	1847	1866
Average number of looms per household	2.71 (1.07)	2.56 (.97)
Average number of residents per household	4.22 (2.00)	3.29 (1.36)
Number of households in sample	175	140
Average ratio of number of relatives of head or spouse to total number of household residents (other than head and spouse)	.55 (.39)	.75 (.37)
Average ratio of number of females to total number of household residents (other than head and spouse)	.49 (.37)	.59 (.41)
Number of households in sample	148	104
Index of familialization of household work force sufficient to occupy active looms (average for all households)[b]	.58 (.42)	.73 (.44)
Proportion of households with one or more nonresident workers	.03	.06
Number of households in sample	167	120

[a]The number in parentheses following each average is the standard deviation for that average.
[b]This index is described in detail in George J. Sheridan, Jr., *The Social and Economic Foundations of Association Among the Silk Weavers of Lyons, 1852–1870* (New York: Arno Press, 1981), pp. 626–630. Briefly, the index rises to the extent that the number of family members of weaving age (members related to the master or to his spouse as indicated by surname) suffices, first, relative to nonfamily household residents of weaving age and, second, relative to nonresidents, for occupying active looms in the household.
Source: Archives municipes de Lyon, *Recensement*, Croix-Rousse, 1847 (samples); Archives départementales du Rhône, 6M-*Dénombrement*, 1866, Lyon 4ème arrondissement, Vols. XVI and XVII (samples).

weavers were known to have found work as "employees on fixed salaries" in the putting-out establishments of merchant-manufacturers of silk.[6] The Vernay household illustrated at least one of these tendencies. One of the sons "in nursing" in 1844 was an *employé* in 1866—perhaps in a silk merchant's establishment.[7]

Nearly all of these changes in weavers' household-shops involved the use of labor in the domestic weaving economy. This essay will explore the nature and sources of master-weavers' demand for labor and of the supply of labor available to them during the period between the 1840s and the 1870s. Special attention will be given to distinctions made by masters between different types of labor, especially between "inside" and "outside" labor.

II. TYPES OF HOUSEHOLD LABOR

Parker's reflections on the American family farm in the nineteenth century have stressed the importance of nonmarket bonds in securing the labor force. Bound by "ties of custom, law, fear and affection" to the ambitions of the head, members of the family remained on the farm for a significant fraction of their working lives, providing labor well below market wage rates.[8] Some of Parker's students have analyzed the institution of slavery in terms of its effects on the farmer's choice between family and nonfamily labor.[9] In the domestic silk-weaving economy of nineteenth-century Lyon, such differences among labor types were equally crucial, but they were not limited to family relationships. Customary and affective ties between masters and their subordinates, regardless of family relation, were established by co-residence, common meals and services carried out in the traditional master–journeyman–apprentice framework. These differences in labor types were commonly associated with different tasks. Besides weaving, these included auxiliary tasks, such as thread reeling (*dévidage*), shuttle spooling (*cannetage*), loom mounting (*remettage, purge, montage de métiers*), warp tying (*tordage*), and combing the thread (*piquage en peigne*). All of these tasks were usually undertaken in the household-shop, owned or rented by the master, on machines also owned by him—looms, reeling machines, and so forth. Normally a different worker performed each task, although occasionally the same worker divided his or her time among two or more tasks. Workers included both members of the master's family residing in the household and nonfamily workers, some of whom lived in the household for a period of time and others of whom worked by day. Residents, both family and nonfamily, received meals, lodging, and certain services, such as laundry, from the master and his wife, while nonresidents received, in addition to the wage for their work, no more than meals and often not even that. Apprentices, in all cases, and nonfamily auxiliary workers, in some cases, were residents. Female *dévideuses* were commonly in the latter category. Journeymen and, less often, journeywomen weavers were as likely to be found among nonresidents as among resident workers. These various distinctions among household workers can be recast and simplified in terms of the proximity of the personal relationship with the master. At one end were workers in closest personal association with him, directly subject to his paternal influence and control, and at the other end were those personally most distant from him, nonresident occasional workers receiving only a wage. This spectrum brings out an important feature of the household-shop's demand for labor, namely, the role of the master's paternal influence in attracting labor into the household economy and in inducing it to remain there.

The distinction between household labor subject to the master's paternal influence and household labor working simply for a wage was closely related to another distinction, maintained in the weaver's account books, between what I call "inside" labor and "outside" labor. Inside labor was that associated most intimately, for accounting purposes, with the labor of the master and his family—both family labor itself and nonfamily labor assimilated to family labor. Outside labor was essentially hired labor, whether resident or nonresident. The criterion for distinguishing between inside and outside labor, as suggested by several master-weavers' budgets of the 1840s, collected and explained by the master Weichmann in 1850,[10] was the extent to which food and lodging of household residents belonged to the home consumption of profit earned by the shop, rather than to shop expenses reducing profit. According to this criterion, master-weavers usually accounted food and lodging of all journeymen weavers and of temporarily employed auxiliary workers—such as warpers (*remetteuses*), other mounters (*purgeuses*), and warp tyers (*tordeuses*)—as part of shop costs and considered upkeep of apprentices and resident reelers (*dévideuses*) as part of the home consumption or family budget.

In Weichmann's budgets, this distinction was evident in the assignment of costs for certain auxiliary tasks, such as shuttle spooling (*cannetage*), loom mounting (*montage de métiers*), and combing the thread (*piquage en peigne*), and for tasks such as "Halfdays lost for *retournage* and for returning the article," number of "trips to the [merchant-manufacturer's] store, not having received the article on the same day" and "accidental trips," to a column labeled *Doit* (saved costs), or "Costs returning to the profit of the *Shop* inventory," when performed "by the *chef de' atelier* or his spouse."[11] Thus, family labor, represented in the budgets by the *chef* and spouse, was paid out of shop profits rather than out of the expense account of the shop. In other words, it was paid implicitly through its consumption of household goods. The same was not true for costs of "upkeep of the bed of the [journey] workers" or of feeding the *remetteuse, purgeuse,* and *tordeuse,* none of which were returned to the profits of the shop, and therefore all of which were considered shop expenses. In practice this meant that the wage paid these outside workers was independent of the incidental expenses, such as food and upkeep, incurred by employing them in the household-shop. In the case of journeymen weavers, custom had established the wage at one-half the piece rate, whether or not the journeyman resided in the household. Inside labor, on the other hand, was paid entirely or in part—usually in large part—by food, lodging, and upkeep, the amount of which was regulated by the consumption standards of the family household. Thus, the wage of inside labor could be adjusted upward or downward as these standards changed, whereas the wage of outside labor was exogenous to the household, determined through supply and demand in the labor market.[12]

Evidence for accounting the room and board of apprentices and resident *dévideuses* as part of household consumption of profits, rather than as shop expenses, is more indirect. None of the 26 budgets collected by Weichmann refers to apprentices, even though apparently apprentice labor was commonly used by masters at the time the budgets were made.[13] Similarly, the reports on costs for *dévidage,* unlike the costs for *remettage* and *tordage,* were limited exclusively to expenses for the service itself, with no reference to costs of food and lodging, even though our knowledge of the profession of *dévideuse,* and the existence of *dévidoirs* in the shop of many masters, suggests that *dévideuses* were usually fed and/or lodged by the masters.[14] The silence of the budgets about both costs may therefore be indirect evidence of masters' accounting the food and lodging of apprentices and *dévideuses* as part of the home consumption of profits as well. Verbal testimony about the conditions of these two workers strengthens this suggestion. Concerning apprentices, the master-weaver Pierre Charnier wrote in 1832: "Apprentices generally mess in their masters' homes, who provide them with food, fire and light."[15] Weichmann noted the same in 1850, stating that it was the "responsibility of the master-weaver to feed [them], to do their laundry, to furnish heat and light. . . ."[16] Concerning *dévideuses,* Jules Simon wrote in 1865: "the most fortunate make an annual contract for food and lodging with an income which varies form 200 to 300 *francs.*" These *dévideuses à gage,* as they were called, were "almost always charged, besides their work, with all the heavy tasks of the house."[17]

The distinction between inside and outside labor was more than an arbitrary bookkeeping practice. It reflected the masters' perceptions of labor supply conditions and strategies for economic survival in the 1850s and 1860s. The remainder of this essay will demonstrate this hypothesis by examining the conditions underlying masters' demand for household labor as well as the supply of labor for work in the household during this period.

III.   HOUSEHOLD DEMAND FOR LABOR

The master's evaluation of the advantage of inside relative to outside labor involved an assessment of economic gains and losses in a context of varying employment, piece rates, and cloth styles in silk manufacture. In this context the master supplied labor—his own labor and that of his household enterprise—and equipment (mainly looms) to the merchant-manufacturer, from whom he received cloth orders, thread to weave these orders, and the piece rate for woven cloth, the only source of the master's earnings. Thus the latter's demand for labor to operate his household-shop originated in the merchant-manufacturer's demand for specific types of cloth. After 1850 this demand was influenced strongly by changes in product markets, in quantities and sources of raw materials, and in location and methods of manufacture.

Fabric markets of the Second Empire were transformed by new tastes and dress designs and by the changing social makeup of consumers. Average annual exports of silk cloth from France—the clearest indication of market size—nearly doubled between the period 1815–1819 (855,000 kg) and the period 1850–1854 (1,643,000 kg), and doubled again in the next 20 years, rising to 3,288,000 kg by 1870–1874. The largest share of this increase was in the plain silk category (*étoffes unies*), which represented 74 percent of total exports in 1815–1819 and 82 percent in 1870–1874. Sales of fancy silks (*étoffes façonnées*) rose through the 1850s but plummeted after 1860, remaining in a depressed state until the late 1870s.[18] (See Figure 1.) The preferences of middle-class consumers for inexpensive fashion fabric and for novelty and variety of style explain some of this growth of plains relative to fancies. Plain silks could be varied more cheaply than the elegant fancies and were, in particular, more adaptable to the cut-and-fold dress design of Charles Worth and other stylists in vogue under the Second

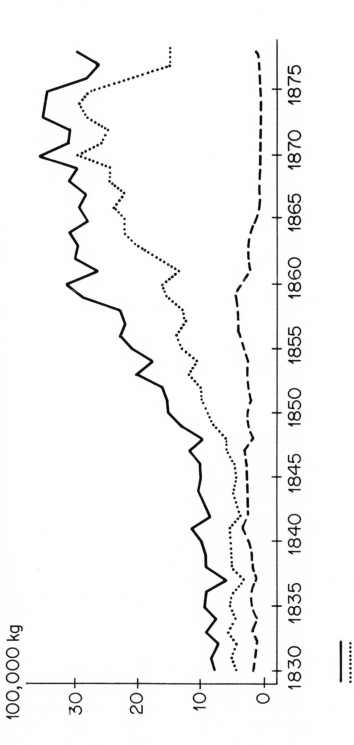

Figure 1. Exports of Silk Cloths from France, Special Commerce (1830–1878). *Key*:— étoffes de soie (all-silk cloths); .... étoffes unies (plain silks); - - - étoffes façonnées (fancy silks). [*Source*: 1830–1836—Ministère des Travaux publics, *Statistique de la France. Commerce extérieur*, Tableaux 193–196. 1837–1878—Administration des douanes, *Tableau décennal du Commerce de la France* (Paris: Imprimerie Nationale), 2 ème Partie, for the years 1837–1846, 1847–1856, 1857–1866, 1867–1876, 1877–1886.]

Empire.[19] Plain silks were also more competitive with woolen and mixed fabrics, whose popularity spread in fashion markets. Finally, the outbreak of the American Civil War in 1860 severely restricted sales of fancy silks to the warring American states. Wartime restrictions, which were partially maintained under the postwar tariff regime, thus eliminated Lyon's single largest buyer of fancies for nearly two decades.[20]

Compounding the effects of changing fabric markets were frequent thread shortages stemming from the silkworm disease *pébrine*. The latter reduced cocoon harvests initially in the French and Italian crops and eventually throughout the entire Mediterranean region. After 1855 prices of silk thread rose and procurement of this costly raw material became uncertain from year to year.[21] Imports of Asiatic cocoons and eggs, notably from Japan, restored the European crop somewhat, and eventually imports of Asiatic fiber and thread more than compensated for the deficit in Mediterranean supplies. However, establishing the necessary commercial links with suppliers of this material and adapting it to French needs, through more extensive throwing, for instance, to strengthen the weak Asian thread, required time and experimentation. Not until 1868, when a secular decline in the price of the imported raw material began, were these adjustments made.[22] In the meantime, prices of raw silk (*grège*) and silk thread fluctuated unpredictably, leading to a search for ways of cutting other production costs. Labor expenses were the obvious candidate for such reductions. Largely in order to lower these, Lyon's merchant-manufacturers put out an increasing share of their cloth orders to rural households in the surrounding countryside. Some manufacturers even set up rural weaving factories, and a few installed mechanical looms. The extent of this shift in the location of production can be seen in the loom data. In 1832, an estimated 22 percent of the looms of the Lyon *fabrique* were rural. From 1840–1848, this percentage fluctuated around 50 percent. By 1861–1865, the great majority of looms—65–70 percent of the 100,000–115,000 looms of the industry—were in the countryside. Of these, 5,000 were operated mechanically.[23] Rural weaving skills and mechanical looms were more readily adapted to the weaving of plain silks than fancies, so the growth of rural industry was well suited to the growing demand for the cheaper silk fabrics.

These various changes in the Lyon silk manufacture introduced much unpredictability and, after 1860, caused stagnation and decline in silk weavers' earnings. During the 1850s, uncertainty about raw silk production and high prices of raw silk deepened depression in seasons of normally low activity or caused the idling of looms to continue beyond these seasons. In 1853, for instance, "heights of prosperity" in August gave way to inactivity in September, as poor cocoon harvests and rising prices of raw silk caused "many establishments" to "refuse large orders." By November one-fourth of the plain cloth looms had ceased production, aggravating the seasonal inactivity of late fall, and in December rumors of war, the high cost of raw silk, or large inventories accumulated during the preceding year led to delays or to postponement of the normal end-of-the-year orders. Production fell through May 1854, idling up to three-quarters of the looms of the *fabrique*.[24] During the next year's cycle—October 1855 to July 1856—this activity followed an opposite course. Instead of a poor beginning in the fall and revival during the following summer, the boom of the previous summer continued through fall 1855, giving silk weavers all the work they could handle, but collapsed by July 1856, when production started to decline because of the high price of raw silk. By the end of October 1856, no more than half of the plain and fancy looms in Lyon were active, and daily earnings of weavers averaged 1.75 to 2.75 francs for fancy cloths and 1 to 2 francs for plain cloths— as compared with 2 to 6 francs for fancies, and 2 to 3 francs for plains, in June 1859, when employment was high. A mild recovery ensued in January only after raw silk arrived from China.[25] Fluctuations of raw silk prices aggravated the usual uncertainties of the industry, eliminating all predictability from the pattern of cloth orders and thus from the pattern of employment. No wonder that Pierre Dronier, a journeyman weaver, remarked in 1860 that fabrics "no longer have their season of manufacture which, in the past, was almost invariable."[26]

After 1860, the loss of the American market, the accelerated putting-out of silk orders to the countryside, and continued shortages of silk thread led to outright stagnation. This especially affected the fancy silks, whose chief foreign buyer had been the United States. Unemployment in this category was so frequent or so continuous that even the relatively high piece rates paid to fancy cloth weavers did not provide them enough income to support more than a modest living. "If labor is compensated better in this article," reported a police agent observing industrial conditions in March 1866, "the fluctuations and unemployment experienced make the situation of most workers as bad as that of workers manufacturing common cloths."[27] Weavers of these "common cloths"—plains (*étoffes unies*) and plain velvets (*velours unis*)—were more securely employed but suffered a decline in piece rates because of the growing competition of rural weaving. Rural weavers could produce ordinary plain fabric as well as urban weavers and accepted lower piece rates for this work, having lower living expenses in the countryside and competing intensely for work because of an abundance of hands. Thus, rural weaving had a depressive effect on the average daily earnings of journeymen weavers in the city, which fell from between 2.50 to 4.50 francs in 1859 to around 1.50, 2.00, or 3.00 francs throughout most of the period 1860–1869.[28]

The experience of unemployment by fancies and plains weavers differed in a manner consistent with these different crises in their trades. From a situation of fluctuating employment and piece rates early in the decade, the fancies category began to experience endemic, long-term unemployment by 1863/64.[29] Especially affected were the "rich" fancy articles—the elegant, embroidered *grands façonnés*—where the "crisis weighing . . . for some 10 or 12 years" was regarded as "almost . . . a normal state" by March 1868. More than two-thirds of the fancies looms in the industry were inactive then.[30] Because of this long inactivity, masters changed their looms to produce "the common articles" and even stopped taking on apprentices.[31] Only the inferior fancy cloths—the *petits façonnés* for ornament and the popular *hautes nouveautés*—occupied "some looms" with regularity, though with frequent "intermittances of work."[32] Small orders for rich articles also arrived on occasion, but these orders were "rare" and "more or less . . . hurried."[33]

In the plains category, the unemployment pattern was very much like that of the 1850s, that is, fluctuating with the changes of cloth seasons and silk thread prices. However, periods of inactivity were apparently much shorter than before 1860. In fact, this category "always occupied the largest number of hands" and was thus "always the main support for the Lyon *fabrique*" during the 1860s.[34] The most common form of "unemployment" consisted of delays experienced by weavers between the time of completing one piece and receiving orders for the next. Controlling timing, merchant-manufacturers could force upon their weavers an increasing share of the risk associated with uncertain future sales or thread prices. In March 1868, merchant-manufacturers were observed to put out orders only "step by step, and a large number of merchants waited eight days between the receipt of a woven piece and the putting out of a new one." Their action was motivated by "the indecision always present in commercial transactions."[35] Since piece rates in this category were usually low, such delays could easily put these weavers in a "very precarious situation."[36] Nevertheless, the regularity of work, at least for the "ordinary" plains, the occasional rises in piece rates in times of brisk demand, and the experience of unemployment as short and rarely deep, kept enough hope alive for improvement in this category so that weavers did not abandon the trade in large numbers. Unlike the workers in the fancies category, where unemployment was long and rarely relieved (at least for the more traditional articles), plain cloth weavers worked regularly, albeit with frequent interruptions and at a generally low level of earnings.

In such contexts of erratic or stagnant employment and generally falling piece rates, master-weavers had to consider two matters especially in assessing the relative advantages of inside and outside labor. These were the risk of assuming responsibility for the upkeep and support of inside labor in times of unemployment and the flexibility of responding to sudden spurts of demand for their services. The master was obliged, by contract or by his interest in maintaining his paternal influence over insiders, to provide food, lodging, and accessory services (laundry and so forth) to insiders during periods of *both* employment and unemployment. Earnings made in times of employment therefore had to finance the upkeep of fallow periods. Expectation of periods of long unemployment and unpredictability in the timing of these periods, as in the 1850s, tended to discourage masters from taking on insiders, at least on long contracts. Relatively low earnings due to low piece rates aggravated this tendency in plain cloth weaving, because of the difficulty of spreading these earnings over the fallow periods. After 1860, stagnant employment made inside labor especially disadvantageous in fancy cloth weaving. Only the weaving of *petits façonnés* and *hautes nouveautés,* where employment was more abundant, and the weaving of more stably occupied plain cloths were likely to benefit from the use of insiders. However, the unusually low level of piece rates in plain cloth weaving after 1860 diminished whatever advantage inside labor gained here.

The substitution of inside for outside labor by households weaving plain cloth, *petits façonnés,* and *hautes nouveautés* was favored more consistently by the flexibility insiders provided for responding to spurts of demand for their services. When cloth orders arrived suddenly and required rapid execution to capture the profits of fleeting demand, inside labor could be employed immediately, without the lure of higher wages, to take advantage of these opportunities. Such sudden demand for labor services was likely to occur in simple fancies and plain cloth weaving during the 1860s, where frequent work interruptions and delays between orders were common. Unpredictable silk harvests, rapid and frequent changes of style, especially for *petits façonnés* and *hautes nouveautés,* and the increasing competitiveness of silk manufacture put a premium on rapid execution of orders arriving at moment's notice during such periods of work stoppage. Inside labor was available for immediate employment without wage incentive, whereas the very unpredictability of labor demand tended to raise both the wage and search costs for outside labor. This availability of insiders more than outweighed the cost of having to support these insiders during periods of interruptions or delays in these cloth categories. Moreover, the relatively low skill requirements and the narrow range of tasks in plain and common fancy cloth manufacture allowed masters to shift insiders from one job to another in the household-shop, keeping them occupied even during interruptions or delays.

Besides employment considerations, costs associated with weaving and auxiliary tasks influenced the master's assessment of the advantage of inside labor. In the fancies category, the major cost item of concern to master-weavers was loom mounting. During the 1850s, when the *grands façonnés* were still selling well, mounting the thread on the loom was probably time consuming and complex, requiring expensive specialized skills. Risks of design failure were the most aggravating feature of this mounting, as a petition of masters to the government suggested in 1860. Masters bore these risks to an unreasonable degree, argued the petition. Merchant-manufacturers of fancy silks required that masters make samples of the ornate fabric, before knowing whether the design would sell. If the sample succeeded, the masters received no share in profits other than orders of the same style at the prevailing piece rate (probably agreed upon at the outset). But if the sample failed, they faced an excessive cost burden in the form of prior investment of time and expense for mounting, and they had no run of cloth orders of the same style to compensate for this burden.[37] Using inside labor for mounting and/or weaving samples had the advantage of reducing these losses by the amount of wages saved from the rate paid to outsiders. In weaving this was the difference between the half piece rate customarily paid to journeyworkers and the wage equivalent paid to inside labor wholly or partially in kind. The level of the latter could be reduced in line with the consumption standards of the household.[38]

During the 1860s this problem of mounting effectively disappeared for the *grands façonnés*, since the market collapsed entirely and few fabrics of this type were made. However, the *petit façonné* for dress ornament and the *haute nouveauté* for assortments had a continuing demand, and mounting was a problem for these as well, though for different reasons. Weavers had to remount their looms frequently for these common fancies, because designs changed often, and the cost of frequent mountings was burdensome. As a result, the "various changes of loom mounts" combined with frequent "interruptions of work" made earnings in this sector little different from those of plain cloth weaving, despite higher piece rates.[39] However, the lesser complexity of most common fancy fabrics reduced the time required for mounting and allowed the substitution of unskilled labor or unspecialized inside labor for skilled workers in these tasks.

In the plain cloth category, the cost situation was somewhat different. During both the 1850s and 1860s, the chief cost concerns of plain cloth masters seem to have been the abnormally large losses (or "wastes") of thread and the high frequency of thread breakage during weaving. In their petition of 1860, masters complained of excessive wastes of thread in *dévidage* and weaving, beyond the amount traditionally allotted by merchant-manufacturers as free *déchets*—that is, as wastes for which masters were not required to reimburse the merchant from whom they received the thread on consignment.[40] Thread breakage during weaving was a more common complaint of the 1860s. In 1867, for instance, frequent breakage caused weavers many delays and perhaps also some additional expense for hiring *tordeuses*. These delays, combined with low piece rates and occasional unemployment, reduced a master's earnings to a level "so low that he [was] no longer able to provide for his needs."[41] Both wastes and breakage resulted from a technique encouraged by merchant-manufacturers in the 1850s and 1860s called "loading" (*charge*) of silk thread. This term referred to the addition of chemicals such as alum or tannin to thread during dyeing to increase its weight and volume. In a period of frequent shortages and wildly fluctuating prices of thread, "loading" compensated somewhat for high or uncertain raw materials costs and thus enhanced the price competitiveness of silk fabrics in a market increasingly sensitive to price differentials.[42] However, this practice also weakened the physical durability and tenacity of the thread, making it more susceptible to breakage.[43] Consequently, plain silk masters may have been more reluctant to have their thread reeled outside the household, where they could not control the amount of waste. They were likely to prefer inside *dévideuses* for this task. They could not only supervise the latter more effectively but also reduce the effective real wage paid for their services to a level below that paid to outsiders, in the form of household consumption. This last consideration also argued for substitution of inside labor in other auxiliary tasks.

The effect of average wages for outside labor on masters' demand for inside labor was somewhat complex. Wages for weaving done by outsiders were, of course, determined by the piece rate, the levels of which fluctuated in the manner described earlier. Wages for auxiliary tasks done by outsiders were determined in the labor market for auxiliary workers and varied according to the task performed. Scattered evidence about piece rates paid for *dévidage* suggests little change in rates between the 1840s and 1860s. Most of Weichmann's budgets for the 1840s list rates of 2.50, 3.50, or 4.00 francs per kilogram of reeled silk, with 3.50 as the most commonly cited rate; the same rate (3.50) was listed on a sample budget in the municipal archives from what seems to be the decade of the 1860s.[44] Average daily earnings of day-laboring *dévideuses* fell to poverty levels of 0.90–1.25 francs by the mid-1860s, down from 1.50–2.00 francs in October 1859, though the former levels did not differ much from the 1.25–1.50 francs earned daily, on the average, in October 1856, when one-half of the *dévideuses* in Lyon were unemployed.[45] What probably distinguished the 1860s from earlier decades was the rarity of these *dévideuses* working by the day for a wage.[46] As police reports repeated throughout the 1860s, the overwhelming majority of *dévideuses* received a 100–130 franc annual stipend, plus food and lodging, rather than a wage.[47] Their employers were required to support them for the period of their contract (usually a year or more), regardless of the state of employment. These employers included not only master-weavers but also, perhaps even more prominently, mistress *dévideuses* who set up shops specializing in the reeling of silk thread. These latter received orders from merchant-manufacturers and master-weavers alike.[48] Thus the masters "very often" had to have, or did have, their reeling done outside the household shop.[49] For this work, they paid rates cited earlier—rates which, in the 1840s, many probably paid to *dévideuses* working in their homes. (One-fourth of the silk weavers' households with looms in the 1847 census sample, for example, also had a reeling machine.[50]) Unfortunately, it is not possible to determine the extent to which masters used specialized shops in the 1860s for *dévidage*. They probably did so for the finer threads requiring closer attention, but for most of the common sorts they could have just as easily (and perhaps more cheaply) used their own household labor or the low-wage *dévideuse* working by the day. For the tasks of *tordage* and *montage de métiers,* however, they did not seem to have as wide a range of alternatives. The earnings of workers specializing in these tasks were relatively high, averaging 200–300 francs per year (plus food) in June 1865, or 2.50–3.50 francs per day in March 1869.[51] This was indeed much lower than the 5.50 to 6.50 francs average daily earnings of *monteurs de métiers* in October 1856,[52] but was nonetheless a significant expense for masters in the 1860s. The very small number of workers in *montage* and *tordage* during this latter decade suggests that these tasks were most commonly undertaken by unspecialized inside labor of the household.[53]

The major expense item for inside labor, both in weaving and in auxiliary work, was the cost of food. As Figure 2 illustrates, food costs fluctuated within a wide range in the period after the potato-wheat famine of 1846/47. The clearest movement was the steep inflation of the mid-1850s, which raised food costs even higher than in the more celebrated crisis years of the 1840s. It too was caused primarily by poor harvests of wheat and potatoes. This inflation produced immense suffering in the silk-weaving communities, where households traditionally depended on bread, meat, and potatoes as staples,[54] the prices of which all rose. Coal prices were high as well, raising the cost of heating households during winter months.[55] In March 1854, the combination of "the high price of food and fuel," "the exceptional severity of the winter," and inactivity of one-quarter of the urban looms, created "greater suffering among the workers than they [were] accustomed to."[56] From the perspective of the master-weaver, high food costs made the acceptance of additional inside laborers (beyond the immediate family, for instance) a more than usually risky enterprise, especially when these laborers were taken on long contracts. The threat of combined inactivity and high food prices, when masters would be required to support insiders with no earnings from their labor in return, reduced the gains of paying them a lower real wage. The end of the inflationary crisis in 1856 restored some of these gains but probably did not eliminate entirely masters' fears of taking on too many insiders for a long period of time. Occasional increases in food costs, as in 1860 and 1867, may have served only to strengthen such fears, at least in the minds of some.

To summarize the effects of these various conditions on the masters' demand for labor, we must distinguish between the periods before and after 1860. In the first period, two countervailing tendencies were apparent. First, masters hesitated to take on inside labor, especially on long contracts, because of the costs involved, and second, masters recognized the advantages of inside over outside labor because of the character of cloth demand and because of costs associated with weaving. Their hesitation was a reaction to the cyclical and "spreadout" nature of unemployment—infrequent but long when it occurred—and to the high cost of food during much of the decade. The cost of one "miss"—that of having to support inside labor in times of unemployment—could be disastrous for the artisanal household, especially if the insider were accepted on a long contract and if the "miss" coincided with a period of food price inflation. As a result, masters either refused to take on inside labor during these latter periods or accepted inside labor only on short-term contracts.

This second alternative had the advantage of capturing some of the advantages of inside over outside labor associated with the character of cloth demand and weaving costs. Mounting costs due to frequent changes of style in fancy cloth manufacture and costs of unforeseen thread breakage and waste were especially acute. The existence of these costs in the 1850s favored inside over outside labor, especially when wages for the more specialized, higher paid auxiliary workers—*remetteuses, tordeuses, monteurs de métiers*—were as high as they were. The

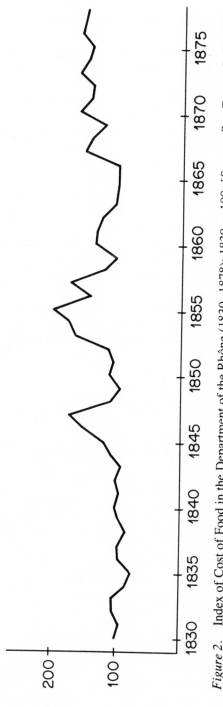

Figure 2. Index of Cost of Food in the Department of the Rhône (1830–1878): 1830 = 100. [*Source:* See George J. Sheridan, Jr. *The Social and Economic Foundations of Association Among the Silk Weavers of Lyons, 1852–1870* (New York: Arno Press, 1981), Appendix II, for construction of this index and for sources used. The index is based on averages of food prices quoted twice each month (*mercuriales*). For 1830–1836 and 1860–1878, the index is based on yearly averages. For 1837–1859, it is based on the January average only.]

generally buoyant demand for cloths after 1854, and the end of the subsistence crisis in 1856, may have tipped the balance even more in favor of inside labor, so that some masters, at least, may have been more willing to accept insiders even on long contracts after the middle of the decade.

The two countervailing tendencies described above affected both plains and fancies weavers in the same direction. After 1860, masters' demand for labor differed for the two cloth categories. In the plain cloth category, the advantages of substituting inside for outside labor were generally clear. Although low profit margins due to low piece rates made the risk of having to support insiders in times of unemployment menacing, the short duration of unemployment and the technical feasibility of shifting insiders from weaving to auxiliary tasks during these fallow periods minimized this threat to household profits. Other considerations then weighed more heavily in favor of taking on insiders. Most important among these were savings in wage payments to outsiders for auxiliary work and greater readiness of the shop for executing orders arriving at a moment's notice. In reeling, the use of inside labor also gave the master greater control over the quality of work, especially over the amount of thread waste, than outwork in specialized reeling shops allowed.

In the fancy cloth category, unemployment, as we saw earlier, became chronic for "rich" fancies and short but frequent for the "common" fancies after 1860. For masters in the first group, inside labor was more a liability than an advantage on balance. Despite the arrival of occasional, even lucrative, orders in a sea of unemployment—a condition normally favoring inside labor for its more ready responsiveness to such orders—the rarity of these orders probably raised the net cost of inside labor because of the support it required in times of unemployment. Masters were therefore more likely to weave these rare orders themselves and to rely on temporarily employed outside labor for extra work. In the 1866 census sample the greater proportion of fancy cloth masters using nonresident weaving labor (11 percent) than plain cloth weavers (3 percent) may have indicated this kind of response.[57] For masters weaving common fancies, the substitution of inside for outside labor was favored by many of the factors encouraging such substitution in the plain cloth category. Common fancies required less specialized weaving and auxiliary skills than rich fancies, so that less specialized or less skilled inside labor could be used for weaving, mounting, and thread preparation. As in plain cloth weaving, masters used such labor to best advantage during short but frequent periods of inactivity affecting each loom, but not all looms at once. Moreover, inside labor had the advantage of "readiness" to execute cloth orders arriving at a moment's notice.

IV.   THE SUPPLY OF LABOR

The character of labor offered for inside and outside status involved three issues. The first was the pool of nonfamily labor, with certain work–leisure preferences, available for recruitment as inside or outside labor on the labor market, as this is normally understood. The second was the opportunity cost of using family labor in weaving or auxiliary tasks in the household-shop rather than in another trade. This was primarily the cost seen from the master's eye but may also be regarded as a cost to the individual family worker, to the extent that it affected each one's willingness to remain in the household-shop. The third issue was the effect of paternal influence on the willingness of all household workers, both family and nonfamily, to work at wages and conditions prevailing in the household-shop. This influence especially affected the master's ability to impose "submarket" wages and working conditions on resident workers, especially on insiders. To some extent all three of these issues were related.

One or several of three factors conditioned the supply of nonfamily labor on the labor market: (1) migration, (2) age and sex distribution of the population, and (3) wage and employment opportunities in trades other than domestic silk weaving. Migration affected labor of two kinds. One of these was temporary outside labor, furnished by the mass of "floating" journeymen who migrated to Lyon from the surrounding countryside in periods of brisk demand and returned there when the demand for labor sagged.[58] The other was nonfamily inside labor recruited from countryside migrants, usually women and children, who settled in Lyon for a longer period to accumulate a dowry or to learn a trade.[59] In Second Empire Lyon, the spread of silk weaving to the countryside tended to reduce the first source of labor supply. Floating journeymen no longer had to travel to the city to find work in the silk industry, and they were indeed reluctant to return to Lyon after long periods of unemployment. During the recovery of 1858 from such a period of work stoppage, "young people sent back to their families during the previous recession hesitate[d] to return" to Lyon, creating an acute labor shortage in the city. As a result of this shortage, merchant-manufacturers "found themselves obliged . . . to increase on their own initiative the amount of the piece rate, which thus rose about 30% in a short period of time."[60] They had to do the same during the spring 1868 recovery, again because of a labor shortage stemming, most probably, from the same cause.[61] Thus, migrant journeyman labor was much less responsive to cyclical opportunities in urban industry than it had been in the past, and its response was elicited only through raising the piece rate—a price merchants were not always willing to pay. From the master-weaver's point of view, these migrant journeymen were a less reliable source of outside labor for executing orders arriving at a moment's notice, especially after long periods of unemployment.

Economic and social conditions of the city as a whole affected the second source of migrant labor, that which settled in the city for a longer period. This migrant labor consisted largely of women and young adolescents. Traditionally, women, especially those who were young and unmarried, sought work as *dévideuses* or as other auxiliary workers in the *fabrique*, while 14- or 15-year-olds, male and female, were placed by their parents as apprentice weavers in the masters' shops.[62] Both groups of workers migrated with the intention of remaining for several years, either to accumulate a dowry or to receive certified training in a craft. Some settled permanently in the city, marrying a weaver or setting up shop on their own. During the 1850s and 1860s this pattern of traditional migration changed as a result of transformations in the silk industry. The city's role as a provider of auxiliary services became more important, giving additional work to *dévideuses* especially, but its role as a cloth-weaving center declined, reducing the demand for apprentices. However, another series of developments—broader industrial expansion and urban renewal—complicated this picture. Such developments provided a wide range of additional employment in skilled trades, which serviced the growing railroad, machinery, and steamboat industries,[63] and also provided both skilled and unskilled work in building projects sponsored by the Second Empire government.[64] This additional demand for labor, beyond that coming from the silk industry, attracted a large number of artisans to the city from surrounding towns and villages.[65] These often came with their families, and their wives and daughters increased the pool of female labor available for work in the silk industry, since most of the new jobs outside of silks were for men. An additional effect of urban renewal was the provision of alternate employment for unskilled journeyman weavers on public works, when looms were inactive in the silk industry.[66] This may have kept some floating journeymen from returning to their villages of origin during periods of slow work in urban silk weaving, thus maintaining a supply of outside labor for temporary employment by masters.

Besides these effects on migration, new urban industries competed for labor with silk manufacture, usually offering better pay and more regular employment to skilled male workers than the silk industry. In October 1856, when average daily earnings of silk weavers ranged from 1.00 to 2.75 francs, reflecting severe unemployment in the trade, average earnings of dyers, stonemasons, carpenters and mechanics ranged from 3.00 francs to 4.00, 5.00, and 6.00 francs. In all of these industries except dyeing there was a shortage of workers.[67] In the last quarter of 1866, when plain cloth weaving languished in the city, when fancy weaving was "still in a bad situation," and when average daily earnings were 1.50 to 3.50 francs for plains and 2.00 to 4.50 francs for fancies, the *Ateliers de la Buire*, a railroad car manufacturer, hired 130 additional workers, paying them 2.75, 5.00, and 6.00 francs per day.[68] Because of these more favorable conditions in other trades, many weavers abandoned their profession during the 1860s. In September 1867 plain velvet weavers were said to prefer work at any task other than weaving, which paid so little, since if one were "hard working," one could "earn more by being a common laborer."[69] In March 1869, those able to find work that was even "a bit continuous," earning 2.00 or 2.50 francs per day, left "weaving aside rather than making two or three pieces and having nothing to do afterwards."[70] Fancy cloth weavers, in particular, tended "bit by bit to renounce a trade whose product [was] insufficient to provide for [their] needs."[71]

This competition for labor by other trades caused the supply curve of outside male labor to shift leftward. In contrast to this tightening, women's labor for weaving and for other household tasks seems to have become more abundant, and therefore cheaper. In September 1868, when the position of men in silk manufacture was "still holding up despite the decline of wages," that of women was "intolerable because their average wage hardly [went] above 1.20 [francs] per day in some privileged categories and certainly [did] not exceed .75 [francs] for the largest number of those employed for ordinary tasks."[72] Besides immigration, which increased the number of women workers in the city in ways described earlier, the lack of better opportunities for women in trades outside of silk weaving or silk-related tasks (such as *dévidage*) probably explains this low wage to a large extent. The availability of cheap female labor gave masters a ready source of inside or outside labor for employment, not only in the auxiliary trades traditionally dominated by women but also in weaving. Even fancy cloth weaving, traditionally dominated by men, became more accessible to women during the 1860s. Among the possible reasons for this were the substitution of common fancies for the more elegant cloths, which required more skill and strength, as the primary source of employment, and the departure of men from fancy cloth weaving to seek employment elsewhere. The increase in the proportion of women in household-shops indicates, to some extent, the new importance of women's work in the domestic weaving economy. This increase was especially strong in fancy-loom households, where the average proportion of women in the census sample rose from 46 to 59 percent between 1847 and 1866, as compared with a milder rise of 58 to 61 percent in plain-loom households.[73] The increase also reflected the growing importance of women as inside workers, for reasons to be discussed shortly.

The availability of alternate sources of employment in Second Empire Lyon raised the opportunity cost of working in the domestic shop for members of the master-weaver's own family as well. From the master's perspective, this cost was essentially the household income foregone by keeping family members at work in the shop instead of having them pursue a trade in a growth industry in the city. Opportunities outside the household-shop were apparently either so lucrative or so secure, in comparison with domestic silk manufacture, that by the late 1860s, "master weavers [were] even having their children learn other trades."[74] Some opportunities became available in the silk industry as well, but outside of the domestic shop. One of these was work as a *commis* (distributing agent) in the establishment of a merchant-manufacturer. This apparently became a common avenue of advancement for master's sons, as a merchant-manufacturer suggested in the early 1870s.[75]

From the family member's own perspective, forsaking such opportunities for better income or advancement was the price paid for the security, affection, authority, sense of family pride, or whatever else the paternal household-shop could offer, and which the family member could not expect to find in work outside the father's or husband's shop. By the early 1870s, opportunities for work outside the domestic shop instilled "ideas of independence" in the masters' children, inducing them to leave "the paternal roof" at "too early" an age. Once having left, they thought only "of their own needs and pleasures" rather than of the "needs of their family."[76] This tendency of course limited the supply of inside labor from this family source.

The master's paternal influence was also a significant factor in inducing non-family workers to accept inside labor status and to remain in that status for a long period. Like family members faced with other opportunities outside the household-shop, these workers valued the intimacy, security, and authority structure they found in the paternal environment as sufficient compensation for the loss of independence, income, or advancement they could attain in another status or trade. To the extent that this paternal influence was strong, the master could effectively "bend" the supply curve of labor in his favor. This strength, however, was dependent both upon other opportunities and upon the cultural-moral climate making workers more or less desirous of the unique benefits of the paternal household-shop. In the 1850s, growing opportunities for employment in the city overall, a brisk demand for labor in silk weaving, and a changed cultural environment made masters' assertion of paternal influence over their journeymen harder than ever before. These journeymen appeared more "unruly" than in the past, at least to some outside observers. Between masters and journeymen, remarked the distinguished sociologist A. Audiganne in 1852, one "hardly sees reigning any more . . . this friendly sympathy which apparently ought to have emerged from the similarity of their situation. The [master] often finds in the worker an unruly collaborator whose peevish and fickle desires he must endure because of commitments made."[77] Journeymen were known to violate work agreements and generally to disregard the quality of their work.[78] The most disturbing feature of this behavior was its extension to even the "most able journeymen, who know that they are needed . . .: they accept the *chef d'atelier* neither as master nor as equal, but as a renter of looms, a sort of co-sharer in the piece-rate."[79] This recalcitrance of journeymen effectively raised their cost to the master, making masters more inclined to replace journeymen with women weavers, apprentices, or family members.

The master's own actions also affected the strength of his paternal influence. In the 1850s, masters' disregard for their traditional obligations toward apprentices, including their failure to observe the traditional formalities of apprentice contracts, provoked a rebellion of sorts among apprentices affecting the quality of their work. In 1855 the president of the *Conseil des prud'hommes* reported a large number of annulments of apprentice contracts made with "children too young and too weak" or "for lack of care on the part of masters who, forgetting the obligations imposed on them by law, exploit their apprentices so badly that they ruin their health. . . ." The same report noted that many contracts were made verbally, causing "the most vigorous contests."[80] In this period of exceptionally high food prices and unpredictable work stoppage, such masters probably sought the maximum advantage from their apprentices for the least cost by making verbal contracts and by dismissing their charges when orders became short. One suspects that the "spirit of insubordination which, for a certain time, has been notable among apprentices," causing "the largest number of annulments" of contracts in 1855, was part of the apprentices' reaction to this poor treatment.[81] This exploitation and insubordination caused a decline in apprenticeship as inside labor in the traditional sense, that is, as labor performed under the master's paternal influence. The insignificant number of apprentices in sample households of master-weavers from the 1866 census[82] and the marked decline in the number of apprentice contracts reported by the *Conseil des prud'hommes* in the same year[83] were signs of this decline.

The effects of these various changes on the supply of inside and outside labor in the domestic economy may be summarized as follows. First, the number of journeyman weavers available to the master on terms suitable to him declined either because of better opportunities for their employment elsewhere or because of a diminished respect for or subservience to the master, making their job performance less satisfactory. Masters were therefore faced with a growing difficulty of recruiting reliable outside male labor for weaving during periods of brisk demand. After 1860 some of the same alternate opportunities and a similar weakening of paternal influence reduced the effective supply of family labor for undertaking these tasks, especially labor of male children. Masters therefore had to turn to other sources of labor, either other inside labor or women's labor working on an inside or outside basis. The crisis of apprenticeship lessened the attractiveness, and indeed the availability, of apprentice insiders as a way of compensating for the smaller number of journeymen. The case was quite different, however, for women's labor. Augmented by a flood of migrants with few better employment alternatives, the supply of women workers available for work in the silk industry increased. Women were cheap to hire, and their inferior social position made them more docile than the unruly journeymen. In fact, as we will see shortly, these women provided masters with a ready solution to the emerging labor shortage in their changing household economy.

V. THE NEW DOMESTIC ECONOMY OF SILK WEAVING

Combining these several effects of demand and supply of household labor, we can now form an image of the weavers' domestic economy. First of all, we observe a strong bias in favor of inside labor. On the demand side, this derived from masters' growing concern for cost savings in auxiliary tasks, and from their need for "readiness" or for productive use of delays between orders. The growing scarcity of the outside labor supply for weaving, because of the diminished importance of floating migration, better opportunities in other trades, and declining paternal influence, heightened the advantages of inside labor from the perspective of "readiness." Moreover, the piece-rate increases required to attract labor in times of brisk demand raised the advantages of replacing outside with inside labor, especially in fancy cloth weaving, through the savings in the half-share of the rate which use of inside labor allowed. Masters discovered, moreover, that they could achieve savings in auxiliary costs by replacing outsiders with insiders in weaving and by shifting inside labor between weaving and auxiliary work as the occasion required. The character of cloth demand in the 1860s, frequent delays between orders, and the small scale of the household-shop enterprise made such shifting both feasible and economical.

The question then arises, where were masters to find an adequate supply of insiders available to work on weaving and auxiliary tasks? Apprentice labor became increasingly problematic, as masters used their apprentices with little concern for their traditional responsibilities toward them and as apprentices responded with insubordination. Verbal agreements between masters and apprentices, which could be broken easily by either party and which freed masters from their obligation of support in times of uncertain employment or high food prices, reflected this crisis of apprenticeship. The supply of female labor available for employment in the household-shop increased in the same period, however. Masters readily took advantage of this additional source of labor for their domestic tasks. By the 1850s, women replaced men as *compagnonnes* in weaving plain silks, for which their weaving skills and physical strength made them as capable as men.[84] In the 1860s women wove fancy silks in large numbers as well, probably the simpler *petits façonnés* and *hautes nouveautés* for the most part.[85] Although, as noted earlier, this female labor was available for both outside and inside status, the relative security and protection which inside status offered probably induced many of these women workers to seek work as insiders. Masters, for their part, found women ideal for inside status. As a result women effectively provided masters a pool of inside labor well suited to their purposes.

Comments by some outside observers suggest that many female weavers, for instance, were treated as insiders, fed and lodged by the master and regarded as "children of the shop . . . attached as to the hearth of the family."[86] As insiders, women weavers received lower wages than journeymen,[87] although one observer, Jules Simon, argued that this was the result of their "natural" physical weakness, reducing their daily output, especially in the weaving of the more complex fabrics, rather than the effect of any discrimination in the amount of the piece rate they received.[88] However, even Simon noted that women weavers ate less food than men in the master's shop,[89] and in this sense their effective real wage as inside labor was less. Women weavers were also more docile than men[90] and therefore could be assigned to additional tasks associated with inside status, such as auxiliary work. Indeed, Simon contrasted their situation with that of men by pointing to their "fatiguing work" along with their lesser needs.[91]

The substitution of women for men in weaving, in short, enabled masters to achieve many of the gains associated with inside labor for a task that had been traditionally performed by outsiders (when performed by workers who were not family members) and to substitute inside for outside work on auxiliary tasks at the same time.

However, this substitution cannot account fully for the observed pattern of predominantly insider household-shops in the 1860s. Some literary evidence of the period suggests that many women workers, both weavers and auxiliary workers, continued to work on an outside, nonresident basis.[92] Moreover, census samples indicate that some 40 percent of the household residents were male.[93] Clearly a large share of the inside labor force came from another source: family labor. The census data show that the proportion of sample households with one or more members not related to master or spouse declined between 1847 and 1866, from 42 to 36 percent for predominantly plain-loom households and from 75 to 33 percent for predominantly fancy-loom households. The average number of nonrelatives fell accordingly—from 1.47 to 1.17 (−20 percent) for plains households and from 1.88 to 1.00 (−47 percent) for fancies households. In both cases the decline was significantly greater than the decline in the number of members related to head or spouse (−2 percent for plains, −24 percent for fancies).[94] Measuring the adequacy of this more familial resident household for occupying active looms, by means of an "entrepreneurial" index, confirms this impression of familialization for the household work force as well. The index represents the sufficiency of the family work force as compared, first, with nonrelative residents of weaving age and, second, with nonresidents, for occupying all active looms in the household. This index was large for both plains and fancies households in 1866 (79 and 67 percent, respectively). For fancies households it was significantly larger than in 1847 (67 percent compared with 49 percent in 1847).[95]

Responses of merchant-manufacturers in the early 1870s to a government enquiry about conditions in the silk industry give a similar impression of both the resident household and the household work force. Nonfamily workers, when present, not only did not live in the household[96] but also rarely took meals with the master and his family.[97] Thus "the journeyman worker [was] no longer included in the family as in the past."[98] But even the presence of such outside workers in the household shop was minimal. There were only "a few" masters with "more than one outside worker."[99] The household shop consisted essentially of the wife working alongside her husband, "either occupying a loom or reeling silk used by her husband,"[100] and of some of their children working as apprentices.[101] Older children tended to drift away from work in the household shop, either to seek better employment elsewhere, as in establishments of merchant-manufacturers,[102] or to cultivate their pleasures.[103] Thus the increasingly familial household-shop was smaller than in the past, as the census data confirm.[104]

However, the household weaving economy did not necessarily coincide with the household (or home) economy, as the Vernay household, described at the beginning of this essay, illustrates. In the Vernay household, there were two older children not involved in the weaving enterprise. Presumably their work as *tailleuse* and *employé*, respectively, added income to the Vernay home budget. This household effectively moved from what Joan Scott and Louise Tilly have called a *family economy*, focused on production within the domestic setting, closer to a *family wage economy*, where household income came largely from wages earned outside.[105] Indeed, the Vernay example underscores the commitment of master-weavers to the preservation of their domestic economy of silk weaving. Masters used all means available from their situation and milieu, especially the varieties of labor, but also the opportunities for outside work for their children, to maintain their household enterprise. This commitment to the domestic economy for its own sake mirrored the attachment of the American farmers of Parker's family farms to their small, predominantly familial enterprise for reasons that were nonpecuniary, even if they were economic in the largest sense of that term. Regarded from the perspective of the silk weavers' experience, such a commitment may also explain a large part of the resilience of this seemingly primitive and fragile type of productive enterprise in a context of profound economic change.

ACKNOWLEDGMENTS

Research for this paper was supported by funds from the Georges Lurcy Trust and the Concilium on International and Area Studies at Yale University. Versions of the paper were presented at the annual meetings of the Economic and Business Historical Society (Los Angeles, April 1979) and the Social Science History Association (Rochester, New York, November 1980). The following people commented on one or the other of these versions: Reed Geiger, William N. Parker, Miriam Cohen, Gavin Wright, and Martha Shiells. I am especially grateful to Ms. Shiells for her close reading and critique.

NOTES

1.   Archives municipales de Lyon (hereafter AML), *Recensement*, Croix-Rousse, 1844, District Enfance, p. 38, household Antoine Vernay.

2.   Archives départementales du Rhône (hereafter ADR), 6M-*Dénombrement*, 1866, Lyon, 4ème arrondissement, 4ème Canton, Vol. XVI, p. 160, household Antoine Vernay.

3.   *Enquête Parlementaire Sur les Conditions du Travail en France* (Rhône, 1872–1875), [Réponses de] Mrs. Faye et Thevenin F[abric]ants de soieries à Lyon (Rhône), Troisième Questionnaire C, 22, 19; Réponses de la Chambre Syndicale des Soieries de Lyon, Troisième Questionnaire C, 19, in Archives nationales (Paris) (hereafter AN), C 3021, *Enquête sur les Conditions du Travail en France (1872 à 1875), Région du Sud-Est (Rhône)*.

4.   Ibid., Réponses de la Chambre Syndicale des Soieries, Premier Questionnaire A. Observations.

5.   "Rapport à Monsieur Delcourt, Commissaire spécial, sur la situation de la fabrique," March 6, 1869, AML, I² 47, No. 312.

6. *Enquête Parlementaire,* Faye et Thevenin, Troisième Questionnaire C, 9.

7. Household Antoine Vernay, AML (1844) and ADR (1866).

8. William N. Parker's essay on "Agriculture" in Lance E. Davis et al., *American Economic Growth: An Economist's History of the United States* (New York: Harper & Row, 1972), pp. 393–396, 403–405.

9. See, for instance, Gavin Wright, *The Political Economy of the Cotton South: Households, Markets and Wealth in the Nineteenth Century* (New York: Norton, 1978), Chap. 3; and Heywood Fleisig, "Slavery, the Supply of Agricultural Labor, and the Industrialization of the South," *Journal of Economic History,* 36 (September 1976): 572–597.

10. "Mémoires recueillis par le citoyen Weichmann, chef d'atelier, rue du sentier, no. 8 à la Croix-Rousse," April 2, 1850, AN, F¹² 2203 (2): *Machines à tisser (1844 à 1866).*

11. 'Compte d'inventaire,' ibid.

12. In a strict economic sense, of course, the incidental expenses of food and upkeep associated with employing outside labor should also be regarded as part of the ''wage'' offered for the services of this labor. This portion of the wage was subject to revision according to the household consumption standards as much as the wage of the inside worker. For this reason it would be more proper to speak of degrees of ''insideness'' or ''outsideness,'' instead of making a sharp distinction between the two types of labor. Making such a distinction does simplify and clarify the analysis, however. It does so in a more or less accurate way, moreover, since the share of the wage independent of household consumption was the major portion of the outsider's wage and the lesser portion of the wage of the inside worker.

13. 'L'Apprentissage' and 'Compte d'inventaire,' "Mémoires recueillis par le citoyen Weichmann''; AML, *Recensement,* Croix-Rousse, 1847.

14. In a sample of 175 households of weavers in the Croix-Rousse, taken from the 1847 census, there were *dévidoirs* in 44, or 25 percent of the households. AML, *Recensement,* Croix-Rousse, 1847, sample.

15. ''Extracts of Communication from *Charnier,* a Chef d'atelier and Prud'homme of Lyons, dated 16th May 1832,'' John Bowring, Esq., report to the Select Committee on the Silk Trade, June 18, 1832, Great Britain, House of Commons, *Report from Select Committee on the Silk Trade With the Minutes of Evidence, an Appendix and Index,* ordered by the House of Commons to be printed, 2 August, 1832 (London, 1832), p. 557, ques. 8930.

16. 'L'Apprentissage,' "Mémoires recueillis par le citoyen Weichmann.''

17. Jules Simon, "L'Apprentissage,'' *Le Progrès* (Lyon), February 13, 1865. This may refer primarily to *dévideuses* taken on by mistress *dévideuses* in specialized reeling shops. However, the context of the quotation and the responses to the article (such as that of César Maire, "A propos d'apprentissage,'' *Le Progrès,* February 26, 1865) suggest that Simon's description of the condition of *dévideuses* applied to shops of master weavers as well.

18. Ministère des travaux publics, de l'agriculture et du commerce, *Statistique de la France. Commerce extérieur* (Paris, 1838), Tableaux 193–6, Commerce spécial; Administration des douanes, *Tableau décennal du commerce de la France. 2e Partie* (Paris: Imprimerie nationale), for the years 1837–1846, 1847–1856, 1857–1866, 1867–1876.

19. Michel Laferrère, *Lyon: ville industrielle* (Paris: Presses universitaires de France, 1960), pp. 126–127 (note 108), 153–154.

20. Ibid., p. 127; *Compte-rendu des travaux de la Chambre de Commerce de Lyon, années 1865, 1866, 1867, 1868,* p. 24, located in Bibliothèque de la Chambre de Commerce de Lyon.

21. E. Pariset, *Histoire de la fabrique lyonnaise* (Lyon: A. Rey, 1901), pp. 339–340; Laferrère, *Lyon: ville industrielle,* pp. 131–132; Pierre Cayez, *Crises et croissance de l'industrie lyonnaise, 1850–1900* (Lyon: Editions du CNRS, 1980), pp. 23–26.

22. Cayez, *Crises et croissance,* pp. 38–41.

23. Estimates of numbers of urban and rural looms based on several detailed sources. The sources are listed in Table 7 of George J. Sheridan, Jr., *Social and Economic Foundations of*

Association Among the Silk Weavers of Lyons, 1852–1870 (New York: Arno Press, 1981), p. 195. See also Cayez, *Crises et croissance*, p. 56.

24. Reports from Prefect of Rhône to Minister of Interior, August 12, September 8, November 9, 1853; January 10, March 10, May 9, 1854, AN, F¹ᶜ III Rhône 5 *Compte-rendus administratifs (An III à 1870)*.

25. Ibid., July 15, October 18, 1855; January 18, April 11, July 14, October 13, 1856; January 15, 1857; report on employment and wages in Lyon industry, October 31, 1856, AML, I² 47, No. 182; "Situation industrielle au 15 Juin 1859," AML, I² 47, No. 166.

26. Dronier, *Essai sur la décadence actuelle de la fabrique lyonnaise*, p. 5.

27. 'Etoffes façonnées,' "Situation industrielle—15 Mars 1866—Soierie et industries qui s'y rattachent," AML, I² 47, No. 186.

28. 'Etoffes unies,' "Situation industrielle," June 15, 1859 through December 1869, AML, I² 47, Nos. 166–212.

29. 'Etoffes façonnées,' "Situation industrielle," June 15, 1860 through June 15, 1864, AML, I² 47, Nos. 169–181.

30. 'Etoffes façonnées,' "Situation industrielle au Mars 1868," AML, I² 47, No. 201.

31. Ibid.; "Situation industrielle au Juin 1868," AML, I² 47, No. 204.

32. 'Etoffes façonnées,' "Situation industrielle au Mars 1869," AML, I² 47, No. 207.

33. 'Etoffes façonnées,' "Situation industrielle," June 1867; June and December 1868; September 1869, AML, I² 47, Nos. 197, 204, 206, 211.

34. 'Etoffes unies,' "Situation industrielle au Juin 1868," AML, I² 47, No. 204.

35. 'Etoffes unies,' "Situation industrielle au Mars 1868," AML, I² 47, No. 201.

36. 'Etoffes unies,' "Situation industrielle au 14 Septembre 1869," AML, I² 47, No. 211.

37. Petition of Tray et al. to Emperor Napoleon III, August 1860, Archives de la Chambre de Commerce de Lyon, *Soieries, Carton 41, I, Législation-Usages (an 8 à 1936)*, liasse 13.

38. This analysis ignores the opportunity cost of using insiders for weaving instead of sending them outside the household to work in other, higher paying jobs. The master's interest in maintaining paternal influence over inside workers probably tended to push down this cost, or at least the perceived opportunity cost. Such influence was most likely fostered by keeping insiders employed in the household-shop rather than by sending them outside the shop to fetch the best possible return.

39. 'Etoffes façonnées,' "Situation de l'Industrie au 15 7bre [sic] 1866," AML, I² 47, No. 192 and 'Etoffes façonnées,' "Situation industrielle au Mars 1869," AML, I² 47, No. 207.

40. Petition of Tray et al. to Emperor Napoleon III.

41. 'Etoffes unies,' "Situation de l'Industrie à Lyon, au 15 Mars 1867," AML, I² 47, No. 196.

42. Laferrère, *Lyon: ville industrielle*, pp. 147–152.

43. 'Etoffes unies,' "Situation industrielle au Juin 1868," AML, I² 47, No. 204.

44. "Mémoires recueillis par le citoyen Weichmann," 2ème Partie, Chap. 2. Inventaire de métier aidant à faire les inventaires d'attelier [sic], définissant les salaires d'ouvriers hommes ou femmes; budget of chef d'atelier, no date (1864–5?), AML, I² 47, No. 921.

45. Report on employment and wages in Lyon industry, October 31, 1856, AML, I² 47, No. 182; 'Dévidage,' "Situation industrielle à Lyon au 3 Octobre 1859," AML, I² 47, No. 168 and 'Dévidage,' "Situation industrielle," March 15, June, September 15, December 1867 and March, June, September 12, 1868, AML, I² 47, Nos. 196–198, 200–201, 204, 205bis.

46. 'Dévidage,' "Situation industrielle—15 Mars 1866—Soieries et industries qui s'y rattachent," AML, I² 47, No. 186.

47. 'Dévidage,' "Situation de l'Industrie à Lyon au 25 Juin 1865," AML, I² 47, No. 183.

48. 'Dévideuses,' "Rapport à Monsieur Delcourt, Commissaire spécial, sur la situation de la fabrique des étoffes de soies au 4ème Trimestre Xbre [sic] 1866," December 8, 1866, AML, I² 47, No. 301; 'Dévidage,' "Situation industrielle au Juin 1868," AML, I² 47, No. 204; E. Pariset, report to the Chamber of Commerce of Lyon concerning children in industry, June 15, 1867, *Compte-rendu des travaux de la Chambre de Commerce de Lyon, années 1865, 1866, 1867, 1868*, pp. 148–150.

49. Petition of Tray et al. to Emperor Napoleon III.

50. AML, *Recensement*, Croix-Rousse, 1847, sample.

51. 'Tordeuses,' "Situation de l'Industrie à Lyon au 25 Juin 1865," AML, I² 47, No. 183; 'Tordeurs de soies et monteurs de métiers,' "Situation industrielle au Mars 1869," AML, I² 47, No. 207.

52. Report on employment and wages in Lyon industry, October 31, 1856, AML, I² 47, No. 182.

53. 'Tordeurs de soies et monteurs de métiers,' "15 Juin 1866," AML, I² 47, No. 187.

54. Yves Lequin, *Les Ouvriers de la région lyonnaise (1848–1914)*, Vol. 2: *Les Intérêts de classe et la république* (Lyon: Presses universitaires de Lyon, 1977), pp. 21–22.

55. Report from Prefect of Rhône to Minister of Interior, September 8, 1853, AN, F¹ᶜ III Rhône 5.

56. Ibid., March 10, 1854.

57. ADR, 6M-*Dénombrement*, 1866, Lyon, 4ème arrondissement, sample.

58. Robert J. Bezucha, *The Lyon Uprising of 1834: Social and Political Conflict in the Early July Monarchy* (Cambridge, Mass.: Harvard University Press, 1974), pp. 55–56, 123.

59. Maurice Garden, *Lyon et les lyonnais au XVIIIe siècle*, Bibliothèque de la Faculté des Lettres de Lyon, XVIII (Paris: Société d'édition 'Les Belles-lettres,' 1970), pp. 52–62; Yves Lequin, *Les Ouvriers de la région lyonnaise (1848–1914)*, Vol. 1: *La Formation de la classe ouvrière régionale* (Lyon: Presses universitaires de Lyon, 1977), pp. 135–136.

60. Report from President of the *Conseil des Prud'hommes de Lyon* to Prefect of Rhône, August 3, 1858, ADR, U-*Prud'hommes de Lyon, Correspondance relative aux élections (1806 à 1870)*: report from Prefect of Rhône to Minister of Interior, January 10, 1859, AN, F¹ᶜ III Rhône 5.

61. 'Etoffes unies,' "Situation industrielle au Juin 1868," AML, I² 47, No. 204.

62. Garden, *Lyon et les lyonnais aux XVIIIe siècle*, pp. 52–62.

63. Laferrère, *Lyon: ville industrielle*, pp. 256–304; Cayez, *Crises et croissance*, pp. 107–122, 280–298; Lequin, *Les Ouvriers de la région lyonnaise*, Vol. 1: 168; Maurice Moissonnier, *La Première internationale et la Commune à Lyon* (Paris: Editions sociales, 1972), p. 27.

64. See Charlene-Marie Leonard, *Lyon Transformed: Public Works of the Second Empire* (Berkeley: University of California Press, 1961).

65. Lequin, *Les Ouvriers de la région lyonnaise*, Vol. 1, pp. 179–180, 221–238, 249–250, 261–266.

66. Reports from Prefect of Rhône to Minister of Interior, July 20, 1857 and April 30, 1858, AN, F¹ᶜ III Rhône 5.

67. Report on employment and wages in Lyon industry, October 31, 1856, AML, I² 47, No. 182.

68. "Situation de l'industrie à Lyon au 15 Décembre 1866," AML, I² 47, No. 193.

69. "Rapport à Monsieur Delcourt, Commissaire spécial sur la situation de la fabrique des étoffes de soies," September 9, 1867, AML, I² 47, No. 305.

70. "Rapport à Monsieur Delcourt, Commissaire spécial sur la situation de la fabrique," March 6, 1869, AML, I² 47, No. 312.

71. 'Etoffes façonnées,' "Situation industrielle au Mars 1869," AML, I² 47, No. 207.

72. "Rapport adressé à Monsieur Delcourt, Commissaire spécial," September 9, 1868, AML, I² 47, No. 309.

73. AML, *Recensement*, Croix-Rousse, 1847, sample; ADR, 6M-*Dénombrement*, 1866, Lyon, 4ème arrondissement, sample. The standard deviations for these averages are 35.4 and 41.7 for fancies and 39.8 and 40.1 for plains.

74. "Rapport à Monsieur Delcourt, Commissaire spécial, sur la situation de la fabrique," March 6, 1869, AML, I² 47, No. 312.

75. *Enquête Parlementaire*, Faye et Thevenin, Troisième Questionnaire C, 9.

76. *Enquête Parlementaire*, Réponses de la Chambre de Commerce de Lyon, Troisième Questionnaire C, 6.

77. A. Audiganne, "Du mouvement intellectual parmi les populations ouvrières—Les ouvriers de Lyon en 1852," *Revue des deux mondes*, 22ème année—nouvelle période, 15 (August 1, 1852), 516–517.

78. Louis Reybaud, *Etudes sur le régime des manufactures: Condition des ouvriers en soie* (Paris, 1859), p. 170.

79. Audiganne, "Du mouvement intellectuel," p. 516.

80. Felix Bertrand, *Compte-rendu des travaux du Conseil des Prud'hommes de Lyon, année 1855* (Lyon: C. Bonnaviat, 1856), p. 9, ADR, U-*Prud'hommes de Lyon, Correspondance relative aux élections (1806 à 1870)*.

81. Ibid.; Bertrand, Report from President of *Conseil des Prud'hommes de Lyon* to Prefect of Rhône, June 29, 1854, ADR, ibid.

82. In the 1866 census sample, only 4 of 181 households of master-weavers had an apprentice identified by the census taker. ADR, 6M-*Dénombrement*, 1866, Lyon, 4ème arrondissement, sample.

83. Jules Bonnet, *Compte-rendu des travaux du Conseil des Prud'hommes pendant la dernière période triennale* (Lyon: C. Bonnaviat, 1866), p. 5, ADR, U-*Prud'hommes de Lyon, Correspondance relative aux élections (1806 à 1870)*.

84. Audiganne, "Du mouvement intellectuel," p. 513.

85. Jules Simon, *L'Ouvrière* (Paris: Hachette, 1861), p. 32. See also announcements of meetings of fancy cloth weavers in 1870 addressed to "masters, male workers, female workers," such as that in *Le Progrès*, March 16, 1870. Also see police report on fancy weavers' strike, July 10, 1870, which refers to men and women journeyworkers in this category, in AML, I² 47 (B), Ouvriers façonnés.

86. Reybaud, *Etudes sur le régime des manufactures*, p. 154.

87. Ibid.

88. Simon, *L'Ouvrière*, p. 32.

89. Ibid, p. 41.

90. Reybaud, *Etudes*, p. 154.

91. Simon, *L'Ouvrière*, p. 41.

92. Ibid., pp. 44–45.

93. See Table 1.

94. Ibid., AML, *Recensement*, Croix-Rousse, 1847, sample.

95. Ibid. These are average figures for households in the sample. The standard deviations are 38.5, 52.6, 52.6, and 40.6 for each figure, respectively.

96. *Enquête Parlementaire*, Réponses de la Chambre Syndicale des Soieries de Lyon, Premier Questionnaire A, IV.

97. Ibid., Réponses de la Chambre de Commerce de Lyon, Premier Questionnaire A, XI.

98. Ibid.

99. Ibid., Faye et Thevenin, Troisième Questionnaire C, 22.

100. Ibid., 21.

101. Ibid., 24, 26; Réponses de la Chambre de Commerce, Second Questionnaire B, I. This is essentially my impression based on these responses and on my analysis of the census samples for 1866.

102. Ibid., Faye et Thevenin, Troisième Questionnaire C, 9.

103. Ibid., Réponses de la Chambre de Commerce, Troisième Questionnaire C, 6.

104. ADR, 6M-*Dénombrement*, 1866, Lyon, 4ème arrondissement, sample.

105. Louise A. Tilly and Joan W. Scott, *Women, Work and Family* (New York: Holt, Rinehart and Winston, 1978), pp. 227–228.

ARE CARTELS UNSTABLE?
THE GERMAN STEEL WORKS ASSOCIATION
BEFORE WORLD WAR I

Lon L. Peters

I. INTRODUCTION

German industrial growth before 1914 has often been traced to the tradition among German businessmen to cooperate, to establish a stable climate where collusive and protected profits promote rapid expansion and related growth in productivity. Large firm size, combined with alleged cooperation with banks and structured formally in organizations known as cartels, is offered as an explanation of the basis for growth before World War I. The existence of interfirm cooperation is clear; a government inquiry into cartels in 1905 discovered 385 such organizations controlling even food and beverages.[1] The motivations, dynamics, and effects of all this cooperation are not, however, straightforward. Trying to explain motivation, Alfred Marshall, usually known for sober insights

Technique, Spirit, and Form in the Making of the Modern Economies:
Essays in Honor of William N. Parker
Research in Economic History, Suppl. 3, pages 61–85
Copyright © 1984 by JAI Press Inc.
All rights of reproduction in any form reserved.
ISBN: 0-89232-414-7

into the economic order, presented in *Industry and Trade* a good example of the "national psychology" school of industrial historiography:

> The tasks involved in cartellization are appropriate to the temper of the German people. The long hours of more or less intensive work, to which they are accustomed, enable them to attend numerous discussions without difficulty; the discipline, to which they have been seasoned in military service, inclines them to submit easily to cartel regulation; and what is perhaps equally important, the semi-military organization of cartels is well adapted to the purposes of autocratic rule, which regards peace as the time of preparation for war.[2]

Written before World War I, these words reflect an almost unanimous international perception of an important component of German industry: an organizational drive singular in its complexity and pervasiveness, characterized by a proliferation of interfirm accords in the form of both bilateral, long-term delivery contracts and multilateral contractual agreements known as cartels.

Some of William N. Parker's earliest research in economic history considered the links between entrepreneurship, industrial organization, and economic growth in Germany. Parker warned explicitly that simple models of entrepreneurial motivation must grow "more complex and subtle" when the economic historian confronts institutions designed to avoid the market.[3] Modern cartel theory, generally avoiding this suggestion, postulates a simple change in price and output when a cartel is formed by previously competitive firms. The maximizing strategy is assumed to shift from individual to collective profits, while the organization of production adjusts to a new, lower level of output. This adjustment is, however, only temporary because some members (which ones is unclear) succumb to individual incentives to "overproduce." Recent work by Thomas Ulen has tied the asymmetry of collusive tendencies more closely to the business cycle, but exogenous changes in demand or technology are not critical to the prediction of cartel instability based on shifting loyalty.[4] But not *all* cartels are unstable. Modern observers are confronted with the survival of OPEC but the failure of many other international primary product cartels. Certainly exogenous forces may differ from one cartel to the next, but we also need to know how these "conspiracies against the public," in Adam Smith's phrase, respond to the shifting sands of demand and technology. The "logic of collective action" for a cartel may deviate widely from the logic of individual entrepreneurship.

There appears to be a consensus that the goals of the German organizations included stabilizing markets and controlling production.[5] Although stabilization and control may seem relatively straightforward concepts, prominent historical questions require additional refinement. Firms and cartels may try to stabilize prices, growth of production, profits, market structure, employment, investment, or even the general social and legal climate in which business is conducted. These are not necessarily compatible goals, and priorities may differ from firm to firm. There is also the question of short-run vs. long-run stability; absence of the former, if it results in the demise of inefficient firms and an increase in industrial concentration, may promote the latter, depending on the behavior of the survivors. Scattered but suggestive evidence indicates that almost all of the above goals found expression at the assemblies of the Rhenish–Westphalian Coal Syndicate and the Steel Works Association before 1914. The only general exception was profits, though of course it is possible for stable profits to result from attention to one or more of the other goals.[6] In the present paper, attention will focus on the stability of a certain mix of production in the Steel Works Association from 1904 to 1912. It will be seen that this element of stability was tied, as one might expect, to investment decisions made during this period, as well as to certain exogenous forces beyond the control of the member firms.

II. INDUSTRIAL INSTABILITY: ENDOGENOUS FORCES

In "The Collapse of the Steel Works Association, 1912–1919," Gerald Feldman describes a process of increasing instability (lack of control over capacity and output) brought about overwhelmingly by the internal dynamics of the Association.[7] In this analysis, building from suggestions of Bogner and Heymann among others, the "beginning of the end" (where "end" means cartel dissolution) was the decision at the May 1912 Association renewal to drop quotas on the so-called B-goods (merchant bars, rolled wire, sheet and plate, pipes, and various cast goods). Before 1912 these B-goods had been loosely regulated only by production quotas, while the so-called A-goods (half-rolled articles, railroad materials, and structural steel) were actually sold by the Association, which thus controlled both price and quantity. From 1904 through 1912, many attempts to "syndicate" (regulate both the prices and quantities of) B-goods, especially merchant bars, failed for various reasons, not least of which was the existence of a host of smaller "outside" mills. The 1903 edition of the *Gemeinfassliche Darstellung der Eisenhüttenwesen* listed 61 locations in western Germany where bars were produced, only 26 of which were regulated in 1905 by quotas of the Association. (Upper Silesia has been omitted from this list due to its effective geographical isolation.) Of the 35 mills outside the Association, 28 were located in Rhineland/Westphalia, and thus posed an obvious local threat to the major integrated firms of the Ruhr. These outsiders were wooed continually by the Steel Association from 1905 through 1911, in an attempt to bring them into the larger cartel or an affiliated bar agreement.

B-good prices were determined in markets with varying degrees of competitiveness and concentration, while A-good prices were set in the Association's internal negotiation process, where decisions of various committees were ratified by an Assembly of Steel Works Owners. Firms were much freer to act in B-good markets than in A-good markets, an imbalance which, according to Feldman, led to "overexpansion," especially in merchant bars (*Stabeisen*). Further, it is argued that the expansion of B-good capacity at the large, vertically integrated firms inhibited attempts to bring B-goods under the same tight controls which were imposed on A-goods in 1904, especially as these larger firms were unwilling to make concessions in the matter of quotas to the smaller unintegrated rolling mills. As the Association moved toward renewal, scheduled for April 1912, conflicts over the syndication of B-goods grew sharper, and individual positions emerged within the Association which reflected the "all or nothing" character of some industrialists' demands. Thus, Feldman notes, August Thyssen demanded "either the syndicalization of the B-Products or the termination of all production limitations on them," a position held by other steel producers at the same time. By 1914 the Association had acquired a "dysfunctional character," suggesting that Germany's collectivist capitalism was fundamentally incapable of creating "mechanisms productive of discipline and sensible planning in such times of need."[8]

Two brief points should be made before proceeding. First, the economic logic of the "all or nothing" demands is not explained by Feldman. It is difficult to understand Thyssen's simultaneous willingness to control *both* prices and outputs, or *neither* variable, if one assumes some interest in stability, or in profits. Controlling both variables assures short-run stability; controlling neither *may* lead to long-run stability via higher concentration, but after a period of intense competition. The simultaneous existence of such extreme positions is not easily explained by the basic economic structure of the industry. Second, the shift from A-goods to B-goods was rather modest. A-goods represented 57 percent of the Association's total allocation of quotas in its first business year (March 1904 through February 1905) and 58 percent of deliveries during those 12 months. In the last full business year when both A- and B-goods were subject to quotas, 1911/12, A-goods' share of quotas had fallen to 50 percent while the corresponding share of deliveries had fallen to 47 percent. This is hardly dramatic.[9]

The shift from A-goods to B-goods is explained by two arguments. First, B-goods may have been more profitable than A-goods:

> Unable to make more than modest profits on the successfully syndicalized A-Products, the large mixed works dominating the Steel Works Association made increasing use of their self-consumption rights to produce B-Products.[10]

Unfortunately, it is doubtful both theoretically and empirically that A-goods were capable of only "modest profits." Assume that A-goods were successfully regulated, and B-goods were traded on (perhaps imperfectly) competitive markets, and note that the price elasticity of demand for B-goods was generally higher than for A-goods, due to the existence of more substitute products and more firms in the former market. We can then conclude that B-goods should have been less profitable than A-goods, if both were priced to maximize profits. If prices were set for other purposes we cannot confidently predict relative profitability. Also, in January 1911 the *Vorstand* of the Rheinische Stahlwerke reported that a request to switch quotas from half-rolled goods to merchant bars was denied by the Association "because the profits from [the former] have been higher than those for bars and sheets."[11] The question of relative profitability obviously merits further investigation.

Feldman's second explanation for the shift in product mix is somewhat circular: stability of A-prices led to "overexpansion" in B-goods in an attempt to "cover fixed costs," which were growing because vertically integrated firms were "at the height of their expansionist propensities." Let us assume that "overexpansion" means investment in new B-capacity (rolling mills) at a pace faster than that which calculations of long-run expected profitability relative to other opportunities would dictate.[12] Contemporary observers decried other manifestations of overexpansion, such as faster rate of growth of B-quotas or B-sales, but within the Association, as we shall see, capacity was indeed perceived to be a problem by 1912. Firms were free to operate independently and competitively to seek profits on B-goods. Depending on market conditions, this could easily imply an expansion of B-capacity. But Feldman argues that A-prices were "too low" given *fixed* costs: "modest profits" on A-production induced firms to expand where possible (increasing fixed cost) at a rate greater than would have occurred had those A-prices been higher. Thus the generally "expansionist" tendencies of the industry were channeled into the addition of new rolling capacity. As this capacity grew, so did the fixed costs of the firms, which further stimulated production and sale of B-goods, and industries fell into the typical cycle of "free competition." The competitive tendencies of steel industrialists were simply redirected, but the virulency of these tendencies produced extreme instability in the B-good sector, according to Feldman.

One test of this scenario would be to compare the relative growth of A- and B-capacity during the tenure of the Steel Works Association. Table 1 illustrates one measure of that comparison. These figures indicate a much faster growth in capacity of steel inputs (pig iron and raw steel) than in capacity for rolling the final steel products, although data limitations force a comparison of unlike quantities.

The accepted explanation of Association "instability" assumes that producers were single-minded entrepreneurs facing markets with fairly elastic demand: vertically integrated firms could all shift heavily into B-goods and sales could increase substantially without someone incurring losses. Such a supply-centered analysis falls short on several counts. Producers are implicitly assumed to adhere rigidly to cartel strictures, but otherwise to push forward oblivious to market signals. The possibility of relative changes in demand for individual steel products is ignored. Also, to ensure profitability in B-goods, one must assume a high price elasticity of demand for these steel products, defend a long-run average cost curve which exhibits enormous economies of scale, or show that the demand for these particular products was growing rapidly enough that prices could fall and still remain above unit costs at quantities actually sold. If on the other hand, for example, demand for merchant bars (a B-good) was growing more rapidly than demand for rails and ties (A-goods), and if producers responded to that shift

Table 1.   Growth in Iron and Steel Capacity, 1903–1912
(%)

A-goods[a]		B-goods[b]	
Blast furnaces	72.5	Bar	18.7
Steel furnaces:		Wire	46.4
Thomas, acid	−51.5	Sheet	−14.3
Thomas, basic	81.6	Girders	59.1
Siemens-Martin, acid	84.4	Bands	127.8
Siemens-Martin, basic	213.0	Plate	−3.6
Cast steel:		Rails	20.7
Acid	154.5	Cast pipes	25.0
Basic	70.3	Rolled pipes[c]	6.5

[a]Measured in metric tons of standing capacity.
[b]Measured in number of locations of rolling mills.
[c]1907–1912 only.
Source: Gemeinfassliche Darstellung der Eisenhüttenwesen, various years.

in demand, production and sales of bars *should* have increased relative to those of rails and ties. Finally, the relative expansion of B-production has been identified as the exlusive cause of the "failure" of May 1912. The negotiations of 1910–1912 show something else: a gradual but marked deterioration in the good will associated with membership in the Steel Association, centered on a relatively few products and firms and on changes in both A- and B-capacity in response to changes in demand.

III. INSTABILITY IN MERCHANT BARS AND PIPES

One major question derives from the assertion that steel firms "overexpanded" bar capacity during the first seven years of the Association, in response presumably to opportunities for profit. "Overexpansion" is a conceptual briar patch. An accurate measure of overexpansion depends on the adjustment of a stock of capital goods to a desired level, defined in terms of the determinants of demand for the final product, in this case bars. For such a short period of time it is almost impossible to estimate a stock adjustment model, even if acceptable data were available. Alternatively, one may compare the rate of return on bar production with that of other rolled steel products. A significantly lower rate of return on bars would indicate "overexpansion." Again, data limitations make such a procedure hazardous. Initially, we may trace the changes in production, quotas, and relative prices which did occur.

As can be seen from Table 2, after extremely rapid growth of quotas in the first few years of the Association, merchant bar quotas leveled off and grew slowly

Table 2. Merchant Bar Quotas and Deliveries

		Growth Rate (%):			Absolute Deviations (%):
		Deliveries		Total	Quotas-Deliveries
Year	Quotas	Domestic	Exports	Deliveries	Deliveries
1905	10.2	7.6	9.4	7.9	−7.8
1906	27.1	19.8	7.4	17.8	−9.6
1907	27.7	9.2	2.9	8.3	7.1
1908	1.6	−9.4	41.6	−2.3	19.8
1909	2.0	12.3	−0.9	9.7	13.6
1910	0.3	15.5	6.0	13.8	2.8
1911	2.5	6.6	21.0	9.0	−4.5

Sources: Historisches Archiv der Gutehoffnungshütte 3000030/2, 3000031/5, Stabeisen-Statistik (December 6, 1914); RheinStahl Archiv 650 00/2; Verein deutscher Eisenhüttenleute Bibliothek (hereafter VdE) Ni 160, Ni 114; Werksarchiv Thyssen AG (hereafter WA/Thyssen) A/652-654.

from 1907 through 1911. Deliveries were of course more erratic; the role of the export market as *Sicherheitsventil* in 1908 seems fairly clear. For 1907–1910 producers were essentially free to sell as many merchant bars as the market would absorb, depending of course on price. It is likely that the quotas achieved in April 1907 exceeded firms' then-current capacity, and there seems to have been little correlation between changes in deliveries and changes in quotas. After 1907 quotas were ineffective in containing merchant bars. What led steel producers to take advantage of this freedom?

From 1904 to 1913, sales of merchant bars in Germany doubled. At the same time the average real price received for this product followed a path alongside most other steel prices, rising through 1906 and 1907 during an expansionary phase of the business cycle, and falling in late 1907 and through 1908. (See Table 3.) The average real price received from 1908 through 1913 was, however, only 114.44 Marks/ton, considerably below the high of over 200 Marks/ton received in 1900, and 26 percent below the average of 154.85 Marks/ton in 1894–1903. These figures lend some support to an interpretation of "overexpansion," unless sufficient technical change or other external economies operated to maintain profitability in the face of falling real prices. Available profit estimates, however, suggest otherwise. At August-Thyssen-Hütte, in the three years for which data are available (1909, 1910, and 1913) billets (an A-good) were always significantly more profitable than merchant bars. At Gutehoffnungshütte, the average unit profit on billets, ingots, and blooms (all half-rolled articles) from 1906 to 1913 was over 11 percent; in *no* year was calculated profit negative. For merchant bars, on the other hand, many years of negative profit were reported, and the average profit for these years was also negative.[13] It appears that merchant bars were a bad gamble, which leaves the question of expansion still

Table 3. Merchant Bar Prices

Year	Wholesale Price Index (1913 = 100)	Market Bar Prices (Marks/ton)	Real Bar Prices (Marks/ton)
1894	73	96.25	131.85
1895	72	96.50	134.03
1896	72	115.88	160.94
1897	76	130.00	171.05
1898	79	119.38	151.11
1899	83	165.83	199.80
1900	90	183.75	204.17
1901	83	110.00	132.53
1902	81	106.88	131.94
1903	82	107.50	131.10
1904	82	109.13	133.08
1905	86	109.00	126.74
1906	92	130.31	141.64
1907	97	142.25	146.65
1908	90	106.25	118.06
1909	91	101.75	111.81
1910	93	110.75	119.09
1911	94	106.00	112.77
1912	102	118.73	116.40
1913	100	108.50	108.50

Sources: Gemeinfassliche Darstellung, 1915 ed., p. 292; Mitchell (1978), Table H1, p. 390.

unanswered. Steel producers appear to have pursued illusory profits, if profit was the target in the short run.

The answer to the question of relative expansion lies in the nature of the demand for this product, something which has not yet been investigated. Steel producers were not only engaged in (not so Smithian) ''higgling and bargaining'' at cartel meetings; they were also firms producing something which had to be sold, if possible at a profit. Conditions during the first decade of the 20th century limited their ability to expand in traditional directions and forced a search for profits in new, expanding markets. A-goods differed from B-goods not only in the style of self-regulation imposed within the Steel Association, but in the nature of the demand for each category of products. There were three groups of A-goods: half-finished articles (ingots, blooms, and billets, which served as inputs for almost all other steel products), railroad materials (rails, ties, and fastenings), and structural items (mainly girders). The B-good category was itself composed of five groups: bars, plate and sheet, wire, pipes, and cast goods. B-goods were used as inputs for nonmetallurgical operations for the most part, and demand was thus affected by conditions both outside and inside the steel industry.

Demand for the half-finished articles, derived from the demand for all other A-goods and B-goods, was price-inelastic because of the absence of realistic substitutes, in part because of tariffs.[14] Demand for railroad materials was also inelastic with respect to price, but sensitive to the overall level of economic activity: public rail authorities allegedly tied their purchases for the national and provincial rail networks to expected tax receipts, lending a definite procyclical force to this market. The elasticity of the demand curve facing the Steel Association for railroad goods was low because of an absence of outside producers large enough to threaten the policies of the cartel. Rail and tie consumers had little choice of supply within Germany apart from the Steel Works Association.[15] Firms were also being forced to adjust their rail mill capacities to changing market conditions. By the 1890s, the growth of the national rail network had slowed perceptibly. At the same time urbanization was accelerating, bringing with it an acceleration in demand for the lighter rails used in trolley and subway systems. Inelasticity was thus compounded by excess capacity in heavier rails. Wolfgang Köllmann has estimated that urban population growth absorbed 85–95 percent of total population increase from 1871 to 1910. The urban areas of Westphalia (which included the Ruhr) grew over 600 percent in these four decades.[16] The number of streetcar rides per annum (admittedly a measure of "production," not of either supply or demand for urban transport alone) rose between 1890 and 1910 at phenomenal rates: in Düsseldorf by 2700 percent, in Duisburg by 1700 percent, in Dortmund and Cologne by over 1000 percent, and in the larger, older cities by 200–800 percent. Also, the urban tramway network (measured in kilometers of track) increased by 178.5 percent from 1895 to 1913, while the national rail network only grew 36.3 percent.[17]

Other products were similarly plagued within the Association. Steel girders (an A-good) and merchant bars (a B-good) were engaged in a battle for the urban construction market, as bars were an important component of reinforced concrete. The Association sponsored investigations which tried to establish the greater "flexibility" and lower long-run cost of girder construction, but these public statements were offset by a price policy which undermined any cost advantage of girder construction.[18] Table 4 shows the relative price of girders and bars during this period. Although loose cartels regulated sales of girders in parts of Germany before 1904, the relative price of girders in the years before the establishment of the Steel Association in March of that year was almost 14 percent lower than under that cartel; from 1896 to 1903 the price ratio averaged 0.870, but under the Association it rose to 0.989. Although this increase was composed mainly of stable girder prices and falling bar prices, the Association was reluctant to use prices to compete with merchant bars. Not surprisingly, sales of girders under the Association stagnated, although the malady was blamed on the interest rate policy of the central bank and on stiff competition from reinforced concrete.[19]

With bar sales increasing at about 10 percent per annum, real prices falling but

Table 4. Relative Market Price
of Girders and Bars

Year	Girders/Bars	Year	Girders/Bars
1896	.831	1905	.964
1897	.804	1906	.885
1898	.905	1907	.881
1899	.714	1908	1.084
1900	.748	1909	1.082
1901	1.006	1910	.994
1902	.971	1911	1.040
1903	.977	1912	.944
1904	.963	1913	1.057

Source: Gemeinfassliche Darstellung, 1915 ed., p. 292.

not plummeting, and complaints about reinforced concrete frequent, one may conclude that both demand and supply curves for merchant bars were shifting out rapidly. If so, this would help explain the expansion of bar quotas from January 1905 through April 1907, reflecting an anticipation of growing demand and in response to rising real prices (see Table 3). It seems clear that the short-run supply curve for merchant bars was shifting out: from 61 locations in 1903, bar manufacture in western Germany had spread to 77 locations by 1912. This is undoubtedly an understatement of expansion, because many locations had multiple bar mills.[20] Stagnant demand for railroad materials and structurals would also imply a larger interest by producers in markets which they thought were expanding: B-goods and by derivation half-rolled inputs. Growth in demand can make the short-run demand curve seem more elastic than it really is, inducing producers to add capacity and increase production in the belief that only small reductions in price will produce dramatic sales increases. As long as demand continues to grow there is no problem with this strategy; we usually applaud markets in which capacity adjusts to long-run demand.

The profit estimates indicate that "overexpansion" in merchant bars was indeed possible during the first few years of the Steel Association. We noted earlier that the current interpretation suggests that the larger members of the Association were reluctant to make concessions to smaller outsiders which might have limited this collusive overexpansion. However, the record of attempts to syndicate bars shows that members of the Association were on occasion willing to grant smaller producers large quota increases, presumably in an effort to induce them to join a Merchant Bar Association. For example, in November 1907 a set of quotas, proposed by a committee established to investigate this market, promised the pure rolling mills and the Siemens-Martin mills a much larger share of the market than they had previously enjoyed. (See Table 5.) When

Table 5.   Proposal for Merchant Bar Quotas, 1907

Faction	Number of Firms	Deliveries (Tons) Apr. 1–Sept. 30	Quota Proposed	Quota/Deliveries (%)
Association	27	988,367	1,179,726	119.4
Siemens-Martin	21	107,210	1,179,910	167.8
Pure mills	25	56,120	171,433	305.5
Total	73	1,151,697	1,531,069	132.9

Sources: Deliveries from HA/GHH 3000031/1, Aufstellung November 4, 1907; quotas from WA/Thyssen A/653, Protokoll November 5, 1907.

this proposal was put to the vote, 15 of the 19 cartel members present voted *ja,* against 1 *nein* and 3 *vorbehalten.* Siemens-Martin firms, of which 13 attended this meeting, split fairly evenly: 6 in favor, 7 either against or abstaining. The pure rolling mills avoided the meeting: only one of the 25 mills included in Table 5 cast a vote, and that firm also abstained.

From the fall of 1909 to March 1911 a Merchant Bar Price Agreement effectively controlled prices separately from the quotas established in the Steel Works Association. This agreement included 27 members of the Association and 10 Siemens-Martin mills by November 1909, although Hösch, a medium-sized producer in Dortmund, proved a continual thorn in the sides of other firms who were interested in colluding. Despite this difficulty, in August 1910 26 members of the Association (including Hösch) and 13 Siemens-Martin firms signed a supplementary Bar Export Contract regulating sales of merchant bars abroad. Prices were raised steadily during these months; one may note that 1910 was the only year of recorded positive profits on bar sales at August-Thyssen-Hütte, rough confirmation of the predicted positive relationship between collusion and profits.

By early 1911 the Price Agreement had been functioning, if somewhat shakily, for about 16 months, and louder voices began to demand an extension of the agreement to control output also. Standing opposite those firms in favor of extending self-regulation beyond prices was a group which considered recent accomplishments quite sufficient. Typical of the first group was Gutehoffnungshütte (GHH), which pressed for a complete syndication of merchant bars as the only guarantee of continued self-regulation, and submitted a long list of topics for discussion which reached far into the activities of individual firms, governing sales reports, fines, security deposits, quotas, a unified surcharge list, export subsidies, freight costs, and rebates to wholesalers. GHH was opposed by Theodor Müller of Gebr. Stumm GmbH (at Neunkirchen in the Saar), who argued that "experience has shown quite explicitly that merchant bars cannot be sold by all firms at the same base price with the same surcharge and rebate structure. On the other hand, neither a common sales office nor a tight cartel could accomplish this without the strictest compulsory measures against the consumers.'' Interfirm differences, Müller continued, touched product quality and mix, rolling programs, capital equipment, accessible sales areas, and export capability. However, the Saar industrialist called for domestic quotas to be established at the level of 1910 sales, since "only in this manner is the Agreement to be extended beyond April 1, 1911."[21]

Notwithstanding the opposition of producers such as Müller, on February 7 the General Assembly of the Bar Price Agreement discussed a new contract to which an "overwhelming majority" gave provisional approval.[22] An important provision of this new agreement was a pledge from Association members to accept established quotas for the duration of the new contract.[23] Those quotas were *not* the then current stratospheric figures of the Association, but were based on deliveries during 1910. Final approval depended on negotiations with six Siemens-Martin firms over their quotas. Because of a last minute concession by GHH which effectively shortened the life of the contract and thus made higher quotas possible at an earlier future date, this list of recalcitrant firms was reduced to one.[24] However, that one holdout proved to be the proverbial weakest link that broke the chain, and on March 31, 1911, both the price and export agreements expired. During the following summer committees were again formed, by which time average prices had fallen over 10 percent.[25]

What caused the breakdown of price and export agreements for merchant bars in March 1911? Differences among potential colluders, the most important source of cartel instability in modern economic theory, were clearly an obstacle to the organization of German bar mills. Interregional differences which were successfully overcome in stretching a cartel over *several* products at the national level were complicated by critical differences in product quality (Thomas steel vs. Siemens-Martin steel) and in the extent of vertical integration (fully integrated firms vs. pure rolling mills). Variations in geographical proximity to markets were offset by the system of multiple base points, which provided some guarantee of continued dominance in traditional markets.[26] But geographic diversity was not the soil in which the seeds of discontent grew to break the Price Agreement for merchant bars.

The Siemens-Martin firms voiced their strongest objections to the collusive prices, as their product traditionally commanded a premium over Thomas bars. Their goal was to maintain that premium, which ceteris paribus should have grown absolutely as Thomas bar prices rose. However, a growing absolute price difference might have begun to encourage switching from Siemens-Martin to Thomas steel, in spite of the difference in quality. It is surprising that, in spite of the relatively small share of the market supplied by the Siemens-Martin firms, Association members considered them almost critical to the success of a bar syndicate. The answer is control of input markets: Siemens-Martin firms relied on the unregulated scrap market for their input; unless controlled, they could have grown into a formidable opposition, possibly organized independently of the Steel Works Association. The pure rolling mills, with perhaps 5 percent of the market, posed less of a threat to the Association members because those mills got all their raw steel input from the Association, and thus their expansion could be regulated by the flow of steel through the supply lines. Again, the pure mills' objections to limited quotas can be seen in terms of the assumption of falling unit costs. These dependencies of the Steel Association were, however, more accommodating, as demonstrated by a draft agreement negotiated in 1905.[27]

The demise on June 30, 1910, of the Boiler Pipe Association (Siederohrverband), sparked by the expiration of a patent on seamless pipes, opened up that market to what was later described as "wild competition." Pipe manufacturing and pipe producers within the Steel Works Association were subject to one formidable force absent in many other markets: Mannesmann AG, a large, relatively young and technically dynamic pipe producer. This "upstart" had thwarted August Thyssen's attempts to lead pipe cartels since the 1890s when Mannesmann introduced a revolutionary pipe-rolling technology which yielded seamless pipes of great strength at relatively low cost.

During the second half of 1910 and through 1911, August Thyssen repeatedly sought to loosen the constraint on his ability to compete with Mannesmann imposed by his pipe quota in the Steel Association. In this campaign he ran full against a form of extracartel interfirm collusion which protected Thyssen's oligopolistic competitors within the Association and simultaneously gave them an incentive to oppose his expansion plans. The extracartel cooperation became important because of the special rules governing B-quota increases in the 1907 contract. Instead of applying for a quota increase for itself alone, the expansion-minded firm had to request an increase (usually expressed as a percentage) for *all* producers of the good in question. Thus Thyssen applied for quota increases for all Association producers with pipe quotas (the "pipe group"), which in April 1910 included the Thyssen concerns (57.3 percent of the total pipe quota), Krupp (with 0.7 percent), and five Upper Silesian firms (the other 42 percent).

An "advise and consent" clause required that the Association's General Assembly, in voting on the requested increase, take into account "market assessments" submitted by all members of the group. This gave other pipe producers a vote disproportionate to their market shares or capacities. Krupp had an incentive to submit a negative assessment because of its unfettered "surrogate pipe quota": a 10-year contract signed in October 1903 to deliver 80 percent of all the steel ingot requirements of Mannesmann's two largest domestic pipe mills.[28] Although sales increased dramatically during 1910, the Association refused to grant Thyssen's repeated requests for higher pipe quotas, relying on "market assessments" submitted not only by Krupp but also by Gelsenkirchener Bergwerks AG (GBAG), which did not even have a pipe quota.[29]

The competition which exploded in late 1910 was sufficiently severe that the Rheinische Stahlwerke, contemplating its expansion program in April 1911, decided at least temporarily to refrain from purchasing a pipe mill, noting that "current pipe prices have fallen so far below average cost that no one, not even the best equipped firms, can make money producing pipes."[30] By February 1912, Thyssen threatened withdrawal from the Steel Association, citing a Reichsgericht decision which allowed unilateral withdrawal when a cartel ceased to strive for the originally stated goals.[31] Not only was Krupp's position bolstered by its delivery contracts, but other Association members were negotiating extra-cartel arrangements with Mannesmann in early 1912. Rheinstahl was planning a special *Verkaufs- und Betriebsgemeinschaft* (Sales and Operations Partnership) which would exploit Mannesmann's technical expertise and sales network by rationalization of pipe production in conjunction with two smaller pipe mills.[32] These disputes helped contribute to strong anticartel attitudes which surfaced in late April 1912.

IV. RENEWAL NEGOTIATIONS, 1910–1912

Although the second contract was scheduled to run from 1907 to 1912, by March 1910 underlying economic conditions had so shifted that concern about renewal began circulating among Association members. An indirect impetus that spring came from a group of unintegrated coal mines, led by Robert Müser, General Director of Harpener Bergbau AG in Dortmund, who in their concern about renewal of the Coal Syndicate (scheduled to expire in 1915!), approached Louis Röchling to inquire when the Steel Association might begin *its* renewal talks. Röchling in turn wrote to Schaltenbrand at the steel cartel outlining the difficulties he perceived for the renewal:[33]

1. The large new plants, mainly in German Lorraine, built by both Rhine/ Ruhr and Southwest firms, and "countless" additions to capacity at all firms.

2. The falling share of A-goods in total production: merchant bars used in reinforced concrete had dealt a heavy blow to girders; railroad expansion was no longer a dependable source of demand for rails and ties; expansion of wire rolling capacity further cut into sales of half-rolled articles, as these were retained in the large vertically integrated plants where the new capacity was built. Emerging excess capacity in heavy rolled products was cutting into the benefits of collusion.

3. The uneven distribution of A-good orders among the individual firms, leading to a faction with disproportionate emphasis on B-goods, and thus "no interest whatsoever" in continuing the Association in its current form; syndication of B-goods was not to be expected, although the current Bar Price Agreement was a "valuable preparation."

The third point implied a division of the Association, Röchling argued, into two camps: (1) those in favor of larger A-quotas *and* syndication of B-goods, who were receiving disproportionate amounts of A-good orders and thus wanted both codification of that imbalance and guaranteed markets for their B-production; and (2) those in favor of shifting quotas from A- to B-goods, to reflect the opposite production emphasis. Overall, Röchling was pessimistic about output restraints, as demands backed by new capacity would be difficult to oppose. A preliminary meeting with limited attendance was held later in March at Röchling's invitation.[34] At that confidential meeting, privately held positions were exposed which are rarely so readily available.[35]

The merchant bar price agreement originally signed in late 1909 was still in force when 13 heavy industry magnates met at the Stahlhof, the steel cartel's headquarters in Düsseldorf, but producers were of different minds about the importance of this limited form of self-regulation for the possibility of full syndication in the B-goods arena. Two factions emerged: those supporting the gradual syndication of one or more B-goods, and those advocating more radical restructuring, including complete dismantling of the cartel or its extension upstream into the regulation of pig iron sales.

The B-syndication faction argued for stronger controls as a means to greater stability. Tables showing the rapid expansion of B-good sales, especially in bars, were introduced to indicate the danger from within of a lack of regulation: if production was shifting away from more tightly controlled products toward a product mix of greater firm discretion, either in response to shifting demand or via attempts to circumvent production controls, the collective benefits of higher collusive prices would eventually be eroded, and the cartel would fall victim to the problems of dividing a shrinking pie. A return to the battlefields of competition would follow, and as Adolf Kirdorf argued, "a later regrouping of those dissipated forces would suffer untold difficulties." The Krupp representative, von Bodenhausen, reported to his Supervisory Board that these prosyndication forces prevailed in the end, as three premises for future negotiations were established: (1) at least merchant bars and steel plate, and possibly rolled wire, were to be syndicated; (2) the renewal would be contingent on the creation of a pig iron syndicate; and (3) the scrap metal market would have to be regulated, at least by controls on price. This last goal was an obvious strike at the freedom of the Siemens-Martin firms. Thus the *Gesamtfacit*, as von Bodenhausen described the overall outcome, was strongly in favor of *more* controls over *more* products. Even more Draconian measures were advocated by Müller, who argued that production should be redistributed so that specialization could lead to lower average costs, and that some plants should be simply shut down. Such a program of "rationalization" would require a contract of at least 10 years' duration, in Kirdorf's view, but importantly, no strong opposition to such radical extension of self-regulation was expressed.

In contrast, when Hugo Stinnes called for a time *without* cartels to achieve the same goal (plant closures), he met multilateral opposition. Stinnes contended that many plants had "no right to exist," and only "free competition" could clear the scene of unhealthy elements, an attitude described as "juvenile" and "short-sighted" by Kirdorf. These industrialists were not opposed to the principle of rationalization, but objected to its "free market" form: simple attrition. Bankruptcy was not the "managed" solution important in an intellectual framework which emphasized minimizing the short-run adjustment costs when resources flow out of industries experiencing excess capacity and negative economic profits.[36] Although this same group of major industrialists was able to agree in 1910 on the principle of expanding self-regulation, specifically into B-goods, changes in demand conditions were building seemingly unobserved outside the wall of cartel regulations which would alter their ability to agree two years later.

During the fall of 1911, members were requested to submit quota demands, although Louis Röchling held to the view that no increases in A-quotas would be possible, due to the difficulty of finding markets for existing quotas. In this he met the determined opposition of Kirdorf (of Gelsenkirchener), Thyssen, Eigenbrodt (of Deutsch-Luxemberg), and Reusch (of Gutehoffnungshütte), all of whom had recently invested substantially in basic steel (A-good) capacity. Röchling's fears of March 1910 were being borne out.[37]

For example, Thyssen had taken advantage of the relative clam of the 1907–1911 period to invest in a new, fully integrated steel works at Hagendingen, in the Lorraine minette region. Based on this new plant and on improvements and expansions in the Ruhr, Thyssen's division captains calculated new quotas to be demanded, with increases of 33 percent in A-goods and 37 percent in B-goods, to be stretched out over two years.[38] In spite of Thyssen's difficulties in pipes, and perhaps vindicating Stinnes's remarks of the previous year, the meeting on October 31, 1911, at which Thyssen's quota demands were discussed internally was surprisingly conciliatory. After considering all the divisions' demands, it was decided "in spite of improvements at old facilities not to request increased quotas for them in the interest of renewing the Association. Increased quota demands will be based only on new capacity, assuming that other firms proceed on the same basis."[39] Thyssen's demands were to be limited to 50 percent of the difference between current total capacity and current total quotas. This conciliatory gesture left them, of course, with considerable bargaining power: the threat of using the other 50 percent.

Toward the end of 1911 specific quota demands were under discussion in the Quota Commission, and, although the demands were high, offers of compromise and cooperation were also forthcoming. Had cooperation been possible at this time, enormous demands in A-goods could have been eliminated or reconciled. As Louis Röchling reported to his Supervisory Board in early December,[40]

[T]he demands for higher quotas are, as expected, quite extraordinarily large and amount to around 1,250,000 tons in A-goods and about 3,500,000 tons in B. [These amounts were about 20 percent and 57 percent of April 1911 levels.] Since sales of A-goods in the last few years have not increased, and cannot be expected to increase for the foreseeable future, we [at Röchling] have not demanded an increase in our A-quota, as that would be pointless. . . . Many of these quota demands are not especially serious, and the Association can only survive if all older plants forego increases in A-quotas and if the three new plants of Thyssen in Hagendingen, Gelsenkirchener in Esch and Burbach in Esch are moderate in their demands. Each of these three has asked for 200,000 to 240,000 tons in A-quotas.

Later in December the outlook darkened even more.

The Quota Commission has determined everywhere that enormous sums are being spent on construction of new capacity, which in general is so large that sales will fall short of capacity. Yesterday [December 21, 1911] the Commission submitted its report to the General Assembly, which concluded that negotiations over B-quotas could not proceed until clarity had been achieved regarding A-quotas.

Accordingly, 15 members agreed at that meeting to withdraw their demands for higher A-quotas, under the conditions that *no* A-quotas be granted to the three new plants in the Lorraine, and that all other members agree also.[41] This slender thread of agreement was quickly broken *not* by Thyssen, Gelsenkirchener, or Burbach, whose new Lorraine plants were both threatening and threatened, but by a number of other firms. For example, the Westfälische Stahlwerke claimed that its current A-quota allowed only 25 percent use of basic capacity: one-half of one normal daily shift. The Bochumer Verein and Stumm also claimed severe underutilization of A-capacity, and other firms not present at the December meeting weighed in with more particular demands in the area of A-goods.[42] This situation led Röchling to report on January 1, 1912, that the negotiations for the renewal of the Association were given up as pointless: "Whether they will be started again in a few months remains to be seen."[43] It should be noted that the obstacle at this early stage was excess capacity in A-goods, not in B-goods.

When the Quota Commission reconvened in mid-March, positions began to converge. Although Thyssen and GBAG agreed on totals for their respective new Lorraine operations and on the condition that B-goods *at least* continue to be subject to quotas, different opinions on the product mix for the Lorraine quotas caused sharp confrontations.[44] By March 21 many members whose recalcitrance in December had caused a near breakdown softened their stands.[45] Whether these firms bowed to retaliation threats from other firms or to the simple economic facts of standing capacity is not clear. However, the Association's Schaltenbrand stated that sales of A-goods would be increasingly difficult due to mergers, partnerships, and new Siemens-Martin plants (which threatened sales of Thomas steel by their higher quality output). A graduated program for Thyssen-Hagendingen and GBAG-Esch was approved by a majority of owners, including those two firms.[46] Having thus momentarily taken care of the A-goods, negotiators ran up against profound discontent with controls on B-goods. As noted by the representative of the Hörder Verein, a division of Phönix,[47] some firms made B-quotas a condition of their continued membership, especially Thyssen, GBAG and Röchling. The last called special attention to the danger to A-quotas posed by freedom in B-goods, as, for example, wire rod users who now roll blooms would instead be delivered only the wire rods. The other firms are against B-quotas, as these have made syndication of B-goods more difficult, and unity over quota levels is not within reach. In this latter group those firms which have recently acquired other companies are especially prominent (Stumm, Krupp, RheinStahl, Königs- und Laurahütte and van der Zypen).

It should be emphasized that those opponents of B-quotas were actually in favor of *stronger* controls in the long run, not weaker regulation or no regulation at all. The comment about recent mergers and attitudes toward the extension of self-regulation indicates that the mergers were not motivated by a desire to escape Association regulations, but were instead based on the risk-spreading grounds often associated with integration into new but related product lines.[48]

In an open letter of April 15, Adolf Kirdorf exhorted all cartel members to keep current controls on B-goods. Kirdorf did recognize that the conditions during 1904–1911 within the Association had led to the impasse over B-quotas.[49]

> The [original] quotas were not based on actual relationships, but were only reached by difficult negotiations. Further, these quotas had no durability because they lacked any justified and sanctioned foundation. Individual firms secured large quotas out of proportion to their then current basic steel capacity and achieved disproportionate profits in those products protected by the Association. Those profits allowed occasional sacrifices in selling prices for their other products, and permitted successful competition against those firms who enjoyed only scanty protection in the Association. At the cost of the latter group, the former firms expanded their basic steel output without limit.

Firms with originally large, better protected sales of A-goods were able to squeeze smaller firms whose product mixes were biased toward less protected B-goods, and simultaneously to increase their raw steel capacity by reinvestment of collusive profits. Kirdorf implied that A-goods were *more* profitable than B-goods, and that firms occasionally relied on financial ''deep pockets'' based on accumulated profits from A-goods. Extra capacity in basic steel was the worst threat to continued stability in the industry, according to Kirdorf. Without limitations on basic steel, negotiations for the complete syndication of B-goods would be much more difficult, so Kirdorf argued for the retention of B-quotas as a partial lid on basic steel production, and therefore as bases for individual B-syndicates:[50]

> Quotas on B-goods provide a brake on basic steel [*Rohstahl*] output. Without them there would be no Steel Works Association. . . . Syndication of B-goods will be made easier if a large group of firms has already reached an understanding on quotas.

The letter further asserted that ''aside from some complaints about B-quotas which stem from the approaching end of the current contract, such complaints have scarcely been heard during the life of the contract.'' By 1912, however, the excess of bar quota over capacity was dwindling, and it should not be surprising that firms began to consider raising that limit.

Kirdorf's letter produced no notable reconciliation. On the 24th of April, a Silesian representative, Nothmann, suggested that firms be allowed to choose three consecutive months in the last two business years for each of the five B-groups, multiply the deliveries during those periods by four and add 20 percent, thus arriving at new B-quotas. This proposal failed in a fairly lopsided vote, as did a proposal for a simple 20 percent across-the-board increase from current quota levels.[51] Why not simply raise quotas? Consider the two factions identified above: those who believed that removal of all controls would prove so devastating that full syndication would result, and those who wanted realistic quotas to provide a basis for future syndication attempts. All quotas, increased or not, would meet *nein* votes from the first group, whereas the roughly 20 percent increase would encounter the opposition of the second. Thus all motions for higher B-quotas had two immediate opposition forces.

On April 29 it was recognized that B-quotas were beyond reach.[52] Although both Adolf Kirdorf and Louis Röchling appealed for more effort and compromise, there was not enough time to consider each member's demands. Jakob Hasslacher of Rheinstahl proposed that a simple trade-off would lure members into syndication of the more finished products:[53]

It is quite possible that firms would be content with lower quotas in B-syndicates which actually promise to quarantee higher net profits, precisely because they would find compensation for the perhaps lower quantities in a substantially higher profit.

The objection might be raised that this stance was pure bluff: Hasslacher was merely interested in complete freedom for B-goods. However, in reporting privately on the final form of the cartel in early May, he explained at greater length:[54]

Quotas for B-goods were completely discarded. On the one hand, a shackle in the form of small quotas which was pressing painfully on our development has been removed. On the other hand, we are convinced that now finally the basis for syndication of individual B-goods has been created. Only negotiations which begin from complete freedom can lead to a recovery [*Gesundung*]; current quotas, in some cases too large, in others too small, make such a recovery unattainable.

High quotas, in Hasslacher's view the only possible compromise which would retain controls, would make it much more difficult to negotiate the trade-off between higher sales and the higher unit profits of lower volume. Standing against this all-or-nothing position was the gradualist approach of men like Kirdorf who argued that B-quotas would serve as a basis for future negotiations with outsiders.[55] Unfortunately, such an approach had not proved especially successful in the past.[56]

After the 1912 renewal, instability continued to plague the Association. Attempts to reopen negotiations on syndicating B-goods failed in the summer of 1913 and were cut short again in August 1914 by the political crisis, which turned attention to production for military purposes and led to a host of new problems and forces.[57] A much different economic story must be told of these years after 1914, with government funding, price controls, and production directives playing important roles. Renewal in 1917 was accomplished with glances over the shoulder to the government, but also with great difficulty. Problems of product mix continued to ensnarl negotiations, as market forces pulled producers' interests farther downstream into more refined steel products. After the war, the strains of shortages, the loss of capacity in the Saar, Lorraine, and Luxembourg, a new political climate, and the disruption of inflation brought about further concentration and new collusive forms. Collusion survived, but continued to be buffeted by exogenous forces as both technology and demand continued to change.[58]

V. CONCLUSION

The possibility of "overexpansion" in merchant bars was confirmed earlier in this paper. Was this growth in capacity based on the peculiar structure of the Steel Works Association? Although the evidence is meager, the answer must be "only partly." Difficulties with respect to B-quotas reflected the pressures of demand-induced expansion upstream in basic steel and preliminary rolling capacity, but also the conflicts between large producers in certain B-markets, for example Thyssen vs. Krupp in pipes. Differential ability to take advantage of cartel restrictions and profits also led to factions which saw self-interest in the removal of B-quotas, giving more freedom to pursue aggressive individual strategies. The expansion in basic steel and preliminary rolling capacity made sense for purposes of diversification in a rapidly growing economy. In addition, more than "modest" profits on A-goods, especially *Halbzeug* (ingots, blooms, and billets), provided a ready source of internal capital for expansion, according to contemporary observers, and probably made access to external sources of capital easier also.

In 1905–1907 Association members negotiated quotas in merchant bars far in excess of quantities demanded at then-current prices. This excess was eroded away as real prices fell after 1907 and sales expansion was hastened by an Association policy which obviously aimed at maintaining high prices for girders, an important substitute for bars in many construction applications. Fortuitously, the excess supply of bar quotas was disappearing by the time the 1907 contract was about to expire. Members of the Steel Association on at least one occasion *were* willing to make concessions to smaller firms with respect to quotas, but the latter probably feared *price* effects even more, especially if they were forced by size to act as price-takers. A guaranteed quota may be useless if revenues earned at or below that output are insufficient to cover costs. Higher quotas also would not be useful to a firm lacking standing capacity or the financial resources capable of increasing that capacity. The percentages put to the vote in November 1907 were obviously unrealistic for most outside *reine Walzwerke* (pure rolling mills). And it was only after Association bar quotas had been roughly stable for over two years (April 1907 to the fall of 1909) that outside Siemens-Martin producers could be persuaded to act in concert with Association members. Reluctance to negotiate with smaller outsiders is thus not evident. However, the larger firms probably had time horizons which allowed them to see beyond the possible flood of output and resulting depressed prices likely if the proposal of November 1907 had been ratified.

Previous explanations of the events of 1912 have suggested a gradient of interest in B-quotas as an inverse function of size. The only real indication we have of the two camps into which the Association split regarding B-quotas is the report of March 1912 from the Hörder Verein. Large, vertically integrated firms actually appeared on both sides of the debate. A significant difference appeared with respect to recent merger activity, however, and the histories of the five firms mentioned show acquisitions downstream.[59] Firms which had recently acquired capacity were anxious to remove restrictions accepted before that capacity was purchased, when their interests lay elsewhere. If the newly acquired capacity was from smaller firms which had recently entered the B-markets, it undoubtedly was more efficient than the facilities of those longer in the market. These firms thus expected to do better than their competitors in a world without B-quotas. As the manager of RheinStahl, Jakob Hasslacher, noted in April 1912, steps were to be taken for the event that *all* quotas were lifted: not only was size important for collusive bargaining sessions, but low unit costs and a full range of products would be of use in a competitive world.[60]

It is not possible to identify factions in the Steel Works Association based solely or even strongly on size and extent of vertical integration, although the conflict between Association members and the pure rolling mills outside the cartel was based on such differences. Rather, firms formed expectations about their relative abilities to compete successfully with and without B-quotas on the basis of many factors, which can be categorized in terms of expected costs and expected revenues. Expected revenues depended less on B-quotas than on the projected growth of various B-markets and the behavior of close competitors. It should not be surprising that August Thyssen took an "all or nothing" position on the regulation of B-goods: specific Association rules had shackled his ability to compete against Krupp and Mannesmann without any apparent limits on the latter pair's expansion. B-quotas as implemented by the Association had provided not an incentive to expand, but a system of discrimination which thereby had little chance of surviving the discontent of its victims. In the end the self-interest of these industrialists was defined in terms of control on A-goods and freedom in B-goods. The Steel Works Association was forced to accommodate cooperation and competition under the same roof.

"Industrial instability" emerges from the investigation, not surprisingly, as a potent force in this era of German steel. The forces of technical change and shifting demand outweighed the bargaining skills of these industrialists. Although this inability to collude successfully had positive implications for the welfare of German consumers, historians may still see in that inability failure in a broader sense. Wilhelmian social economists decried the "adjustment costs" borne by both capital and labor in this period of rapid technical change and growth.[61] Although the simple removal of output controls on merchant bars which had been largely fictitious since 1907 cannot be considered symptomatic of a more serious malaise, a closer look at those "costs" might lead to the formulation of more specific charges against Germany's collectivist capitalism.

ACKNOWLEDGMENTS

A previous version of this paper was presented to the Economics and Business Historical Society in April 1981. The underlying research was supported by the Social Science Research Council, the Yale University Council on West European Studies, the National Science Foundation (Grant No. SOC-7901429), and the Mellon Foundation (through Reed College). I would like to thank Gavin Wright and Steven Webb for their comments on earlier versions, without of course implicating them in my conclusions.

NOTES

1.   Stockder (1924), p. xix.
2.   Marshall (1920), p. 850.
3.   Parker (1954b), p. 382. See also Parker (1954a).
4.   Ulen (1979a, 1979b).
5.   See the preambles to the contracts of the Steel Works Association, available at the library of the Verein deutscher Eisenhüttenleute (hereafter VdE); also Feldman (1974), p. 575.
6.   For the evidence on motivations, see Peters (1981), especially Chap. III and IV. For a concise review of stabilization cartels, see Scherer (1980), pp. 212–220.
7.   Feldman (1974). See also Feldman (1977), especially the Introduction.
8.   Feldman (1974), pp. 576–578, 590.
9.   Calculated from data in the *Jahrbuch für den Oberbergamtsbezirk Dortmund,* Vol. 12, 1911/12, p. 758, and the business reports of the Steel Works Association, VdE Wo 344.
10.   Feldman (1974), p. 577.
11.   RheinStahl Archiv, Essen, 120 00/1, Mappe 2, *Vorstand* meeting January 23, 1911. Steven Webb (1980) has also shown that the cartel-tariff system led in general to higher effective protection for A-goods after 1879.
12.   Of course, aiming at long-run profits may lead to excess capacity in the short run.
13.   These percentages are generally calculated as the difference between market price and average cost of production, and expressed as a percentage of cost. For more details and sources, see Peters (1981), pp. 314–316.
14.   See Webb (1980).

15. See Peters (1981), Chap. V.

16. Köllman (1969), Table 2; see also McKay (1976) and the business reports of the Steel Works Association, VdE Wo 344.

17. Calculated from McKay (1976), Tables 7 and 9, and from Mitchell (1978), Tables A2 and F1.

18. See Peters (1981), Chap. V for a more complete discussion.

19. See the annual business reports of the Association, VdE Wo 344.

20. See, for example, the descriptions of firm installations in the *Jahrbuch für den Ober-bergamtsbezirk Dortmund,* beginning with the 1901–1904 edition.

21. Historisches Archiv der Gutehoffnungshütte (hereafter HA/GHH), GHH to Schumann January 11, 1911, and Rundschreiben 88, January 31, 1911.

22. *Stahl und Eisen* 31(1911), February 16, p. 290; Mannesmann-Archiv P5 25 64, Rundschreiben 91, February 2, 1911.

23. Also, Association members agreed to pay a fee for export subsidies of 4 Marks per ton as against only 1.50 Marks for nonmembers of the cartel (i.e., the Siemens-Martin firms).

24. Mannesmann-Archiv P5 25 64, Rundschreiben 94, and Protokoll, Hauptversammlung, February 22–23, 1911.

25. From 113.50 Marks in 1910-IV and 1911-I to 100.50 Marks by 1911-III. *Gemeinfassliche Darstellung der Eisenhüttenwesen* 1915 edition, p. 292.

26. See Peters (1981), Chap. VII, especially the section entitled "Overcoming Geographical Dispersion."

27. See Peters (1981), Chap. VII.

28. This was augmented by a three-year contract signed January 21, 1910, and amended May 4, 1910, scheduled to run until January 1, 1924. The 1903 contract is mentioned in Mannesmann's official history [Mannesmann (1965)], but the later contracts are ignored there. Documentation is at Mannesmann-Archiv M 60 011, Verträge, pp. 158–159.

29. For a fuller discussion of this episode, see Peters (1981), Chap. VII, the section entitled "Oligopolistic Rivalry in the Pipe Group."

30. RheinStahl Archiv 123 00/16, *Vorstand* to *Aufsichtsrat* April 11, 1911.

31. Simultaneously a disagreement over the definition of pipes was filtering through the cartel's committees. Werksarchiv Thyssen AG (hereafter WA/Thyssen) A/654, and Mannesmann-Archiv P5 25 64, December 1911 to February 1912.

32. Balcke, Tellering & Cie in Benrath, and the Wittener Stahlröhren-Werke AG in Witten. RheinStahl's purchase of 90 percent of Balcke, Tellering's shares in late 1911 was followed by the plan to expand the latter's product line into large pipes, and to expand sales generally in South Africa. Obviously, by late 1911 RheinStahl's pessimism earlier in the year had eased.

33. Mannesmann-Archiv P5 25 64, Mappe 1, Röchling to Schaltenbrand, March 9, 1910. The following is a paraphrase of Röchling's main points.

34. Mannesmann-Archiv P5 25 64, Röchling to Beukenberg, March 14, 1910.

35. The following discussion is based on the report prepared by Eberhard von Bodenhausen-Degener for Krupp. Historisches Archiv der Fried. Krupp AG FAH, IV E81.

36. See Peters (1981), Chap. II. There is some possibility that Stinnes's recommendation was the result of a running battle with August Thyssen, a ploy designed to force Thyssen to support renewal of the Rhenish-Westphalian Coal Syndicate. By threatening to blockade the Steel Works Association, more important to Thyssen than the coal cartel according to Stinnes, the younger industrialist may have sought to force withdrawal of a similar blockade threat by Thyssen directed at the Coal Syndicate.

37. Mannesmann-Archiv P5 25 64, Sitzung des Stahlwerks-Verbandes October 24, 1911.

38. WA/Thyssen A/654, Aufstellung October 1911, Anlage 1.

39. Ibid.

40. Werksarchiv Röchling (Völklingen) (hereafter WA/Röchling) D 177, Röchling to the Supervisory Board December 2 and 22, 1911.

41. Mannesmann-Archiv P5 25 67, Association (Abt. G) to Phönix January 2, 1912.

42. Mannesmann-Archiv P5 25 67, letters to the Association from various members November and December 1911 and January 1912.

43. WA/Röchling D 177, January 5, 1912.

44. Mannesmann-Archiv P5 25 67, Beukenberg to Schaltenbrand January 16, 1912, and Protokoll March 13, 1912.

45. Stumm and Deutsch-Luxemberg, for example.

46. Dissenting votes were cast by Gutehoffnungshütte, Deutsch-Lux, Stumm, de Wendel, Dillingen and Königs- und Laurahütte.

47. Mannesmann-Archiv P5 25 67, Betr. Verhandlungen über Verbandsverlängerung 21.3.1912, vermerkt Hörde 22.3.1912.

48. The possibility of "economies of scope" is also very strong. See Bailey and Friedlaender (1982).

49. Mannesmann-Archiv P5 25 67.

50. Ibid.

51. On Nothmann's proposal: *in favor*—Rote Erde, Hösch, Bochumer Verein, Röchling, Osnabrück, and Friedenshütte; *abstaining*—Haspe, Westfälische Stahlwerke, Rodingen, and Bismarckhütte; *against*—all other firms (18 in number). Details on the second vote are not available. Mannesmann-Archiv P5 25 67, Protokoll, Besprechung der Verbands-Erneuerung April 24, 1912.

52. For details of firms' late quota demands, see Mannesmann-Archiv P5 25 67, Zusammenstellung, Erneuerung des Stahlwerks-Verbandes 19.4.1912, Betr: Quoten im neuen Stahlwerks-Verband.

53. HA/GHH 3000030/16, April 29, 1912.

54. RheinStahl Archiv 1 23 00/16, Hasslacher to Aufsichtsrat May 1, 1912, and 1 20 00/2, Vorstandssitzungsprotokolle.

55. It is perhaps not surprising to find a coincidence between the gradualism in practice espoused by Adolf Kirdorf and the gradualism called for in general by his brother Emil, head of the Rhenish–Westphalian Coal Syndicate. See Peters (1981), Chap. II.

56. HA/GHH 3000030/16, April 29, 1912; Mannesmann-Archiv P5 25 67, April 29, 1912; WA Thyssen A/654, April 29, 1912.

57. HA/GHH, 3000031/4 and 3000031/5.

58. Parker (1954a, 1954b) and Feldman (1974, 1977) have brought much of these years to light.

59. For short firm histories, see the *Jahrbuch für den Oberbergamtsbezirk Dortmund*.

60. RheinStahl 1 23 00/16, Hasslacher to the Aufsichtsrat, April 11, 1911.

61. See Peters (1981), Chap. II, for a review of this debate on adjustment costs.

REFERENCES

Bailey, E. E., and A. Friedlaender (1982). "Market Structure and Multiproduct Industries." *Journal of Economic Literature* 20(September): 1024–1048.

Feldman, Gerald (1974). "The Collapse of the Steel Works Association, 1912–1919." Pp. 575–593 in *Sozialgeschichte Heute*, edited by Hans-Ulrich Wehler. Göttingen: Vandenhoeck & Ruprecht, 1974.

Feldman, Gerald (1977). *Iron and Steel in the German Inflation, 1916–1923*. Princeton, N.J.: Princeton University Press.

Jahrbuch für den Oberbergamtsbezirk Dortmund. Essen: Baedeker, 1894–1921.

Köllman, Wolfgang (1969). "The Process of Urbanization in Germany at the Height of the Industrialization Period." *Journal of Contemporary History*, 4: 59–76.

McKay, John P. (1976). *Tramways and Trolleys: The Rise of Urban Mass Transport in Europe*. Princeton, N.J.: Princeton University Press.

[Mannesmann, A. G. (1965)]. *75 Jahre Mannesmann.* Düsseldorf: Mannesmann.

Marshall, Alfred (1920). *Industry and Trade,* 3rd ed. London: Macmillan.

Mitchell, B. R. (1978). *European Historical Statistics, 1750–1970,* abridged ed. New York: Columbia University Press.

Parker, William N. (1954a). "Entrepreneurial Opportunity and Response in the German Economy." *Explorations in Entrepreneurial History,* 7: 26–36.

Parker, William N. (1954b). "Entrepreneurship, Industrial Organization and Economic Growth: A German Example." *Journal of Economic History* 14: 380–400.

Peters, Lon L. (1981). "Cooperative Competition in German Coal and Steel, 1893–1914" Ph.D. dissertation, Yale University.

Scherer, F. M. (1980). *Industrial Market Structure and Economic Performance,* 2nd ed. Chicago: Rand-McNally.

Stockder, Archibald (1924). *History of the Trade Associations of the German Coal Industry.* New York: Holt.

Ulen, Thomas (1979a). "Cyclical Factors in Cartel Stability: Theory." Working Paper No. 572, Department of Economics, University of Illinois at Urbana–Champaign, May.

Ulen, Thomas (1979b). "A Critique of Cartel Theory." Working Paper No. 599, Department of Economics, University of Illinois at Urbana–Champaign, August.

Webb, Steven B. (1980). "Tariffs, Cartels, Technology and Growth in the German Steel Industry, 1879 to 1914." *Journal of Economic History* 40: 309–330.

CURRENCY AND CREDIT IN
THE GILDED AGE

Barry Eichengreen

I. INTRODUCTION

The rapid industrialization of the United States in the half-century following the Civil War required a sound banking system able to mobilize savings and transfer funds between regions and sectors of the economy. An extensive literature documents the success with which, despite its imperfections, the postbellum money market helped to perform these functions.[1] To its contemporary critics, the major defect of the American financial system was neither the endurance of local market power and interregional interest differentials on otherwise comparable assets, nor the failure of the money supply to respond countercyclically to changing economic conditions. Rather, the major deficiency perceived in the operation of the postbellum banking system was its difficulty in accommodating seasonal variations in money market conditions. To the extent that the money supply varied seasonally, it exhibited "perverse elasticity," declining in the autumn and

Technique, Spirit, and Form in the Making of the Modern Economies:
Essays in Honor of William N. Parker
Research in Economic History, Suppl. 3, pages 87–114
Copyright © 1984 by JAI Press Inc.
All rights of reproduction in any form reserved.
ISBN: 0-89232-414-7

early winter months precisely when the demand for money to move crops was greatest. This perverse response is accused of exacerbating interest rate fluctuations and blamed for the concentration of bank failures and financial crises in the final quarter of the year.

The source of these seasonal fluctuations in the money supply was a regional differential in the use of currency and credit. American economic historians long have told us that by 1860 the United States was divided into three regions: Northeast, South, and West. In each region "the population had developed a characteristic social organization and with it a characteristic culture. . . ."[2] After the Civil War, these regional identities manifested themselves in attitudes toward currency and credit. In the Northeast, a region blessed with a well-articulated financial system, residents relied heavily on bank deposits and checks for the provision of liquidity. In the South, where a sound banking system was seriously weakened by the war and the federal banking laws of 1863–1865, the propensity to utilize personal checks and bank drafts for transactions purposes was considerably lower. Every harvest season, as funds were shifted from Northeast to South and West, they passed from regions where residents held a high ratio of bank deposits to currency into regions where the deposit/currency ratio was low. As the ratio of deposits to currency declined, reserves were drained from the banking system, and financial intermediaries holding fractional reserves were forced to contract their outstanding liabilities by a multiple of the reserve loss. The consequent decline in the money supply is thought to have heightened seasonal interest rate fluctuations, and to have forced the banking sector to make difficult adjustments on both the asset and liability sides of its balance sheet. In years when the impact of this portfolio adjustment was particularly severe, it may have been a major factor contributing to the incidence of bank failures.

There has been rather more speculation than evidence on the determinants of this regional differential in the use of currency. After reviewing the debate over the operation of the National Banking System, this paper presents evidence on the use of currency and credit. While the paper's analytical framework is choice-theoretic, it recognizes the role played by social organization and culture in the decision problem. The individual's choice of whether to use currency or credit instruments to complete a transaction is related not only to observed and unobserved attributes of the two means of payment and the transaction, but also to attributes of the individual and his environment. Individuals are assumed to base their decisions on utility-maximization, but their utility functions are allowed to vary in a specified stochastic fashion.

Economists and historians have advanced a variety of explanations for the existence of a regional differential in currency use during the Gilded Age. Some have argued that the roots of this regional differential lie in the early emergence of a regional banking system in the Northeast in the first half of the nineteenth century. The banking habit gradually spread outward from the Northeast to other parts of the continent, but several decades were to pass before the advantages of deposit banking were equally well appreciated in the rest of the country. According to this view, the source of the regional differential in currency use was institutional: it can be traced to the structure of regional banking systems and the extent to which regional economies were suited to the banking systems at hand.

Other observers have emphasized the personal characteristics of individuals engaged in transactions, including their wealth, race, and occupation, as well as characteristics of their environment, such as population density and the extent of urbanization. Perhaps the most controversial hypothesis is the racial explanation for the regional differential in currency use. In this view, the tendency of blacks to rely unusually heavily on currency helps to account for the South's exceptionally low deposit/currency ratio. In fact, the findings reported here provide little support for this racial explanation. They indicate that regional differentials in the demand for currency and credit are explicable largely in terms of differences in financial structure, the extent of wage labor, and population density. The racial composition of a region's population appears to have had relatively little effect on its use of currency and credit.

II. THE OPERATION OF THE NATIONAL BANKING SYSTEM

At the beginning of the Civil War, the only significant financial intermediary in the United States was the banking system. That system consisted of approximately 1300 commercial banks, chartered by the states and heavily concentrated along the Atlantic coast, plus some 300 mutual savings banks, which were largely restricted to the New York and New England regions. At midcentury these banks accounted for more than 80 percent of the assets of American financial intermediaries.

By 1860 the confusing variety of state bank notes, many of which traded at substantial discounts, and the questionable investment practices of certain state banks, which threatened to render them unsafe as depositories, had created considerable support in Washington for federal banking regulation. The Civil War, which posed new financial difficulties for a U.S. Treasury required to finance unprecedented military expenditures, provided the impetus for reform. The National Currency Acts of 1863 and 1864 enhanced the Treasury's ability to raise war finance by creating a system of federally chartered banks entitled to issue notes only by purchasing federal bonds. In 1865, to encourage state banks to join the national system and provide the country with a uniform national currency, Congress imposed a 10 percent tax on state bank notes, effective as of July 1, 1866. Due in large part to this legislation, circulation of state bank notes fell from $143 million in 1865 to $20 million in 1866 and to $3 million the following year.

Since issuing bank notes remained a profitable activity, at least initially, and since for a considerable period it remained impractical to introduce checking accounts in regions where familiarity with deposit banking was limited, many state banks joined the federal system. However, some intermediaries, particularly in the South, found it difficult to satisfy other restrictions imposed on federal banks. The 1864 Act mandated minimum capital requirements of $50,000 for national banks in cities with populations of 6000 or less, $100,000 for banks in cities with 6000 to 50,000 residents, and $200,000 for banks in more populous cities.[3] In addition, national banks were prohibited from issuing certain classes of mortgage loans, a particularly burdensome restriction in agricultural regions where land was the most important asset. As a result, in the immediate postwar years the vast majority of national banks came to be located east of the Mississippi and north of the Ohio: no more than 20 of the 1688 national banks organized in the three immediate postwar years were located in the Cotton South. The combined impact of the Civil War and the federal banking laws reduced the South's percentage of national bank deposits from 28.6 percent in 1860 to 5.8 percent in 1870.[4]

As note issue gradually became less important, the number of state banks, with less stringent regulations, lower capital requirements, and frequently nonexistent reserve requirements, grew at an accelerating rate. In the five decades following the Civil War, the number of banks grew five times faster than population. The assets of commercial banks and of mutual savings banks increased by twentyfold over the same period, while the assets of life insurance companies and building and loan associations expanded even more rapidly. But the South continued to lag behind the rest of the nation, less in number of banks than in their size. By 1909 the South had 28 percent of the nation's population and 24 percent of its banks, but only 7 percent of its deposits.[5]

A.   The Network of Interbank Balances

Well before the Civil War, country banks throughout the United States had come to rely on deposits with city banks in regional financial centers for the provision of highly liquid interest-bearing assets. These city banks, as well as some country banks, in turn maintained bankers' balances with correspondent banks in New York City. New York served in turn as an intermediary between Europe and the South and West. This hierarchy of interbank balances was institutionalized by the National Currency Act of 1864, which required banks in reserve cities and central reserve cities to maintain reserves in lawful money equal to 25 percent of their deposits, but allowed reserve city banks to keep half their reserves as deposits at central reserve city banks. Country banks, which were required to hold reserves amounting to 15 percent of deposits, could keep up to 60 percent of that amount in the form of deposits at banks in reserve or central reserve cities.

Country banks turned naturally to their correspondents in regional financial centers when they wished to acquire additional interest-bearing assets in periods of slack loan demand. Interbank balances soon reached substantial proportions:

in Chicago and Kansas City, for example, at the turn of the century correspondent balances accounted for approximately one-half of total national bank deposits.[6] Banks in these and other regional reserve cities relied in turn on their New York correspondents for the provision of similar services. Since bankers' balances were a volatile liability, New York banks tended to invest an amount proportional to the interbank balances on deposit in call loans on the New York money market, often securing the loans with stock as collateral. When a country bank liquidated its balances with its reserve city correspondent, the reserve city bank would run down its own balances with its New York correspondent, and the New York bank would call some of its loans. In effect, New York banks provided their Southern and Western counterparts a supply of highly liquid assets with stable rates of return in exchange for a commission amounting to the difference between the rate on bankers' balances, typically 1 percent, and the call loan rate, which might vary from 1 or 2 percent in mid-summer to 25 percent in November.[7] Contemporaries noted that the volume of bankers' balances fluctuated seasonally, rising in periods when the demand for currency and credit in the countryside was depressed, and falling in periods of increased agricultural activity such as the "spring revival" of March, April, and early May and the crop-moving months in the late autumn.[8]

The planting season in the spring and the crop-moving months of October and November marked seasonal peaks in the transactions demand for money, not just in the heavily agricultural South and West but for the nation as a whole.[9] Kemmerer's study of the 1890–1908 period shows that average weekly bank clearings in the continental United States reached their annual high in the third week of November.[10] The secondary peak in the volume of transactions which took place during the planting season became more important in later years as the use of purchased inputs, such as hybrid seed and fertilizer, grew increasingly prevalent. These seasonal variations in the value of transactions were especially pronounced in agricultural areas. In New Orleans, an important marketing center for cotton, sugar, and rice, the value of bank clearings varied on average by 125 percent between its annual peak and trough, compared with a 35 percent variance for the country as a whole.

Interest rate movements provide evidence of regular seasonal swings in money market conditions. Figure 1 presents a spectral density function for the average monthly renewal rate on call loans in New York City. It confirms that annual cycles were that interest rate's most prominent cyclical characteristic. While an important secondary cycle at a frequency corresponding to 2.5 months is evident in the density function, there is not enough data to reveal the existence of longer cycles.[11]

B.   The Interregional Balance of Payments

Substantial cash flows between New York and predominantly agricultural regions of the United States took place over the course of the year. These

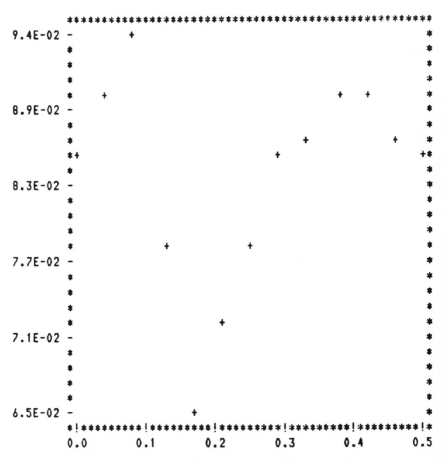

Figure 1. Spectral Density Function for New York Call Rate[1]

[1]Maximum lag = 12. The peak in the density function at a frequency of 0.08333 corresponds to a periodicity of 12 months.

seasonal flows of money balances are evident both in the statistics on net cash flows into and out of New York City reported weekly by the *Commercial and Financial Chronicle* and in 1907 survey data gathered for the National Monetary Commission.[12] Both sets of figures show that the first signs of the crop-moving demand for money appeared around mid-August. As interest rates began to rise in the autumn, bankers' balances in the East were liquidated and funds were transferred to the South and West. Transfers continued through September and October, but by January the return movement of funds to the East was dominant.

There exist two competing theories of the mechanism which effected the interregional flow of funds required by seasonal variations in money demand. The traditional view emphasizes the response of capital flows to interregional interest differentials.[13] It is argued that, as money demand rose in the interior during periods of increasing economic activity, interest rates were pushed upward and opportunities were created for arbitrage between regional financial markets. Southern and Western banks exploited these opportunities by liquidating their correspondent balances in the East as soon as they observed a rise in local interest rates relative to the rate on bankers' balances in New York.

Charles Goodhart and Allyn Young before him have suggested that the traditional emphasis on the role of capital movements in the interregional balance of payments may be misleading.[14] Goodhart argues that the current account rather than the capital account was the primary source of the interregional flow of funds that occurred during the crop-moving season. In the winter, spring, and summer, agricultural regions typically ran current account deficits with the East, importing more goods and services than they exported. During the fall, however, the eastward movement of crops generated a substantial current account surplus. The autumnal flow of funds westward and southward in payment for the agricultural regions' current account surpluses more than satisfied the interior's demand for funds and depleted the Eastern money supply. Consequently, interest rates in New York rose relative to those in the South and the West, attracting short-term capital from the interior. Thus, Goodhart not only attributes the westward flow of funds to the current account, but suggests that to the extent that there existed capital transactions of any significance, they actually operated in the opposite direction from that hypothesized in the traditional view.

Proponents of both views draw support from Leonard Watkins's figures on bankers' balances in New York. The change in bankers' balances is taken as a proxy for the capital account on the grounds that the banking system was responsible for the largest part of the capital transfer and that bankers' balances were the proximate repository for such funds. Goodhart's estimates of the seasonal component in Watkins's data are reproduced in Table 1.[15] Assuming that New York is representative of the eastern region, we observe bankers' balances in the East reaching their lowest level at the Comptroller of the Currency's fifth call, which occurred in the final months of the year. The third column, containing data on total bankers' balances, supports the traditional view. Yet if it is assumed, following Goodhart, that nonnational banks maintaining correspondent balances in New York tended to be upstate banks which regarded New York City as their regional financial center, and that national banks maintaining correspondent balances in New York City were largely reserve city banks located in other regions of the country, then the figures in Table 1 are not nearly so supportive of the conventional view. According to Goodhart, the flow of national bankers' balances from New York to the interior reflected in the figures in column 1 is too small to be consistent with the traditional view. Moreover, the observed flow of funds from New York to the interior during the summer months is totally incon-

Table 1.   Seasonal Variations in Bankers' Balances
at New York ($ millions)[a]

	Balances Held with New York Banks by Other National Banks	Balances Held with New York Banks by Other Nonnational Banks	Total
1st call	9.9	−2.2	7.7
2nd call	3.9	−7.0	−3.1
3rd call	−1.6	18.0	16.4
4th call	0.8	13.9	14.7
5th call	−12.6	−22.9	−35.5

[a]Calls were requests by the Comptroller of the Currency to national banks for information on their assets and liabilities. The dates of the five calls varied periodically—the first falling in January or February; the second in March, April, or May; the third in May, June, or July; the fourth in July, August, or (in 1913) October; and the fifth in the final months of the year.
Source: Goodhart (1969, pp. 98–100).

sistent with that view. However, counterarguments can be made. For example, had a significant proportion of state banks outside of New York maintained bankers' balances directly with their correspondents in New York City, then both of Goodhart's objections would be eliminated. In fact, it was not uncommon for nonnational banks in the interior to maintain accounts in New York City to facilitate their customers' transactions in eastern markets. Since these transactions caused a large number of state bank notes to pass through New York, even prior to the Civil War many banks in the interior of the country had adopted the practice of maintaining balances with a New York bank as a way of facilitating redemption. We know little of the prevalence of such practices, but their existence renders estimates of the national/nonnational composition of bankers' balances held in New York insufficient for distinguishing the two views.

An alternative is to use observed interest rate differentials as a basis on which to infer the likely direction of capital movements. Goodhart has observed that, even while interest rates rose in the interior during the crop moving months of October and November, they rose more dramatically in New York. With the growth of the interest differential favoring New York, Goodhart argues, capital would have flowed in that direction. A problem with this argument is that the interest differential measures the incentive to shift capital only in the absence of risk premia; otherwise, interest rates must be adjusted for investors' perceptions of risk before inferences can be drawn. Given the association of high interest rates and money market stringency with the perceived danger of bank failures, it is plausible that risk premia in different markets were positively associated with the level of interest rates in those markets. In this case, as the demand for money increased, interest rates in the high-interest-rate center would have had to rise by a greater amount than rates in the low-interest-rate center for capital flows to be prevented. Thus, it is not clear that sound inferences about the direction of capital flows can be drawn on the basis of interest differentials.

Another approach is to compare the timing of interest rate movements in New York and in the interior. If an excess demand for money which developed first in the interior caused capital to be pulled westward, leading subsequently to a rise in interest rates in New York, then one would expect to observe interest rate movements in the interior occurring prior to interest rate movements in New York. Conversely, if current account settlements enabled money market equilibrium in the interior to be maintained at stable interest rates but gave rise to an excess demand for money in the East, leading to a capital flow eastward and to a subsequent rise interest rates in the interior, then one would expect to find interest rate movements in New York occurring prior to interest rate movements in the West. In fact, cross-spectral analysis for the period 1902–1913 indicates that loan rate cycles in St. Louis occurred one to one-and-a-half months prior to loan rate cycles in New York.[16] This provides some support for the traditional view. However, timing relationships alone are an imperfect guide to the underlying economic relationships.[17] Ultimately, it is difficult to resolve this debate in the absence of reliable data on capital flows.

C.   Regional Differentials in Currency and Credit

To understand how shifts in the regional distribution of money balances gave rise to the perverse elasticity of the money supply, it is necessary to consider the changing composition of the money stock. Following the end of the Civil War, it took a mere 15 years for the deposit/currency ratio to double and another 20 years for it to double again. Associated with this shift in the composition of portfolios was a change in means of payment. The postbellum period was marked by the increasing use of credit instruments such as bank drafts, bills of exhange, promissory notes, and, most importantly, checks drawn upon bank accounts. Checks had first come to be as important as currency during the late 1830s in urban areas and during the 1850s in the country as a whole, and their use continued to increase over the course of the century. By 1900, perhaps 85 percent of the nation's business was transacted with checks.[18]

Residents in different regions of the country neither employed credit instruments to the same extent nor held the same proportion of their money balances in the form of bank deposits. Financial experts took note of the exceptionally high propensity of Southerners to employ currency in transactions. This regional differential in the use of currency and credit is apparent in Table 2, where the percentage of bank deposits paid in by check in selected Southern states is compared with the national average. The figures for different years are not directly comparable, due to the omission of reserve cities in 1890 and the fact that information was gathered at different times of year. But in comparison with

Table 2. Percentage of All Bank Deposits or Receipts in the
Form of Checks

State	June 30, 1881[a]	July 1, 1890[b]	Sept. 15, 1892[c]	July 1, 1896[d]	March 1909[e]
Alabama	72.0	77.6	78.0	82.3	83.6
Arkansas	66.2	75.4	80.0	82.1	79.2
Florida	23.7	84.2	84.0	84.2	86.4
Georgia	69.5	81.3	84.3	77.3	85.3
Kentucky	86.8	79.3	83.5	86.3	89.0
Louisiana	89.8[f]	55.7	60.9	88.1	90.5
Mississippi	NA[g]	72.6	74.2	83.8	82.5
N. Carolina	85.0	88.1	79.9	79.3	85.2
Oklahoma	NA	NA	42.3	77.2	82.0
S. Carolina	85.9	83.0	92.2	86.6	78.6
Tennessee	63.9	82.4	83.2	86.5	87.3
Texas	67.8	76.5	80.4	78.9	88.3
Virginia	89.5	92.1	90.0	89.6	88.3
W. Virginia	65.1	86.0	85.9	82.3	81.7
Total U.S.	95.1	84.1	84.9	93.4	94.0

[a]Percentage of national bank receipts taken as checks. Comptroller of the Currency, *Annual Report* (Washington, D.C.: Government Printing Office, 1881), p. 96.
[b]Percentage of national bank receipts taken as checks exclusive of reserve cities. Secretary of the Treasury, *Annual Report on the State of Finances for the Year 1890* (Washington, D.C.: Government Printing Office, 1891), p. 387.
[c]Percentage of national bank receipts taken as checks. Comptroller of the Currency, *Annual Report* (Washington, D.C.: Government Printing Office, 1892), p. 34.
[d]Percentage of total deposits made by checks for all banks. Comptroller of the Currency, *Annual Report* (Washington, D.C.: Government Printing Office, 1896), p. 68.
[e]Percentage of total deposits made by checks for all banks. David Kinley, *The Use of Credit Instruments in Payments in the United States* (Washington, D.C.: Government Printing Office, 1910), pp. 181–182.
[f]Figures for the city of New Orleans only.
[g]NA = Not available.

other regions, an unusually low percentage of deposits made by check is evident for the states of the Deep South in every year for which these data are available.
The impact on the money supply of seasonal shifts in cash balances from regions with high deposit/currency ratios to regions with low deposit/currency ratios can be illustrated with a simple accounting framework. Under a mixed specie–fiduciary standard like that maintained in the United States during the Gilded Age, the supply of money (M2) depends on the circulation of currency (C), the ratio of deposits to reserves maintained by commercial banks (D/R), and the ratio of deposits to currency held by the public (D/C).

$$M2 = C \frac{D/R(1 + D/C)}{D/R + D/C} . \tag{1}$$

Here the monetary base is composed entirely of currency (gold and silver certificates, U.S. notes, national bank notes, and Treasury notes of 1890). Under a fractional reserve banking system in which the deposit/reserve ratio is greater than unity, a decline in the public's deposit/currency ratio, holding other variables constant, reduces the money supply.

$$\frac{\partial M2}{\partial D/C} = C\frac{D/R(D/R - 1)}{(D/R + D/C)^2} > 0. \tag{2}$$

A rise in the monetary base or a fall in the deposit/reserve ratio conceivably could offset the impact on the money supply of a decline in the deposit/currency ratio; this possibility is discussed below. Yet few contemporaries were confident that this was the case. In fact, the tendency of the money supply to contract in the autumn due to the transfer of cash balances from the East to the South and West, where lower deposit/currency ratios were maintained, was one of the principal concerns of commentators who complained of the "inelasticity" or "perverse elasticity" of the money supply.

Of course, the complaint that the currency was inelastic meant different things to different people. To members of the cheap-money–greenback movement, the inelasticity of the currency referred to the failure of the money supply to grow as rapidly as output and the consequent tendency of prices to fall. To others, inelasticity implied the absence of a lender of last resort able to ensure the effective convertibility of deposits into currency during banking panics. At times these meanings were inadequately distinguished.[19] For example, in a speech to the U.S. Senate in 1874, John Gordon of Georgia found the causes of both the 1873 financial crisis and the downward trend of prices in "the rigidity of volume, the non-elasticity and therefore insufficiency of the currency."[20]

By the turn of the century, the inelasticity of the currency had come to mean the slight or perverse response of the money supply to seasonal variations in money demand. As James Forgan, President of the First National Bank of Chicago, told an assemblage of bankers in 1903,

the supply of money periodically oscillates between overabundance and inadequacy, in accordance with the demand for it, which varies with the seasons. The supply being arbitrarily fixed in quantity, bears no relation to the varying demands of commerce, and there is not even an attempt in our monetary system to adjust the supply to the demand.[21]

To some, the regular seasonal pattern in money demand meant not just that the Treasury should act to prevent the money supply from declining in the autumn, but that it should actively intervene to stabilize interest rates by maintaining a fixed relation between the supply of notes and the volume of transactions. This view was an outgrowth of the real bills doctrine. According to this doctrine, currency should be issued to finance merchandise trade and loans for carrying goods, but not to facilitate transactions in financial markets or fixed investment.

Modern critics of this doctrine have faulted it for neglecting the role of higher interest rates in equilibrating the money market during periods of increased transactions demand.[22] However, contemporaries feared interest rate fluctuations with good reason: high rates were a sign of strain in the money market and brought to mind the threat of a banking panic. Indeed, financial crises and seasonal fluctuations in the money market were seen as closely related. Financial crises were attributed not to cyclical factors but to the recurring autumnal pressures on the money market. As contemporaries saw matters, these seasonal pressures were so severe that only a little extra strain, brought on by a speculative boom on Wall Street, a bank failure, or the coincidence of the harvest season with a business cycle peak, might be sufficient to transform pressure into panic.[23] As O. M. W. Sprague wrote in his influential history of American financial panics, ''With few exceptions all our crises, panics and periods of more severe monetary stringency occurred in the autumn, when the western banks, through the sale of cereal crops, were in a position to withdraw large sums of money from the East.''[24] Thus, the panic of 1873 began shortly after the middle of September, the crisis of 1890 began early in November, and the 1907 crisis began in October. While the crisis of 1893 deviates from this pattern, its onset in May was identified with the heightened seasonal demand for money associated with the planting season.

In the early years of the 20th Century, the Treasury sometimes responded actively to a decline in bank deposits. Treasury Secretary Shaw restored an earlier policy of running down the available cash balance in the Treasury in response to seasonal variations in the tightness of the money market. The Treasury was compelled to hold only $150 million as a reserve to back the circulation of U.S. notes and could exercise discretion over the disposition of its other balances. In the fall, Shaw transferred Treasury deposits from subtreasuries to national banks designated as depositories for public funds, and augmented the public's currency holdings by purchasing government bonds or prepaying interest due. State and national banks helped to accommodate seasonal fluctuations in the demand for money by reducing their reserve/deposit ratios in the late summer and early fall.[25] On the other hand, there was little seasonal variation in the supply of national bank notes, since issuing and retiring them was a costly process. On balance, few experts in or out of government were confident that Treasury and commercial bank operations were sufficient to neutralize the contractionary pressure on the money stock caused by the transfer of funds from the Northeast.

III. DETERMINANTS OF THE USE OF CURRENCY AND CREDIT

In the absence of information about the distribution of currency by state, little is known about the magnitude of regional differentials in the deposit/currency ratio. However, if it is assumed that the deposit/currency ratio is correlated with reliance on currency and checks in business and personal transactions, then information on the proportion of bank deposits paid in by currency can be used to test various explanations for this regional differential.

The assumption that the flow of transactions using currency or checks was proportional to the stock of currency or demand deposits maintained by transactors is reasonable so long as both instruments were demanded for transactions purposes but were not held as assets. Standard models of the transactions demand for money imply that each component of the money stock will be held for use in transactions to the point where the marginal cost of interest earnings foregone is just equal to the marginal benefit of an additional transaction.[26] However, to the extent that there existed a demand for money due to the riskiness of nominal returns on other assets, the flow of transactions is an imperfect guide to holdings of currency and demand deposits.[27] Furthermore, in interior regions where money and capital markets were quite imperfect, interest-bearing demand deposits may have provided an important repository for wealth, particularly in light of their liquidity. Therefore, the proportion of bank deposits paid in by currency would seem to be a reliable proxy for the share of currency in money holdings only for years after the turn of the century, by which time the distinction between savings deposits and demand deposits was clear and savings accounts were more likely to dominate both currency and interest-bearing demand deposits in investors' portfolios.

Economists have not been at a loss for explanations of regional differences in the proportion of transactions using currency. When Goodhart recently speculated that the unusually high proportion of deposits paid in by currency in the postbellum South was due to its "lack of urbanization, a relatively weak banking system, and a large Negro population . . . ," he was echoing the observations of previous writers.[28] The first expert on this question was David Kinley, who in fact designed the questionnaires used by the Comptroller of the Currency to gather information on the composition of bank receipts. In his early writings, Kinley focused on the relationship between population density and credit use. He posited the existence of a nonlinear relationship between the two variables, suggesting that the percentage of transactions using credit "increases until a certain point of density of population is reached, after which the percentage continues to decline relatively to total business."[29] Others have recast Kinley's population density hypothesis in terms of urbanization: Cagan, for instance, has suggested that urban life provided familiarity with the advantages of credit while at the same time increasing the tendency to trade with strangers, thereby discouraging its use.[30]

In subsequent studies, Kinley continued to regard population density as a critical determinant of credit use. In addition, he nominated race, employment, and national origin as additional determinants of the regional differential in the use of checks. For the South in particular he argued that the large black popula-

tion, ''in which the use of checks practically does not exist . . . ,'' was an
important part of the explanation for that region's unusual reliance on currency.[31] Kinley also suggested that the high proportion of immigrants from countries where deposit banking was unfamiliar tended to depress the proportion of
bank deposits paid in by check in certain urban areas and portions of the Far
West.

Employment influenced the use of currency because, except in the Far West
and portions of the Midwest, wage payrolls traditionally were paid in cash.
David Kinley noted in 1910 that three-quarters of the wage payrolls made up by
national banks took the form of cash.[32] As Irving Fisher put it, the preference for
paying wages in cash was so strong that ''we could not imagine [it] overridden
except temporarily and to a small degree. . . .''[33] While Fisher's assertion may
be an accurate characterization of the state of affairs in the Northeast, it neglects
significant regional differentials in the form of wage payment.[34] In 1894, for
instance, the ratio of wage payrolls made up in checks to those dispersed in cash
ranged from 9.7 in Colorado to 0.07 in Vermont.[35] By the time of Kinley's 1909
study, regional differentials in the form of wage payment had diminished somewhat. Still, wages typically were paid out in cash in the industrial states of the
East and by check in western areas of relatively recent settlement. It may be that
the prevalence of wage labor had different implications for currency use in
different regions; while workers in the Northeast receiving wages in cash may
have relied heavily on currency for transactions purposes, workers in the West
who were familiar with the virtues of banking through the receipt of payroll
checks may have relied to a considerably lesser extent on currency. The fact that
the payment period varied with the form of payment may help to eliminate the
apparent discrepancy. In the South and West, where wages typically were paid
out by check, monthly payments predominated, in contrast to the Northeast,
where weekly cash payments were usual. Workers paid by check presumably
deposited their wages and then conducted the greater portion of the month's
transactions with currency, while workers paid in cash used that cash for the
subsequent week's transactions. Though this suggests that the prevalence of
wage labor may have had different implications for the use of currency and credit
depending on region, the fact remains that contemporary observers believed the
prevalence of wage labor to be a crucial determinant of currency use.

Farmers were another group unlikely to accept payment by check, because
trips to the bank were costly in time and effort.[36] Fisher and others also noted
that the proportion of business transacted by check tended to rise with income
and wealth.

The availability of banking facilities was another factor mentioned frequently
in discussions of currency use. The closer and more convenient the bank, the
lower the effective cost of maintaining a bank balance and accepting payment by
check. Thus, in the South, with few banks relative to area or population, the
higher effective cost of deposit banking deterred the use of credit. Another factor
influencing the tendency to rely on currency and credit was the interest rate

differential on checking and savings account balances.[37] In the immediate postbellum period, comparable rates of interest were paid on demand and time deposits alike, and checks could be written against both types of accounts. As the distinction between checking and savings accounts became clearer, a rise in the interest rate paid on savings accounts should have raised or lowered the deposit/currency ratio depending on whether currency or demand deposits were closer substitutes for savings deposits.

A. A Model of the Choice Between Currency and Credit

The preceding analysis suggests that in choosing whether to use currency or credit instruments in a particular transaction, individuals considered the cost and riskiness of the two means of payment. Their decision also may have been affected by the special attributes of the transaction (such the value of the commodity exchanged or the timing of the exchange) and by the individual's own characteristics (familiarity with deposit banking, reputation, other socioeconomic variables, or simply random variations in tastes). In turn, the attributes of the transaction and the attitudes of the individual may have been a function of social organization and cultural background. Since the individual's decision problem was to select one means of payment from various alternatives each time payment was to be made, standard utility analysis of marginal trade-offs between commodities is inappropriate. Rather, it is necessary to assume that the individual considered the alternatives and selected the means of payment which maximized utility. By imposing further assumptions on the problem it is possible to derive a logit model similar to that applied by McFadden and others to problems in decision analysis.[38]

Assume that the utility of each means of payment depends on a vector of its own observed characteristics, a vector of observed characteristics of the individual facing the decision problem, a vector of observed characteristics of the commodity exchanged, a vector of observed characteristics of the choice environment, and a vector of unobserved characteristics of the individual, commodity, and environment. The unobserved component of utility may include purely random variation in tastes. Thus, the utility to an individual of each means of payment can be described by the stochastic utility function:

$$U_i = U_i(C_i, I, \mu_i) \qquad (i = 1, \ldots, n), \qquad (3)$$

where U_i = utility of means of payment i;

C_i = vector of observed characteristics of means of payment i;

I = vector of observed characteristics of the individual, the commodity exchanged, and the environment;

μ_i = vector of unobserved characteristics of means of payment i, the individual, the commodity, and the environment.

Assume further that the stochastic utility function U_i can be separated into two parts: $V(C_i, I)$, which is a function of observed characteristics, and ϵ_i, the unobserved component of utility, which is a random variable.

$$U_i = V(C_i, I) + \epsilon_i. \tag{4}$$

Here V can be referred to as representative utility, since it reflects the representative tastes of the population, while the ϵ_i reflect the idiosyncrasies in individuals' tastes.

From utility maximization it follows that in a given instance an individual will choose alternative i over alternative j if and only if $U_i > U_j$ for $i \neq j$ among the alternative means of payment. Since the ϵ_i are random variables, the event $U_i > U_j$ is itself random. The probability that means of payment i will be chosen can be written:

$$p_i = p(U_i > U_j) \tag{5}$$
$$= p[\epsilon_j - \epsilon_i < V(C_i, I) - V(C_j, I)] \quad \text{(for all } i \neq j\text{)}.$$

To compute p_i, knowledge about the probability distribution of ϵ_i is required. To keep the problem tractable, assume that the ϵ_i are identically and independently distributed across the two alternatives according to the Weibull distribution.

$$p(\epsilon_i \leq \epsilon) = \exp(-e^{-\epsilon}). \tag{6}$$

The corresponding frequency function has the same general shape as the normal, but it is skewed to the right. Thus, the probability of selecting means of payment i is given by

$$p_i = \frac{e^{V(C_i, I)}}{\sum\limits_{j=1}^{n} e^{V(C_j, I)}}. \tag{7}$$

B. Implementing the Model

The problem at hand is to estimate the effect of the observed attributes of the means of payment, environment, commodities, and individuals on the probability that a transaction is completed by check or currency. Assuming the representative utility functions to be linear in their parameters, equation (7) can be transformed so that

$$\log\left(\frac{p_1}{1 - p_1}\right) = a + \sum\limits_{k=1}^{K} b_k C_k + \sum\limits_{m=1}^{M} B_m I_m. \tag{8}$$

Here p_1 denotes the share of checks in total transactions. The C_k variables represent the difference between checks and currency of attribute k of the two means of payment, while the I_m variables represent the difference between checks and currency in the value of attribute m of the individual, commodity or environment.

Despite the fact that it is derived under the assumption that there exist random variations of tastes, the logit model in equation (8) contains no error term. However, since the units of observation are aggregations of samples of individual decisions, an observed market share f is only an estimate of p, the true probability of choosing a means of payment. It can be shown that

$$\log\left(\frac{f_1}{1 - f_1}\right) = \log\left(\frac{p_1}{1 - p_1}\right) + \alpha, \qquad (9)$$

where α is a normally distributed random variable with zero mean. The error term in the estimating equation will be heteroskedastic, since the logit has variance $p_1(1 - p_1)/n$, where n is the number of observations in a cell. After weighing each observation by $p_1(1 - p_1)n$, using total deposits as the measure of n, standard tests for heteroskedasticity provided no indication of its presence.[39] Note that, although the probability of making a deposit by check p_1 is bounded by zero and one, the transformed variable, the log odds of making a deposit by check $\log[p_1/(1 - p_1)]$ ranges from $-\infty$ when $p_1 = 0$ to ∞ when $p_1 = 1$. Given the transformation, the estimated standard errors of the regression coefficients follow a t distribution.[40]

C. Data and Results

Hypotheses concerning the determinants of interstate differences in the use of currency and credit can be tested with data for 1909 on the proportion of bank deposits paid in by check in 48 states and the District of Columbia.[41] This information was solicited by the Comptroller of the Currency from all banks known to exist in the United States on March 16, 1909. Out of approximately 25,000 banks contacted by the Comptroller, 12,190 responded. 698 of the forms returned were rejected because they were completed incorrectly, received too late, or among seven returns received from Alaska and Hawaii likely to reveal confidential information about the operation of individual banks.

It is evident from Table 2 that similar information is available for other years in the postbellum period. However, the March 1909 survey is preferable to previous inquiries in several respects. Survey data for the middle of the month should be relatively free of the dominating effects of wage payments, which is a problem with other surveys conducted at the beginning or end of months. Unlike all earlier surveys except that conducted in 1896, information was solicited not just from national banks but also from state and private banks, savings banks, and loan and trust companies. Coverage improved somewhat between 1896 and

1909: the ratio of acceptable replies to total banks surveyed rose from 0.42 to 0.46. A further advantage of the 1909 survey is that it can be linked to data gathered by the National Monetary Commission on bank assets and liabilities as of April 28, 1909.[42] Finally, as indicated above, it is desirable to utilize data for years close to World War I, when the distinction between savings and checking accounts was widely made and the former clearly dominated both currency and demand deposits in asset portfolios.

Even apart from the adequacy of data on deposit flows as a measure of stocks of credit instruments, the 1909 survey is not without its problems. Due to the gradual decline of regional differentials in credit use, the 1909 survey may not be as informative as those conducted earlier. Coverage was considerably more complete for national banks than for state and private banks. The nonreporting banks were smaller than average and tended to be located in the agricultural communites of the West. Thus, there may be a problem of overrepresentation of urban areas with large numbers of foreign-born residents and workers engaged in wage labor. Moreover, statistics tabulated by state inevitably entail problems of aggregation. There is no alternative, for instance, to aggregating together deposits made by wholesale and retail establishments.

Explanatory variables were selected to measure the characteristics of the alternative means of payment, the individuals facing the decision problem, and their environment. Personal characteristics include per capita wealth and the percentages of the population which were black, foreign-born, wage-earners, and farm operators. Proxies for the characteristics of the environment include the interest rate paid on savings deposits, the average size of banks (as measured by the value of liabilities), the number of banks, and the number of banks per square mile.

Figures on the number of banks and the value of total liabilities and current accounts by state are taken from the Federal Reserve System's *All-Bank Statistics*.[43] The principal sources used by the Federal Reserve Board in compiling these figures were the annual reports of the Comptroller of the Currency, but supplementary information was secured from state banking departments and the 1909 report of the National Monetary Commission. The average rate of interest paid on savings accounts by 6592 national banks at the close of business on June 30, 1909, also is taken from the National Monetary Commission report.[44]

Estimates of wealth by state for 1909 are constructed by interpolating the Census Bureau's figures for the true value of all property (including real estate and improvements, livestock, farm implements and machinery, manufacturing equipment, bullion, and transportation equipment) for 1904 and 1912.[45] The remaining variables, which are defined in Table 3, are taken from the Abstract to the 1910 Census.[46]

Results are reported in Tables 4 and 5. Table 5 includes the adjustment for heteroskedasticity while Table 4 does not. Significant variables include population density, percentage of the population classified as wage-earners, the interest rate paid on savings accounts, and the proxies for the structure of the banking

Table 3.   Variable Definitions

BLACK	Percent of population classified as black
URBAN	Percent of population residing in urban areas
DENSITY	Population per square mile
FOREIGN	Percent of population classified as foreign born
FARMERS	Percent of population classified as farm operators
EARNERS	Percent of population classified as wage earners
WEALTH	Per capita wealth (estimated true value of all property)
BANKSIZE	Ratio of bank liabilities to number of banks
BANKDEN	Banks per square mile
BANKNUM	Number of banks
INTEREST	Interest rate paid on savings deposits

industry. Population density enters with a negative coefficient, suggesting that, on balance, density depressed check usage by increasing the proportion of transactions between individuals with little information about one another's creditworthiness. While there is no evidence of a nonlinear relationship between the use of credit instruments and population density like that hypothesized by Kinley, the existence of a nonlinear relationship between urbanization and credit use, as suggested by Cagan, finds some support.[47]

An increase in the percentage of the population engaged in wage labor has a large, consistently significant, and negative impact on the odds of making a payment by check. Whether this finding results from the tendency of workers to be paid in cash or from their preferences concerning the instruments with which to carry out other transactions remains uncertain. Of the other personal characteristics considered, only per capita wealth is significant, confirming the obvious presumption that wealthy individuals used a higher proportion of checks.[48]

The negative coefficient on the rate of interest paid on savings accounts suggests that demand deposits were better substitutes for time deposits than was currency. The various measures of the structure of the banking industry also are significant. The variable measuring bank size (average value of bank liabilities) has a positive coefficient: larger banks may have more effectively promoted the virtues of deposit banking and, in any case, they tended to be located in older states where the virtues of banking had long been familiar. The variables measuring the availability of banking services—number of banks and banks per square mile—enter with positive coefficients and can be interpreted as indicating that a reduction in the effective cost of using checks increased the odds of a transaction being completed by credit instrument.

It should be noted that the coefficient on the percentage of blacks in a state's population is uniformly insignificant. Once the economic characteristics of the population and the banking system are taken into account, the racial composition

Table 4. Determinants of the Use of Credit Instruments[a]

Equation	C	INTEREST	BANKSIZE	BANKDEN	BANKNUM	WEALTH	DENSITY	BLACK	FARMERS	EARNERS	FOREIGN	R^2
(1)	1.94 (4.33)	-0.28 (2.11)	0.24 (3.73)		0.34 (2.58)	0.25 (2.66)	-0.37 (4.20)	0.34 (0.77)	2.63 (1.10)			.57
(2)	2.13 (3.80)	-0.35 (2.42)	0.26 (3.80)	2.80 (0.30)		0.29 (2.94)	-0.65 (0.86)	0.29 (0.61)	4.40 (1.77)			.49
(3)	3.05 (5.08)	-0.36 (2.85)	0.31 (4.69)		0.31 (2.47)	0.10 (1.10)	-0.46 (5.12)	0.11 (0.25)	-0.66 (0.26)	-484.0 (2.58)		.63
(4)	3.24 (5.31)	-0.38 (2.88)	0.36 (5.19)	16.52 (1.84)		0.10 (0.92)	-1.85 (2.40)	0.10 (0.21)	-0.59 (0.22)	-699.2 (3.25)		.60
(5)	1.93 (4.20)	-0.28 (2.39)	0.23 (3.16)		0.35 (2.56)	0.24 (2.56)	-0.37 (3.78)	0.41 (0.81)	2.87 (1.12)		0.30 (0.28)	.57
(6)	2.14 (3.76)	-0.35 (2.25)	0.27 (3.45)	2.96 (0.31)		0.30 (2.81)	-0.67 (0.87)	0.25 (0.46)	4.24 (1.56)		-0.19 (0.16)	.50
(7)	3.34 (5.52)	-0.44 (3.39)	0.28 (4.08)		0.34 (2.75)	-0.01 (0.08)	-0.43 (4.80)	0.49 (1.06)	-0.34 (0.13)	-663.5 (3.19)	1.98 (1.80)	.66
(8)	3.53 (5.69)	-0.45 (3.47)	0.32 (4.69)	18.91 (2.01)		-0.01 (0.12)	-2.02 (2.65)	0.46 (0.97)	-0.33 (0.12)	-902.9 (3.72)	1.93 (1.69)	.63

[a]Dependent variable is $\log(p/(1-p))$, where p is the probability that a deposit is paid in by check. Coefficients on BANKSIZE and BANKNUM have been multiplied by 1000. Figures in parentheses are t-statistics. Number of observations = 49.

Table 5. Further Determinants of the Use of Credit Instruments[a]

Equation	C	INTEREST	BANKSIZE	BANKDEN	BANKNUM	WEALTH	DENSITY	BLACK	FARMERS	EARNERS	FOREIGN	R^2
(9)	2.48 (0.89)	-1.19 (1.48)	3.43 (8.56)		4.26 (5.20)	0.94 (1.64)	-2.16 (3.86)	3.81 (1.41)	21.65 (1.45)			.79
(10)	0.81 (0.19)	-2.33 (2.15)	3.71 (7.23)	7.47 (0.11)		1.47 (2.00)	-3.38 (0.60)	2.95 (0.83)	43.64 (2.37)			.65
(11)	8.15 (2.51)	-2.14 (2.94)	4.11 (11.41)		3.94 (5.83)	-0.43 (0.78)	-2.99 (6.07)	1.56 (0.69)	-10.19 (0.72)	-4663.5 (4.59)		.86
(12)	11.36 (2.76)	-2.58 (2.91)	4.59 (9.95)	138.56 (2.17)		0.38 (0.52)	-14.88 (2.86)	1.05 (0.36)	-4.10 (0.22)	-6682.6 (4.60)		.77
(13)	2.13 (0.76)	-1.04 (1.26)	3.61 (7.98)		4.15 (4.97)	1.11 (1.82)	-2.34 (3.90)	2.49 (0.80)	17.24 (1.09)		5.63 (0.87)	.79
(14)	1.00 (0.24)	-1.91 (2.34)	4.04 (7.17)	16.81 (0.24)		1.79 (2.34)	-4.44 (0.80)	0.44 (0.11)	33.66 (1.71)		-11.21 (1.35)	.67
(15)	9.32 (2.79)	-2.35 (3.25)	3.97 (10.62)		4.05 (1.37)	-0.89 (3.25)	-2.86 (5.75)	3.10 (1.23)	-8.87 (0.64)	-5390.5 (4.70)	8.02 (1.32)	.87
(16)	1.23 (2.85)	-2.82 (2.97)	4.50 (9.36)	145.87 (2.24)		-0.72 (0.84)	-15.40 (2.91)	2.91 (0.66)	-3.30 (0.18)	-7307.1 (4.34)	5.92 (0.75)	.78

[a]Dependent variable is $p(1 - p)n * \log(p/(1 - p))$, where p is the probability that a deposit is paid in by check and n is the value of deposits. Coefficients on all variables except BANKSIZE and BANKNUM have been divided by 1000. Figures in parentheses are t-statistics. Number of observations = 49.

107

of the population does not appear to have affected its reliance on currency and credit. Southern states with large proportions of black residents tended to rely heavily on currency for transactions purposes not because blacks and whites had different tastes, but because Southern blacks tended to be poor, because Southerners faced relatively high interest rates on savings accounts (3.77 percent vs. a national average of 3.34 percent in 1909), and because they had access only to poorly articulated and relatively underdeveloped banking systems.

Thus, institutional factors—notably the differences in regional banking systems bequeathed by the Federal Banking Laws—emerge as significant determinants of the use of currency and credit. Although certain personal characteristics, such as wealth and occupation, also appear to have influenced demands for credit instruments, others such as race do not appear to have been strongly related to those demands. While the concentration of industry and wage-labor in the Eastern part of the country and agricultural self-employment in the West contributed to the perverse elasticity of the currency, so did the institutions established by Congress in response to the weaknesses of nineteenth-century money and capital markets. If the source of the problem was institutional, so was the response, which took the form of the Federal Reserve System. The Federal Reserve Act which established it was entitled "An Act to provide for the establishment of Federal Reserve Banks, [and] to furnish an elastic currency . . . ."[49]

IV. CONCLUSION

This paper has examined the operation of American money and capital markets in the heyday of the National Banking System. The interaction of distinct regional economies and the implications of that interaction for the resilience of the American financial system have been at the center of the analysis. Since the annual shift out of demand deposits and into currency after the harvest has been blamed for the concentration of episodes of financial stringency and bank failure in the late autumn and early winter months, considerable attention has been devoted to explanations for regional differentials in the demand for currency. The model used to analyze these questions relates the individual's decision of whether to use currency or credit instruments in a given transaction to the attributes of the two means of payment, the environment in which the transaction takes place, and the participants in the exchange. Estimation of the model indicates that the important determinants of the probability of using credit instruments include population density, the extent of wage labor, and the structure of the region's banking industry. The racial composition of the population does not emerge as a significant determinant of the use of currency.

These findings direct our attention once more to the regional factor in American economic history. This would not surprise William N. Parker: the uniqueness of regional experience and the role of the regional factor in American growth feature prominently in his writings and lectures alike.

ACKNOWLEDGMENTS

The origins of this paper can be traced to a presentation made to Professor William N. Parker's Economic History Seminar at Yale University. To Bill go thanks for encouraging my interest in this topic. In addition, the helpful comments of Stanley Engerman, Gary Gorton, Zvi Griliches, William Hutchinson, John James, and Richard Sylla are gratefully acknowledged.

NOTES

1. Recent contributions include C. A. E. Goodhart, *The New York Money Market and the Finance of Trade, 1900–1913* (Cambridge, Mass.: Harvard University Press, 1969); John A. James, *Money and Capital Markets in Postbellum America* (Princeton, N.J.: Princeton University Press, 1978); Richard Sylla, "The United States, 1863–1913," in Rondo Cameron (ed.), *Banking and Economic Development* (New York: Oxford University Press, 1972), pp. 232–262; Barry Eichengreen, "Mortgage Interest Rates in the Populist Era," *American Economic Review* 75 (March 1985), forthcoming. The classic works on the role of financial intermediation in economic growth include Raymond Goldsmith, *Financial Structure and Development* (New Haven, Conn.: Yale University Press, 1969); Ronald I. McKinnon, *Money and Capital in Economic Development* (Washington, D.C.: The Brookings Institution, 1973); Edward S. Shaw, *Financial Deepening and Economic Development* (New York: Oxford University Press, 1973).

2. William N. Parker, "From Northwest to Midwest: Social Bases of a Regional History," in David C. Klingaman and Richard K. Vedder (eds.), *Essays in Nineteenth Century Economic History: The Old Northwest* (Athens: Ohio State University Press, 1975), p. 3.

3. The Gold Standard Act of 1900, which established a capital requirement of $25,000 for national banks in cities with populations under 3000, encouraged the establishment of 4600 new national banks, two-thirds with capital of less than $50,000, in the first decade of the twentieth century. See Sylla, "United States," p. 241.

4. Roger L. Ransom and Richard Sutch, *One Kind of Freedom* (New York: Cambridge University Press, 1977), p. 110; Richard Sylla, "Federal Policy, Banking Market Structure and Capital Mobilization in the United States, 1863–1913," *Journal of Economic History* 29(December 1969): 658–660. The implications of these developments for Southern society and economy are critically examined in William N. Parker, "The South in the National Economy, 1865–1970," *Southern Economic Journal* 46(April 1980): 1037–1038.

5. Figures in the text are calculated from National Monetary Commission, *Special Report from the Banks of the United States* (Washington, D.C.: Government Printing Office, 1909), Tables 1 and 5. Here, as in what follows, the Southern states are taken to include Virginia, West Virginia, North Carolina, South Carolina, Georgia, Florida, Alabama, Mississippi, Louisiana, Texas, Arkansas, Kentucky, and Tennessee. See also Ransom and Sutch, *Freedom*, p. 113.

6. James, *Money and Capital,* p. 110; Margaret G. Myers, *The New York Money Market* (New York: Columbia University Press, 1931), Chap. 6.

7. Richard H. Timberlake, Jr., "Mr. Shaw and his Critics: Monetary Policy in the Golden Era Reviewed," *Quarterly Journal of Economics* 77(February 1963): 45.

8.   E. W. Kemmerer, *Seasonal Variations in the Relative Demand for Money and Capital in the United States* (Washington, D.C.: Government Printing Office, 1910), p. 223.

9.   For contemporary views of this phenomenon, see Horace White, *Money and Banking* (Boston: Ginn, 1911), p. 402; Henry Parker Willis, *The Federal Reserve* (New York: Doubleday, Page, 1915), p. 250.

10.   Kemmerer, *Seasonal Variations*, p. 161.

11.   Spectral density functions were estimated using a variety of smoothing windows and maximum lags, after prefiltering the interest rates to obtain a flat power spectrum. The results reported here do not appear to be sensitive to different methods of smoothing and filtering or different maximum lags. Interest rate data for the period January 1857–December 1912 are from F. R. Macaulay, *The Movements of Interest Rates, Bond Yields, and Stock Prices in the United States since 1856* (New York: National Bureau of Economic Research, 1938), Appendix Table 10.

12.   Goodhart, *New York Market*, p. 184; Kemmerer, *Seasonal Variations*, p. 53.

13.   Edward S. Meade, "The Deposit Reserve System of the National Bank Law," *Journal of Political Economy* 6(1898): 209–224; A. P. Andrew, "The Influence of Crops on Business in America," *Quarterly Journal of Economics* 20(May 1906): 323–353; O. M. W. Sprague, *History of Crises under the National Banking System* (Washington, D.C.: Government Printing Office, 1910), p. 33; Kemmerer, *Seasonal Variations*, pp. 113–114; Jacob H. Hollander, "Security Holdings of National Banks," *American Economic Review* 3(December 1919): 793–814.

14.   Goodhart, *New York Market, passim;* Allyn A. Young, *An Analysis of Bank Statistics for the United States* (Cambridge, Mass.: Harvard University Press, 1928), p. 36.

15.   Leonard L. Watkins, *Bankers' Balances* (Chicago: Shaw, 1929), Table IV. Goodhart's estimates of the seasonal component in Watkin's figures are reported despite James's criticisms because they are the figures most favorable to Goodhart's argument. See James, *Money and Capital*, p. 134.

16.   Estimates of the lag between interest rate cycles in St. Louis and New York, which are sensitive to the choice of prewhitening filter, range from 0.98 to 1.51 months. The largest cross-correlation between the two series occurs when the New York rate lags one period behind the St. Louis rate. Interest rate data are from Macaulay, *Movements*, Appendix Table 10, and Goodhart, *New York Market*, Appendix D.

17.   For a discussion of these limitations, see Barry Eichengreen, "The Causes of British Business Cycles, 1833–1913," *Journal of European Economic History* 12 (Spring 1983), pp. 145–161.

18.   E. W. Kemmerer, *Money and Credit Instruments in Their Relation to General Prices* (New York: Holt, 1907), p. 71.

19.   This was not always the case. For academic analyses which carefully distinguish the various meanings of inelasticity, see the article by the noted opponent of the quantity theory, J. Lawrence Laughlin, "Bank Notes and Lending Power," in Henry Raymond Mussey (ed.), *The Reform of the Currency* (New York: Columbia University, 1911), 258–260; and David Kinley, *Money: A Study of the Theory of the Medium of Exchange* (New York: Macmillan, 1903), p. 360. The literature on inelasticity is reviewed by Lloyd W. Mints, *A History of Banking* (Chicago: University of Chicago Press, 1945), Chap. XII.

20.   Quoted in Richard H. Timberlake, Jr., *The Origins of Central Banking in the United States* (Cambridge, Mass.: Harvard University Press, 1978), p. 109.

21.   James B. Forgan, "The Money Supply of the United States," in Walter Henry Hull (ed.), *Practical Problems in Banking and Currency* (New York: Macmillan, 1907), p. 307.

22.   Phillip Cagan, "The First Fifty Years of the National Banking System: An Historical Appraisal," in Deane Carson (ed.), *Banking and Monetary Studies* (Homewood, Ill.: Irwin, 1963), p. 21; Milton Friedman and Anna Jacobson Schwartz, *A Monetary History of the United States* (Princeton, N.J.: Princeton University Press, 1963), p. 169.

23.   The last few sentences follow closely the argument in Goodhart, *New York Market*, pp. 2–3.

See also Alexander J. Field, "Asset Exchanges and the Demand for Money, 1919–29," *American Economic Review* 74 (1984):43–59; Mints, *History of Banking Theory,* pp. 224–225.

24. Sprague, *Crises,* p. 127. See also E. W. Kemmerer, "American Banks in Times of Crisis under the National Banking System," in Henry Raymond Mussey (ed.), *The Reform of the Currency* (New York: Columbia University Press, 1911), p. 249.

25. Kemmerer, *Seasonal Variations,* p. 27.

26. W. J. Baumol, "The Transactions Demand for Cash: An Inventory-Theoretic Approach," *Quarterly Journal of Economics* 66(November 1952): 545–556; James Tobin, "The Interest-Elasticity of the Transactions Demand for Cash," *Review of Economics and Statistics* 38(September 1956): 241–247.

27. James Tobin, "Liquidity Preference as Behavior Toward Risk," *Review of Economic Studies* 25(February 1958): 65–86.

28. Goodhart, *New York Market,* p. 40.

29. David Kinley, "Credit Instruments in Retail Trade," *Journal of Political Economy* 3(March 1895): 209.

30. Phillip Cagan, "The Demand for Currency Relative to Total Money Supply," Occasional Paper No. 62, National Bureau of Economic Research, New York, 1958, pp. 6–7.

31. David Kinley, *The Use of Credit Instruments in Payments in the United States* (Washington, D.C.: Government Printing Office, 1910), p. 86.

32. Kinley, *Use of Credit,* pp. 100, 200–201.

33. Irving Fisher, *The Purchasing Power of Money* (New York: Kelly, 1911), pp. 50–51. See also Laughlin, "Bank Notes," p. 255.

34. I am grateful to Gary Gorton for this point.

35. Comptroller of the Currency, *Annual Report* (Washington, D.C.: Government Printing Office, 1894), Vol. 1, p. 23; Kinley, *Use of Credit,* p. 97.

36. Margaret G. Myers, *A Financial History of the United States* (New York: Columbia University Press, 1970), p. 247; Paul Studenski and Herman E. Krooss, *Financial History of the United States* (New York: McGraw-Hill, 1963), p. 178. Note, however, the dissenting view in Kinley, *Use of Credit,* p. 77.

37. Friedman and Schwartz, *Monetary History,* p. 122; Cagan, "Demand," p.3.

38. See D. A. McFadden, "Conditional Logit Analysis of Qualitative Choice Behavior," in Paul Zarembka (ed.), *Frontiers in Econometrics* (New York: Academic Press, 1974), pp. 105–143. Nowhere is it assumed that individuals rely exclusively on currency or checks for transactions purposes. However, each time a transaction is contemplated, individuals face an either/or decision of whether to complete it (or any portion thereof) with currency or credit. The binomial logit model is applied to an aggregation of such decisions.

39. This correction for heteroskedasticity is suggested by J. Berkson, "A Statistically Precise and Relatively Simple Method of Estimating Bio-assay with Quantal Response, Based on the Logistic Function," *Journal of the American Statistical Association* 48(September 1953): 565. See also S. M. Goldfeld and R. E. Quandt, "Some Tests for Homoscedasticity," *Journal of the American Statistical Association* 60(1965): 539–547.

40. See J. Berkson, "Application of the Logistic Function to Bio-assay," *Journal of the American Statistical Association* 39(September 1944): 357–365.

41. Deposits were classified as checks, currency, specie, silver, and gold. In 1909, specie, silver, and gold accounted for 2 percent of the total. See Kinley (1910, p. 182).

42. National Monetary Commission, *Special Report from the Banks of the United States* (Washington, D.C.: Government Printing Office, 1909).

43. Board of Governors of the Federal Reserve System, *All-Bank Statistics* (Washington, D.C.: Government Printing Office, 1959).

44. National Monetary Commission, *Report,* p. 36.

45. U.S. Department of Commerce, Bureau of Foreign and Domestic Commerce, *Statistical Abstract of the United States* (Washington, D.C.: Government Printing Office, 1917), pp. 652–655.

46. Bureau of the Census, *Abstract of the Thirteenth Census of the United States* (Washington, D.C.: Government Printing Office, 1913).

47. For example:

$$\log \frac{p_1}{1 - p_1} = 0.95 + 0.03 \text{ URBAN} - 0.001 \text{ (URBAN)}^2 + 0.54 \text{ BLACK} + 7.68 \text{ FARMERS}$$
$$\phantom{\log \frac{p_1}{1 - p_1} = } (1.09) \quad (2.13) \qquad\qquad (1.87) \qquad\qquad (1.06) \qquad\quad (2.28)$$

$$+ 0.31 \text{ BANKSIZE} - 4.48 \text{ BANKDEN} + 0.32 \text{ WEALTH} - 0.29 \text{ INTEREST}$$
$$(3.41) \qquad\qquad (3.05) \qquad\qquad (3.01) \qquad\qquad (2.02)$$

$$R^2 = .54$$

48. The insignificance of the percentage of farmers in a state's population may be due in part to this variable's collinearity with other population measures. Substituting the percentage of land in farms for the percentage of the population classified as farm operators yielded a consistently significant negative coefficient. However, it is unclear what interpretation should be attached to this result. In seeking to explain regional differentials in currency use, it seems more appropriate to use a measure of the share of transactions or transactors associated with farming than a measure of the size and number of farms. For this reason, only equations with the percentage of farm operators are reported in Tables 4 and 5.

49. *Federal Reserve Act of 1913, with Amendments and Laws Relating to Banking* (Washington, D.C.: Government Printing Office, 1913), p. 1.

REFERENCES

Andrew, A. P. (1906). ''The Influence of Crops on Business in America.'' *Quarterly Journal of Economics* 20(May): 323–353.

Baumol, W. J. (1952). ''The Transactions Demand for Cash: An Inventory-Theoretic Approach.'' *Quarterly Journal of Economics* 66(November): 545–556.

Berkson, J. (1944). ''Application of the Logistic Function to Bio-assay.'' *Journal of the American Statistical Association* 39(September): 357–385.

———— (1953). ''A Statistically Precise and Relatively Simple Method of Estimating Bio-assay with Quantal Response, Based on the Logistic Function.''Journal of the American Statistical Association 48(September): 565–599.

Board of Governors of the Federal Reserve System (1959). *All-Bank Statistics*. Washington, D.C.: Government Printing Office.

Bureau of the Census (1910). *Abstract of the Thirteenth Census of the United States*. Washington, D.C.: Government Printing Office.

Cagan, Phillip (1958). ''The Demand for Currency Relative to Total Money Supply.'' Occasional Paper, No. 62, National Bureau of Economic Research, New York.

———— (1963). ''The First Fifty Years of the National Banking System: An Historical Appraisal.'' Pp. 15–42 in Deane Carson (ed.), *Banking and Monetary Studies*. Homewood: Irwin.

Comptroller of the Currency (1881). *Annual Report*. Washington, D.C.: Government Printing Office.

———— (1890). *Annual Report*. Washington, D.C.: Government Printing Office.

———— (1892). *Annual Report*. Washington, D.C.: Government Printing Office.

———— (1894). *Annual Report*. Washington, D.C.: Government Printing Office.

Eichengreen, Barry (1982). ''The Causes of British Business Cycles, 1833–1913.'' *Journal of European Economic History* 12 (Spring 1983): 145–161.

———— (1985). "Mortgage Interest Rates in the Populist Era," *American Economic Review*, forthcoming.

Federal Reserve Act (1913). *Federal Reserve Act of 1913, with Amendments and Laws Relating to Banking*. Washington, D.C.: Government Printing Office (reprinted 1966).

Field, Alexander J. (1984). "Asset Exchanges and the Demand for Money, 1919–1929," *American Economic Review* 74 (March): 43–59.

Fisher, Irving (1911). *The Purchasing Power of Money*. New York: Kelly (reprinted 1963).

Forgan, James R. (1907). "The Money Supply of the United States." Pp. 307–314 in Walter Henry Hull (ed.), *Practical Problems in Banking and Currency*. New York: Macmillan.

Friedman, Milton, and Anna Jacobson Schwartz (1963). *A Monetary History of the United States*. Princeton, N.J.: Princeton University Press.

Goldfeld, S. M., and R. E. Quandt (1965). "Some Tests for Homoscedasticity." *Journal of the American Statistical Association* 60: 539–547.

Goldsmith, Raymond (1969). *Financial Structure and Development*. New Haven, Conn.: Yale University Press.

Goodhart, C. A. E. (1969). *The New York Money Market and the Finance of Trade, 1900–1913*. Cambridge, Mass.: Harvard University Press.

Hollander, Jacob H. (1913). "Security Holdings of National Banks." *American Economic Review* 3(December): 793–814.

James, John A. (1978). *Money and Capital Markets in Postbellum America*. Princeton, N.J.: Princeton University Press.

Kemmerer, Edwin Walter (1907). *Money and Credit Instruments in Their Relation to General Prices*. New York: Holt.

———— (1910). *Seasonal Variations in the Relative Demand for Money and Capital in the United States*. Washington, D.C.: Government Printing Office.

———— (1911). "American Banks in Times of Crisis under the National Banking System." Pp. 233–253 in Henry Raymond Mussey (ed.), *The Reform of the Currency*. New York: Columbia University.

Kinley, David (1895). "Credit Instruments in Retail Trade." *Journal of Political Economy* 3: 203–217.

———— (1904). *Money: A Study of the Theory of the Medium of Exchange*. New York: Macmillan.

———— (1910). *The Use of Credit Instruments in Payments in the United States*. Washington, D.C.: Government Printing Office.

Laughlin, J. Laurence (1911). "Bank Notes and Lending Power." Pp. 254–269 in Henry Raymond Mussey (ed.), *The Reform of the Currency*. New York: Columbia University.

Macaulay, F. R. (1938). *The Movements of Interest Rates, Bond Yields, and Stock Prices in the United States Since 1856*. New York: National Bureau of Economic Research.

McFadden, D. A. (1974). "Conditional Logit Analysis of Qualitative Choice Behavior." Pp. 105–142 in Paul Zarembka (ed.), *Frontiers in Econometrics*. New York: Academic Press.

McKinnon, Ronald I. (1973). *Money and Capital in Economic Development*. Washington, D.C.: Brookings Institution.

Meade, Edward S. (1898). "The Deposit-Reserve System of the National Bank Law." *Journal of Political Economy* 6: 209–224.

Mints, Lloyd W. (1945). *A History of Banking Theory*. Chicago: University of Chicago Press.

Myers, Margaret G. (1931). *The New York Money Market*. New York: Columbia University Press (reprinted 1971).

———— (1970). *A Financial History of the United States*. New York: Columbia University Press.

National Monetary Commission (1909). *Special Report from the Banks of the United States*. Washington, D.C.: Government Printing Office.

Parker, William N. (1975). "From Northwest to Midwest: Social Bases of a Regional History." Pp. 3–34 in David C. Klingaman and Richard K. Vedder (eds.), *Essays in Nineteenth Century Economic History: The Old Northwest*. Athens: Ohio State University Press.

———— (1980). "The South in the National Economy, 1865–1970." *Southern Economic Journal* 46(April): 1019–1048.

Ransom, Roger L., and Richard Sutch (1977). *One Kind of Freedom.* New York: Cambridge University Press.

Secretary of the Treasury (1890). *Annual Report on the State of Finances.* Washington, D.C.: Government Printing Office.

Shaw, Edward S. (1973). *Financial Deepening and Economic Development.* New York: Oxford University Press.

Sprague, O. M. W. (1910). *History of Crises under the National Banking System.* Washington, D.C.: Government Printing Office.

Studenski, Paul, and Herman E. Krooss (1963). *Financial History of the United States.* New York: McGraw-Hill.

Sylla, Richard (1969). "Federal Policy, Banking Market Structure and Capital Mobilization in the United States, 1863–1913." *Journal of Economic History* 29(December): 657–686.

———— (1972). "The United States, 1863–1913," Pp. 232–262 in Rondo Cameron (ed.), *Banking and Economic Development.* New York: Oxford University Press.

Timberlake, Richard, Jr. (1963). "Mr. Shaw and His Critics: Monetary Policy in the Golden Era Reviewed." *Quarterly Journal of Economics* 78(February): 40–54.

———— (1978). *The Origins of Central Banking in the United States.* Cambridge, Mass.: Harvard University Press.

Tobin, James (1956). "The Interest Elasticity of the Demand for Cash." *Review of Economics and Statistics* 38(September): 241–247.

———— (1958). "Liquidity Preference as Behavior Toward Risk." *Review of Economic Studies* 25(February): 65–86.

U.S. Department of Commerce, Bureau of Foreign and Domestic Commerce (1917). *Statistical Abstract of the United States, 1916.* Washington, D.C.: Government Printing Office.

Watkins, Leonard L. (1929). *Bankers' Balances.* Chicago: Shaw.

White, Horace (1911). *Money and Banking.* Boston: Ginn.

Willis, Henry Parker (1915). *The Federal Reserve.* New York: Doubleday, Page.

Young, Allyn A. (1928). *An Analysis of Bank Statistics for the United States.* Cambridge, Mass.: Harvard University Press.

PEASANTS, POTATOES, AND POVERTY:

TRANSACTIONS COSTS IN PREFAMINE IRELAND

Elizabeth Hoffman and Joel Mokyr

I. INTRODUCTION

Are technical change and productivity growth always beneficial? Economists often seem to assume so. After all, if a new technique is not an improvement, why would it be adopted? The present paper derives its inspiration from a cryptic but thought-provoking passage on this subject by William Parker (1971, p. 176):

> the word 'productivity' pushes a historian toward economics, but the term 'productivity growth' pushes an economist toward history. The economist who uses it must ask himself, how over history can productivity change?

One interpretation of this remark is that historical productivity measurement is always endangered by the possibility that some apparent gains in productivity

Technique, Spirit, and Form in the Making of the Modern Economies:
Essays in Honor of William N. Parker
Research in Economic History, Suppl. 3, pages 115–145
Copyright © 1984 by JAI Press Inc.
All rights of reproduction in any form reserved.
ISBN: 0-89232-414-7

may be the result of "unaccounted-for" inputs. If these inputs are scarce but from some reason not paid for, the gains in productivity could be in part imaginary and indeed could ultimately plunge the system into a regime of lower productivity.

Examples of such temporary gains are by no means novel. They often stem from productivity changes which lead to intensified exploitation of a resource which, due to some market failure, is in danger of being overexploited. A striking example is the California sardines industry, which was all but annihilated by the introduction of diesel engines in fishing vessels (McEvoy, 1979).

In this paper we examine an example of a case of apparent technological improvement which may have had serious negative consequences for the rest of the economy, and which ultimately may have led the entire country into unprecedented disaster. The innovation we have in mind is the introduction of the potato as a staple food in Ireland in the seventeenth and eighteenth centuries. Can this new crop be blamed for the poverty of Ireland before the Great Famine of 1845–1850?

II.   IRISH POTATOES: A BRIEF SURVEY

In the first half of the nineteenth century, Ireland was utterly dependent on potatoes. In 1845, on the eve of the Great Famine, about 2.1 million acres were planted with potatoes. This area amounts to one-seventh of total land under cultivation and about one-third of land under tillage. At some reasonable assumptions concerning per acre output and the proportions of the crop directly consumed by humans, the per capita consumption of potatoes in Ireland before the Famine was five to six pounds per capita per day, providing around 1750 calories per person per day. The vast majority of the Irish depended almost exclusively on potatoes. Potatoes were the mainstay of the Irish diet, even in urban areas and among the better to do classes, although the dependency on potatoes understandably diminished with income. For the sake of comparison, note that in East-Elbian Prussia, where potatoes were also playing a crucial role in the economy, only 4.3 percent of the arable land was planted with potatoes (Dickler, 1975, p. 288).

The literature on Irish agricultural history has traditionally emphasized two aspects of the impact of the potato on Ireland: productivity growth and population growth. If output is measured in terms of nutritional value instead of money, the potato represents a wondrous gain in productivity in food production, a property which was well-known to contemporaries. Potatoes can be grown in almost any soil conditions, including steep mountain soils not otherwise usable for field crops. The output of an acre of potatoes in terms of calories is between 2 and 3.5 times that of cereals. Potatoes contain proteins as well as a wealth of other nutrients such as iron, niacin, vitamin C, and thiamin.

Little wonder, then, that this "gift, humble and unobtrusive" (Salaman,

1949) as one historian has called it in an irresistible phrase, revolutionized Irish agriculture to an extent at least comparable to the effect of the enclosures on British agriculture. Indeed, it seems that what has to be explained is the slowness with which other regions in Europe overcame their reluctance to adopt potatoes. The great spurt in potato cultivation in Eastern Europe did not come until 1770 (and in some regions considerably later still). In 1770 the potato was clearly the main staple in Ireland, although it may not yet have been as indispensable as it became in the 1830s and 1840s.

At first sight, then, the potato seems a classic case of productivity growth. It seems reasonable to conclude that potatoes were a superior crop at any set of factor prices, although it is hard to demonstrate that unequivocally, since potatoes are a labor- and fertilizer-intensive crop. Cullen (1968), for example, argues that potato cultivation only became profitable in low wage societies. Mokyr (1981) explores that hypothesis further. In any event, the potato increased both the quantity and the quality of the food supply, and in the process allowed more land to be brought into cultivation, or shifted from pasturage to more intensive tillage. Moreover, until the onslaught of the blight in 1845, major crop failures in Ireland were rare.

The second hypothesized effect of the potato on Ireland, widely discussed in the literature, is the possible positive effect it had on population growth. In this view (Connell, 1950; Salaman, 1949) the potato allowed the Irish to marry younger and relax all constraints on fertility. The marginal cost of feeding a family was very low if the individuals were willing to subsist on a diet consisting exclusively of potatoes. One and a half acres of potatoes could provide about 12,500 calories per day for humans, after the animals were fed (see Bourke, 1968). According to this interpretation, which maintains that the potato was an exogenous source of productivity growth and led to a Malthusian response, the short-run positive effects of the potato were offset by long-run population growth.

While this simple-minded Malthusian model has been criticized (Mokyr, 1982b), it is still widely regarded as part of the conventional wisdom of Irish economic history. If it is accepted, it follows that the introduction of the potato was at best a mixed blessing for Ireland, since its adoption allowed population to grow under the false assumption that this rich and cheap source of food was secure forever. The blight and the disillusionment with the potato are seen as forcing the Irish economy to contract severely after 1845, a process accompanied by immense human suffering. The implications for this view as far as the analysis of productivity growth is concerned are that the *measured* gains in average annual output were bought at the price of a significant but unrealized increase in the probability of a major famine, since a large and growing population depended completely on the harvest of one crop. According to this view a long string of good harvests lulled the Irish into thinking they could abandon the prudential approach to childbearing which was the norm in Western Europe at that time (Flinn, 1981). Productivity growth led to the growth of an input, labor, which then became totally dependent on the maintenance of high average productivity with very low variance.

Despite the widespread appeal of the population growth hypothesis, however, there is little empirical support for it. Yet, historians continue to stress a link between potato growing and poverty (Morineau, 1979, pp. 24–25; Davidson and Passmore, 1965, p. 285) and contemporaries warned strongly against reliance on potato subsistence (Blum, 1978). D. Warriner called them "poor man's crops and poor man's foods" (cited by Blum, 1978, p. 271).

In this paper we focus on the possibility that the potato may have led to impoverishment and economic backwardness through mechanisms independent of population growth, despite an initial appearance that it was a more efficient way of producing food. Our argument is that even if there had been no famine and if it is concluded that the potato was not associated with unusually high rates of population growth, reliance on the potato may have had long-run negative effects on the Irish economy.

Ireland before the Famine was already one of the most backward regions in Europe. At the same time, as we have seen, Ireland was firmly committed to the potato. Were these two phenomena related? At first glance it seems far-fetched to blame the potato for Ireland's backwardness. If anything, it would seem that Ireland was poor *despite* its dependence on the potato diet. While housing, clothing, household implements, education, transportation, and personal comforts were all highly deficient in both quantity and quality, the Irish were comparatively well fed from a nutritional if not a culinary point of view.

To understand how the potato might have contributed to Ireland's backwardness, we will consider the restrictions which the potato imposed on the Irish economy. As we shall see below, the potato was characterized by high costs of storage, transportation, and marketing. Although some potatoes were bought and sold in both urban and rural markets, high costs of transacting and transporting them dictated that wherever the potato was grown, the bulk of the crop was consumed either by the same people who produced it or by their immediate neighbors. Dickler (1975) discusses the local and limited nature of trade in potatoes in Eastern Europe.

The Irish potato came to play a role comparable to that of the turnip in the light-soil agriculture in Britain. Like turnips, potatoes were grown in rotation with grains (Donnelly, 1975; Mokyr, 1981). The difficulty was that once a rotation system like this was firmly entrenched, it became difficult to change it. Grain crops required soil preparations; so farmers who might have wished to experiment with other foods had to continue to grow potatoes or overhaul the entire setup of agricultural production. On the other hand, potatoes required the cash crop not only for purposes of crop rotation, but also because rent (and thus money) was a necessary input in the growing of potatoes. Had the potato been widely marketed, a peasant could have exercised more flexibility in his decision making, either by selling potatoes to raise cash, or by experimenting with other crops and buying food. The particular situation in Ireland tended to lock peasants increasingly into both potato production and potato subsistence. Peasants were unwilling or unable to change technology themselves and they fought their landlords who wanted to introduce scale economics which would have significantly reduced demand for peasant labor per unit of land (Mokyr, 1982a,b).

The social cost which the potato inflicted on the Irish economy can be examined on three levels. First, the gains in total food output resulting from the adoption of the potato were bought at the price of increases in vulnerability and risk, so that the potato left the Irish peasants increasingly open to disaster. Second, the potato contributed to the decommercialization of Ireland and was therefore likely to have stifled the process of modern economic growth. Third, we shall indicate how certain exogenous "shocks" imposed on the Irish economy before the Famine were likely to have reinforced the decommercialization of the rural economy.

In the next section we lay out in some detail the theoretical framework in which these issues can be analyzed. We return to the pre-Famine economy in the following section, in which the relevance of the models will be demonstrated. We then attempt to utilize cross-sectional aggregate data to test the hypothesis that potatoes affected the level of income in the pre-Famine economy and present our conclusions.

III. MODELS OF THE POTATO ECONOMY

The models we present below formalize some of the constraints which the potato imposed on an economy dependent on it and explore some of the ways in which it could lead ultimately to impoverishment. The models are "neoclassical" in that they assume that peasants do not waste resources in a systematic way. In other words, in the long run the economy will drift toward an efficient allocation of resources, subject to the various constraints on its operation. It is on these constraints that we wish to concentrate.

A. Risk and Uncertainty

It is best to start with the simple model of a peasant economy. At least since Adam Smith economists have known that there are two distinct sources of increased productivity and welfare. One source is an outward shift of the product possibility frontier due to technological progress (including new crops). The other source is through exchange. The demonstration that exchange between different economic agents (or economies) can lead to increased welfare for all without any shift in the product possibility frontier is one of the most triumphant moments in any course in price theory or international trade and a fundamental justification of free enterprise economics. The standard model is illustrated in

Figure 1, and "Smithian growth" is demonstrated by the move from the lower indifference curve at the self-sufficiency point to the higher level at the trade–consumption point.

For the economic historian concerned with the agricultural societies of pre-modern Europe, the simple production and exchange model of Figure 1 is interesting but basically not much more than a foundation on which to build further. From the point of view of the description of the individual peasant or peasant community, it abstracts from a crucial element, namely, risk. Risk, defined as undesired variation in consumption, can be reduced in three ways: (1) diversifying the portfolio of lots cultivated and crops grown; (2) trading; and (3) storage of buffer stocks. A combination of the latter two is holding inventories of money, buying and selling in years of scarcity and plenty, respectively.

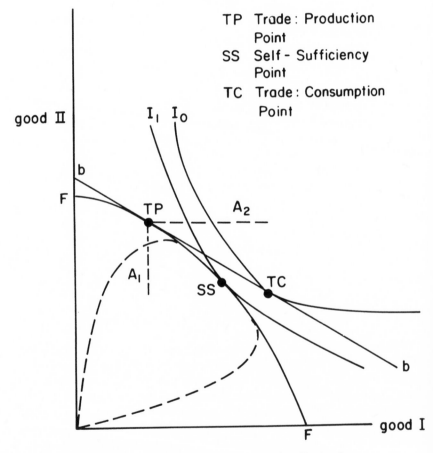

Figure 1. Welfare Gains from Market Production

1. Risk Reduction Through Trade

To show how trade can provide a means of reducing risk, assume that peasants produce only one crop and that all land is homogeneous. Despite this homogeneity peasants can still reduce the variance of their consumption if they exchange in a market all their produced output for the goods they wish to consume. The intuitive explanation of the risk-reducing effect of commerce is simply that the demand curve facing the community in question serves as a cushion absorbing stochastic shocks in physical output: In years in which physical output is small, prices are high and vice versa.

Formally, let physical output in year i be X_i. For the self-sufficient peasant who does not trade or store

$$Y_i = X_i \quad \text{for each peasant,} \tag{1}$$

so that var(Y) = var(X), that is, the variance in consumption equals the variance in production. Now suppose that there is trade but no storage. Then for each year:

$$Y_i = P_i X_i, \tag{2}$$

where Y is income in terms of the consumption good (potatoes) and P is the relative price of the marketed good in terms of the consumption good. Let the demand curve facing the unit under discussion be of the constant elasticity variety (suppressing subscripts):

$$X = BP^{-\beta} \quad (\beta > 0), \tag{3}$$

so that

$$P = AX^{-1/\beta} \quad (A = B^{1/\beta}) \tag{4}$$

and thus

$$Y = AX^{(1 - 1/\beta)}. \tag{5}$$

Having defined equation (3) as a constant elasticity function, the methodology employed is to compare the variance of the logarithm of Y with the variance of the logarithm of X. To the extent that trade can make the former smaller than the latter, it is true that trade reduces the variance in consumption. We are assuming for simplicity that the consumer would prefer to consume the same quantities in each year i, so that *any* variance is undesirable, and that the random variables are distributed normally or approximately so. Taking logarithms on both sides of equation (5):

$$\log(Y) = \log(A) + (1 - 1/\beta)\log(X) \tag{6}$$

$$\text{var}[\log(Y)R = \text{var}[\log(A)] + (1 - 1/\beta)^2 \text{var}[\log(X)]$$
$$+ 2(1 - 1/\beta) \text{cov}[\log(A), \log(X)]. \tag{7}$$

If the demand curve is stable, the first and last terms on the right-hand side of equation (7) drop out, and the condition for trade to be risk-reducing is

$$(1 - 1/\beta)^2 < 1, \tag{8}$$

or

$$\beta > 1/2. \tag{9}$$

Actually, the relation between the elasticity of demand β and risk-reduction is nonmonotonic. For $\beta = 1$, equation (7) implies that variance is zero. Clearly, unitary elasticity of demand implies constant revenue. For $\beta \to \infty$ and for $\beta = \frac{1}{2}$, there is no gain in trading as far as risk-reduction is concerned, and for $\beta < \frac{1}{2}$, the risk is actually increased. For the single individual, it is likely that β is quite large and possibly infinite.

In the above analysis A was assumed fixed. However, it is more likely to be both variable and correlated with X. In fact, the smaller the unit under consideration, the larger the elasticity of demand it faces and the higher is the likelihood that A and X are correlated. For instance, a case of harvest failure (low X) is likely to be associated with harvest failure among other units, which will result in a rise in A and vice versa (i.e., shifts in the demand curve facing the individual unit). This is equivalent to saying that when all harvests are low the demand for the output of each individual farmer shifts out at every price. Thus, cov[log(A),log(X)] is negative. For $\beta > 1$, this means that the market can absorb some of the fluctuation in X. If the demand curve is unstable so that A is subject to annual variations, equation (8) can be generalized to

$$\left[\gamma + 1 - \left(\frac{1}{\beta}\right)\right]^2 < 1 - \frac{\text{var}(\log e)}{\text{var}(\log X)}, \tag{10}$$

where γ is the (negatve) partial regression coefficient of log(A) with respect to log(X), and e is the random factor affecting A but not X. Equation (10) is derived by decomposing A into a component which is correlated with X and is a purely random component. Write: $A = ZX^\gamma e$, where Z is a constant and e is the random component of A. Taking logs implies $\log(A) = \log Z + \gamma \log(X) + \log(e)$. This equation can be used to show that $\gamma = \text{cov}[\log(X),\log(A)]/\text{var}[\log(X)]$, and that $\text{var}[\log(A)] = \gamma^2\text{var}[\log(X)] + \text{var}[\log(e)]$. Substituting these into equation (7) and comparing to var[log(X)] leads to equation (10).

Comparing equations (8) and (10) we can see that if $\beta > 1$ and $\gamma < 0$ and sufficiently large in absolute value, the stochastic demand curve may increase the risk-reducing effect of trade. On the other hand, if the variance of the random component is very large relative to the variance of X, the risk-reducing effects of trade are diminished. It is even possible that trade is more risky than self-sufficiency. The conditions under which this could happen are strong but cannot be ruled out. These conditions are a very inelastic demand ($\beta \to 0$) or a very volatile demand curve ($\text{var}[\log(e)] > \text{var}[\log(X)]$). The economy as a whole obviously cannot gain from trade without storage, since the variance in aggregate output is not reduced by internal trade. Each subset of the economy can, however, achieve a real reduction in consumption variance due to trade. When transportation or similar costs make trade expensive and rare, this opportunity is lost.

In the more general case, some proportion k of the farm output is retained and the rest is sold. Clearly, k will be larger the higher the transactions and marketing costs. It can also be shown that if the market demand curve is elastic, an increase in k will increase the variance of total income. If the demand curve is inelastic, this could still be the case depending on the values of k and the demand elasticity. In any event, only if equation (10) is violated or demand is inelastic are Wright and Kunreuther (1979, p. 217) correct when they maintain that "the cash crop is in fact the risky choice for a subsistence farmer. . . . A farmer who buys his food must consider the yield variance of the cash crop as well as the price variance . . . for the farmer who grows and consumes his own crop, only the yield variance is relevant."

2. Risk Reduction Through Storage

When storage is introduced, the variance of consumption can be reduced further simply by means of buffer stocks. If storage costs (including interest) are zero, there is no reason why the actual consumption pattern should not be equal to the desired pattern—possibly reducing variance to zero. With storage, the role of trade as an activity which reduces the variance of consumption is altered. If there are no storage costs, obviously storage alone will be used to reduce variance. If storage is costly, however, the peasant may find it cheaper to store money than commodities for a rainy day.

It is possible to construct a formal model of a peasant economy with storage and transactions costs. Details of that model are presented in the mathematical appendix to this paper, which can be obtained from the authors, and here we shall only provide a rough outline and the principal results. The model postulates a peasant producing a crop X, which is a random variable. For simplicity we assume that annual output takes only two values, a high value X_h and a low value X_1. At the end of each period, the peasant determines his buffer stock S and the amount he markets M. Define S_1 and S_h as the size of the buffer stock under low and high "states of the world" respectively, and define M_1, M_h, Q_1, and Q_h

(consumption) in corresponding fashion. Storage is subject to a cost C_s per unit stored and marketing to a cost C_m per unit marketed. The solution of the dynamic programming problem leads to the optimal values S^* and M^*.

The following theorems can be proven about this economy:

T.1. An optimal storage or marketing policy needs to consider only the effect of current storage or marketing on current consumption and next period consumption. Other consumption periods are covered by the optimal storage decision. This follows from the envelope theorem.

T.2. An increase in the cost of storage or marketing reduces storage or marketing through a substitution effect, but increases storage or marketing through a next period income effect (i.e., lower storage or marketing reduces potential consumption next period).

T.3. $dS^*/dC_s < 0$ and $dM^*/dC_m < 0$ if the substitution effect outweights the income effect. This follows from T.2.

T.4. If $dS^*/dC_s > 0$, $dm^*/dC_m < 0$, and $Q_h > Q_1$, then

$$\frac{d[\text{var}(Q)]}{dC_s} > 0 \quad \text{and} \quad \frac{d[\text{var}(Q)]}{dC_m} > 0 \quad \text{if} \quad \frac{dS_l^*}{dC_s} - \frac{dS_h^*}{dC_s} > 0$$

$$\text{and} \quad \frac{dM_l^*}{dC_m} - \frac{dM_l^*}{dC_m} > 0,$$

respectively.

The conditions $dS_l^*/dC_s - dS_h^*/dC_s < 0$ and $dM_l^*/dC_m - dM_h^*/dC_m < 0$ in T.4 imply that the storage and marketing functions must be less steeply sloped for any level of C when X is low than when X is high. In other words, given C, buffer stocks and amounts marketed decline at a slower rate when X is low. This is so because when X is high, the peasant can afford to reduce next period's buffer stocks faster in response to price changes than when X is low. This income effect occurs because the expected value of next period's consumption is higher when X is higher.

B. The Effects of Transactions Costs

We now leave the world in which potatoes are the only good produced, and examine the effect of transactions costs of potatoes on other crops (which are assumed to be free of them). Of particular interest is the effect of a change in the terms of trade between the two types of crops.

In the simplest models, it is assumed that the two goods compete for the same factors of production but otherwise are produced independently of each other. This assumption is patently unrealistic in agricultural societies. Even before root crops were widely cultivated, "joint production" was universal. Livestock and cereals (*bêtes et blé*) were unthinkable without each other: Livestock pulled ploughs and harrows and provided manure. They also ate oats and straw and grazed on crop land after harvest. In the new husbandry in England as well as in Ireland, root crops and cereals were jointly produced in a crop cycle. It can be shown without much difficulty that if the two products are necessary inputs into each other (i.e., the production function is nonseparable), the product possibility frontier will be balloon-shaped like the broken line in Figure 1. Only the negatively sloped segment of the curve is economically relevant to our peasant, however, since on the upward segments of the frontier more of both goods can be produced by reshuffling the resources.

The simple model of Figure 1 is further complicated by the existence of transactions costs. By that term we designate any cost which is incurred in selling A_1 or buying A_2. Transaction costs change the location and shape of the line bb facing the individual trader. The exact nature of the effect depends on the form of the transactions costs function. For instance, if the transactions costs are essentially informational, the function may have a fixed-cost quality: regardless of market conditions, fixed costs reduce the number of traders, but do not affect marginal decisions. If transportation costs are dominant, there will probably be both a fixed and a variable component.

Regardless of the form of the transactions costs, their existence implies in general a discontinuity in the choices made. In the simple world of Figure 1, there is a possibility of autarky only if by fluke the consumption point and the production point coincide. *Any* kind of transactions costs will result in a region of autarky in which the gains from trade are outweighed by the costs of transactions. Once the gains from trade exceed the costs, there is likely to be a discontinuous "leap" from autarky to substantial levels of trade.

A diagrammatic presentation of the historical situation runs into the dilemma that the Irish farmers were never wholly autarkic. Even the poorest tenants had to sell some part of their output in order to acquire a minimum level of cash. This cash was then used to pay rents and tithes and purchase some goods which could not be produced on the farm. A large number of smallholders and cottiers thus found themselves self-sufficient in food and fuel, but still having to sell some output on the market. Four "cash" goods were of importance in this respect: butter, pigs, grain crops, and nonagricultural goods produced in domestic industry. These cash crops were exchanged for other commodities (tobacco, drink, religious services, salt) or paid in rent. In addition there were the "subsistence" crops, potatoes and peat. In some ways, peat resembled the potato in the type of constraint it imposed on the economy. Like potatoes, it was a cheap and ubiquitous source of energy. Peat, too, was largely used in the area where it was cut, and most of it was extracted by the user himself. We assume that the subsistence goods are subject to transactions costs whereas the cash goods are not. With these "stylized facts" in mind, we can proceed with the construction of our model.

We assume an economy of peasants which produces two composite goods: a cash crop and a subsistence crop. The cash crop is grown exclusively for sale on the world market and the proceeds are used to purchase other goods. The subsistence crop may be bought or sold in the market or used exclusively for subsistence. The two goods differ in two important ways. First, the subsistence crop, if sold, implies a "marketing" cost paid by the seller. In practice, the marketing cost will be shared by the seller and the buyer, but in order to keep the analysis simple, we shall abstract from its distribution. Second, the cash crop has no use value for the producer, but this is irrelevant because it can be costlessly converted into other goods or inputs which do. The two production functions are interdependent so that each crop is a necessary input into the other's production.

Definitions:

L_i = labor supplied by peasant i

A_i = land area farmed by peasant i

P_i = $g(L_i,A_i,V_i)$ = the quantity of the subsistence crop (e.g., potatoes) produced by peasant i

V_i = $f(L_i,A_i,P_i)$ = the quantity of the cash crop (e.g., grain) produced by peasant i

P_i^m = quantity of the subsistence crop sold by peasant i in the market

P_i^b = quantity of the subsistence crop bought by i in the market

q = market price of the subsistence crop

π = market price of the cash crop

Y_i = $\pi V_i + q(P_i^m - P_i^b)$ = money income of peasant i

d_i = i's distance from the market

C_i = $C(P_i^m,d_i)$ = the marketing cost function

P_i^c = $P_i - P_i^m - C_i + P_i^b$ = the quantity of the subsistence crop consumed by i

U_i = $U_i(Y_i,P_i^c)$ = the utility function of peasant i

We now make the following assumptions:

A.1. L, A, and d are fixed for each i. This assumption allows us to focus on the joint products and variable features of the model. Dropping this assumption only complicates the mathematics without changing the results.

A.2. The production functions f and g are continuous and have the standard properties of differentiability and concavity

A.3. The transactions cost function C is concave, i.e., $\partial C_i/\partial P_i^m > 0$ and $\partial^2 C_i/\partial(P_i^m)^2 < 0$. This assumption reflects the existence of economies of scale in transportation.

A.4. The peasant's utility function has the standard mathematical properties.

A.5. Cash and subsistence crops are gross complements in consumption, that is, $\partial^2 U_i / \partial Y_i \partial P_i^c > 0$. This assumption means that having more of one good increases the marginal utility derived from the other.

A.6. The product possibility frontier can be written as

$$P_i = g_i(V_i) = g_i[f_i(P_i)] \text{ or } g_i^{-1} = V_i = f_i(P_i) \tag{11}$$

for each peasant, although the functions g and f are different from peasant to peasant, as allocations of land, labor, and capital vary. This assumption implies that the transformation curve is balloon shaped so that $f'(0) > 0$ and $g'(0) > 0$, where g is the inverse of f.

A.7. The transformation function of the cash crop as a function of the subsistence crop is not so sharply convex to preclude marginal adjustments in production in response to changes in relative prices:

$$\left| \frac{\partial f_i / \partial P_i}{f_i} \right| \geq \frac{\partial^2 f_i / \partial P_i^2}{\partial f_i / \partial P_i} .$$

Dropping constants and subscripts and substituting income, production, and transactions costs into the utility function, the maximization problem is as follows:

$$\max_{P,P^m,P^b} U\{[\pi f(P) + q(P^m - P^b)], [g(f(P)) - P^m - C(P^m) + P^b]\} \tag{12}$$

The following three properties of the model are immediate:

L.1. Given any ratio of prices, $g' < 0$ and $g'' < 0$, $f' < 0$ and $f'' < 0$ at a utility maximum. Thus, the peasant will only operate at the *downward sloping* segment of the product possibility curve.

L.2. No agent will be both a buyer and a seller of subsistence crops at the same time. Of course, a peasant may be a seller in one year and a buyer in another, if the parameters change over time.

L.3. An agent will buy the subsistence crop as long as $-qg' < \pi$, sell if $-qg' > \pi(1 + c')$, and not participate in the market as long as $\pi < -qg' < \pi(1 + c')$.

We now turn to the important properties of the model. Since the cash crop is traded at the world market, its price is exogenously given to the peasant. Since changes in the terms of trade in the cash sector reflect many of the shocks to which Ireland was subject in the pre-Famine years, it is interesting to examine the effects of these shocks on the subsistence sector. The following properties can be shown from a comparative statics analysis of equation (12).

T.1.   Buyers of the subsistence crop have downward-sloping demand curves for the subsistence crop.

T.2.   Sellers of the subsistence crop have upward-sloping supply curves for the subsistence crop as long as they derive most of their income from the cash crop, i.e., as long as $\pi f > qP^m$.

T.3.   A decline in the price of the cash crop causes both buyers and sellers of the subsistence crop to produce more of it. The converse holds, too. In other words, in a partial equilibrium setting, a decline (rise) in the price of the cash crop increases (decreases) the supply curve and reduces (increases) the demand curve of the subsistence crop.

T.4.   (Follows immediately from T.3): A decline (rise) in the price of the cash crop causes a fall (rise) in the equilibrium market price of the subsistence crop.

As Figure 2 shows, the net effect of a fall in the world market price of the cash crop could easily be a decline in the quantity of the subsistence crop transacted (from P_1^e to P_2^e). As T.4 shows, the price of the subsistence crop is a positive function of the price of the cash crop. As the price of the cash crop declines, some of the former buyers of the subsistence crop will now start producing their own food. Thus, the demand for the subsistence crop falls and the supply rises. This leads to an unambiguous decline in the price and the possibility that the quantity transacted will fall.

While this possibility is an intriguing counterintuitive result, it is not necessarily a general result. What makes the problem mathematically difficult is that the marginal sellers who retire do not become buyers but are likely to become self-sufficient. Similarly, the new buyers do not come from the ranks of sellers but were probably self-sufficient before. Consequently, we have not been able to describe the second derivatives of the aggregate demand and supply functions. Our model predicts that anyone who changes, switches from cash-crop production to subsistence crops. If Figure 2 describes the net result, however, we expect a "decommercialization" of the subsistence sector in addition to the contraction of the cash-crop sector. Such a decommercialization would have been a rather unique experience in Europe in the first half of the nineteenth century.

We can now see the rather subtle sense in which the potato may have been a mixed blessing to the economies which adopted it. If it is true that it induced a reduction in market orientation and specialization in Ireland at a time when increased market specialization was one of the chief dynamic elements in the development of Europe, some of the mystery of Ireland's amazing backwardness is removed. Moreover, as we will show below, the two characteristics of the potato widely lamented by contemporaries, lack of portability (i.e., transactions costs as defined here) and lack of long-term storability, implied a slightly different but equally pernicious influence of the potato.

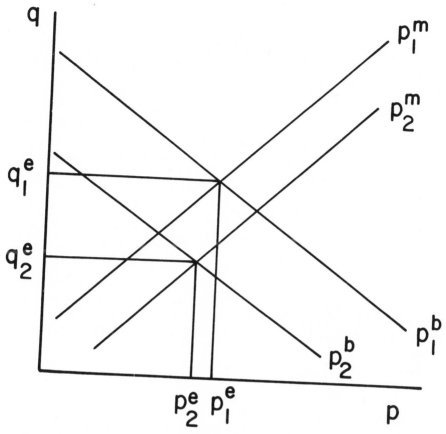

Figure 2. The Effect on the Potato Market of an Exogenous Decline in the Cash Crop Price

C.   Further Consequences of the Potato

There is another way in which potatoes could have been a liability to the Irish economy in the pre-Famine years in spite of their apparent superior efficiency as a means of extracting food from the earth. In order to illustrate this mechanism, we make a few simplifying assumptions. First, assume that there are two groups of individuals in the economy, landlords and peasants. The peasants consume both potatoes and "other goods" or "money income," whereas the landlords are interested in money income only and do not consume potatoes. To stress the issue at hand, make the extreme assumption that the costs are such that potatoes are not traded at all, and have to be produced on the spot to be consumed, while there are no transactions costs associated with the cash crop. From the point of view of the landlord, this means that he will always want to produce cash crops since the market price of potatoes is zero. However, the peasant maximizes utility, not income, and will prefer an interior solution. Transactions costs drive a "wedge" between potatoes and income, and a conflict of interest thus emerges between landlord and peasant. The conflict is illustrated in Figure 3.

The product possibility frontier is denoted by the line FG and a peasant's indifference curve by I. With an effective zero price for potatoes, landlords clearly wish to be at F, where income is maximized. Peasants will prefer to be at E where their utility is maximized. The striking feature of this model is that it is not likely that side-payments can be arranged so that landlords and tenants can negotiate themselves into the core of the economy. The landlords cannot bribe the peasants with money to agree to be at point F, since the peasants have only limited use for money, which cannot buy potatoes. The peasants cannot afford to pay the higher money rent implied at point F since they have to produce potatoes for their own consumption.

More formally, consider a world in which landlords maximize rents subject to a production function and a given money wage rate. The solution which maximizes rent is to devote the proportion Q^* to cash crops and $(1 - Q^*)$ to subsistence crops. Under the assumptions made above, $Q^* = 1$, but that result is not necessary. The peasant maximizes a nonseparable utility function subject to the production function and a given level of rent, which implies the optimal proportions Q^{**} and $(1 - Q^{**})$. If Q^* and Q^{**} differ, it is quite possible that a

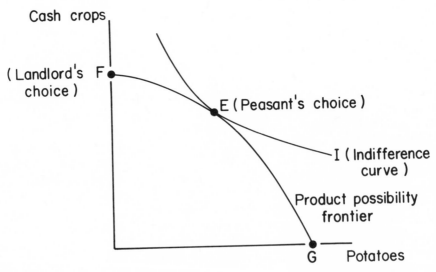

Figure 3. One Source of the Irish Land War

conflict will erupt on the question *what* to produce. The history of pre-Famine Ireland suggests indeed that the conflict was not resolved peacefully (Lewis, 1836).

Needless to say, this model is heavily oversimplified, and a more detailed exposition can be found in Mokyr (1982b, Chap. V). Peasants—to some extent—did consume oatmeal and, in some regions, bread. The adversary of the smallholder and the landless laborer in these clashes was not always the landlord or his agent, but often a large farmer or grazier, who let out small potato gardens for money or as payment for labor services (Lee, 1973). Nonetheless, the struggle for the "right" to grow potatoes cannot be understood without realizing the "wedge" which transactions costs drove between potatoes and cash crops. This conflict was an important component of the violence which marred the Irish countryside before the Great Famine. The transactions costs of potatoes thus had severe consequences for the entire economy: unrest and lack of security had devastating spillover effects on investment and economic initiative.

IV. SOME EVIDENCE

By far the best and most detailed evidence on the cost of the potato in terms of portability and storability is contained in Appendix E of the massive Poor Law Commission Report of 1836.[1] The "baronial examinations" (Parliamentary Papers,[2] 1825) dealing with food provide detailed comments on the effects of potatoes on local conditions, comparing potatoes and grains in a variety of aspects. The baronial examinations were based on about a thousand witnesses from 20 counties. The testimonies unanimously pointed out that the high transportation costs of potatoes greatly curtailed commerce in them. A Galway witness observed, for instance, that although potatoes were traded to some extent, a cart hauling 2.5 barrels of potatoes would feed an adult man for 120 days. The same cart could haul 20 cwts. of meal, which could feed an adult man for 640 days (PLR, 1836, XXXII, p. 4). "The large amount of nourishment contained in a small space makes corn much easy and cheap of carriage than potatoes," noted another witness. A witness from Dublin maintained that potatoes were never carried over land for more than 20 miles (PLR, 1836, XXXII, p. 11). A Wicklow witness estimated that there was "no increase in price" which would permit the farmers to carry potatoes for more than 40 miles and that then only on extraordinary occasions, scarcely worth the price of carriage (PLR, 1836, XXXII, p. 11).

It may be added that the natural disadvantages under which potatoes were traded were compounded by man-made obstacles. One such obstacle was tolls on potatoes which were charged by some market towns. Although this custom was not general, it could be occasionally serious. The town of Tralee (County Kerry) charged 30 percent of the value of potatoes (Great Britain, H.C., *Parliamentary Papers*, 1825, Vol. VIII, p. 317). Secondly, the quantities of potatoes were measured in a bewildering myriad of inconsistent and incompatible weights and measures. Potatoes were sometimes sold by weight and sometimes by volume. Wakefield (1812) presents a table of weights and measures which indicates that, for example, in the city of Londonderry oats and potatoes were sold by the stone but in the rural parts by the bushel (Vol. II, p. 199). To confound things further, "a measure of potatoes weighs more winter than in spring and summer." The barrel of potatoes was equal to 40 stones in Tyrone, 21 stones in Kilkenny, 25 stones in Meath, 28 stones 8 lbs. in Monaghan. Even when measured in terms of weight alone, consistency left much to be desired: in Clare a stone of potatoes was 16 lbs. in summer and 18 lbs. in winter. An exasperated correspondent from County Cork added that the measures of potatoes "vary much in neighboring parishes and require to be regulated in all the South and West of Ireland" (ibid., pp. 197–202).

It is thus not surprising that the low tradeability of the main food crop led often to famine and abundance in adjacent regions. Although the term "famine" should not be mistaken for a situation that even remotely resembled the cataclysmic events of 1845–1850, local scarcities could be serious enough. A Leitrim witness noted that "there have been instances of the peasantry being in a state of starvation in one district, while in a neighboring district potatoes have been abundant" (PLR, 1836, XXXII, pp. 4–5). Similar complaints come from other parts of Ireland, although one witness contended that the reason for such discrepancies was simply that "the people in the starved district had no money to pay for them" (PLR, 1836, XXXII, p. 19). A County Mayo witness points out, however, that "last Monday potatoes were selling at Ballina, a distance of 15 miles, at 2d. a stone and on the same day they could not be had here under 3d. . . . although the road is excellent" (PLR, 1836, XXXII, p. 8).

The large dispersion in potato prices confirms the importance of transactions costs. An 1843 source on food prices in Scotland yields a cross-sectional coefficient of variation of .249 for potato prices and only .109 for oatmeal. The larger dispersion of potato prices was due to the bulkiness of potatoes relative to their selling price. (Levitt and Smout, 1979, pp. 61–62). Looking at potato prices in Ireland for the years 1840–1846 (PP, 1846, XXXVII, pp. 489–495), for about 400 observations each year, the coefficient of variation is between .27 and .31 in the pre-Famine years. These values are consistent with the Scottish data.

Transportation cost data themselves are fragmentary at best. A large collection of them can be found in Wakefield's *Ireland*. Wakefield (1812) collected information from over 50 correspondents from all over Ireland. The data pertain to 1811, a year of high prices, but since we are chiefly interested in the relative price of transportation, this is of no concern. The transportation costs were compute from the entries of the item "land carriage from you to Dublin per cwt." The (unweighted) provincial means are presented in Table 1. The most interesting variable is K, which is the cost per mile divided by the price of the

Table 1. Transportation Costs in Ireland, 1811[a]

Province	No. of Observations	Cost per Mile	Price of Potatoes	K (Potatoes)	K (Wheat)	K (Oats)
Ulster	12	.71 (.024)	27.9 (1.35)	2.63 (.19)	.36 (.015)	.85 (.07)
Leinster	22	.75 (.095)	26.4 (2.03)	2.79 (.45)	.37 (.047)	1.14 (.21)
Munster	11	.63 (.086)	32.8 (4.40)	2.10 (.25)	.31 (.048)	.85 (.16)
Connaught	7	.56 (.036)	30.8 (3.06)	2.00 (.20)	.34 (.045)	1.02 (.11)
Ireland	52	.69 (.044)	29.1 (1.31)	2.52 (.22)	.36 (.024)	1.01 (.10)

[a]The numbers in parentheses are standard errors of the means.
Source: Wakefield (1812), Vol. 2, pp. 208–229.

good times 100, which is thus the percentage of the value of the good which "evaporates" due to transportation over one mile.

The data indicate that potatoes cost, on average, about 2.5 percent of their value for each mile that they were transported. An indication of the significance of that number can be obtained by comparing it to modern underdeveloped economies: Clark and Haswell (1970, p. 19) assert that when the cost of transport comprises three-fifths of the value, "transporting grain to market . . . is economically out of the question." The Wakefield data are confirmed by data from the 1830s. The manuscript collection known as the Ordnance Survey Memoirs reports a cost of 7.2d. per ton/mile in 1835, which amounts to 0.36d. per cwt./mile (Ordnance Survey Memoirs,[3] Box 31, file I). Since the price level in 1811 was roughly 75 percent higher than in 1835, and since some technological progress in land transport had occurred in the meanwhile, these data are consistent with those in Table 1. Weld (1832) produces a set of estimates of transport costs for County Roscommon in 1832, which average to 0.25d. per cwt./mile (p. 175). With potatoes at 1.5d. to 2d. per stone the implied value of K is between 1.5 and 2.00 for this period. Slightly higher are the figures provided by a witness from Tipperary before the Poor Law Commission (PLR, 1836, XXXII, p. 8), who estimated the cost of carrying potatoes over a distance of 24 miles at 1s. As the price of a cwt. of potatoes was 1s. 6d., a value of K = 2.78 is implied.

Furthermore, the cost of transportation is not the only cost incurred in shipping potatoes. Irregularly shaped, poorly packed, moved along bumpy roads on primitive vehicles, the product lost much of its value in transit. For example, a relief shipment sent by sloop from Wexford to Westport in 1835, which had been en route for only 12 days and had been shipped in a "sound and dry state," arrived in very poor condition. The potatoes had turned soft and sprouted and fermentation had set in (PLR, 1836, XXXII, p. 30).

Some idea of the vulnerability of potatoes to handling and transportation can be gained from modern studies. One study (Burton, 1968, pp. 197–209) examining nine 50-kg. bags of potatoes at point of wholesale, found two to have less than 5 percent serious damage, four to have between 9 and 14 percent damage, and three to have over 27 percent damage (of which one had just over 50 percent). The main damage is caused by a phenomenon known as "internal bruising" or "blue spot." Even under modern transportation conditions, shipments of potatoes have been rejected because of high incidence of internal bruising after travelling 50 km. by road. In pre-Famine Ireland, the spoilage problem was aggravated because most trade in potatoes took place in open carts in the early summer. Exposed to higher temperatures, potatoes were damaged by accelerated sprouting as well as by "black heart," a phenomenon of discoloration and breakdown of the inner tissue of the tuber due to asphyxiation (Burton, 1968, pp. 230–231).

The same witnesses who emphasized the lack of portability spoke also at length of the storage problems of the potato. Potatoes could be stored cheaply in so-called clamps. Clamps are heaps of potatoes, covered with straw and turf or earth, usually set up on the side of the field. If the water table was sufficiently low, the clamp would be a pit covered with straw (Salaman, 1949, pp. 235–236). The efficiency and low cost of this method is demonstrated by the fact that in 1963, 48 percent of the potatoes stored in Great Britain were clamped (Burton, 1968, p. 266). While the storage costs of potatoes for a period of up to 10 months was thus very low, the cost function leaps up steeply after that and becomes essentially infinite after 12 months. In general, potatoes spoil after about 10 months of storage in clamps. Buffer stocks, consequently, were totally out of the question.

There are three reasons for the limited storability of potatoes: disease, evaporation, and sprouting. Although all three can be controlled to some extent under modern conditions, it is clear that the Irish peasant was largely unaware of the mechanisms involved and powerless to prevent spoilage. Storage diseases were largely caused by fungi and bacteria. In particular, the disease known today as "soft rot" or "black leg," caused by bacteria, seems to have been prevalent. Bacterial multiplication is a rising function of external temperature, which explains the rotting of the potatoes by mid-summer. In clamps, things were made worse by the lack of ventilation and the consequent accumulation of metabolic heat and carbon dioxide.

The effects of these technological and physiological constraints were that every year in mid-summer the Irish peasant class started to run out of food. In Galway and Kerry, around the first Sunday of August ("Garlick Sunday") potatoes of the "lumper" variety were getting bad and all those who could switched to other kinds of food. The "apple" variety typically kept two months longer but was more expensive and even it did not last longer than 12 months. In short, there were no "means known by which potatoes can be preserved for the next season when there is a superabundant supply." The situation is neatly summarized by a witness from Kilkenny: "the supply of the principal food of the laboring classes is . . . altogether dependent on the produce of one year and (from the bulkiness of the article) almost of one place . . . if the crop of any year fails, distress is inevitable to the extent of the failure" (PLR, 1836, XXXII, p. 427). A Leitrim witness assessed his region to be fortunate because "with us, the interval between the old crop becoming unfit and the new becoming fit has never been more than a month" (PLR, 1836, XXXII, p. 6). In Sligo, a witness said, the "lumper" and "cup" varieties began to deteriorate as early as June (PLR, 1836, XXXII, p. 9). In Wicklow, the months of July and August were times of great distress and "an annual return of temporary half-famine" (PLR, 1836, XXXII, p. 25).

Potatoes were generally consumed by the people who grew them, though trade in potatoes always existed. Lord Carbery, testifying before a Parliamentary Commission in 1825, pointed out that "as long as the potato is the staple food, we cannot reckon much on the home market for the peasantry, for each provides for his year's subsistence . . . he does not think of the market" (PP, 1825, VIII, p. 615). The potato led to some peculiar features in the Irish economy. One of those unique characteristics was the practice of con-acre, in which a landless laborer rented at high cost a fertilized and prepared plot of an acre or less and raised his and his family's annual food supply on it (Beames, 1975; Donnelly, 1975). Less well-known but equally telling about the effect of the potato is the fact that many urban residents rented little plots of land just outside the town confines. On these plots they grew potatoes—presumably just for their own consumption (PLR, 1836, XXXIII, p. 240 for Kilkenny; OSM, Box 27, file I for Enniskillen; OSM, Box 39, file II for Dungiven, County Londonderry). Thus, while growing urban demand was providing an incentive to commercialize agriculture in the rest of Europe, Irish urban dwellers were often growing their own potatoes instead of registering a market demand for more potatoes. This is just one more way that the potato stifled the growth of commercial agriculture in Ireland.

There is also some evidence to support the hypothesis that the reliance on potatoes worsened in the period 1815–1845, at least as far as the mass of smallholders and landless laborers were concerned. The 1841 *Census of Ireland* (PP, 1843, XXIV, pp. xvii–xix) reported that 67.9 percent of the rural population of Ireland were laborers, smallholders, and other persons "without capital, in either money, land, or acquired knowledge." The Poor Law Unions' data on farm size show that 75.2 percent of all farms were under 20 acres, of which 55.0 percent were under 10 acres.

In part, the increased dependence was caused by a growth of population. But there was another element operating here, namely, the worsening of the terms of trade of the "cash crops" bought by the smallholders and laborers in terms of those that they sold. The primary factor which reduced the cash-generating capacity of the Irish peasant in the first half of the nineteenth century was the decline and almost total collapse of the rural cottage industries, which had provided much of the cash income earned by Irish peasants, especially in Ulster and Connaught (Gill, 1925, pp. 322–329; Almquist, 1977).

The demise of spinning and, a bit later, weaving, was swift, brutal, and total. Within a few years an indispensable source of "cash" had vanished. A County Tyrone witness before the Poor Law Commissioners described the consequence as a "scramble for cash" (PLR, 1836, XXXI, p. 391). The collapse of the demand for industrial products produced by manual methods in the countryside, led to an exodus of labor back into agriculture. Much of that labor, inevitably, went into the production of potatoes (OSM, Box 3, file V; Box 9, file VI; Box 13, file I; Box 36, file VI). Trade in agricultural goods declined. A County Down witness pointed out that he could still recall the days when spinners could get 3s. per web, and never had to sell any corn, in many cases buying their food. Where the prices of textile products declined to a fraction, they were forced to depend on potatoes and sell corn to get cash (PLR, 1836, XXXII, p. 312).

The decline of nonagricultural cash-generating activities was compounded by the movement of rents. Rent was the one item in the peasant's expenditure which required cash and could not be postponed. Nonpayment of rent was formally a cause for eviction, an option which many Irish landlords were often all too eager to exercise. In the three decades following Waterloo, all prices, including agricultural prices, fell. Most of the land in Ireland was leased at rents specified in money terms. Although the nominal value of rents declined between 1815 and 1845, real rents actually paid by the tenants rose. While many landlords realized the peasants' inability to pay higher rents, many others demanded payment in full. Unlike the decline of cottage industries, the increase in real rents hit the middle-sized farmers (holding between 10 and 50 acres) most severely. Many farmers, one witness explained, speculated on the high Napoleonic War prices and had rented land much above its value now, and "many of the landlords holding them nearly to their original engagement, have brought them to a low condition" (PLR, 1836, XXXI, p. 329). For these farmers, too, this change in prices implied a greater dependence on potatoes. A rise in rents implied that peasants had to sell a larger part of the edible cash crop (oats, dairy products, pork) to pay rents. Consequently they were forced to rely more heavily on potatoes for subsistence. The model suggests that the increase in potato subsistence was accompanied by a decline in trade in potatoes. The result was what may be called an "encapsulation" of the subsistence sector, reducing further what little trade there was in potatoes.

As peasants became more dependent on the potato, the reliability of the potato crop became of paramount importance. Without the opportunity to store or equalize regional differences through trade, high variance in output could lead to disasters since bad years in one area could not be made up by storage or transport. Were potatoes more volatile than cereals in the sense that the crop fluctuated more violently? Although what matters ultimately is the variance of consumption and not that of production, the latter is not without interest, since if the variance in potato production was very small, the issues of storability and tradeability became irrelevant. The answer to the question depends on time series of yields, which are not available for Ireland. In the second half of the eighteenth century, potato famines were rare. Connell (1950) speaks of a "gap in famines" between 1742 and 1815 during which "even the rumblings of disaster were seldom heard." Contemporary evidence confirms this view. In 1802 William Tighe (1802) wrote in his magisterial work on County Kilkenny that "it is a happy circumstance that the food of the majority of the inhabitants in this country consists of potatoes which are more certain in produce and less liable to injuries, and that wheat is an article of commerce rather than of food" (p. 191). Maria Edgeworth spoke of "clear headed farmers," who told her in 1822, without hesitation, that there was more chance of a failure of the wheat or oats harvest than the potato harvest (Ricardo, 1952, p. 253). Very similar views were expressed by witnesses before the 1825 *Select Committee on the State of Ireland* (PP, 1825, VIII, pp. 312, 416, 615).

After 1820, however, the yield of potatoes seems to have become more variable, and complaints about bad harvests more frequent (O'Rourke, 1902, p. 34; PP, 1830, VII, p. 378); although Bicheno (1830, pp. 20–21) was cautious on that point. Combinations of frost and curl (a viral disease) seem to have been largely responsible (Mokyr, 1982a). The adoption of the "lumper" variety in this period may have contributed to the vulnerability of the potato crops (Davidson, 1937, p. 64). A list of crop failures was compiled by William Wilde and published in the 1851 Census (PP, 1856, XXIX, pp. 502–506). Wilde pointed to the 1813/14 season as the season which was the "forerunner of other calamities . . . a new pestilential constitution now commenced."

It thus seems likely that in the 30 years before the Great Famine, the Irish were slowly becoming aware of the higher vulnerability of their "potato economy." It could be reasoned that a sufficient number of local failures coupled with a lack of cushions to absorb these shocks would have led the Irish to try to reduce their dependence on their staple diet. However, for the vast majority of the Irish peasants such a reversal was nearly impossible. Moreover, as we argued above, there were strong forces which led to an *increasing* dependence on the potato. The potato had become deeply entrenched in the agrarian economy as part of the crop cycle, and breaking out of that cycle required capital and expertise beyond the reach of the bulk of the peasantry. Furthermore, the potato had led to the disappearance of the ''infrastructure'' necessary to consume other forms of food. Millers, bakers, and even domestic utensils other than those necessary to boil potatoes were rare, especially in the south and west. In a real sense, Ireland was ''locked'' into a potato culture.

V. AN ECONOMETRIC APPROACH

Is it possible that the cultivation of potatoes was a factor in the impoverishment of the pre-Famine Irish economy? The above suggests a number of mechanisms by which the potato could have been, in the final analysis, more a curse than a blessing. It is not clear, however, that potatoes actually *reduced* average income per capita. After all, potatoes raised the productivity of labor in food production. To a large extent, the models developed above point to a reduction in security and a higher vulnerability to exogenous shocks, but not necessarily to a lower average *level* of income per capita. Potatoes protected the self-sufficient subsistence sector from the encroachment of commercialized agriculture, an encroachment which was occurring inexorably almost everywhere in Europe. But income, by necessity, is measured in the cash sector. Is there any reason to suppose that the cultivation of potatoes had adverse effects on the commercialized sector as well?

The classical approach of nineteenth-century political economy, as adopted by historians such as K. H. Connell, presented a straightforward argument: potato cultivation led to increased population which, by the principle of diminishing returns, reduced income per capita. While theoretically attractive, the difficulty is that there is very little hard evidence for this hypothesis (Mokyr, 1982b). While the evidence is perhaps not strong enough to rule out the classical theory altogether, a further search for the effects of the potato on income per capita is indicated. As noted, the chief effect of the potato was to increase the dependence of the peasant on his own harvest. At first sight, it might seem as if that dependence should show up in the variance of consumption but not in the *level* of income. However, if the peasant is risk averse, he would try to make an attempt to reduce his risk in other ways. Alternative forms of insurance inevitably cost something in terms of income. For instance, if the Bloch–McCloskey view of open fields is correct, peasants reduced their variance by scattering their plots. The inefficient (and thus costly) custom of scattering known as ''rundale'' was still widely practiced in such counties as Donegal and Mayo, which were very poor and highly dependent on potatoes (Almquist, 1977).

A further mechanism by which potatoes could have actually reduced income is by the absence of positive ''spillover effects'' of trade. Commerce has always meant more than static ''gains from trade.'' The flow of goods is accompanied by flows of men, and with men come ideas, new technologies, and other stimuli to the production process. Learning by doing effects lead to continuous improvements in transport technology, financial and commercial practices, and backward linkages to the industries catering to commerce. It would be misleading to say that Ireland with its thousands of local county fairs and advanced road system was incapable of generating these externalities. And yet, for a Western European country in the middle of the nineteenth century, Ireland's commercialization and monetization appear stunted. Wages to laborers were often paid in provisions or con-acre land. Smallholders and cottagers, comprising over two-thirds of the rural population, were by and large self-sufficient in food and fuel production. Although the use of money had reached everywhere, in much of the country a majority of the peasantry carried out only a small number of monetary transactions each year. Much of rural Ireland lacked retail trade networks. The province of Connaught, for instance, with a total occupied adult population of 560,000 in 1841, had less than 0.5 percent of them in occupations which fall under the heading of "commerce and finance." Many of these were wholesale traders of cattle produced by the large grazier farms in the west (PP, 1843, XXIV, p. 430). By comparison, in 1846, 5.2 percent of the French occupied population were classified in commerce and finance, 3.5 percent of the Belgian workers, and 1.8 percent of the British (Mitchell, 1975, pp .153–163). Although inconsistencies in definitions present many pitfalls in the comparison of different countries, the gap between the Irish west and the other countries is striking.

Transportation to market was also primitive. Railroads, canals, and harbors were backward and few. Even the much-praised Irish roads were better adapted for the carriage of tourists and commercial travellers than for heavy and bulky goods (O'Tuathaigh, 1972, p. 121). It would be foolish to blame only the potato for the underdevelopment of the commercial infrastructure of Ireland. Nonetheless, the decommercializing effects of potato cultivation cannot wholly be absolved from responsibility for this state of affairs.

A further difficulty with the potato was that it did not seem to lend itself to productivity growth in the long run, as beneficial as it may have seemed as a new technology in the short run. If it is accepted that a large proportion of technological progress was "local" around the technique in use, then the heavy reliance on potatoes may have turned out, ex post, to have been a costly decision. Technological progress in potato cultivation after 1800 was slow compared to other crops. In 1771 Arthur Young's calculations implied that the calorific value of an acre of potatoes was three times that of an acre of grain. Today, that gap has been entirely eliminated because the increase in grain yields has been much larger than the increase in potato yields (Burton, 1968, p. 181; Davidson and Passmore, 1965, p. 181).

Furthermore, savings and investment are definitely encumbered if one of the chief sources of income consists of a crop which is *both* perishable and difficult to transport. In the extreme case, the budget constraint in the standard Fisherian two-period diagram is confined to a single point, with no possibility of reallocation between the two periods.

These considerations suggest that the potato crop may possibly also have reduced income per capita in pre-Famine Ireland, although we emphasize that the costs of specializing in potatoes extended beyond the simple reduction of *average* income. To test whether that hypothesis is consistent with available data, we have to formulate a model in which income per capita is determined by the degree of dependence of the population on potatoes. Simple OLS regressions would be misleading here, since income per capita simultaneously determines the demand for potatoes through the (presumably negative) income elasticity. We use therefore a two-equation simultaneous model, in which both income per capita and potatoes are endogenous.

$$INCOME = a_0 + a_1 POT + a_2 CAPLAB + a_3 LANDQUAL$$
$$+ a_4 LIT + a_5 EMPIN + a_6 PERURB \qquad (12)$$

and

$$POT = b_0 + b_1 INCOME + b_2 CAPLAB + b_3 INFER$$
$$+ b_4 FMSIZE + b_5 PERURB, \qquad (13)$$

where INCOME = income per capita around 1840;
           POT = indexes of potato acreage on the eve of the Famine.
       CAPLAB = capital/labor ratio in 1841;
   LANDQUAL = indexes of land quality;
           LIT = proportion adult population who could both read and write in 1841;
        EMPIN = proportion employed population in nonagricultural occupations;
      PERURB = percentage of persons living in towns over 2000 in 1841;
         INFER = proportion mountain and bog land presently uncultivated which is suitable for potato cultivation;
      FMSIZE = average size of farms, Poor Law Union data, 1845.

A full description of the data and their sources, and the justification for their inclusion in these equations cannot be attempted here (see Mokyr, 1981, 1982b). The two equations were estimated using generalized two-stage least squares on county data (32 observations). The results are presented in Tables 2 and 3. Two columns of the same number constitute a "compatable pair" of equations in the sense that all variables are consistently defined and each equation uses the exogenous variables of the other as its instruments, in addition to its own.

Table 2. Regression Results of Equation 1

Dependent Variable	Income	Income	Income	Income
Constant	16.09	8.85	9.13	8.27
	(1.69)	(2.78)	(3.22)	(2.54)
Potato acr. per cultivated area	−52.83			
	(−1.38)			
Potato acr. per capita		−14.98		−17.19
		(−1.65)		(−1.63)
Potato acr. per rural capita			−15.29	
			(−1.98)	
CAPLAB	.96	1.75	1.83	1.88
	(1.42)	(4.77)	(5.00)	(4.58)
LANDQUAL1				2.83
				(1.76)
LANDQUAL2		1.01	1.12	
		(1.88)	(2.11)	
LANDQUAL3	.0098			
	(1.18)			
LIT	−7.76	6.23	4.98	3.97
	(−.45)	(1.01)	(.82)	(.55)
EMPIN	13.29	10.29	10.11	10.54
	(2.53)	(3.17)	(3.17)	(3.11)
PERURB	12.19	6.08	10.14	6.35
	(1.91)	(2.37)	(2.98)	(2.38)

Table 2 indicates that potato dependence did indeed tend to reduce income per capita, even when mutual determination is accounted for (see Table 3). Potato acreage is consistently negative and significant at the 10 percent level (one tailed test) or better. The other variables all perform satisfactorily. Percentage urban, nonagricultural employment, land quality, and the capital/labor ratio all have the expected positive influence on income per capita. Only literacy is disappointing.

These regressions suggest that there was a twofold relation between poverty and potatoes. Potatoes were an inferior good, and poor people ate proportionately more of them. At the same time, however, there was a feedback effect, leading from a dependence on potatoes to more poverty. This feedback effect helps to explain the existence of poverty "traps" of various kinds. Although potatoes were not the sole factor responsible for such traps, the results presented above indicate that they made a contribution in this respect.

Table 3.   Regression Results of Equation 2

Dependent Variable	Potato Acr. per Cultivated Acre	Potato Acr. per Capita	Potato Acr. per Rural Capita	Potato Acr. per Capita
CONSTANT	.21 (3.11)	.34 (4.15)	.36 (3.73)	.33 (3.55)
INCOME	−.0028 (−.53)	−.013 (−2.10)	−.015 (−2.06)	−.012 (−1.67)
CAPLAB	−.031 (−1.64)	.021 (.85)	.018 (.62)	.019 (.71)
INFER	.26 (2.97)	.075 (.66)	.079 (.59)	.085 (.69)
FMSIZE	.0028 (1.28)	.0034 (1.20)	.0052 (1.55)	.0036 (1.20)
PERURB	.56 (.56)	.029 (1.23)	.027 (1.89)	.017 (.13)

Figures in parentheses are asymptotic t-statistics.
The land quality variables are defined as follows: LANDQUAL 1 is the proportion of all land under cultivation in 1841. LANDQUAL 2 is a nonlinear transformation of LANDQUAL 1. LANDQUAL 3 is the standard deviation of absolute elevation above sea level. For a discussion of the theory behind these proxies, cf. Mokyr, *Why Ireland Starved*, Ch. III, Appendix B.

VI.   CONCLUSIONS

The question posed in this paper is not new. Classical political economists wondered about the effects of potato cultivation on the people dependent on it, long before anybody suspected that a catastrophe like the Great Famine was possible. Some of them, like Adam Smith (1976, p. 179), cheered the potato as a plentiful and healthy food. Malthus (1826, p. 393), on the other hand, viewed the potato with suspicion, maintaining that it led to higher birth rates, and encouraged "idleness and turbulence." From our point of view, there is perhaps more interest in the curious correspondence between David Ricardo and Maria Edgeworth, the Anglo-Irish novelist, on "the question *for* and *against* the potato which has for some hundred years past been alternately cried up as the blessing and cried down as the bane of Ireland," as Edgeworth put it (Ricardo, 1952, Vol. IX, p. 231). Ricardo, who had been a member of an 1823 *Select Committee on the Condition of the Laboring Poor in Ireland*, remained somewhat dubious of the beneficial effects of the potato. Only if it could be demonstrated conclusively to him that potatoes could be stored and that speculators would carry buffer stocks, Ricardo wrote, would he "fight to the death in favor of the potato" (p. 259). Edgeworth assured him that farmers in Ireland considered the potato more reliable and secure than corn, but Ricardo still had his doubts: he insisted that one had to know something about the proportional difference between an average and a deficient crop of potatoes and wheat, which determined the "comparative hazard" (p. 259) of the two crops.

The net effect of the potato on the Irish economy is ambiguous and multidimensional. There can be no question that most of the positive and the negative consequences mentioned in the writings of contemporaries contained some truth. At first, the potato was undoubtedly a blessing. Yet, in the final analysis, the kind of economy the potato made was rigid, vulnerable, and backward. The worries of Malthus and Ricardo turned out to be more realistic than the exuberance of Arthur Young or Adam Smith. Needless to say, the potato was only one element in a complex mechanism leading Ireland to poverty and then to disaster in the nineteenth century; but it should be recognized as such.

"No ground is darker or bloodier than Europe's agrarian past," wrote William Parker in 1975 (Parker and Jones, 1975, p. 3). Surely, this statement holds with particular force for the hapless Irish. In the grim history of this plagued economy, the role of the potato was in small part hero, in large part villain. The counterfactual question seems unavoidable: what would Ireland's history have been like without the potato? It seems hard to imagine that without the potato Irish history could have been more tragic.

ACKNOWLEDGMENTS

The comments and help of Letty Anderson, Brian Binger, Cormac O'Grada, Aba Schwartz, and Gavin Wright are acknowledged. Evelyne Seebauer provided excellent research assistance.

NOTES

1. Henceforth referred to as PLR (1836).
2. Henceforth referred to as PP (date).
3. Henceforth referred to as OSM (Box and file numbers).

REFERENCES

Almquist, Eric L. (1977). "Mayo and Beyond: Land, Domestic Industry, and Rural Transformation in the Irish West." Unpublished Ph.D. dissertation, Boston University.

Beames, M. R. (1975). "Cottiers and Conacre in Pre-Famine Ireland." *Journal of Peasant Studies* 2(3): 352–55.

Bicheno, James (1830). *Ireland and its Economy.* London: Murray.

Blum, Jerome (1978). *The End of the Old Order in Rural Europe.* Princeton, N.J.: Princeton University Press.

Bourke, P. M. Austin (1968). "The Use of the Potato Crop in Pre-Famine Ireland." *Journal of the Statistical and Social Inquiry Society of Ireland* 12(4): 72–96.

Burton, W. G. (1968). *The Potato: A Survey of Its History and of Factors Influencing its Yield, Nutritive Value, Quality, and Storage,* 2nd ed. Wageningen, Netherlands: Veenman & Zonen.

Clark, Colin, and Margaret Haswell (1970). *The Economics of Subsistence Agriculture,* 4th ed. New York: Macmillan.

Connell, K. H. (1950). *The Population of Ireland, 1750–1845.* New York: Oxford University Press (Clarendon).

Cullen, L. M. (1968). "Irish History Without the Potato." *Past and Present* 40: 72–83.

Davidson, Stanley, and R. Passmore (1965). *Human Nutrition and Dietetics.* Baltimore: Williams & Wilkins.

Davidson, W. D. (1937). "History of Potato Varieties." *Journal of the Department of Agriculture* 34(2).

Dickler, Robert A. (1975). "Organization and Change in Productivity in Eastern Prussia." In W. N. Parker and E. L. Jones (eds.), *European Peasants and Their Markets.* Princeton, N.J.: Princeton University Press.

Donnelly, J. S. (1975). *The Land and People of Nineteenth Century Cork.* Boston: Routledge & Kegan Paul).

Flinn, Michael (1981). *The European Demographic System, 1500–1820.* Baltimore: Johns Hopkins University Press.

Gill, Conrad (1925). *The Rise of the Irish Linen Industry.* New York: Oxford University Press (Clarendon).

Great Britain, H.C. (1825). *Parliamentary Papers,* Vol. VIII: "Reports from the Select Committee on the State of Ireland."

———— (1830). *Parliamentary Papers,* Vol. VII: "Second Report of Evidence from the Select Committee on the State of the Poor in Ireland."

———— (1836). *Parliamentary Papers,* Vol. XXXI–XXXIV: "Reports of the Commissioners for Inquiry into the Conditions of the Poorer Classes in Ireland."

———— (1843). *Parliamentary Papers,* Vol. XXIV: "1841 *Census of Ireland.*"

———— (1846). *Parliamentary Papers,* Vol. XXXVII: "Return Relative to the Prices of Potatoes in Ireland."

———— (1856). *Parliamentary Papers,* Vol. XXIX: "The Census of Ireland for the Year 1851."

Kunreuther, Howard, and Gavin Wright (1979). "Safety-first, Gambling, and the Subsistence Farmer." In J. A. Roumasset et al. (eds.) *Risk, Uncertainty and Agricultural Development.* College Laguna, Philippines: Southeast Asia Regional Center for Graduate Study and Research in Agriculture.

Lee, Joseph (1973). "The Ribbonmen." Pp. 26–35 in T. D. Williams (ed.), *Secret Societies in Ireland.* Dublin: Gill & Macmillan.

Levitt, Ian, and T. C. Smout (1979). *The State of the Scottish Working-Class in 1843.* Edinburgh: Scottish Academic Press.

Lewis, George Cornewall (1836). *On Local Disturbances in Ireland.* London: Fellowes.

McEvoy, Arthur (1979). "Economy, Law, and Ecology in the California Fisheries to 1925." Unpublished Ph.D. dissertation, University of California, San Diego.

Malthus, Thomas R. (1826). *An Essay on the Principle of Population,* 6th ed. London: Murray, Vol. II.

Mitchell, Brian R. (1975). *European Historical Statistics, 1750–1970.* New York: Macmillan.

Mokyr, Joel (1981). "Irish History With the Potato." *Irish Economic and Social History* 8: 8–29.

———— (1982a). "Uncertainty and Prefamine Irish Agriculture." In D. Dickson and T. M. Devine (eds.), *Ireland and Scotland: Economic and Social Developments, 1650–1850.* Edinburgh: Donald.

———— (1982b). *Why Ireland Starved: A Quantitative and Analytical History of the Irish Economy, 1800–1850.* London: Allen & Unwin.

Morineau, M. (1979). "The Potato in the Eighteenth Century." In Robert Forster and Orest Ranum (eds.), *Food and Drink in History* (Baltimore: 1979).

O'Rourke, J. (1902). *The History of the Great Irish Famine of 1847, with Notices of Earlier Irish Famines.* Dublin: Duffy.

O'Tuathaigh, Gearoid (1972). *Ireland Before the Famine.* Dublin: Gill & Macmillan.

Parker, William N. (1971). "Productivity Growth in American Grain Farming: An Analysis of its 19th Century Sources." In R. W. Fogel and S. L. Engerman (eds.), *The Reinterpretation of American Economic History.* New York: Harper & Row.

———— and Eric L. Jones (eds.) (1975). *European Peasants and Their Markets.* Princeton, N.J.: Princeton University Press.

Ricardo, David (1952). *The Work and Correspondence of David Ricardo,* Piero Straffa (ed.). New York: Cambridge University Press, Vol. IX.

Royal Irish Academy, Dublin, Ordnance Survey Memoirs (undated manuscripts designated by file boxes):

Box 3, file V;
Box 9, file VI;
Box 13, file I;
Box 27, file I, pertaining to Enniskillen;
Box 31, file I, pertaining to the parish of Ballywellen Co. Londenderry;
Box 36, file VI;
Box 39, file II, pertaining to Dungiven, Co. Londenberry.

Salaman, N. Redcliffe (1949). *The History and Social Influence of the Potato.* New York: Cambridge University Press.

Smith, Adam (1976). *The Wealth of Nations,* Edwin Cannan (ed.). Chicago: University of Chicago Press.

Tighe, William (1802). *Statistical Observations Relative to the County of Kilkenny.* Dublin: Graisberry & Campbell.

Wakefield, Edward (1812). *An Account of Ireland, Statistical and Political.* London: Longmans.

Weld, Isaac (1832). *Statistical Survey of the County of Roscommon.* Dublin: Graisberry.

PART II

SCIENCE, TECHNOLOGY, AND PRODUCTIVITY

THE DECLINE AND RISE OF THE
DUTCH ECONOMY, 1675–1900

J. de Vries

I. CONNECTING TWO HISTORIES

In the seventeenth century the economy of the Dutch Republic reached a position of international influence and material prosperity that elicited the envy of its neighbors and, since then, the curiosity of generations of historians. That "Golden Age" ended, as they all do. Opinions vary about the dating of the Golden Age's expiration, but it is generally agreed to end sometime in the last third of the seventeenth century.

The Kingdom of the Netherlands began to experience modern economic growth, growth closely linked to industrialization and associated technological transformation, no earlier than the last quarter of the nineteenth century. Indeed one of the few aspects of its nineteenth century economic advance to attract international attention is its lateness.[1]

In this paper I am concerned with the intervening two centuries of Dutch economic history. My objective is to assess what can now be said about the

Technique, Spirit, and Form in the Making of the Modern Economies:
Essays in Honor of William N. Parker
Research in Economic History, Suppl. 3, pages 149–189
Copyright © 1984 by JAI Press Inc.
ISBN: 0-89232-414-7

course of national income and related quantitative indicators of economic activity between the end of the Golden Age in the late seventeenth century and the onset of modern industrial growth at the end of the nineteenth century.

The eighteenth and nineteenth centuries are not often studied together. An obvious reason for this is the general perception that the French and Industrial Revolutions constitute a great watershed separating two utterly dissimilar epochs. This dogma is now occasionally challenged, and rightfully so,[2] but a second obstacle remains to make difficult the unified study of this period. The various ''schools'' of economic history are often regarded as in competition with each other, but in fact each has staked out a ''temporal turf'' that seems most congenial to the methodology and ideology of the school. Thus, the French historical school, or Annales school, regards the eighteenth century as the end of an era of ''quasi-immobile history,'' and its practitioners tend to grow weary of their monitoring of the respiration of the social order well before the French Revolution, which is the terrain of another sort of historian.[3] Likewise, the New Economic History might be thought to enjoy general applicability. In practice it is closely associated with a specific era, in this case the nineteenth century. It is the exceptional cliometrician who has pushed back beyond the British Industrial Revolution; more surprisingly, few have proceeded beyond World War I into the twentieth century.[4]

It is perhaps no accident that I should embark on the task of examining Dutch economic performance over a span of years divided between such dissimilar historical schools. As an economic historian of preindustrial Europe I have been much influenced by the French historical school, although I must admit that it inspires more readily than it instructs. On the other hand, my training in economic history emphasized the work of the then still new New Economic History. Economic history lives at the intersection of two proud disciplines, and my guidance as a graduate student came from someone prepared to work in industry as well as agriculture, in Europe as well as in America. Now it must be seen whether the rigor of the New Economic History can be crossbred with the insight of the French historical school.

II. LOOKING BACK FROM THE TWENTIETH CENTURY

The first step in plotting the likely course of Dutch national income from the end of the Golden Age to the onset of modern economic growth must be an assessment of the literature, to establish what is now thought to be true and to identify areas of controversy and ignorance.

In a reconnaissance of this kind a sensible strategy is to begin from a known point and move from there to the unknown. In this case that requires looking back into the past from the twentieth century, for the Dutch series of national income accounts extends back no further than 1900. The Dutch economists Jan

Tinbergen and J. B. D. Derksen produced this series of net national income on the eve of World War II, and it has been incorporated into the official Central Statistical Bureau series of national accounts.[5] All estimates of pre-1900 national income are back projections from an early twentieth century base; none is founded upon direct estimations of either output or income. Derksen, a participant in the project that yielded the official twentieth-century series, tried his hand at estimating national income at 10-year intervals back to 1860. Regrettably, he has never published his study. The results of his efforts have been published, and I will allude to them later in this survey, but since it is not possible to evaluate his estimates, it is also not possible to lend them much credence.[6]

The back projections of Dutch national income most worthy of consideration are the product of J. Teijl, who in 1971 offered two separately calculated series of estimates extending back at five-year intervals of 1850.[7] One series is based on Dutch government tax revenues. Teijl observed that total tax revenues strayed but little from a fixed relationship to national income in the period 1900–1915. He then satisfied himself that such changes as were introduced to the structure of taxation between 1850 and 1900 did not affect the relative tax burden. Armed with such assumptions, the estimation of national income became a straightforward matter: it was a constant multiple of total tax revenue.

Teijl's second estimate was based on the estimation of a Cobb–Douglas production function for the Dutch economy. With parameters estimated on the basis of 1900–1940 data, he "postdicted" net domestic product by introducing nineteenth-century data on the size of the labor force and, as a proxy for the capital stock, the annual consumption of energy. Net domestic income became net national income with the addition of independent estimates of foreign income.

The two series follow very different courses on a decade-by-decade basis, but they cross each other and end up in close agreement in 1850. This has led some observers to suppose that the two series confirm each other; indeed, J. H. van Stuijvenberg offers averages of the two series as the best available estimates of national income.[8]

It is hard to suppress the thought that the rough conformity of the two series is sheer coincidence. The tax-based estimate is an ad hoc procedure that depends entirely on the assumption that the tax burden remained constant. In discussing the reasonableness of this assumption, Teijl rests his case on the fact that the economy was relatively static and the role of government changed but little in the nineteenth century.

Even if Teijl's justification is accepted, a second problem remains: is the estimate of national income measured in constant or current guilders? If the tax system were based primarily on a proportional income tax, the results of Teijl's exercise would be national income in current guilders. Before 1893 there was no income tax. If most tax revenues were raised by indirect levies such as fixed excise taxes and license fees (as opposed to ad valorem taxes), the result might approximate national income in constant guilders. Teijl *appears* to interpret his results in this latter way, and the users of his estimates assume that they are expressed in constant 1900–1910 guilders.[9] If tax revenues actually grew at the rate of real national income, they would have become a steadily larger percentage of money income during the sharp deflation of the period 1873–1896. Since Teijl did not discuss this problem, the meaning he imputes to the concept of "constant tax burden" must remain uncertain.

The production function–based estimates depend on time series of labor inputs and energy consumption. Since the input of labor is simply assumed to grow at the rate of population growth (unemployment is assumed to be constant), the estimates of per capita national income depend entirely on the energy series, a product of Teijl's own research. Richard Griffiths has correctly remarked of this approach that it is likely to underestimate the growth of productivity in an economy, such as the Netherlands', in which agriculture, services, and transportation (where technological change was energy-saving) are of great importance relative to industry.[10]

Teijl's estimates describe the Dutch economy as growing at 0.7 percent per annum over the period 1850–1910. Our reservations suggest the possibility of more rapid growth, implying a lower 1850 income than Teijl estimates. Derksen, whose never-published estimates go back to 1860, set national income at a level 15 percent above those of Teijl.

Since the estimates of 1850 national income are anything but firm, projections further back would appear foolhardy; nevertheless, two Dutch scholars have ventured to make them. J. H. van Stuijvenberg, in a recent essay on the Dutch economy during the past two centuries, concluded that between 1770 and 1850 productivity advances were so minor that their effect on national income were fully negated by a long-term rise in the unemployment rate. He guesses that real 1770 net national income was roughly equal to Teijl's estimate for 1850.[11] Th. P. M. de Jong, whose research has concentrated on the late-eighteenth-century economy, made rough estimates of the capital stock in 1780 that he interpreted as support for the view that real per capita income was stagnant between then and 1860 (he preferred to rely on Derksen's estimates).[12] Both Van Stuijvenberg and De Jong restate a view widely shared by historians and deriving from nineteenth-century liberal polemicists that the Dutch economy broke out of a long-term stagnation only after 1850 (that is, after promulgation of the liberal constitution of 1848).

A revisionist position has recently been staked out by Richard Griffiths. In his 1980 inaugural address at the Free University of Amsterdam he extended the analysis of his book *Industrial Retardation in the Netherlands 1830–1850* to argue that the Dutch economy experienced balanced growth—he called it *stiekeme groei* (surreptitious growth)—that had not been appreciated fully because of the relative absence of dynamic industrial expansion.[13] Griffiths offers no national income estimates, but he makes two assertions relevant to our subject: (1) Teijl underestimates 1850–1910 growth, and (2) the growth path of

1850–1910 should be extended back to 1830, since there is no basis for supposing the midcentury to be an economic turning point.

Since Teijl's estimate of the long-run rate of per capita growth is 0.7 percent per annum, it seems reasonable to interpret Griffiths's statements to mean that the Dutch economy grew at a rate of approximately 1.0 percent per annum over the period 1830–1910, i.e., that per capita income roughly doubled during the interval.

The literature on the nineteenth century now offers something for everyone. At one extreme, real income stood at f 250 (i.e., 1900 guilders) in 1770, stood no higher until after 1850, and rose to f 353 in 1900; at the other extreme, it stood at about f 175 in 1830, on the order of f 215 in 1850, and f 353 in 1900.

III. LOOKING FORWARD FROM THE GOLDEN AGE

The view backward from 1900 is still shrouded in mist. If we now position ourselves at the apogee of the Golden Age and gaze forward into the eighteenth and nineteenth centuries, is it possible that some orienting landmarks will be revealed?

The literature on the aggregate economy in these centuries is primarily concerned with establishing trends, turning points, and crises. These efforts are based primarily on time series of demographic, price, and trade statistics and are not readily usable as indicators of national income. Indeed, no modern historian has ever attempted the estimation of the level, that is, the valuation, of national income or product. Only contemporaries of that era had the temerity to venture onto that treacherous terrain.

Gregory King, the celebrated English political arithmetician, made estimates of Dutch and French national income for 1688 and 1695 in conjunction with his more familiar efforts concerning England.[14] Economic historians have an obvious interest in defending King's reputation for sagacity. It is convenient to imagine that he had access to voluminous and accurate information that is regrettably no longer extant. Indeed, his writings on the quantitative dimensions of England's population and economy remain well regarded after a generation of scholarly scrutiny.[15]

The same cannot be said for his French estimates, which have been savaged by E. Le Roy Ladurie.[16] What of King's national income estimates for the Dutch Republic, where he sets per capita income in 1688 at £8.5, or 7 percent above his estimate for England? King's own published works reveal next to nothing about the basis for his figures, but his manuscript notebook, happily preserved and published, permits an evaluation of his method.[17]

King's approach to national income accounting in this case was to estimate the returns to the factors of production, albeit in a desperately abbreviated way. The total rent receipts, including dwellings and urban property, he set at £4 million, the result of multiplying the 8 million acres surface area of the Republic (an accurate figure) by an assumed average rent of 10 shillings per acre. He had reckoned English rents to average 5 shillings per acre and reasoned that the higher population density of the Republic warranted a doubling of that figure. In this regard it is worth noting that in 1835–1840, just after the completion of the first Dutch cadastral survey, the Netherlands had 2.1 million hectares (5.25 million acres) of cultivated land, which had an average rental value of f 31.2 per hectare.[18] Average rents before the decline in agricultural prices that sets in by the 1670s may not have stood far below the 1835 level.[19] Even if they were set at two-thirds of the 1835 level, which is 20 percent below the average 1650 rental price found in a survey of 177 parcels in Holland, the agricultural rents of the Netherlands would have totaled some £4 million. To that figure one would need to add the rental value of woodlands and rural dwellings, not to mention all urban property, which accommodated some 40 percent of the population in 1675. An indication of the probable importance of such property is available in 1808, when the nation's 400,947 residential dwellings were taxed on the basis of their rental value. The total assessed value was then f 21 million, or nearly £2 million. This figure may well have been substantially higher in the seventeenth century.[20]

The returns to labor and capital King collapsed into a single estimate of "trade and business," elsewhere labeled "improvements by labor." There is nothing in his notes to hint at the source of this estimate except perhaps some marginalia about the importance of the fishing industry and a tenuously reasoned estimate of the total capital stock (£71 million, implying a capital–output ratio of 5.5:1).

The incomes to trade and business he estimates at £13 million for 1688 and £14 million (and also apparently £15 million) in 1695, making his total estimate for national income range from £17 million to £19 million. King divided these national income figures by the population of the Republic, which he set at 2 million in 1688 and thought had risen to 2.2 million by 1695. Modern estimates are very close to the 2 million figure. However, there is no evidence that the population was growing; the reverse is more likely. King's per capita income figures for 1688 through 1695 range between £8.14 and £8.64, equivalent to 90–94 guilders at the ruling exchange rates of those years.

King's next step was to split the total into its component parts of national expenditure: consumption, government, and savings. Here we come to the motivation for King's excursion into comparative national income accounting. He wished to advance an argument about how best to finance the wars then being waged against France. For present purposes it should be noted that his figure for Dutch tax revenues is apparently based on contemporary evidence and that his estimate of savings was likely dictated by the needs of his political argument. Private consumption expenditure is almost certainly a residual figure. Although King estimated Dutch per capita income to be 7 percent above the English level, he was left with a figure for Dutch consumption that was only three-quarters of the English figure. This, despite his remark in the notebook that "Ye necessaries in Holland in many things, especially Food and Rayment and other matters of Importance being generally a 5th or 4th part dearer than in England, Excepting Fish. . . ."[21]

It suited King to put this image of Dutch frugality before his English readers, but his estimates cannot stand as an adequate characterization of Dutch national income. The fact is that King's notebook reveals little more knowledge of the Republic than its size, population, and government revenues.

The only other estimates of Dutch national income date from the early nineteenth century.[22] The more informative of the two is W. M. Keuchenius' *Nationaale Balans der Bataafsche Republiek,* which refers to an unspecified year around 1800. Keuchenius furnishes his study with a table itemizing the national income in one column and national expenditure in another. Unfortunately, Keuchenius shows himself to be an inconsistent physiocrat. His assessment of national income and "expenditure" is concerned primarily with the value of domestic agricultural and fishing output, to which he adds exports. All domestic trade, transport, and manufacturing he dismisses, "since the profit passes from hand to hand without enriching the country or increasing the [quantity of] money." Ironically, he does include under national income the classic transfer payment, interest on the public debt.

Little can be done with Keuchenius's study to estimate national income, but, assuming that the component estimates can be trusted, his work can serve to reconstruct the chief components of the Dutch balance of payments. Table 1 shows that Keuchenius—either directly or by implication—believed foreign earnings to total 96 million guilders, only 14 million of which consisted of domestically produced exports. On the other hand, foreign payments totalled 79 million guilders, all of which went for commodity imports. Were one to accept Keuchenius' estimate of national income, 221 million guilders, or *f* 126 per capita, this would imply that 43 percent of national income was earned abroad. The conclusion cannot be avoided that either his individual estimates are very far from the mark, or national income stood far above *f* 126 per capita, or both.

A second source, written at about the same time but with knowledge of Keuchenius's estimates, is Rutger Metelerkamp's *De toestand van Nederland in vergelijking gebragt met die van enige andere landen van Europa.* He begins by estimating the average annual payments to the owners of real property (*f* 45 million—compare to Gregory King's £4 million ≅ *f* 44 million in 1688), to the owners of domestic and foreign government bonds (*f* 70 million, *f* 30 million of which is from domestic debt) and then plunges into the commercial sector. Foreign trade and shipping, by Metelerkamp's reckoning, yielded *f* 36 million on a capital investment of *f* 350 million. Further calculations were apparently beyond him, for he then moves on to offer an overall estimate of national income of *f* 250 million, or *f* 125 per capita, and an estimate of the "national wealth"—the capital stock—of *f* 3500 million! These estimates he placed in the context of a

Table 1. The Balance of Payments of the Batavian Republic, circa 1800, According to the Estimates of W. M. Keuchenius (in millions of guilders)

Receipts from Abroad			*Payments to Foreigners*		
Exports			*Imports*		
Agricultural products	10		Agricultural products	33	
Fish	1		Raw materials	11.5	
Manufactures	3		Manufactures	26.5	
Colonial commodities	12*a*		Colonial commodities	8*a*	
Subtotal		26	*Subtotal*		79
Invisibles					
Shipping, banking, insurance	30*b*				
Investments					
Income from foreign government debt	40				
Total		96			79

*a*Keuchenius estimates that the Dutch East Indies and West Indies possessions yielded an income from the sale of delivered commodities of *f*20 million. He then reckons that the domestic consumption of these goods accounted for *f*8 million. I am treating the *f*20 million as net proceeds from all colonial activities. I suspect that this results in a substantial overestimate of colonial earnings.
*b*Keuchenius' estimate of these earnings from "invisibles" is for "years of peace."
Source: W. M. Keuchenius, *De inkomsten en uitgaven der Bataafsche Republiek voorgesteld in eene nationale balans* (Amsterdam: 1803), p. 139.

large table entitled "Comparison of the situation of the Netherlands and several other countries in various periods." He compared eight European nations in a variety of quantitative dimensions (among others, value of foreign trade, size of armies) in the course of which he displays evidence of familiarity with the work of Gregory King and Patrick Colquhoun. Unfortunately, his Dutch estimates give even less evidence than those of Keuchenius of an understanding of the elements of national income.

Neither King nor Keuchenius and Metelerkamp can be of much use in pegging the level of Dutch national income in the seventeenth and eighteenth centuries. The first reveals too little knowledge; the two others, too much ignorance.

We must turn then to the modern scholars who have sought to establish the trends in the volume of seventeenth- and eighteenth-century economic activity. Still the most comprehensive study of the eighteenth-century Dutch economy is Johan de Vries's *De economische achteruitgang der Republiek in de achttiende eeuw.*[23]

In a sector-by-sector assessment, De Vries emphasized the structural changes taking place in the Dutch economy and concluded that the economy was overshadowed by others, that is, had suffered relative decline. A loss of position seemed unquestionable; a loss of real income was more doubtful. De Vries ventured to guess that real national income remained constant into the 1780s but that per capita income may have fallen slightly.[24]

Since Johan de Vries wrote, several monographs and articles have added a great deal to our knowledge of trends in the domestic economy. A. M. van der Woude demonstrated that the region of North Holland experienced a severe demographic and economic contraction between the 1670s and the 1740s.[25] J. A. Faber noted a somewhat milder contraction in the primarily agricultural economy of Friesland in the same period. In both areas the second half of the eighteenth century brought some respite, but only in Friesland was a marked recovery observable. These regional studies portray an economy of more discontinuous change than did Johan de Vries, and they regard as likely an absolute decline of the economy up to the mid–eighteenth century. But in a complex, urbanized economy, studies of several rural regions cannot alone reveal the overall trends.

I have claimed that the acceptance of Gregory King's estimate of Dutch national income for 1688–1695 cannot be justified. But, in order to get a clear picture of the present status of our knowledge, I now ask the reader to suspend disbelief for the moment and accept King's figures as roughly correct. They suggest a per capita income of 90–95 guilders. No reliable price deflator is available to express this amount in 1900 guilders, since no comprehensive Dutch price index has ever been constructed for the nineteenth century. Van Stuijvenberg and De Vrijer have put together a series that links the seventeenth- and eighteenth-century price history of N. W. Posthumus with twentieth-century data by splicing them to English and German wholesale price indices.[26] The open character of the nineteenth-century Dutch economy gives a certain justification for this expedient, but the fact remains that this spliced series is subject to substantial error, particularly in the calculation of long-term price trends. Compounding this problem is the fact that 1688–1695 was itself a period of rapidly increasing prices. The composite wholesale price series, indexed to 1900–1910 = 100, sets prices in 1685–1689 at 66 and in 1690–1694 at 85. It is indisputable that prices in 1688 were substantially below those of the Napoleonic era, and it is probable that the 1900–1909 level, while lower than a century earlier, had not descended to the level of the 1680s. In King's day 90–95 guilders certainly possessed greater purchasing power than it did in 1900; it may have been the equivalent of 105–115 guilders of the 1900–1910 period.

If we attach the King estimate of income *level* to the Johan de Vries assessment of income *trend,* the conclusion must be that Dutch per capita income at the end of the eighteenth century could not have stood far above *f* 100 (in 1900 guilders) but was certainly above the level set in Keuchenius's incomplete analysis.

IV. AN AWKWARD JOIN

A large gap yawns between the late-seventeenth-century estimate of Gregory King (105–115 guilders) and the several mid-nineteenth-century estimates

(215–250 guilders). One need not place a great deal of faith in the price adjustments to be led to the observation that per capita income appears roughly to have doubled. How is that gap to be bridged?

In fact, few scholars have addressed that problem; while many have expressed themselves about income trends in one period or another, they have rarely considered the implications of their views for later or earlier periods. It is obvious that the orthodox belief of the early modernists in eighteenth-century stagnation and that of the specialists in the nineteenth and twentieth centuries in stagnation before 1850 is not compatible with the available estimates of income level. What is not obvious is which element—the estimates of trend, level, or both—is most in need of revision.

Recently two scholars have ventured to trace a path linking the Dutch Golden Age to the twentieth century. One is Angus Maddison, an economist whose chief interests are in the industrial era; the other is James Riley, an historian of the early modern period.

Angus Maddison, a veteran analyst of national income data, addresses the question of Dutch growth in his study *Phases of Capitalist Development*.[27] He focuses on the successive leaders in productivity in order to develop an argument about gaps between performance and potential, or actual and best practice in the various capitalist economies. He proposes that an envelope curve of per capita output—ideally gross domestic product per man-hour—in the successive leaders in economic performance defines the long-run pace of technological progress in the global economy. In order to establish the contours of his envelope of growth rates from the seventeenth century onward, Maddison had to identify the leading economies in each period and construct for them time series of national income. He asserts that in the twentieth century the United States growth curve traced the uppermost national growth trajectory, having surpassed that of the United Kingdom around 1890. Britain, in turn, held the top honors for approximately a century, having surpassed the Dutch around 1780. The Dutch lead extends back into the seventeenth century, the starting point of Maddison's analysis.

Maddison, now a professor at the University of Groningen, inaugurates his study of long-term economic growth with an analysis of the Dutch Republic, regarding it to have been the first economy to advance beyond the economic constraints of an agrarian society on a national scale. This seventeenth century achievement endowed the Republic with productivity levels that he estimates as 50 percent above the level established by Gregory King for England in 1688. Maddison justifies this steep upward revision of King's implied ratio of Dutch to English incomes by observing that (1) upwards to two-thirds of the Dutch labor

---

Figure 1. Locus of Productivity Leadership, 1700–1979. Gross domestic product (GDP) per man-hour in 1970 U.S. dollars. [From Angus Maddison, *Phases of Capitalist Development* (Oxford: 1982), pp. 30–31.]

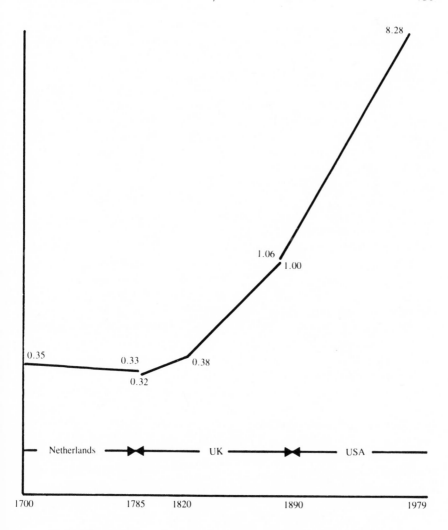

		Annual Average Compound Growth Rate of:	
Lead Country	Date	GDP per Man-Hour	Gross Fixed Nonresidential Capital Stock per Man-Hour
Netherlands	1700–1785	−0.07	N.A.
UK	1785–1820	0.5	0.0
UK	1820–1890	1.4	0.9
USA	1890–1979	2.3	2.4

force found employment outside of agriculture, where incomes are usually higher; (2) the high-income foreign trade and services sectors were equal in size to England's, and on a per capita basis much larger; (3) agriculture was highly specialized and presumably more productive; (4) the industrial structure was diversified and benefited from a low-cost energy source in the form of peat; and (5) the investment rate ran higher in the Republic than in England, and this must have provided for some measure of technical progress.[28]

Having set Dutch income 50 percent above the English level in 1700, Maddison proceeds by accepting Johan de Vries's assessment of the eighteenth century economy: national income remained about the same, but per capita gross domestic product, which excludes income from foreign investments, fell by about 10 percent between 1700 and 1760, remaining constant from then until 1820. After 1820 Maddison makes no direct estimates of Dutch growth. Since Dutch national income by then stood well within the envelope curve of the lead countries, he understandably turns his attention elsewhere. But an unavoidable consequence of connecting Maddison's eighteenth-century scenario to the available estimates for the late nineteenth century is an amazingly high rate of growth, one of the highest in all of Europe.[29] Much the same comment can be made about the GNP estimates for the Netherlands presented by Paul Bairoch.[30] Bairoch does not describe the basis for his Dutch estimates, which is all the more puzzling when one notes that they reflect a growth rate in the period 1820 to 1870 of 1.5 percent per annum, higher than any other European national economies except Switzerland and Belgium. Even Richard Griffiths, the most vigorous exponent of the nineteenth-century growth hypothesis, writes only of "surreptitious growth" and "some measure of economic growth."

James C. Riley suggests a very different growth path for the Dutch economy between the seventeenth and twentieth centuries. He is suspicious of the orthodox image of a lethargic, outmaneuvered eighteenth-century economy. His own work on the Amsterdam capital market showed a rapid growth of Dutch foreign investment in the second half of the century. In addition recent work on Dutch shipping suggests that the decline of Holland's entrepôt function found compensation in the rise of direct Dutch shipping services that bypassed the Republic's ports. On these twin pillars he bases his case for eighteenth-century growth.[31]

Riley, just as Maddison, starts with Gregory King, and just as Maddison he suspects that the gap between England and the Republic was greater than King allowed. Riley suggests a maximum figure for Dutch per capita income about 25 percent higher than King's figure for England. Riley then turns to the mid–nineteenth century, calling on Derksen rather than Teijl, and proposes that the apparent doubling of real income between 1688 and 1860 was chiefly an achievement of the eighteenth century. He agrees that stagnation ruled in the first half of the nineteenth century and suggests that undramatic but persistent growth characterized the eighteenth century, as continued commercial vitality and its multiplier effects plus the addition of a flourishing financial sector sustained employment, increased incomes from abroad, and secured lower prices for Dutch consumers.

Figure 2 brings together the various more or less explicit estimates and guesses embodied in the literature. No graceful way has yet been found to join the Golden Age to the Industrial Age.

V. AN AWKWARD COMPARISON

The estimates of Dutch national income made by Gregory King, Angus Maddison, and James Riley depend on their respective views about English national income. That is, their judgments about Dutch income are essentially statements about the relationship of Dutch to English national income. It follows that the level at which Dutch income is set in 1688 and later is not independent of our understanding of England's national income at the same time. Unavoidably, this

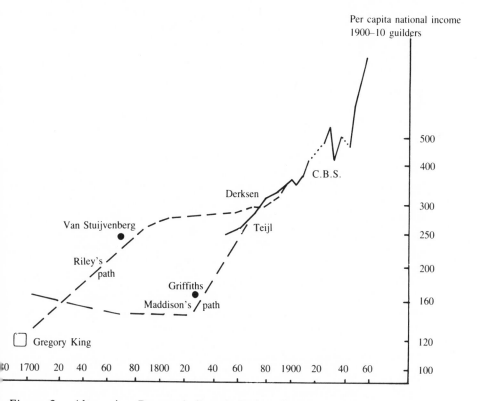

Figure 2. Alternative Proposed Growth Paths of Dutch National Income, 1688–1900.

investigation of the Dutch economy must turn its attention to the other side of the North Sea. What is now known about British national income in the eighteenth and nineteenth centuries, that is to say, during the Industrial Revolution?

The standard source on this subject is Phyllis Deane and W. A. Cole's *British Economic Growth 1688–1959.*[32] There the authors produced an index of real output for the eighteenth century comprising decennial estimates of activity in agriculture, export industries, domestic industries, government, and rents. They concluded that total output had grown 2.5-fold over the century, and on a per capita basis by 60 percent. Among the critics of this output series, Nicholas Crafts has argued cogently that they underestimated the growth of agricultural output in the first half of the eighteenth century.[33] The publication of the *Economic History of Britain Since 1700*, edited by Roderick Floud and Donald McCloskey, provided an opportunity for Cole to offer a revised total output series incorporating Crafts's suggestions.[34] Total output is now thought to have grown by 2.7-fold. But since new calculations of English population show more rapid growth in the early eighteenth century than Deane and Cole had originally assumed, the per capita output estimates remain essentially unchanged, although it is not clear that this was the intention of either Cole or Crafts.

Deane and Cole made no effort to cast their output index in monetary terms, but when the 1800 estimate is linked to their nineteenth-century national income series, the implied 1700 income is roughly consistent with Gregory King's 1688 estimates, which they discuss approvingly. Cole's revisions are also capable of incorporating King's vision of the English economy and Cole ventures to estimate total and per capita national product. Table 2 displays Cole's series and converts it into guilders at prevailing exchange rates.[35]

From the early nineteenth century onward the Deane and Cole estimates of national product of *Great Britain,* and from 1855 their series for the net national product of the *United Kingdom* (i.e., including Ireland), can serve our purposes, once they are expressed in 1900–1909 prices and converted to guilders at current exchange rates.[36] Cole's eighteenth-century estimates yield a 57 percent growth of *English* per capita real income. Deane and Cole's nineteenth-century estimates yield, for *Great Britain,* a 408 percent increase. The entire two-century period therefore experienced per capita income growth, in real terms, of 640 percent. When expressed in guilders the rise is just under sevenfold, reflecting a diminution in the exchange value of the guilder after the period of French domination ending in 1814.

On the basis of this evidence Dutch per capita national income in the first decade of the twentieth century stood at approximately 63 percent of Great Britain's (somewhat higher relative to U.K. national product). If we accept the accuracy of the twentieth-century relationship, then the issues involving Dutch growth and stagnation and their timing will be affected sensitively by what is thought to be true of the Dutch–English income ratios in the late seventeenth century, and this, in turn, will hinge on one's perceptions of the eighteenth-century English economy.

Table 2.   W. A. Cole's Estimates of
English Per Capita National Product in
1700 Pounds and Guilders

Year	In Pounds	In Guilders
1700	£9.45	ƒ103
1720	10.16	111
1740	10.80	118
1760	12.40	135
1780	12.20	133
1800	14.80	161

	In Current Pounds and Guilders	In 1700 Guilders	Source
1688	£7.91 ƒ84	ƒ98	Gregory King

Sources: W. A. Cole, "Factors in Demand, 1700–80,"
in Roderick Floud and Donald McCloskey, eds.,
The Economic History of Britain Since 1700,
Vol. 1 (Cambridge: 1981), p. 64; Gregory King,
"Natural and Physical Observations Upon the
State and Condition of England," in Peter Las-
lett (ed.), *The Earliest Classics . . .* (London:
1973).

If one accepts Gregory King's figures and holds to the view that Dutch income at the end of the eighteenth century was no higher than in 1688, then Dutch income circa 1800 would be no more than 67 percent of the British level. Since Dutch income in 1900–1909 stood in about the same relationship to British income, an implication of this view is that the nineteenth-century Dutch economy grew at the same overall rate as Britain's, or 1.4 percent per annum throughout the century. No student of the nineteenth-century Dutch economy has ever advanced such a view.

Implications of Deane and Cole, and King,
Regarding Eighteenth-Century Stagnation

	1700	1800	1900
Britain	100	157	698
Netherlands	107	107	440
Neth./Britain	107	67	63

If one accepts Maddison's position that Dutch per capita income was half again the English level in 1700 and declined by 10 percent thereafter, England surpasses the Dutch in 1780, as Maddison claimed. In 1800 Dutch income is at 81 percent of the British level. This assumption, too, requires very rapid nineteenth-century growth. The major problem here is to find a period after 1800 when Dutch per capita income could have grown 3.6-fold. Accordingly to Teijl the second half of the nineteenth century booked only a 43 percent increase. That is, in the period when industrial growth and structural change began to take hold, Dutch growth was less than half that of Britain. If one follows Griffiths in rejecting Teijl's estimates as too low, and assumes 1.0 percent per annum growth from 1830 to 1900, a gap still looms in the period 1800–1830 requiring a rate of growth exceeding Britain's in those years, and far exceeding later Dutch growth.

Implications of Deane and Cole, and Maddison, Regarding the Eighteenth-Century Decline and 1% Per Annum Growth after 1830

	1700	1780	1800	1830	1900
Britain	100	130	157	254	698
Netherlands	150	135	135	220	440
Neth./Britain	150	104	86	87	63

If we now turn our attention to the nineteenth century, the comparison of Dutch and English data uncovers several different but equally unlikely growth scenarios.

Teijl's back projections imply that British per capita income exceeded the Dutch level only after 1860—after a century of vigorous growth that is witness to the Industrial Revolution. A comparison with U.K. income, would push the crossing point forward even further. Could it be that Britain's time at Maddison's productivity frontier (Figure 1) lasted only 25 years, years that provoked so much wringing of British hands about industrial retardation?

An equally iconoclastic conclusion must be drawn if one embraces the orthodox position that the Dutch economy achieved no, or next to no, per capita growth in the 70 or 80 years before 1850. Van Stuijvenberg's analysis requires us to believe that Dutch per capita income in the 1770s stood at two and a half times the English level.

Finally, we must consider Riley's argument that eighteenth-century growth bridged the gap between the Golden Age and the mid–nineteenth century. By his own estimate of the size of the gap (he uses Derksen's nineteenth-century estimates, inflates King's 1695 Dutch income figure by some 25 percent, and believes there was little growth after 1800) real per capita income needed to grow at 0.6 to 0.8 percent per annum from 1695 to 1800.[37] Teijl and the official twentieth-century national income series yield no more than 0.7 percent per annum for the period 1850–1939, and the highest estimates of English growth in the eighteenth century yield no more than 0.5 percent overall. It is difficult to accept that such an impressive "preindustrial" growth rate could have been sustained for over a century without anyone noticing.

My purpose here can be compared to clearing out the attic of an elderly and absent-minded relative. Many of the accumulated possessions obviously should have been disposed of years ago. Others reputed to be valuable heirlooms are found to be as worthless as the rest. In such a situation it is desirable, albeit painful, to be candid about just how little of value there is. It is best to face one's tasks without illusion. Gregory King's estimates of Dutch income are without merit; Teijl's back projections rest on dubious interpretations and data, while his results are difficult to explain. The assumptions made by most economic historians about Dutch income trends are mutually incompatible and at certain points implausible in the extreme.

We now see more clearly what could not have happened; there remains the task of establishing what did. In the course of dusting off and scrutinizing the artifacts in the attic of Dutch economic history I came more and more to feel that the greatest obstacle to achieving a better appreciation of their true value was, ironically enough, one of the treasured relics in a neighbor's attic: the long-reigning interpretation of the English Industrial Revolution as a momentous discontinuity bringing about rapid economic growth in a brief period of time. No plausible account of the Dutch economy's history can be made to rhyme with that interpretation.

I came to the (perverse) conclusion that English quantitative economic history would have to be changed in the interest of achieving a better understanding of the Dutch experience. No sooner had this heretical thought asserted itself than there appeared within one year, in a remarkable example of intellectual convergence, three articles produced by four economic historians working in three countries, all arguing variously and vigorously that the English economy grew much less rapidly in the eighteenth century than has hitherto been believed. Directly or by implication they all regard England before the Industrial Revolu- .tion to have been more industrial and enjoying a larger income than the literature reviewed above could admit to.

Peter Lindert and Jeffrey Williamson, reexamining the work of the political arithmeticians Gregory King, Joseph Massie, and Patrick Colquhoun (who all estimate flows of income rather than Deane and Cole's volumes of output), came to the conclusion that King underestimated English national income by 25 percent, that Massie did so by 16 percent, and that Colquhoun's totals were approximately correct.[38] The result, obviously, is to reduce greatly the estimated rates of eighteenth-century income growth.

By their calculations the adjustments to Deane and Cole's series must come almost entirely in the period before 1760. By inflating King's figures by 25

Table 3. Revisionist Estimates of English Rates of National Income Growth, 1700–1841

A. *Average annual rates of growth:*

Lindert and Williamson	*1700–1760* .39		*1760–1800* 1.01	
Harley	*1700–1770* .56		*1770–1815* 1.31	*1815–1841* 2.23
Crafts (1982)	*1700–1760* .66	*1760–1780* .83	*1780–1801* 1.27	*1801–1831* 1.93
Dean and Cole	.66	.65	2.06	2.86
Cole (revision)	.84	.65	2.06	

B. *Average annual rates of per capita growth:*

Lindert and Williamson	*1700–1760* .19		*1760–1800* .14	
Harley	*1700–1770* .27		*1770–1815* .33	*1815–1841* .86
Crafts (1982)	*1700–1760* .28	*1760–1780* .14	*1780–1801* .30	*1801–1831* .48
Dean and Cole	.45	−.04	1.08	1.41
Cole (revision)	.46	−.09	1.00	

C. *Chronology of per capita income growth (1688–1700 = 100):*

Year	Lindert and Williamson	Harley	Crafts	Deane and Cole
1688	100			
1700		100	100	100
1760	115		118	130
1770		119		122
1780			122	129
1800	122		130	160
1815		140		
1831			150	237
1841		175		265

Sources: Peter H. Lindert and Jeffrey G. Williamson, "Revising England's Social Tables, 1688–1867," *Explorations in Economic History* 19 (1982) 385–408; C. Knick Harley, "British Industrialization before 1841: Evidence of Slower Growth During the Industrial Revolution," *Journal of Economic History* 42 (1982): 267–90; N. F. R. Crafts, "British Economic Growth, 1700–1831," *Economic History Review* 36 (1983) 177–99; Phyllis Deane and W. A. Cole, *British Economic Growth, 1688–1959* (Cambridge: 1967).

percent, Lindert and Williamson set the rate of growth in 1688–1760 at 0.39 percent per annum, whereas Deane and Cole had it 0.64 percent. Per capita growth Lindert and Williamson estimate at under 0.2 percent per annum while Deane, Cole, and Crafts (1981) all put it at more than double that level.

C. Knick Harley set about recomputing industrial output indices as well as consumption estimates. He concluded that "the growth of industrial production was much slower between 1770 and 1815 than either most narrative accounts of the industrial revolution or the quantitative research of Walter Hoffman and of Phyllis Deane and W. A. Cole have suggested."[39] His computation of English national income reveals a per annum growth rate of 0.56 percent from 1700 to 1770 and 2.23 percent from 1815 to 1841. Both of these are within striking distance of the Deane and Cole estimates. He departs from this orthodoxy, however, in the classic period of English industrialization, 1770–1815. Here he sets per annum growth at 1.31 percent, little more than half the rate advanced by Deane and Cole. In Harley's words: "The indices imply that the industrial sector in the eighteenth century was nearly twice as large as previous estimates indicated."[40]

Finally, Nicholas Crafts reviewed afresh the evidence of British economic growth. While his earlier critique of Deane and Cole (discussed above) had the effect of increasing their estimates of early-eighteenth-century growth, his most recent utterances have the opposite effect, particularly on the estimates for the post–1760 period.[41] Table 3 displays a summary of the estimates put forward by these exponents of the "slow-growth" school.

It is apparent that the three revisionist works are not of one mind on certain critical issues, but they share the position, of importance for present purposes, that the English economy before 1760 was more industrial and generated a higher national income than has hitherto been accepted. Instead of an economy with a per capita income level in 1700 that was less than 40 percent of the 1840 level (as Deane and Cole had it), we must now consider the well-supported view that England's 1700 per capita income stood at nearly 60 percent of the 1840 level.

VI. A NEW ASSESSMENT

This hydra-headed reassessment of the quantitative dimensions of the English economy opens the way to the construction of a plausible account of the long eighteenth- and nineteenth-century readjustment process of the already "modern" Dutch economy. Figure 3 presents a sketch of my hypotheses concerning the trends and levels of Dutch national income, comparing this to Harley's reassessment of pre-1840 English growth. I will argue that (1) the Dutch economy declined absolutely during the period 1675–1813, with most, if not all, of the decline occurring before 1750; (2) from 1813 to 1850 the economy recovered

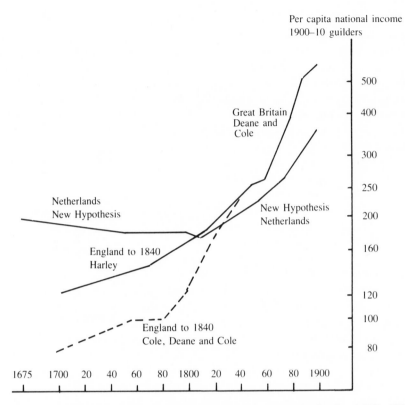

Figure 3. Proposed Growth Paths, Britain and the Netherlands, 1675–1900.

from severe depression in the Napoleonic period, but could not have grown rapidly; and (3) per capita income in the third quarter of the seventeenth century stood at double the level identified by Gregory King—a revision that is based in roughly equal parts on a revision of England's income in 1700 and an argument that the Republic's income could have exceeded England's by two-thirds. The reader must not expect a comprehensive set of Dutch national income estimates; the foundations for such an enterprise simply have not yet been built. What one can expect is a marshaling of evidence, some new, to assess the plausibility of the hypotheses.

A. Trends

One approach to the question of Dutch economic trends is to survey the economy sector by sector, industry by industry, noting the fortunes of each. This is not the place to review the available evidence; several works do an adequate job of that.[42]

Industry and regional studies have established beyond a reasonable doubt that commodity production declined in the course of the eighteenth century, as such major industries as Leiden woolen textiles, Haarlem linen bleaching, Gouda and Delft ceramics, and Zaandam shipbuilding fell into irremediable decay, while sailmaking, fishing, and the activities of industrial windmills declined substantially. Certain industries resisted these trends—papermaking, tobacco processing, and gin distilling are perhaps the most important—and many smaller crafts may have shown greater stability than the export industries mentioned here, but the basic direction of change is clear.[43]

Eighteenth-century commentators often wrote of the flood of imports in the Republic.[44] Indeed, Keuchenius, in his incomplete assessment of Dutch national income circa 1800, set final imports at 36 percent of national income and estimated that the value of imported manufactures exceeded that of exported manufactures by a factor of nine.[45]

At present the course of agricultural output can only be inferred from evidence about the timing of investment, land abandonment, volumes of marketed dairy products, and incidental information. In the western half of the Republic it seems probable that output declined substantially between the 1660s and 1740s. The growing pressure of taxation forced land abandonment; reclamation activities sank to zero; the epizootics of 1713–1719 and 1744–1765 severely depressed dairy output, and the pressure of costs encouraged more land-extensive production techniques. Certain compensatory activities in the eastern provinces, particularly tobacco production, relieve this litany of gloom.[46] In the second half of the eighteenth century the evidence all points to expansion, a trend that is not broken by the political disturbances of the Napoleonic era and that continues into the nineteenth century.[47]

Commercial, banking, and shipping services form the most debated sector of the eighteenth-century economy. There is no doubt that these activities suffered severely during the Napoleonic period, never again to enjoy their earlier importance. But the course of affairs before 1795 is not at all clear. The financial role of Amsterdam grew throughout the second half of the eighteenth century, although it too suffered greatly during the Napoleonic period.[48] It is arguable that Amsterdam's commercial activities did not decline until 1780 (although the emphasis shifted from commodity trade to financial services), but it is difficult to be as charitable about the numerous lesser ports of the Republic. There are many indicators that eighteenth-century Amsterdam attracted to itself the remnants of a previously more broadly distributed commercial life.

Our perceptions about the various sectors of economic life, even if they were unerring, cannot form the basis of national income estimates when the relative size of these sectors is unknown and changing. With so many imponderables standing in the way of direct estimation of national income, it seems advisable to turn our attention to less direct but aggregative economic indicators.

One such indicator is the time series of intercity passenger travel by barge on the canal network connecting almost all the major cities of the Republic's maritime provinces. From the mid–seventeenth century until the mid–nineteenth century, when railways replaced the barge services, hundreds of thousands of passengers per year made use of this backbone of the Republic's transportation system. The long-term pattern of demand for these services is displayed in Figure 4. In *Barges and Capitalism* I sought to identify the variables that most affected the demand for intercity passenger transportation and to measure their impact.[49] A reduction of per capita urban incomes emerged as the most important variable, although in the absence of reliable knowledge of the income elasticity of demand for passenger transportation no firm estimate of the decline in income could be made. This decline was concentrated in the period 1675–1745. Thereafter the demand for passenger travel revived slightly, suggesting that in the second half of the eighteenth century Dutch cities did not experience further income decline.

This indicator of the direction of change illuminates only the urban sector of the Republic's maritime provinces, and must certainly be used with caution. Layer upon layer of assumption and inference envelop the model that yielded these insights, and it would certainly be comforting to be able to reinforce these findings with independent evidence.

In the modern economy economic growth is generally associated with changes in structure that find their reflection in urbanization and a reduction of the relative importance of agriculture. It has also been associated strongly with population growth.[50] From this perspective the case for substantial economic growth in the Netherlands during the two centuries after 1675 must appear weak indeed. Table 4 summarizes our present understanding of Dutch population growth and urbanization.[51] By preindustrial standards the total population grew rapidly from about 1520 until the mid–seventeenth century, and the cities absorbed most of the increase. The rural sector grew at only half of the total rate, while cities grew dramatically, accounting for over 40 percent of the total population by 1675. From then until the first decade of the nineteenth century overall population growth was all but imperceptible. After 1750, as the rate of population growth rose throughout Europe. he Dutch population remained all but stationary, such growth as there was being located primarily in the poorest, most rural regions.

Nineteenth-century population growth was substantial, but the 1800 level of urbanization was not exceeded until after 1870, implying that the rural sector had to accommodate ever larger numbers at just the time that industrial mechanization, chiefly beyond the Dutch borders, reduced rural nonagricultural employment possibilities.

In 1849 the first occupational census showed 44 percent of the male labor force to be engaged in agriculture.[52] It is possible to doubt that agriculture

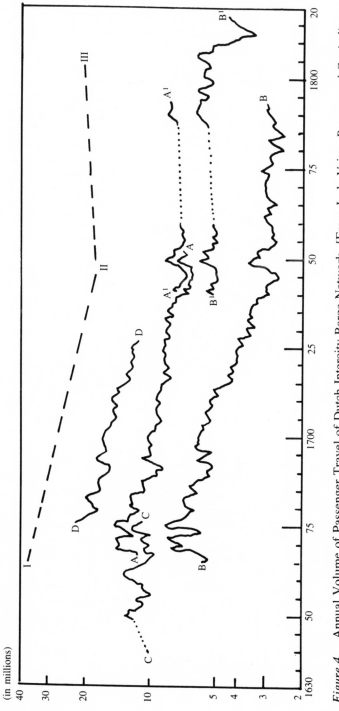

Figure 4. Annual Volume of Passenger Travel of Dutch Intercity Barge Network. [From J. de Vries, *Barges and Capitalism.* (Utrecht: 1981).] p. 223. A, B, C, and D refer to various combinations of routes; I, II, and III represent estimates of the total volume of traffic on the entire network.

171

Table 4. Dutch Population and Urbanization, 1500–1900 (in thousands)

Year	Total Population	Population of Holland	Rural Population	Percentage Urban Population		
				>2500	>10,000	>20,000
1500	900–1000					
1525		275[a]	800	27	15	5.5
1550	1200–1300				15	
1600	1400–1600	672[b]			24	
1650	1850–1900				32	
1675		883	1085	42		24.5
1700	1850–1950				34	
1750	1900–1950	783	1150	39	30	21.8
1800	2100	783	1300	37	29	20.8
1815	2202	764		35	26	17.5
1830	2613	894		39	26	
1840	2860	969		39	28	21.3
1850	3049	1039	1830	39	29	
1860	3309	1143				24.7
1870	3580	1266	2140			28.9
1880	4013	1484				30.5
1900	5104	2113				35.6

[a]In 1514.
[b]In 1622.
Sources: A. M. van der Woude, "Demografische ontwikkeling van de Noordelijke Nederlanden, 1500–1800," in *Algemene Geschiedenis der Nederlanden,* Vol. 5, pp. 102–168; E. W. Hofstee, *De demografische ontwikkeling van Nederland in de eerste helft van de negentiende eeuw,* Table IA; M. C. Deurloo and G. A. Hoekveld, "The Population Growth of the Urban Municipalities in the Netherlands Between 1849 and 1970," in H. Schmal (ed.), *Patterns of European Urbanisation since 1500,* pp. 247–283.

absorbed so large a percentage of the labor force in the third quarter of the seventeenth century. This is so in part because of the intervening minor deurbanization, in part because post–1675 population growth was concentrated in the more agrarian eastern provinces, and in part because seventeenth- and eighteenth-century regional occupational censuses and estimates show the agricultural population to have been proportionally smaller than in the nineteenth century. Agriculture may well have occupied under 40 percent of the mid–seventeenth-century labor force.[53]

Given the evidence calling attention to the relative prosperity of the agricultural sector in the century after 1750, such an occupational shift should not be altogether unexpected. Moreover, the gap typically observed between urban and rural incomes was undoubtedly relatively small, certainly in the maritime provinces. The mid–ninteenth-century level of urbanization, even after 150 years of stagnation, was still high by European standards. These features help explain why Dutch income *levels* may have been high even after a long stagnation, but they are difficult to reconcile with an argument for rapid *growth* of incomes.

The final approach to be considered here is to examine a principal component of national income, payments to labor. In most preindustrial economies true wage earners were rather uncommon and the wage bill could not have formed a large part of national income. In the Dutch Republic, where the urban population approached 40 percent of the total and agriculture in many regions was commercialized, wage and salaried labor could easily have approached half the adult labor force.[54] What can now be said about the course of wages and salaries and their purchasing power after the mid–seventeenth century?

The most abundant data refer to craftsmen and laborers in the building trades and related outdoor employments such as road, canal, and dike maintenance. A valuable source of wage data is the archives of the regional drainage authority of Rijnland (serving central Holland), which employed numerous carpenters, masons, and common laborers in the maintenance of sluices and dikes at several rural locations.[55] At Spaarndam, a village near Haarlem, the daily pay of such workers reached a plateau in the 1640s of 16 stuivers (st.) for common labor, 24 st. for craftsmen, and 28 st. for master craftsmen. In 1679 each of these wage rates rose by 2 st. per day to compensate the workers for the discontinuation of the beer ration. The wages of common labor fell back by 2 st. in 1739. Otherwise only temporary adjustments interrupted the maintenance of this wage scale until after 1860.

This constancy is typical of the wages of craftsmen and common laborers throughout the Netherlands. Small adjustments were sometimes made, but these did not form a consistent pattern. Table 5 presents a summary of the unweighted mean daily wage paid to common labor and craftsmen in the places for which I have assembled data. The number of observations per entry varies from 7 to 14.

Few sources stand ready to illuminate the course of wages in the industrial sector, or, indeed, in nongovernmental employment generally. However, one might hope that the industrial enterprises of government agencies would pay wages that bear some relation to those paid by their private counterparts. The ropeworks and ship wharves of the Admiralties employed large numbers of workers, and the records of their wages and salary payments are available from the eighteenth century onward. The ropeworks of the Amsterdam Admiralty employed scores of spinners and ropemakers whose standard daily pay stood at 16 st. in the summer and 14 st. in the winter from 1719, when the sources begin, to 1795.[56] In the following year (the first of the Batavian Republic) the wages rose by 25 percent to 20 st., at which level they remained until 1870; then the nominal wages were raised at frequent intervals, reaching a new plateau of 32 st. (double the eighteenth-century level) by 1887.

The naval shipyards of Amsterdam and its counterpart at Rotterdam employed many hundreds of workmen.[57] Besides numerous shipwrights and unskilled

Table 5. Unweighted Mean Daily Summer Wages Paid
to Common Labor and Skilled Labor in the Building Trades
in the Western and Eastern Netherlands, 1550–1854,
in Current Stuivers (20st = 1 guilder)

| | Common Labor | | Skilled Labor | |
Period	Western	Eastern	Western	Eastern
1550–1558	4.5	3.0	6.5	5.0
1583–1592	9.0	6.9	11.5	10.5
1650–1679	18.7	13.6	25.1	18.6
1745–1754	18.1	13.6	25.2	18.9
1790–1799	17.9	13.1	24.8	19.5
1820–1829	17.8	—	25.2	—
1840–1854	18.0	—	26.2	18.0

Source: Dutch labor market study, in progress.

laborers, the Admiralty payrolls recorded the pay of a wide variety of building crafts. Here we will content ourselves with averages of annual earnings (assuming full employment) of all skilled and unskilled employees. The eighteenth-century pay scales were established well before 1700, but the initiation date is not known. From then until after 1847 nominal wages held constant for skilled workers and rose slightly after 1815 for unskilled workers. From 1847 to 1902 they all rose by two-thirds. This post–1850 experience is consistent with a survey of wages in the building trades which found the 1900–1910 level of nominal pay to exceed that of 1869–1873 by two-thirds (see Table 6).

The final series to be introduced concerns salaried employees. Assembling data on salaried members of the labor force is a daunting task, since the number of separate occupations was enormous and salary variations among individuals within an occupation was common. All that is attempted here is an overall salary index that represents the unweighted index of 9 separate series, each for a group of differently salaried individuals ranging in number from 7 to 27. The index is composed of the salaries of city officials, teachers, pastors, orphanage employees, and rural windmill operators. It differs from the wage indices in that the salaries crept upward throughout the late seventeenth and eighteenth centuries. By the beginning of the nineteenth century the composite index stood 32.6 percent higher than in the mid–seventeenth century (see Table 7).

For the purpose at hand it is not sufficient to establish the course of nominal wages; annual earnings are, of course, what one needs to estimate the size of the wage bill in national income. In the case of salary earners we can risk making the convenient assumption that annual salaries equal annual earnings; analogous assumptions cannot be made with regard to wage earners. Fortunately, the detailed wage records of the drainage authority and the Amsterdam ropeworks,

Table 6. Nominal Pay of Workers at the Admiralty Shipyards
of Amsterdam and Rotterdam
(in current guilders; pay is expressed as annual earnings at full employment)

Period	Average for Skilled Workers	Index	Average for Unskilled Workers	Index
Before 1695 to after 1780	ƒ391.44	100	ƒ238.42	100
1815	377.66	96	248.64	104
1847	401.52	103	297.64	125
1902	660.15	169	498.05	209

Source: Dutch labor market study, in progress.

make possible the specification of how, in these two cases, nominal wages were related to annual earnings.

At the sluices at Spaarndam the permanently employed craftsmen and laborers worked 260 to 270 days per year throughout the eighteenth century until 1784. Then the drainage authority made the first of a series of adjustments that had the effect of transforming a day of work from a real to a notional "day." By 1798 workers were being paid for at least 325 "days" per year, even though they did not physically labor more than before. The long summer days then counted for more than one day for pay purposes. In short, the wage rate had risen by 22 percent in a series of steps between 1784 and 1798.

The Amsterdam ropeworks introduced a similar but smaller hidden wage increase in 1774. The observed wage increase of 1796 abolished the fictive days, with the effect that full-employment earnings remained constant. But after 1816 piece rates were introduced for certain activities that had the effect of raising total earnings once again. The next wage increase in 1872 was, just as the last one in 1796, coupled with cancellation of the piecework practices, negating much of the effect of the increase.

Two organizations do not form a sufficient basis for generalization about labor compensation practices in the Netherlands, but these findings should certainly warn us that the stated daily wages may understate actual pay and that the timing of effective nominal wage increases could differ substantially from the apparent pattern.

We have seen that the pattern of maximum annual earnings of ropeworks employees differed significantly from the stated daily wages. The actual earnings—taking unemployment into account—alters the picture once again. The early-eighteenth-century work force typically labored 250–270 days, and in the 1740s and 1750s regular employees worked even less, often under 200 days per year. After 1770 the real days of employment rose sharply, and in the first half of the nineteenth century most workers logged upward of 300 days per year. The relative importance of changes in the demand for labor and changes in the supply

Table 7. Trends in Salary Earnings, 1582–1894

Year	Middelburg, Seven Occupations, Municipal Government	Middelburg, Teachers at Latin School	Goes, Ten Occupations, Municipal Government	Amsterdam, Eight Employees, Burger's Orphanage	Amsterdam, All Teachers in Municipal Schools	Amsterdam, Rectors and Correctors of Municipal Schools	Utrecht, Six Employees, Burger's Orphanage	Amsterdam, Reformed Clergymen	Smaller Cities of the Netherlands, Reformed Clergymen	Rural Areas and Western Provinces, Reformed Clergymen	Central Holland, Seven Windmill Operators for Hoogheemraadschap van Rijnland	Unweighted Average of All Series
1582		25							39	36	41[b]	
1584		38										
1600		52			40	32						
1605		60									72	
1620		60	59		59							
1630		75		58	65	38		75				
1650	94		85	81	73	53	105				106	86
1664					77		94	91			107	
1680		86		103			83				98	96
1700	105	100	86			94	96	91			99	
1720–1744	100	100	100	100	100	100	100	100	100	100	100	100
1750	100	100		105	100	111	100				101	
1778		111									120	
1790	132	118	103	103	100		108	100			126	114
1815					120[a]	121[a]					134	
1849			128	220					208	218		
1894								124				

[a] 1800.
[b] 1590.

Source: Dutch labor market study, in progress.

cannot now be determined. For whatever reason, the ropeworks employees experienced large swings in their actual annual earnings, which often rose most in periods when the purchasing power of wages was under pressure.

This brings us to the final step in the analysis of the earnings of Dutch labor, the calculating of purchasing power. N. W. Posthumus laid the foundation for the study of Dutch prices in two great studies: a two-volume compendium of prices and a three-volume history of the Leiden textile industry that included a wealth of price data and a consumer price index. That index and the several wholesale and other commodity price indices in his price series span the seventeenth and eighteenth centuries. They either end in 1800 or peter out in the course of the first half of the nineteenth century. We have already noted that no broadly based price index exists for the nineteenth century. The single effort to link Posthumus's work with the twentieth century series relied on German and British wholesale price series.[58]

The various series display substantial differences during the periods of rapid price increases in the 1690s, 1860s, and, most seriously, during the French Revolution and Napoleonic Wars.

On the basis of Posthumus's compilations, I have constructed a cost-of-living index based on a basket of goods designed after the manner of the Phelps-Brown and Hopkins index of consumables prices.[59] Unfortunately, the full index ends in 1800, after which date industrial prices become scarce. After 1800 the foodstuffs portion of the index continues to 1850, when it too must end. A separate index of food and drink prices constructed by J. A. de Jonge is available for the period 1852–1911.[60] Regrettably, it cannot yet objectively be linked to the earlier series.

Figures 5, 6a,b, and 7 present the real wage and real earnings trends for the wage data introduced above, adjusted by the new cost-of-living index and, after 1850, the index of food and beverage prices prepared by De Jonge. Given the constancy of nominal wages, the real wage is a faithful mirror of price trends, peaking in the 1680s and again in the 1720–1740 period, when prices are low, and plunging during the high price periods associated with the Napoleonic Wars, the First and Second Anglo–Dutch Wars and the "hungry forties" of the nineteenth century. When the surreptitious wage increases described above are taken into account in Figures 5 and 6, the late-eighteenth-century earnings crisis is somewhat moderated. If the consumer price index were to be adjusted after 1780 so that potatoes substituted for half the previous level of rye bread consumption, the crisis would be further moderated, particularly in the worst years.[61] Finally, when actual real annual earnings are plotted, which can be done only for the employees of the Amsterdam ropeworks, a pattern arises that deviates markedly from the real wage trend.

The basic trends in the real wage can be summarized as follows:

1. Real wages rose erratically from the mid–sixteenth century to the 1680s,

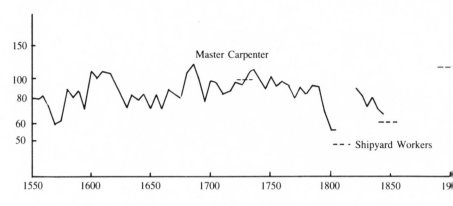

Real wages = daily wages (summer)/cost of living index.
Real earnings = daily wages adjusted for changes in the definition of the work day/cost of liv
   index.
Real earnings* = same as ''real earnings, except the cost of living index is altered by substitut
   potatoes for a portion of the rye in the basket of consumables.

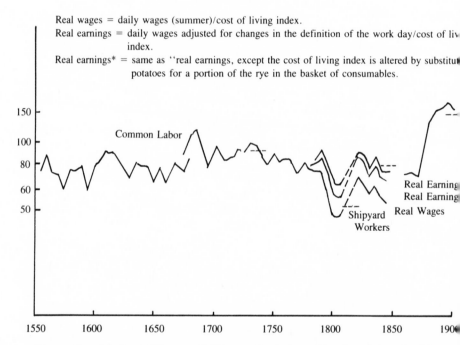

Figure 5. (a) Real Wages of Master Carpenters Employed by the Hoogheemraadschap van Rijnland at Spaarndam, 1550–1849. Real wages of all skilled workmen employed at the Amsterdam shipwharves of the Dutch Navy, 1720–
1902 (1720–1744 = 100). (b) Real Wages of Common Laborers Employed by
the Hoogheemraadschap van Rijnland at Spaarndam and Katwijk, 1550–1900.
Real annual earnings of all unskilled workmen employed at the Amsterdam
shipwharves of the Dutch Navy, 1720–1902 (1720–1744 = 100).

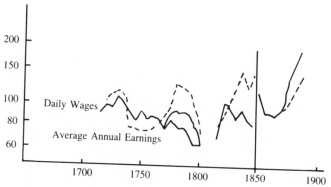

Figure 6. Real Wages and Earnings of Laborers at the Ropeworks of the Amsterdam Admiralty, 1715–1890 (1720–1744 = 100; 1850–1859 = 100).

the rise being interrupted most notably by the many years of high prices during the wars of the 1650s and 1660s. The wage increases dominated the pattern to the 1640s; thereafter price changes generated the changes.

2. From the real wage peaks extending from the 1680s through the 1730s, a new trend of declining real wages set in that reached its nadir shortly after 1800. Price changes dominated this trend, but from the 1770s onward various stratagems to increase earnings reduced the erosion of purchasing power for at least some workers.

3. The recovery of real wages after the Napoleonic era was only partial and was determined by price changes. Only after the 1860s does a combination of rising wages and falling prices push up the real wage to unprecedented levels. This breakthrough was concentrated in the 1870s and 1880s.

The attentive reader will have noted that real wages stand at their highest levels in precisely the period, 1680–1740, for which I hypothesize declining national income. What is more, they tend inexorably downward in the second half of the eighteenth century, when I suspect that the decline of national income had already run most of its course.

The contemplation of the ironic character of these trends in real wages, and similar trends at other times and places, has more than once led historians into debates where one scholar's depression is another's Golden Age.[62] Indeed, the apparent contradictions of these and similar findings are at the root of the skepticism expressed by "Annales school" historians concerning the concept of national income when applied to the preindustrial economy.[63]

A proper understanding of these real wage trends require that we address the causes of the price movements that play the dominant role in driving real wages between 1640 and 1870. When prices fall as a response to growth in the volume

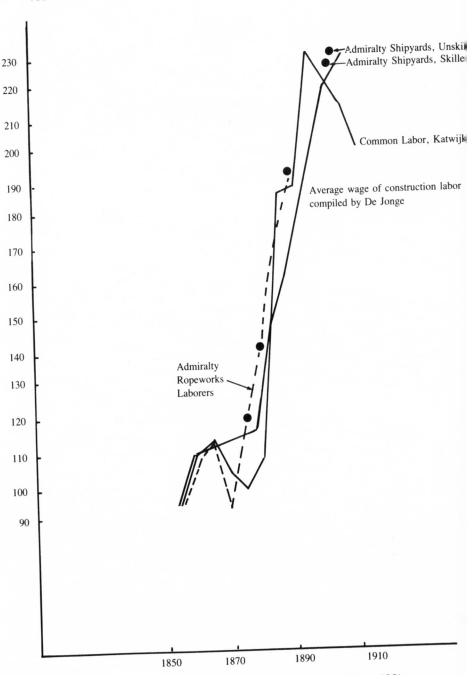

Figure 7. Real wages, 1850–1910 (1852–1861 = 100).

of output or because of cost-reducing investment or both, there is reason to expect rising real wages will be associated with rising per capita national income. The argument that the decline in grain prices in early-eighteenth-century England was paired with the diffusion of the "new husbandry," reducing the costs of production as it increased output per acre, would be consistent with this view.[64] When a fall in prices is not associated with output growth and cost-reducing investment, it takes the form of an exogenous shock to the economy. In the absence of adjustments in nominal wages, such exogenous price changes have the effect of redistributing income, in this case from capital and rents to the wage bill. The high real wage is compensated for in depressed land values and low returns to capital and, eventually, unemployment.

This scenario seems consistent with what is known about the Dutch economy from 1680 to 1740. In these decades commodity production declined as capital was withdrawn particularly from labor-intensive industries. Agriculture, too, was depressed, as high costs pressed on the farmers, forcing the abandonment of land, the adoption of less labor-intensive production techniques, and bringing about the collapse of rental values.

In the following period of falling real wages, exogenous factors again dominated the movement of prices, shifting income away from labor. The population growth that might have pressed down on agricultural productivity in most preindustrial societies was largely absent in the Netherlands at this time. The increased number of real days of work and the effective increases in nominal wages observed at the ropeworks in Amsterdam and at the workplaces of the Rijnland drainage authority are consistent with one's expectations in a situation where the real cost of labor of constant productivity was falling.

What still needs explanation, of course, is the labor market structure that held nominal wages all but fixed through these long swings in price level. For present purposes it is enough to observe its probable effect: labor's share of national income rose to a high level during the period 1680–1740, undermining the demand for labor in the agricultural and industrial sectors. Thereafter labor's share declined, reviving the possibilities for agricultural prosperity and investment, but the latter came to be directed almost entirely abroad, limiting the extent to which the domestic demand for labor could rise. Only after 1870 is there a growth of real income that seems to have sources in domestic productivity improvements and increased production.

B. Levels

The third hypothesis of this study concerns the *level* of Dutch national income. Indeed, it was present by implication in the preceding discussion of the relationship of real wage trends to national income.

In the absence of sufficient data for direct estimation of national income, I will

focus attention here on the level of Dutch wages in relation to neighboring
economies. Table 8 represents crude estimates of the nominal wage for skilled
and unskilled labor in the building trades. The wages are unweighted averages
drawn from such time series as I have found for Germany, the Southern
Netherlands, and England. The English wages for 1583–1592 are based exclusively on the Phelps-Brown and Hopkins series for southern England; all the
others are based on at least four independent series. The wages are expressed in
Dutch currency, the basis for conversion being current exchange rates in all years
except the 1580s, when the intrinsic silver content of the currencies was relied
upon. One might think of the resulting wage estimates as expressing the relative
cost of labor to a prospective employer producing for an international market.

Table 8. Unweighted Mean Daily Summer Wage
Paid to Labor in the Building Trades in Four Countries,
Expressed in Current Stuivers

Place	1582–1592	1650–1679	1745–1754	1790–1799
Unskilled Labor·				
Holland	9.0	18.7	18.3	17.9
E. Netherlands	6.9	13.6	13.6	13.1
Belgium	9.5	13.8	12.0	11.9
Germany	5.3	9.0	7.9	7.6
England	6.0	12.1	14.2	19.9
Journeymen				
Holland	11.5	25.1	25.2	24.8
E. Netherlands	10.5	18.6	18.9	19.5
Belgium	16.1	25.0	22.5	22.3
Germany	7.5	15.0	12.0	11.4
England	9.0	18.7	20.4	27.9
Wage Rate Index				
(100 = highest average wage in each time period)				
W. Netherlands	95	100	100	90
E. Netherlands	73	73	74	66
Belgium	100	74	66	60
Germany	56	48	43	38
England	63	65	78	100
Journeymen				
W. Netherlands	71	100	100	89
E. Netherlands	65	74	75	70
Belgium	100	99	89	80
Germany	47	60	48	41
England	56	75	81	100

Source: Dutch labor market study, in progress.

The estimates must not be pressed very far, but they are probably sufficiently accurate to permit the observation that wages in the maritime provinces of the Netherlands surpassed the Belgian level after 1600 and reigned as the highest in northern Europe until the end of the eighteenth century, when English wages assume that position.

Since the comparison with England has functioned as an orientation point in this study of Dutch national income, we should now look more closely at the course of wages in the two countries. Figure 8 shows the course of real wages in England and the Netherlands. It includes a 25-year moving average of southern English craftsmen's real wages as calculated by Phelps-Brown and Hopkins and adjusted by Wrigley and Schofield,[65] a 25-year moving average of real wages of common labor at Spaarndam, and the more broadly based Dutch real wage levels at selected intervals. Since each national series is expressed in its own currency and adjusted by its own cost of living index, comparisons of the level (as opposed to the trends) of the purchasing power of English and Dutch laborers cannot avoid a degree of arbitrariness. But two facts can help reduce the likelihood of misinterpretation. First, the silver values of wages were roughly equal in the first half of the sixteenth century and again, more briefly, around 1800. Second, the close economic relations of the two countries enforced a high degree of correlation in their commodity prices.

These considerations have emboldened me to join the English and Dutch series as shown in the figure. It must be emphasized that their position on the graph is purely a matter of judgment. While this exercise is not without its dangers, it has the redeeming academic virtue of calling attention to the important differences in the histories of Dutch and English real wages.

The central feature of the graph is the dramatic divergence between Dutch and English wages between 1580 and 1620. English real wages fall by half while Dutch wages rise. England was not alone in suffering falling real wages in this period; students of the sixteenth-century price revolution have established that plunging real wages characterized most of Europe. In this perspective a great achievement of the Dutch Golden Age was to prevent the fall of real wages and, indeed, allow for a measurable increase in the purchasing power of many categories of labor.

The effect was to open an enormous gap between real wages in the two countries that was gradually reduced to zero over the course of the eighteenth century. The gap diminished as English nominal wages rose step by step to reach the level attained by the Dutch in the mid–seventeenth century. Seen in this light, the English economy of the eighteenth century appears to be proceeding through an extended catch-up or recovery phase. It would be surprising if in the 1680s Dutch per capita income stood only 7 percent above the depressed English levels, as Gregory King had it.

In the "good" years (i.e., nonwar years) of the seventeenth century, Dutch real incomes stood far above the English level and European levels more gener-

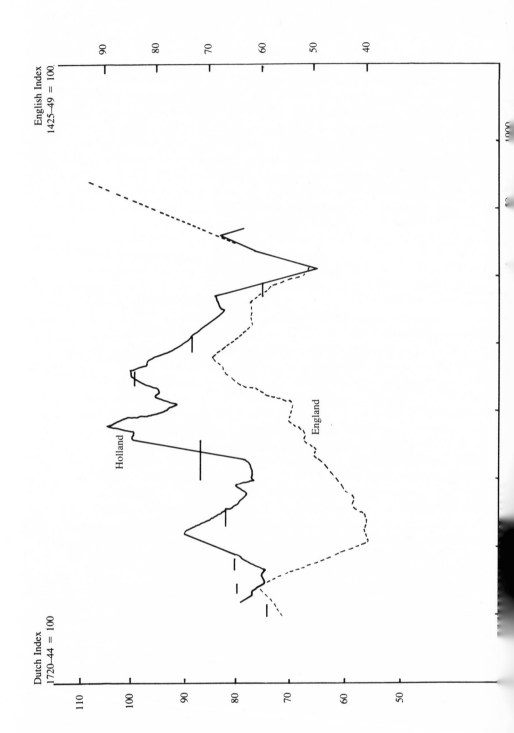

English Index
1425–49 = 100

Dutch Index
1720–44 = 100

Holland

England

184

ally because the Republic's economic expansion had sheltered it from the sharp decline in purchasing power experienced by neighboring countries. The high wage position of the Republic proved to be a problem during the long-term deflation culminating in the period 1680–1740. Just as real wages reached their apogee, employment-generating activities became unprofitable in the Republic while the economies that had not been able to raise wages in earlier decades were well placed to expand. If this scenario has merit, then a central issue of Dutch economic history must be why the restoration of equilibrium to the Dutch labor markets took well over a century to achieve.

VII. CONCLUSION

Of the tasks I set for myself in this study, establishing the *level* of Dutch natural income is the most difficult. Much more evidence is needed to confirm my hypothesis that Dutch per capita income in the third quarter of the seventeenth century stood at double the level estimated by Gregory King for 1688. But its plausibility now rests on two legs. The first is a revision in our understanding of the growth of the English economy before and during its Industrial Revolution. The chasm separating economic life before and after the initial decades of classic industrialization appear to have been overdrawn, resulting in an underestimation of the size of the early-eighteenth-century economy. The second element rendering this hypothesis plausible is an improved understanding of the substantial real wage differences then prevailing between the Republic and England, and of the scope of the structural differences between the economies.

The issues relating to the *trends* of Dutch national income between 1675 and 1900 have elicited sharply contrasting viewpoints, but I believe the general contours of decline and growth to be evident.

The Dutch faced, by the late seventeenth century, problems requiring structural change in their economy, as the deterioration of their ability to export commodities idled labor and the rising wage bill squeezed profits. Capital then left labor-intensive sectors to be reinvested, more often than not, abroad. Labor reacted in ways more difficult to fathom, but the response included a diminution in the size of the urban labor force and long-term structural unemployment. This process was interrupted by intervals of stabilization and regional prosperity, but the economic dislocations brought on during the Revolutionary and Napoleonic periods certainly depressed incomes further across a broad front.

Figure 8. Real Wage Indices for Southern England and Holland in 25-Year Moving Averages. (Also, average real wage of construction labor in the western Netherlands in selected periods.)

The high initial Dutch level was such that it took a long period of vigorous British growth for it to be surpassed. However, it would be surprising if the British surpassed Dutch income levels only after 1860, as Teijl's GNP estimates imply. By then British nominal wages were easily double those of the Dutch, which had continued to stand where they had been set more than two centuries earlier. Likewise, British income from foreign investments had become a large multiple of Dutch foreign investment income, which had shrunk to a fraction of its late-eighteenth–century level.

In assessing this long period of Dutch economic history, two distinct emphases are possible, and legitimate. On the one hand, there is the loss of leadership and innovativeness across a broad range of activities, leading to idle resources and creating over time an economy that was obsolete and subordinate. On the other hand, there is the survival of the basic attributes of a diversified economy and the preservation of its capital in a situation where there was both much to defend and few means to defend it. Which of these two realities one wishes to emphasize is largely a question of taste about which observers will continue to differ.

ACKNOWLEDGMENTS

The author wishes to express his thanks to Richard Griffiths, Peter Lindert, Angus Maddison, and James Riley, whose corrections and suggestions have improved this article at many points. Indeed, recent publications by each of these scholars (referred to below) created the intellectual environment in which this article could be written. I also benefitted from the comments of many seminar participants at Indiana, Harvard, Berkeley, Amsterdam, Groningen, Leuven, and Brussels. The research on the Dutch labor market presented here is being supported by a National Science Foundation grant.

NOTES

1.   The standard authority on nineteenth-century industrialization is J. de Jonge, *De Industrialisatie in Nederland tussen 1850 en 1914* (Amsterdam: 1968).

2.   See, for example, Roger Price, *The Economic Modernization of France, 1730–1880* (London: 1975).

3.   See, for example, A. M. van der Woude, *Het Noorderkwartier* 3 vols. (Wageningen: 1972); J. A. Faber, *Drie eeuwen Friesland*, 2 vols. (Wageningen: 1972); B. H. Slicher van Bath, *Een samenleving onder spanning* (Assen: 1957).

4.   Works of this genre on the Dutch economy are not numerous. See Joel Mokyr, *Industrialization in the Low Countries* (New Haven, Conn.: 1976).

5.   Centraal Bureau voor de Statistiek, *Berekeningen over het nationale inkomen van Nederland voor de periode 1900–1920* (The Hague: 1941); C.B.S., *De Nederlandsche Conjunctuur, Speciale onderzoekingen No. 4;* C.B.S., *Het nationale inkomen van Nederland 1921–1939* (Utrecht: 1948).

6.   Derksen's estimates, but not his methods, are published in J. H. van Stuijvenberg, "Economische groei in Nederland in de negentiende eeuw: een terreinverkenning," in J. H. van Stuijvenberg (ed.), *Bedrijf en samenleving* (Alphen aan den Rijn: 1967), p. 73. There Van Stuijvenberg introduces an error in presenting Derksen's estimates for 1860. The correct figure is about equal to Teijl's

estimate for that year. I have not corrected the error in Figure 2 or in the text since the subsequent literature always referred to the erroneous transmission of Derksen's views, and not the unpublished original source. See: R. T. Griffiths and J. M. M. de Meere, "The Growth of the Dutch Economy in the Nineteenth Century: Back to Basics?" *Tijdschrift voor geschiedenis* (forthcoming).

7. J. Teijl, "Nationaal inkomen van Nederland in de periode 1850–1900. Tasten en testen," *Economisch- en Sociaal-Historisch Jaarboek* 34(1971), 232–263.

8. J. H. van Stuijvenberg, "De economie in de noordelijke Nederlanden, 1770–1970," *Algemene geschiedenis der Nederlanden* Vol. 10 (Haarlem: 1981), pp. 106–07; J. H. van Stuijvenberg and J. E. J. de Vrijer, "Prices, Population and National Income in the Netherlands, 1620–1978," *Journal of European Economic History* 11(1982): 699–711.

9. This is assumed by Van Stuijvenberg, "economie," pp. 106–107; J. M. M. de Meere and L. Blok, "Welstand, ongelijkheid in welstand en censuskiesrecht in Nederland omstreeks het midden van de 19 de eeuw," *Economisch- en Sociaal-Historisch Jaarboek* 41(1978): 175–293; Richard T. Griffiths, "Achterlijk, Achter of Anders," Inaugural lecture, Free University of Amsterdam, December 4, 1980; and others.

10. Griffiths, "Achterlijk," p. 11. Griffiths also notes that Teijl published elsewhere estimates of energy consumption in the period 1834–1864 that do not agree with those used in his national income estimations. The more recent estimates show a more rapid growth of consumption around the middle of the nineteenth century. J. Teijl, "Brandstoffaccijns en nijverheid in Nederland gedurende de periode 1834–1864," in J. van Herwaarden (ed.), *Lof der historie, Opstellen over geschiedenis en maatschappij* (Rotterdam: 1973), p. 164.

11. Van Stuijvenberg, "Economie," p. 107.

12. Th. P. M. de Jong, "Sociale verandering in de neergaande republiek," *Economisch- en Sociaal Historisch Jaarboek* 35(1972), 3.

13. Griffiths, "Achterlijk," p. 10.

14. Gregory King, "Natural and Political Observations and Conclusions Upon the State and Condition of England," in Peter Laslett (ed.), *The Earliest Classics . . .* (London: 1973).

15. See Phyllis Deane, "The Implications of Early National Income Estimates," and D. V. Glass, "Two Papers on Gregory King," in D. V. Glass and D. E. C. Eversley (eds.), *Population in History* (London: 1965), pp. 159–220.

16. E. Le Roy Ladurie, "Les comptes fantastiques de Gregory King," *Annales E.S.C.* 5(1968): 1086–1102.

17. "'The LCC Burns Journal,' A Manuscript Notebook Containing Workings for Several Projected Works," in Laslett, *Earliest Classics*, pp. 227–229.

18. Blok and de Meere, "Welstand," pp. 187–188.

19. This impression is gleaned from scattered observations cited in Van der Woude, *Noorderkwartier*, Vol. III, Figures 7.2–7.5; C. Baars, *De geschiedenis van delandbouw in de Beijerlanden* (Wageningen: 1973), pp. 114–116; Jan de Vries, "Landbouw in de noordelijke Nederlanden, 1490–1650," *Algemene geschiedenis der Nederlanden* (Haarlem: 1980), Vol. 7, p. 41; J. Kuys and J. T. Schoenmakers, *Landpachten in Holland 1500–1650* (Amsterdam: 1981).

20. I. J. A. Gogel, *Memoriën en Correspondentiën betreffende den Staat van 's Rijks Geldmiddelen in den Jare 1820* (Amsterdam, 1844), Bijlage B, p. 31.

21. King, "Manuscript Notebook," p. 228.

22. W. M. Keuchenius, *De inkomsten en uitgaven der Bataafsche Republiek voorgesteld in eene nationale balans* (Amsterdam, 1803); R. Metelerkamp, *De toestand van Nederland in vergelijking gebragt met die van enige andere landen van Europa* (n.p., 1804).

23. Johan de Vries, *De economische achteruitgang der Republiek in de achttiende eeuw* (1959; 2nd ed., Leiden: 1968).

24. Ibid., p. 167.

25. Van der Woude, *Noorderkwartier*, Vol. I, pp. 256–257; Vol. II, pp. 609–610.

26. Van Stuijvenberg and De Vrijer, pp. 700–701.

27.   Angus Maddison, *Phases of Capitalist Development* (Oxford: 1982).

28.   *Ibid.*, pp. 31–32; 165–66.

29.   *Ibid.*, p. 44.

30.   Paul Bairoch, "Europe's Gross National Product: 1800–1975," *Journal of European Economic History* 5(1976): 286. For another view, see: N. F. R. Crafts, "Gross National Product in Europe 1870–1910: some new estimates," *Explorations in Economic History* 20(1983): 387–401.

31.   James C. Riley, "The Dutch Economy after 1650: Decline or Growth?" *Journal of European Economic History* (forthcoming). Riley bases his revisionist view on his own work, *International Government Finance and the Amsterdam Capital Market, 1740–1815* (Cambridge, 1980); and also Marten G. Buist, *At Spes Non Fracta: Hope & Co., 1770–1815* (The Hague: 1974); Jake V. T. Knoppers, *Dutch Trade with Russia from the Time of Peter I to Alexander I: A Quantitative Study in Eighteenth Century Shipping*, 3 Vols. (Montreal: 1976); Jake V. T. Knoppers and F. Snapper, "De Nederlandse scheepvaart op de Oostzee vanaf het eind van de 17de eeuw tot het begin van de 19de eeuw," *Economisch- en Sociaal-Historish Jaarboek* 41(1978): 115–153; M. Morineau, "La balance du commerce franco-néerlandais et le reserrement économique des Provinces-Unies au XVIIIeme siècle," *Economisch-Historisch Jaarboek* 30(1963/64): 170–235.

33.   Nicholas F. R. Crafts, "English Economic Growth in the Eighteenth Century: A Re-examination of Deane and Cole's Estimates," *Economic History Review*, 2nd ser. 29(1976): 226–235.

34.   W. A. Cole, "Factors in Demand, 1700–1780," in R. Floud and D. N. McCloskey (eds.), *The Economic History of Britain since 1700*, Vol. I (Cambridge: 1981), p. 64.

35.   Quotations of exchange rates between London and Amsterdam are provided in N. W. Posthumus, *Inquiry into the History of Prices in Holland*, Vol. I (Leiden: 1946), pp. 590–595. The use of foreign exchange market rates for the comparison of national incomes is not without its problems. For a discussion of the "exchange rate problem" see Patrick O'Brien and Caglar Keyder, *Economic Growth in Britain and France, 1780–1914* (London: 1978), pp. 34–47. I have not pursued their suggestions in this study, fearing that any revision of official rates would be as likely to diminish as to improve the accuracy of the conversions. However, I take comfort in calling attention to the fact that the two economies were as unified by trade and by common tastes and patterns of consumption as any two in Europe.

36.   Deane and Cole, *British Economic Growth*, pp. 282, 329–331.

37.   Riley, "Decline or Growth?", Tables 4 and 5.

38.   Peter H. Lindert and Jeffrey G. Williamson, "Revising England's Social Tables, 1688–1812," *Explorations in Economic History* 19(1982): 385–408; *Ibid.*, "Reinterpreting Britain's Social Tables, 1688–1913," *Explorations in Economic History* 20(1983): 94–109.

39.   C. Knick Harley, "British Industrialization Before 1841: Evidence of Slower Growth During the Industrial Revolution," *Journal of Economic History* 42(1982): 285.

40.   Idem.

41.   N. F. R. Crafts "British Economic Growth, 1700–1831," *Economic History Review* 36(1983): 177–199.

42.   For surveys of Dutch industry see P. C. Jansen, "Nijverheid in de noordelijke Nederlanden, 1650–1780," in *Algemene geschiedenis der Nederlanden*, Vol. 8 (Haarlem: 1979), pp. 102–123, and Richard Griffiths, "Ambachten nijverheid in de noordelijke Nederlanden, 1770–1844," *Algemene geschiedenis der Nederlanden*, Vol. 10 (Haarlem: 1981), pp. 219–52. Both are supplied with annotated bibliographies.

43.   N. W. Posthumus, *De geschiedenis van de Leidsche lakenindustrie*, 3 vols. (The Hague, 1908–1939); S. C. Regtdoorzee Greup-Roldanus, *Geschiedenis der Haarlemmer bleekerijen* (The Hague: 1936); Van der Woude, *Noorderkwartier*, Vol. 2, pp. 457–472.

44.   Johan de Vries, *Achteruitgang*, Appendix V, pp. 198–199, provides a summary of contemporary opinion.

45.   Keuchenius, pp. 110–111.

46.   For summaries of agrarian activity see: Jan de Vries, "Landbouw," pp. 12–43, and H. K.

Roessingh, "Landbouw in de noordelijke Nederlanden 1650–1815," *Algemene geschiedenis der Nederlanden*, Vol. 8 (Haarlem: 1979), pp. 16–72.

47. Griffiths, "Achterlijk," pp. 16–20, for data on early-nineteenth-century expansion.

48. Riley, *International Government Finance;* Buist, *At Spes Non Fracta.*

49. Jan de Vries, *Barges and Capitalism: Passenger Transportation in the Dutch Economy, 1632–1839* (Utrecht: 1981); also published in *A.A.G. Bijdragen* 21(1978), pp. 231–303.

50. These overly familiar generalizations are most comprehensively described and defended in Simon Kuznets, *Modern Economic Growth* (New Haven, Conn.: 1966).

51. For sources, see Table 4.

52. J. A. de Jonge, *De industrialisatie in Nederland tussen 1850 en 1914* (Amsterdam: 1968), p. 296.

53. Jan de Vries, "Landbouw," pp. 36–37.

54. Deane and Cole, *British Economic Growth,* p. 251, estimate the British wage bill in 1801 to be 45 percent of national income.

55. Hoogheemraadschap van Rijnland, oud archief, Nos. 9510–10263, Bijlagen tot de rekeningen; Nos. 10917–10932, werklijsten.

56. Algemene Rijksarchief, The Hague, Archief van de Lijnbaan te Amsterdam, Nos. 8–20, Betalingsboek van spinders en draijers; Nos. 121–124, 186, 188, Betaallijsten.

57. Gemeentearchief van Amsterdam, Part. archief 310, Rijksmarinewerf Nos. 1514, 1516, 2278, 4351–4352; Algemene Rijksarchief, The Hague, Admiraliteitscolleges, No. 786; Verzameling Van der Heim, Nos. 432, 447; Verzameling Van Alphen, No. 4.

58. N. W. Posthumus, *Inquiry into the History of Prices in Holland,* 2 vols. (Leiden, 1946–1964); Posthumus, *Lakenindustrie,* Vols. 2 and 3. The spliced series based on Posthumus and foreign series is in Van Stuijvenberg and De Vrijer, "Prices, population and national income in the Netherlands, 1620–1978," pp. 707–710.

59. The basket of consumables consists of the following items: Rye (1050 kg), yellow peas (143.5 kg), stockfish (25 kg), meat (100 kg), cheese (50 kg), butter (50 kg), beer (621 liters) [for which coffee, tea, and gin are substituted in the second half of the eighteenth century], peat (100 turf tons), and a composite of industrial product prices weighted to equal 25 percent of the food subtotal in the period 1575–1599.

60. De Jonge, *Industrialisatie,* p. 435.

61. In the basket of goods described in note 59, the cost of 1050 kg of rye is replaced with the cost of 525 kg of rye and 1400 kg of potatoes (the caloric equivalent of the missing rye). Potato prices varied locally since this commodity was not widely traded; however, the available price series confirm that the consumption of potatoes did not result in an enormous cost reduction in years of relatively low rye prices in the 1780s but made a great deal of difference in the crisis years of the early nineteenth century.

62. Both the "late feudal crisis" of the fifteenth century and the "great depression of 1873–1896" generated contradictory economic phenomena that have fueled scholarly debate.

63. Van der Woude, *Het Noorderkwartier,* Vol. II, pp. 607–608.

64. N. F. R. Crafts, "English Economic Growth in the Eighteenth Century: A Reexamination of Deane and Cole's Estimates," *Economic History Review* 29(1976): 226–235.

65. E. A. Wrigley and R. S. Schofield, *Population History of England: A Reconstruction* (London: 1982), Appendix 9, pp. 638–644. The real wage series constructed by Phelps-Brown and Hopkins contains gaps, and their nominal wage series often changes abruptly. Wrigley and Schofield introduced linear interpolations to fill the gaps and dampen abrupt changes. As a consequence, the English trends in Figure 8 appear much smoother than the Dutch series, for which no such adjustments have been made.

THE SHIFTING LOCUS OF AGRICULTURAL INNOVATION IN NINETEENTH-CENTURY EUROPE:

THE CASE OF THE AGRICULTURAL EXPERIMENT STATIONS

George Grantham

I. INTRODUCTION

One of William Parker's more intriguing speculations about the course of productivity growth in the West is that its underlying technology and governing institutions seem to display a logical sequence of stages.[1] In the first phase the expansion of trade brought forth its fruits through Smithian processes of regional and occupational specialization. In the second labor shortages and rising fuel costs induced craftsmen to invent the wave of gadgets that marks the first indus-

Technique, Spirit, and Form in the Making of the Modern Economies:
Essays in Honor of William N. Parker
Research in Economic History, Suppl. 3, pages 191–214

trial revolution. In these early stages the process of invention seems to have been well served by an atomistic society of family firms and craftsmen responding to market signals and to obvious technical problems growing out of increased speed and scale of production. Confined at first to inventions having well-defined property rights and to fields where a strong demand for labor and shortages of specific materials interacted with men possessing appropriate inventive skills, the locus of invention spread in the late nineteenth century to areas that were less accessible to the society of farmers and craftsmen who had generated the first wave of discovery. The technologies based on electricity, chemistry, and biology had few roots in the traditional crafts. Their social home was the laboratory, the scientific society, and higher education. To develop and apply this knowledge required new kinds of men and new institutions that were only loosely connected to the market. Nowhere, perhaps, was the institutional gap as large as it was in nineteenth-century agriculture, where the sciences of chemistry, physics, and biology confronted an occupation founded on the particularistic knowledge of the properties of individual places.

This essay explores some of the issues surrounding the emergence of agricultural science as a source of innovations. The principal institutional event in this process was the emergence of publically funded agricultural research stations staffed and directed by professional scientists. From its beginnings at the Leipzig Economic Society's farm in Mockern, Saxony, in 1851, the agricultural research "movement" grew to over 90 stations by 1875 and more than 500 by 1900. By the beginning of the twentieth century there were research stations throughout the temperate agricultural belt. In Europe the annual expenditures on agricultural research amounted to roughly $2 million and the various research organizations employed about 1500 professional scientists. Almost all of these institutions were supported by governments or by producers' associations. Although many of them drew revenue from fees charged for soil and fertilizer analyses, virtually none survived as private enterprises.[2] The agricultural research station constituted a significant displacement of innovative activity from the small firm and the private sector toward the public sector. It cannot be viewed, therefore, as a natural evolution out of a preexisting set of institutions. This essay is concerned mainly with the reasons for this institutional jump. The study of the efficiency of agricultural innovations under the new form as compared to more traditional methods needs more quantitative information than is at present available.

From the perspective of the economics of institutional change, the rapid growth in the number of experiment stations after 1850 seems to reflect a rise in the value of research. However, it is extremely difficult to identify exactly what this value was before 1880. Nineteenth-century data are simply too error-ridden to provide statistically secure estimates of the contribution of research expenditures to the growth of agricultural output. Without more direct evidence bearing on the diffusion of techniques directly attributable to research, one is left with the impression that it must have had some use, but with no precise sense of what exactly it was. Most of the early work at the experiment stations was devoted to soil and fertilizer analysis, to studies of plant nutrition, and to investigations of the metabolism of farm animals. Probably the most valuable contribution was Millardet's discovery of the Bourdeaux mixture, which opened the way to fungicidal control of plant diseases; but his work dates from the 1880s. The discovery of the nitrogen-fixing bacteria in legumes was another major advance, but its immediate consequence for agricultural techniques appears to have been very limited. The work on soils and fertilizers probably helped to increase the use of fertilizers, but this evidence constitutes neither a measure of the impact nor an estimate of the demand price of agricultural research before 1880.

The development of a network of research stations, then, was only in part attributable to well-defined economic forces. Expectations probably outstripped performance in the early years. The first historical question is what led to expectations that science could significantly improve agricultural performance and what institutional arrangements seem to have been best adapted to translating these expectations into reality. The argument advanced below is that the people whose expectations mattered were government officials with some discretion to spend money on research independently of popular demand. One reason for this is that in the beginning the benefits from research were too uncertain to support sustained demand. Another more subtle reason lies in the need for agricultural scientists to distance themselves from the direct demands of farmers for useful information. To uncover Nature's laws as they applied to farming was a work that needed as much care in measurement and in the design of experiments as any "pure" science, and the social institutions needed to induce and sustain this activity were the same. Thus, although agricultural science was ultimately practical in its aims and drew its finance from those who expected to benefit from its findings, it was nevertheless a science with all the social mechanisms of control that this implied. The institutional innovation was to bring these social mechanisms into the service of farmers. The timing of this innovation can be explained by the inadequacy of traditional methods of generating new knowledge in agriculture as the pace of change quickened in the first half of the nineteenth century.

II. TRADITIONAL INNOVATION

Students of innovation describe the act of insight marking the moment of discovery as a piecing together of preexisting physical and intellectual material into new patterns. Before the middle of the nineteenth century most agricultural innovation was a by-product of general farming. Unlike American farmers, who from the beginning had to innovate in response to rapidly evolving physical and economic environments, European farmers before 1800 faced relatively stable conditions. The long rise in productivity after 1500 was mainly due to intensified mixed husbandry, which combined existing crops and animals in new ways in response to opportunities created by rising demands for cash crops, meat, and dairy products in the larger towns and cities. Agricultural improvements reflected materials locally available. Farmers used manures, lime, salt, sand, night soil, and town garbage soil, and garbage as soil amendments.[3] Pesticidal uses were found for such industrial products as soap, alum, arsenic, rendered tallow, the less of olive oil and bittern, as well as for newly imported substances such as nicotine or pyrethrum.[4] No doubt some of these discoveries were owing to plain luck, as when a farmer discovered the smut-inhibiting properties of brine steeps by leaving his seeds on a beach below high tide;[5] but others must have come about as a result of the availability of materials providing occasions for new observations. The large number of reported early applications of copper compounds as fungicides must have owed much to the ubiquity of copper pots and stills in the countryside.[6] Chance, trade, and industrial development, then, sustained slow rates of technological change at isolated points, but these processes did little to speed generalization and diffusion of new discoveries beyond their point of origin.

Traditional agriculture and its capitalistic adjuncts had a limited capacity to improve crop strains and livestock, but the data do not as yet allow one to distinguish between the genetic and environmental sources of this improvement. Better feeding and more intensive manuring raised yields independently of any genetic improvements, and much of the improvement in meat and dairy yields from the mid-eighteenth century is simply the result of farmers specializing animals to uses for which market premiums had emerged.[7] The proliferation of ornamental plants and flowers for sale illustrates the speed with which farmers could respond to market incentives in the absence of genetic barriers to change. At the beginning of the nineteenth century, English fanciers could choose from among 700 different kinds of tulips, 500 types of ranunculus, 350 carnations and 1450 varieties of roses.[8] This diversity depended on the ability of gardeners to clone these plants and protect them from the consequences of Mendelian segregation. In this highly commercializable sector, nature and the market cooperated to raise the private returns to genetic innovation.

This was not so easily accomplished in the main food crops. Farmers traded seed, and specialized firms for collecting and redistributing regional varieties can be traced to the late seventeenth century, but it was virtually impossible to maintain pure strains in the easily hybridized cereals. Even under the best conditions it takes from six to eight generations to stabilize the genetic constitution of wheat varieties.[9] The great seed collection built-up by the firm of Vilmorin-Andrieux between 1785 and 1815 did not acquire enough genetic fixity to be listed in their catalogue until 1850.[10] These were slowly maturing investments. Traditional agriculture could not be expected to respond to opportunities for making them.

There are reasons to suppose that the potential demand for new information about plants and biological processes grew after 1820. This was due not so much to sharply rising pressure on food supplies, which eased after the Napoleonic Wars, but to changes in the ecological balance in Western Europe and to the appearance of new but costly inputs. The ecological changes consisted mainly in increased crop losses resulting from the larger and more uniform strands of grain induced by the commercialization of agriculture and the introduction on a large scale of imported crops that were vulnerable to local fungal or insect pests. Heavier manuring also took its toll at the same time that it raised yields, because the extra nitrogen distended cells and weakened them, making the grains susceptible to parasites. Although less severe than the disturbances brought on by rapid settlement in America and Australia, the biological consequences of accelerated agricultural change were also felt in Europe. Casual surveys indicate that the incidence of insect and fungal pathogens was increasing toward the end of the eighteenth century. A search of the literature on rust in small grains shows a rise in outbreaks from once every 20 years between 1650 and 1750 to once every seven years between 1750 and 1825. Between 1825 and 1850 there was rust every 27 months, and after 1850 every 15.[11] Other pests appear to have increased in frequency after the Napoleonic Wars. The entomologist John Curtis noted an increase in wireworms in the 1830s. In France grasshopper and locust plagues appear to have been more common after 1830.[12]

What is important about these problems is that their solution required skills not readily available in traditional farming communities. What is interesting is that although governments commissioned individual scientists to investigate the causes of crop losses, there were no research institutes to study plant or insect diseases before the mid-1860s. Potential demand for knowledge did not automatically translate itself into permanent research institutions.

III. SCIENTIFIC INNOVATION

Applying science to agriculture was difficult because the phenomena to be studied were far more complex than phenomena in industrial fields. The adaptability of living things to small ecological "niches" and the complexity of their mutual adaptations greatly multiplied the number of facts that had to be mastered and frustrated the design of simple experiments. A fruitful science requires a lengthy gestation period for gathering, verifying, and classifying the facts of plant and animal growth. To protect property rights and product "quality" in circumstances where the market admits of few pecuniary returns to research, organized science employs a highly artificial environment of easy communication and peer review.[13] The necessary institutional foundation for accurate scientific work had emerged by the end of the eighteenth century, but it was confined to the elitist domains of "pure" science. Since similar problems existed in applied sciences like agronomy, the institutional apparatus of organized science had to be transferred to the literally down-to-earth realm of crop and livestock science. Agricultural science, therefore, meant more than simply hiring scientists. It was as well a matter of subsidizing a scientific community having ties both to academic science and to the economic needs of the farming community. A kind of indivisibility is at work here. A group of scientists working on similar problems and criticizing each other's work is more productive than the same number of scientists working singly and in isolation.

We will argue below that the early development of experiment stations in Europe was powerfully influenced by the form of the organizations responsible for purchasing agricultural public goods. Given the high degree of uncertainty, indeed the almost total ignorance, of what investments in research might yield, the transactions costs of organizing an effective demand for research were extraordinarily high. Thus, circumstances that on the surface appear to have had little relation to agriculture or science, such as the training of bureaucrats, the organizational forms of agricultural scientists, and the methods of recruiting and training professional pharmacists, played significant roles in bringing about an effective demand for science in agriculture.

IV. MOCKERN—AN INSTITUTIONAL INNOVATION

The modern agricultural experiment station traces its origins to Emil Wolff's arrival at the small farm owned by the Leipzig Economic Society at Mockern. Mockern was not the first institution to conduct chemical studies of agricultural substances. Boussingault was already carrying out experiments on his wife's estate in Alsace by the mid 1830s, and Lawes had begun his and Gilbert's work on his Rothamsted estate in the early 1840s. What gives Mockern its significance is the degree of state support it received and the way that it spawned the first wave of experiment stations. In 1853 Wolf left the station to take up a chair in agricultural chemistry at Hohenheim, where he pursued researches along the lines he had begun in Saxony. In 1856 his two assistants and successors both left Mockern to found experiment stations in Silesia. By the early 1860s there were over a dozen active experiment stations in Germany, and by 1863 the experimenters had their own journals and annual professional meetings where they presented and discussed their findings.[14] In contrast, Rothamsted, much better financed than any of the early German stations, had no immediate offspring. The expansion of English agricultural experimentation had to wait until the 1890s, when funds from the Whiskey Excise were made available to finance a network of agricultural colleges.[15] In France the expansion of a modest network dates from 1875. National differences in form and timing of agricultural research institutions provide a crude way of examining the causes of their development.

When Wolff was called to Mockern he was teaching science at a secondary school near Halle. Possessing a degree in chemistry he had published some of his private experiments in agricultural chemistry in a textbook inspired by Justus

Liebig's enunciation of the chemical principles of plant nutrition and animal metabolism. Wolff saw his mandate as a purely scientific one. His program of research at Mockern included studies of the interaction of nitrogen, phosphates, and alkalis in plant nutrition, the analysis of the chemical composition of plants at different stages of growth, and the nutritional value of different fodders for the production of milk. He did not claim that these researches would yield productive results immediately but argued that they would help to uncover the basic "laws" that governed the growth of plants and animals. Although from the mid-1850s Mockern had a "practical" division that occupied itself in fertilizer and seed analyses, the original and continuing purpose was scientific study of agriculturally relevant problems.

According to Gustav Kuhn's history of Mockern, the station owed its birth and survival to the efforts of three men: Adolph Stockhardt, whose enthusiastic advocacy of state-financed agricultural chemistry before and after his appointment to the School of Forestry at Tharand earned him the sobriquet "Tharand Feldprediger"; Wilhelm Crusius, who as President of the Leipzig Economic Society, co-founder of the All-German Congress of Agricultural Societies, and lord of a progressive estate of Sahlis, was one of Saxony's movers and shakers;[16] and Theodor Reuning, the Saxon official responsible for agricultural development.[17] The biographies of these three men illustrate some of the more general forces at work to concentrate an effective demand for agricultural science between 1840 and 1860.

At first, the station's resources were very modest. The Leipzig Economic Society, which had received the farm as a bequest from one of its members a half century before, assumed the cost of erecting the laboratory. In the absence of promised government funds, its president Wilhelm Crusius paid Wolff's salary of 300 taler and managed to secure him the position of Secretary to the Society, carrying a stipend of 150 taler. Crusius's appeal for support from the Knights' Estate of Saxony was unsuccessful, but in 1852 he obtained a gift of 800 talers from the All-German Congress of Landowners. In 1852 the Saxon Ministry of the Interior agreed to match the contribution of farmers' societies to the research station, assuring its financial stability.

Stockhardt was the propagandist. He typifies the first generation of agricultural scientists in Germany, almost all of whom came from the middle class of clerical families, pharmacists, and physicians. He was a pastor's son who, having shown an early interest in chemistry, was apprenticed to an apothecary. After he passed his examinations, he went to Berlin to work in a pharmacy and attend lectures at the university. In 1833 he passed the Prussian apothecaries' examinations and undertook a *wanderjahr* through Europe which took him to the laboratories of Gay-Lussac, Dumas, Faraday, and Jussieu. On his return to Saxony he accepted a job with a mineral water firm, completed his doctoral dissertation at Leipzig, and in 1838 accepted an appointment to teach at the Gewerbeschule in Chemnitz. To this point his formation and interests were nonagricultural.[18]

Agriculture for him, as for many other chemically trained persons in 1840, became a passion with the publication of Justus Liebig's *Organic Chemistry in its Application to Agriculture and Physiology* in 1840. This survey by Europe's leading organic chemist was the catalyst if not the ultimate cause of the development of agricultural experiment stations in Europe. It laid out a practical program of research that seemed to offer fairly immediate returns in higher crop and livestock yields.[19] As such it seemed to touch a strain of idealism in many young chemists. Liebig himself was ignorant of farm practices. His influential book owes more to developments in organic chemistry than to any immediate triggering signal from the agricultural economy. Stockhardt began to give public lectures on the new science to farmers' associations and to the small intellectual societies that were a hallmark of Biedermeier society. It was though routes such as this that opinions favorable to agricultural science began to form. It was here that Liebig's scientific eminence was crucial.

As the leading chemist of his day, Liebig had been invited by the British Association in 1837 to prepare a survey of organic chemistry. Evidently, while he was preparing his text, he read an article by Saussure on fermentation in humus which led him to review the existing literature on plant nutrition. He synthesized this literature and enunciated new principles of nutrition based on concepts of conservation of matter and emerging notions of the conservation of energy.[20] Liebig's basic notions were easy enough for laymen to understand. Nature had to balance her books. Chemistry was simply a means to more accurate accounting. Not given to understatement he warned of the dangers of soil depletion which threatened to provoke cruel wars caused by famine, when "mothers, as during the Thirty Years War, will drag home the bodies of the slain enemy in order to still with their flesh the hunger of their children. . . . These are not vague and dark predictions, images of a sick phantasy; for science does not prophesy, it calculates: not *if,* but *when,* is undecided."[21]

The English background to Liebig's invitation and the enthusiastic reception his book received there (which as we shall see had repercussions in Germany) have a prehistory. An organized lobby for the possible application of chemistry to agriculture had emerged in England during the 1830s as an offshoot of the prevailing interest in geology. In 1838 Henry de la Beche, director of the Geological Survey, urged the creation of an adjunct museum and curator to whom soil samples could be sent to be analyzed and classified. The curator was to serve as a kind of government chemist at large for landowners and farmers. The museum would be a central depository of geological and chemical information. In 1839, the government gave him £1500 to this end. The same year the British Association for the Advancement of Science heard two other reports dealing with the application of chemistry to agriculture. From its establishment in 1838 the Royal Agricultural Society expected to fund a chemical laboratory for its members. In 1841 and 1842 the British government gave serious consideration to a proposal to establish a department of agricultural chemistry at the University of

Durham. Another plan involved carrying out soil analysis on a nationwide scale by the Museum of Economic Geology, which was to function both as an institute for agricultural research and a training ground for agricultural chemists. In the course of these discussions, Peel's advisor Buckland noted that Peel was trying to find a way to do what "has been begun in France and Germany, but hitherto been much neglected in England as to the extent which a knowledge of organic chemistry may be applied to the improvement of agriculture." In 1844 the British Association voted £50 to encourage a national program of plant ash analysis, and convinced the Royal Agricultural Society to contribute a further £350. Liebig, who had been in correspondence with Peel, was present at these meetings and the enthusiasm for his ideas must have convinced him that a large-scale effort was not far-off.[22]

The results of all this hustle and bustle were more strongly felt in Germany than in England, and testify to the power of implicit competition among nineteenth century states to elicit public action. Stockhardt had been lecturing enthusiastically on Liebig's ideas when it was announced in 1844 that the great man was about to establish a fertilizer factory in England. This led to a demand for a similar facility in Saxony, and Stockhardt seems to have persuaded the *vereine* that the appointment of agricultural chemists to serve as extension agents was crucial to the success of any such enterprise. In 1845 he drafted a petition urging the government to appoint chemists to analyze soils and advise farmers on manures and rotations. The petition was turned down, but as a partial response Reuning appointed Stockhardt to a chair in agricultural chemistry at the Forestry School in Tharand. His lectures and books helped to create a favorable public for agricultural chemistry as a state-supported enterprise. A few years later he was instrumental in founding a station at Jena.

Agricultural chemistry was in the air in the 1840s. At virtually the same time as Liebig's book, there appeared new and more powerful fertilizers that seemed to substantiate his chemical view of life and provided a new set of reasons for chemical analysis of agricultural processes. French explorers had discovered guano and nitrates on the Peruvian coast in the early eighteenth century and Humboldt had brought back some samples in 1804 for analysis; but it was only in 1840 that a shipment of 10 casks of guano to Liverpool proved their worth as manure, setting off a sudden boom in shipments.[23] Guano was an all-purpose manure, containing both phosphates and nitrates, but it was costly and subject to wide natural variations in its active ingredients, which gave unpredictable results and made it difficult to detect fraud.[24] Chemical analysis seemed to offer a means of reducing the cost of using these and other new substances.

In the early 1840s, then, two streams joined: the one stemming from improvements in organic chemistry that had been taking place since around 1810, and the other the quickening flow of new concentrated fertilizers that can be traced to the 1820s.[25] The streams came together in Saxony, in part because the rapid growth of intensive husbandry attendant upon industrialization and population growth was making new demands on the soil. Sugar beets were especially demanding of and responsive to mineral fertilizers, and, as the center of sugar beet farming in Germany, Saxony was the major importer of commercial fertilizers in Germany before 1870.[26] Until the 1840s the failure of innumerable trials and ill-considered experiments with different dungs and amendments to yield reliable results had not mattered much. The emergence of concentrated fertilizers raised the value of losses caused by faulty information.[27] The impact of this revolution can be seen in topics raised for discussion at the annual Congress of German Landowners. In 1841 they were still considering the effects of different animal dungs on crop yields and the length of years a crop could continuously be sown. By 1845 the agenda dealt with the importance of ammonia, the fertilizing power of nitrogen in organic substances, and the relation of animal manures to the constituents of different organs of plants.[28] It was in these meetings that the organized demand for chemical studies of soils, plants, and fertilizers began to form. The associations of landowners were economically the "natural" purchasers of such public goods as could be produced by agricultural science. However, it was at first only in Germany that demand for them became effective.

V. AGRICULTURAL ASSOCIATIONS AS DEMANDERS OF RESEARCH

In 1840 Saxony was one of Germany's most industrialized states. Less than one-third of its population was agricultural, and there was free trade in grain. Serfdom and the manorial and communal restrictions on land transfers had been abolished in 1832 and, on the assumption then common in Germany that the transition to laissez-faire could best be achieved through the guidance of enlightened bureaucrats, the state appropriated modest sums to encourage the diffusion of better techniques. Most of these funds were channeled through local agricultural societies (*landwirtschaftlichen vereine*).[29] The German *vereine* date from the Napoleonic period. In contrast to the agricultural societies of the late eighteenth century with which they are sometimes confused, the *vereine* were not merely discussion clubs, but constituted a part of the corporate state dear to the hearts of contemporary German political theorists and bureaucrats.[30] The legislation creating legal status for the Prussian associations was passed on the same day that Prussia abolished "feudalism."[31] The task of the associations was "the perfection of agriculture," in which "not only every individual farmer has an interest, but pre-eminently also the State, which must work to raise the production of the soil, so that the nation will be independent in foodstuffs for a growing population."[32] Within these associations patriotic landowners were expected to associate to purchase improved stock and new implements, try out new techniques, aid their diffusion among the newly liberated peasantry, and advise government on ways to encourage agriculture. Growth in the number and membership of the *vereine* dates from the 1840s, when they were receiving subsidies from the government.[33] What makes them unique among contemporary agricultural associations was the interpenetration at their apex of scientific, agricultural, and government interests.

Composed for the most part of well-off farmers and dominated by the larger landowners, the German agricultural societies were convenient receptacles for new ideas about possible applications of science to farming. They had a quasi-governmental status from the beginning in Prussia and after 1848 in Saxony, when the government established a council (*landeskulturrat*) to supervise and direct their work.[34] As a bureaucratic expedient for gathering and transmitting information, they were a wonderful mechanism for reducing the transaction costs of organizing demand for an obviously public good.

This institutional form gave representation but not authority to important agricultural interests (an instance of what Wolfram Fischer has termed government "for the common interest of, but not through, its citizens").[35] It seems to have been an unusually suitable organization for channeling the demand for something as uncertain as agricultural science. One of the fundamental organizational problems in funding agricultural science was how to persuade its potential users that it might possess some value.[36] The German *vereine,* unlike the French and English agricultural societies, had a structure that gave considerable governmental direction to their affairs. This meant that when a bureaucrat like Reuning was persuaded of the value of pure science for agriculture he could use the *vereine* to build support for his ideas. Differences in economic situation and variations in the capacity to evaluate the likely benefits of and to appreciate the need for lengthy research made a popular demand for government funding of agricultural science highly unlikely. The more authoritarian German agricultural associations permitted a few well-placed and well-informed persons to respond to scientific opportunities in ways that were difficult if not impossible for more popularly based institutions.

British and French agricultural associations lacked this easy combination of public and private interest. In France the principal local associations for improving techniques were the *comices agricoles,* which after 1815 busied themselves with holding fairs and awarding prizes and medals. After 1848 they were supplemented by *chambres d'agriculture,* which were departmental bodies charged with advising the government on agricultural matters and collecting agricultural statistics.[37] By 1861 there were 561 *comices* and 141 agricultural societies organized along the older lines of the *académies* and choosing their members by co-optation.[38] Despite a formal resemblance to the German organizations, the *chambres* and the *comices* do not seem to have played a large role in forming opinion about using science to improve agriculture. This was perhaps because their influence was mainly local, whereas decisions about allocating funds to research stations were taken in Paris.[39] In 1848, when the Second Republic discussed and then voted an ambitious project to establish an agronomy institute and a network of agricultural education institutes and model farms, the initiative came from the Ministry of Agriculture. It was opposed (though eventually passed) in the Assemblée Nationale as being too ''elitist.''[40]

In Britain, the control of government by the great landlords provided ample scope for supplying agricultural research with government funds, but to the extent these functions were undertaken at all, they were conducted by voluntary associations. The earliest of these seems to have been the Dublin Society, organized in 1731 by a group of landowners who wanted to raise their rents by introducing English techniques.[41] The Society established a botanical garden for research into useful plants in 1732, and in the 1760s employed John Wynn Baker to conduct experiments on the basis of the ''new husbandry.'' Hiring experimental farmers proved to be the source of many persistent problems, because the agricultural societies wanted their farmers to demonstrate what was then believed to be the best practice rather than to design new experiments and test hypotheses. As a result, the ''experiments'' produced little of scientific worth.[42]

By far the most common means in England by which landlords acquired the services of scientists was to keep specialists on retainer.[43] The Royal Agricultural Society granted funds to the London Veterinary College, hitherto exclusively preoccupied with the medical problems of horses, to study diseases in sheep and cattle. In 1841 the Highland Agricultural Society retained the Edinburgh chemist James T. Johnston and shortly after the Royal Society procured the services of Lyon Playfair, lately returned from Justus Leibig's laboratory in Giessen. In 1849 the Royal Society appointed its own veterinary inspector making his services freely available to members. In 1871 it retained a consulting botanist to examine seeds and plants and in 1872 appointed the great mycologist Anton De Bary to study the life cycle of the blight fungus in potatoes.[44]

Retaining scientists made it easy to direct their skills toward immediate problems. Its disadvantage lay in its inability to support research that required lengthy preliminary work not immediately related to agricultural issues. Thus, although the Royal Society's early chemical consultants carried out original research at the Society's London laboratory, the greater part of their time was taken up in testing soils and certifying fertilizers. The only long-run research supported by the Royal Society came about in the early 1870s when, as a result of the new Agricultural Holdings Act, it became necessary to determine methods of ascertaining the unexpired fertility in improved lands. British reluctance to engage government in agricultural research predates the period of free trade. Sir John Sinclair's suggestion at the beginning of the century that the government endow a research farm was ignored, as was Major Le Couteur's proposal in the 1830s that Parliament subsidize a farm to identify and test the different varieties of wheat.[4] In the 1880s none of the commissions established to look into England's agricultural problems recommended state support for improving productivity. This dilatory response is no doubt due to British preference for voluntary action; but i is likely that the absence of a government department for agriculture allowed this popular sentiment to maintain its force.

VI. BUREAUCRATS AND DEMAND FORMATION

One of the institutional requirements of a new science for agriculture was that its practitioners be shielded from demands for immediate practical results. At Mockern, the Saxon official responsible for agricultural affairs, Theodor Reuning, protected the station from the demands of the farmers who were to be its ultimate beneficiaries and were in the short run its main source of finance through their associations. Reuning's ability to maintain a steady scientific orientation was owing to the centralized organization of the Saxon *vereine,* the head of which was appointed by the government, and to his place on the station's board of governors. The presence of bureaucrats seems to have been critical in the early years of the agricultural experiment station movement. Neither the academic institutions (universities and agricultural academies) nor the larger landowners seem to have been capable of establishing and maintaining chemical research stations. This is only partly because of the problems of funding. As Table 1 shows, the Saxon government provided an important but not overwhelming share of the monies needed to finance the first five years of experimentation. Rather, it appears that bureaucrats in the centralized administrations of the German states were the main effective demanders of the new knowledge in the years before it was capable of giving practical results. One can ask, therefore, where the bureaucrats acquired the information needed to evaluate the possible benefits of investing in science, and why, as nonfarmers, they chose to do so.

Table 1.   Sources of Funds: Mockern, 1853–1856
(in Saxon talers)

Sources of Funds	1853	1854	1855	1856	1860
Saxon Government	350	350	500	415	500
Leipzig Economic Society	150	150	150	50	50
District *Vereine*	400	550	400	500	700
Special *Vereine*	—	—	—	—	—
Crusius	200	200	200	200	—
Interest on Thaer Endowment	32	36	36	36	36
Other	—	—	—	—	—
Total	1.132	1.286	1.286	1.281	2.112

Source: Gustav Kuhn, *Geschichtliches über die landwirtschaftlichen Versuchs-station Mockern,* in *Die landwirtschaftlichen Versuchs-Stationen,* Vol. 22 (1877), p. 145. The data have been transformed from marks to taler at the rate of 3 marks per Saxon taler.

The answer to the second question probably lies in the relation between government income and population. As small independent principalities German states before 1870 had an interest in taking measures to raise their national output. The Vienna treaty of 1815 guaranteed inhabitants of the German states the right to emigrate, which they did not hesitate to exercise in times of difficulty.[46] After 1834 (earlier for some states), customs duties collected on the external frontier of the *zollverein* were divided among member states according to their population, further raising the value to the state and its servants of keeping people at home. This was best accomplished by promoting local prosperity. One can, therefore, argue a mercantilistic case for state entrepreneurship in early nineteenth century Germany, which to a degree overcame the problems of aggregation associated with making the demand for public goods effective.

The paternalistic strain in German economic administration has its roots in the late seventeenth century when the newly reconstituted principalities were trying to become states. Administrators quickly learned the relation between higher productivity and higher revenues. The odd mixture of economic and administrative learning that constituted *kameralwissenschaft* thus came to embody a substantial amount of purely technological information.[47] For example, when the brothers Humboldt went up to the Prussian University at Frankfurt/Oder in 1787 they learned, besides much else, the number of threads in the warp and woof of silk and linen cloth, how to design tar kilns, flour mills, and brandy distilleries, and what to do about caterpillars and other insect pests.[48] By the late eighteenth century bureaucratic office required university training.[49] Since bureaucrats administered the extensive estates of the crown it was natural that they be introduced to industrial and agricultural techniques, with emphasis on the more advanced methods used in economies to the west. The exigencies of lecturing and textbooks did the rest. "Principles" of agriculture compiling various techniques and attempting to systematize or rationalize them began to appear in the 1750s and 1760s.[50] From the early nineteenth century, some of these were embodying primitive "chemical" analyses. Most German administrators at the beginning of the nineteenth century, therefore, not only had a superficial exposure to the different technologies then in use, but also were taught to expect benefits from scientific "perfection" of these techniques.

This educational background may account for observed differences in the accessibility of scientific ideas to French, English, and German administrators. Such differences cannot be measured, but it is known that the French administration drew its cadres from the faculties of law and arts, where rhetoric and jurisprudence dominated the curricula, while the British drew their cadres from the universities where much the same conditions prevailed. At the very least, this must have raised the costs of informing government decision-makers about opportunities involving science.[51] But more than this, it tended to produce a different set of tastes, showing up in different marginal valuations of expenditures on research into agriculture. Given equal opportunity, German administrators were more likely to respond quickly.

VII. EDUCATION

Educational institutions predating the rise in demand for highly skilled specialists and technicians also played a role in determining the timing and spread of formal agricultural science. This influence was exerted through two distinct routes. The first was the development in Germany and France before 1850 of agricultural colleges providing higher instruction in agriculture and making place for specialized professors and some limited facilities for research.[52] The second was the way higher education served to screen as well as train specialists for service in the various professions. Each of these bears on the economic question whether training was provided ahead of demand, which in turn bears on the issue of whether demand or supply forces dominated the movement to create new experiment stations. Institutional education, as opposed to apprenticeship or other forms of on-the-job training, is relatively indivisible, due to the fixed costs (and advantages of) a central library, a curriculum, and a permanent staff of full-time teachers. This gives rise to economies of scale as a function of enrollments. Because of these indivisibilities, anything that tended to promote early institutionalization also made possible relatively abundant supplies of specialists at low marginal costs. This relationship seems to explain some of the differences in the supply of specialists available in Germany and in the rest of Europe.

Before 1850 the growth of the economy everywhere did not create much demand for specialized skills of advanced science. The main outlets for graduates in science in the early nineteenth century were the armed forces, pharmacy, medicine, and the secondary schools. The demand from the private sector for technically skilled personnel seems on the whole to have been met as well by informal as by formal methods of instruction. Indeed, it seems that private demand before 1850 and even later was insufficient to sustain formal educational systems for imparting scientific skills. The major demand for scientific training came from government—which was a major consumer of engineering skills on the continent and which financed the lower levels of education—and from the medical sector.[53]

French, British, and German systems of recruiting professionals differed markedly in the early nineteenth century. In Germany access to the professions, as well as to the higher bureaucracy, was by examination taken on completion of, but supplementary to, university education.[54] In France, examinations also played a key role in assigning men to the professions, but here they were conducted as part of the higher educational establishment—the ''University,'' as the corps of secondary and higher school teachers were called—with the result that higher instruction was a function of the written and oral examinations rather than the imparting of techniques for further learning.[55] Since students did not have to attend classes, but had only to pass exams, the French system for screening applicants to the professions did not generate as high enrollments as in Germany. In England, certification was in the hands of private corporations like the College of Physicians or the London Apothecaries. Exams were required, but teaching normally took the form of apprenticeship-like arrangements. When special facilities such as laboratories or botanical gardens were needed, they emerged to service distinct clienteles, which made for great heterogeneity and limited the extent of scale economies realizable through concentrating the basic courses in single institutions.[56] These differences, all of which seem related to the need to train and screen professionals, appear to have had a marked effect on the supply price of agricultural scientists.

The development of advanced scientific instruction outside the medical facilities in Germany seems to have been a stroke of good luck, in that it developed within the philosophical faculty, which traditionally imparted preliminary teaching and remedial education for students intending to matriculate in the higher faculties of law, theology, and medicine. In the eighteenth century, as noted above, a university degree was required for higher bureaucratic office; at the beginning of the nineteenth century it became mandatory for secondary school teachers. Thus there was created a demand for some scientific education as students prepared to take their state examinations. This feature of German education became even more marked in the 1830s when the slowdown in the expansion of secondary education and the civil service led to a sharp increase in the difficulty of exams and entry requirements as a means of limiting the numbers of unemployed intellectuals.[57] The university degree and advanced training were a signaling device for upwardly mobile young men. In such situations, private demand can exceed what is socially optimal.[58] Supplies could not be expected to adjust immediately to changes in demand. Some of the excess supply was available for agricultural research.

The second peculiarity of higher education in Germany was the multiplicity of small state-supported universities. According to Paulsen this was due to the desire of the territorial princes to control the training and recruitment of their officials. As noted above, the number of institutions and their competition for a fixed student population facilitated the expansion of scientific employment and accentuated the movement to promote and appoint university professors on the basis of published research.

In France, certification dominated the educational functions of higher education with the result that there was much less provision of scientific education than in Germany. The philosophical faculty had withered away in the seventeenth century when its functions were transferred to the *collèges classiques,* leaving the university to give professional training in the "higher" faculties of law, medicine, and theology. By the late eighteenth century many of these institutions had degenerated into examination boards. When the Revolution destroyed the old universities (by seizing their endowments) it created a problem of training and certifying professionals. Military exigency led to the establishment of an engineering school (the Ecole Polytechnique), but by the beginning of the nineteenth century, egalitarian principles were also receding in the face of popular demand to provide some kind of screen for entry to the medical pharmaceutical and legal professions. The screen was provided by higher education. The "University" was a Napoleonic creation consisting of the entire body of secondary school teachers and faculty professors, organized as a hierarchical corps, whose main function was to set and mark degree examinations.[59]

The prerequisite for access to this corps was the bachelor's degree, while the professional "faculties" gave the examinations that awarded access to law, medicine and pharmacy. The system was designed to secure equality of opportunity by means of common examinations for every "grade." The result was that teaching was oriented towards the examinations rather than towards development of research skills.

The significance of this for the supply of scientists is that the meager opportunities provided in Germany by the professional chairs of the numerous universities were lacking in France. Membership in a faculty carried no obligation to conduct research and it provided few or no facilities for advanced instruction. It was simply a mandate to grade. On the whole this seems to be what the French public wanted—theoretically open access to the learned professions combined with strict quality control. It meant, however, that the curriculum was controlled by the content of examinations, which in turn limited the development of new fields. The stress on faculties as mere examination boards or "juries de baccalauréats" meant that they were small, unequipped with laboratory facilities or even libraries outside Paris, and thus unable to take advantage of educational scale economies. Even in Paris these economies were realized not by institutional integration, but by geographical proximity of a number of organizationally distinct institutes and museums. As a result, advanced scientific training was limited to the institutions providing specialists for the state, and to public lectures at the Museum of Natural History or the Conservatory of Arts and Crafts. The recruitment of scientists was thus more strongly determined by the weak private demand for them than was the case in Germany where, because the examinations upon leaving the university and the professional examinations were separate, scientific instruction could develop life of its own.

In England scientific instruction was even more determined by private demand. Medical practitioners below the level of physicians, who took a B.A. entirely unrelated to their prospective careers, and pharmacists, for example, did not need university degrees, but acquired the right to practice by apprenticeships followed by examinations. Their training involved formal instruction, but the teaching was done in separate establishments that had emerged to meet particular demands. Natural scientists and mathematicians taught at the Universities, but their subjects did not compose a central part of the curriculum.

These educational differences show up in the differing prices and apparent supply elasticities of scientists in mid-nineteenth-century Europe. In the 1840s and 1850s skilled chemists could be attracted to agricultural work for about 1000 marks; in England the consulting chemist for the Royal Agricultural Society received the equivalent of 4000 marks. Even at the end of the century beginning chemists at experiment stations in Germany were earning only 1200 marks, while the comparable starting salaries in England and France were closer to 2000.[60] However, it is the early years, when chemists seem temporarily to have been in excess supply, that matters. Their relative abundance in Germany permitted an early and smooth expansion.

VIII. CONCLUSION

This brief account has attempted to draw attention to the institutional factors at work in determining the timing and geographical incidence of early institutions for formal agricultural research. The key elements seem to be the greater responsiveness of authoritarian organizations to perceived opportunity and the differences in the supply of scientists that stemmed from different educational training institutions. The account neglects factors operating on the demand side, of which the uncertainty attached to new inputs, the changes in ecology attendant on the intensification and commercialization of European agriculture, and the need to adjust to more rapidly changing relative prices, were dominant. All these factors helped to create a demand for more precise knowledge that could only be obtained from careful investigations of the properties of living nature. What I have attempted to recount here is how these vague perceptions of opportunity were focussed to produce institutions to study what Benjamin Franklin called "a kind of continuous miracle, wrought by the hand of God . . . as a reward for his innocent life and virtuous industry."

NOTES

1. W. N. Parker, "On a Certain Parallelism Between Two Historical Processes of Productivity Growth," *Agricultural History* 50(1976).

2. These figures are calculated from the lists in A. C. True and D. J. Crosby, *Agricultural Experiment Stations in Foreign Countries* (Washington: 1902). USDA Office of Experiment Stations Bulletin No. 112. The list for 1875 is taken from *Die Landwirtschaftlichen Versuchs-stationen* 22(1877), which describes each station then in existence.

3. G. E. Fussell, *Crop Nutrition: Science and Practice Before Liebig* (London: 1972), pp. 50, 69.

4. See Allan Smith and Diane M. Secoy, "Organic Materials used in European Crop Protection

Before 1850,'' *Chemistry and Industry* 5(November 1977): 863–869; ''Early Chemical Control of Weeds in Europe,'' *Weed Science* 24(November 1976): 594–597; ''A Compendium of Inorganic Substances Used in European Pest Control Before 1850,'' *Agricultural and Food Chemistry* 24(November–December 1976): 1180–1186; and ''Salt as a Pesticide, Manure and Seed Steep,'' *Agricultural History* 50(July 1976): 506–516. I am indebted to Alan Fusonie of the National Agricultural Library for drawing my attention to this material.

5. F. A. Buttress and F. A. Dennis, ''The Early History of Cereal Seed Treatment in England,'' *Agricultural History* 21(1947): 95.

6. E. C. Large, *The Advance of the Fungi* (London: 1938), pp. 78–79. A similar happy coincidence permitted the Abbé Prévost to discover copper's fungicidal properties when he noticed that water distilled in his copper alembic prevented the bunt spores from germinating. Millardet's discovery was also prefigured by peasant use of copper preparations to deter moulds. See George F. Johnson, ''The Early History of Copper Fungicides,'' *Agricultural History* 9(1933): 76–78; and E. G. Lodeman, *The Spraying of Plants* (New York: 1897), pp. 9–10.

7. See the discussion and references in G. W. Grantham, ''The Diffusion of the New Husbandry in Northern France, 1815–1840,''*Journal of Economic History* 38(June 1978): 332–333.

8. Richardson Wright, *The Story of Gardening* (New York: 1934), p. 400.

9. See Moshe Feldman and Ernest R. Sears, ''The Wild Gene Resources of Wheat,'' *Scientific American* 244(January 1981): 102–112; and John Percival, *The Wheat Plant* (London: 1921), p. 410. On the general problems that farmers and breeders faced in distinguishing phenotypes from genotypes, see F. Roberts, *Plant Hybridization Before Mendel* (Princeton: 1929); Hans Stubbe, *History of Genetics, from Prehistoric Times to the Rediscovery of Mendel's Law* (Cambridge: 1972); and Donald F. Jones, *Genetics in Plant and Animal Improvement* (New York: 1925).

10. Jean Meuvret, *Le Problème des subsistances à l'époque de Louis XIV* (Paris: 1978), Vol. 2, p. 136; and the obituary of Louis Vilmorin in the *Journal d'agriculture pratique* (1860): 295.

11. Jakob Eriksson and Ernst Henning, *Die Getreideroste* (Stockholm: 1896), pp. 443–454. Although general predators were always present, mass plagues of the more specialized fungal and insect parasites seem to have been kept in check before 1750 by the complexity of European cropping patterns, which limited the possibilities for rapid expansion of host-specific parasites, and also by the mountain and forest barriers of Eastern Europe, which appear to have protected Western Europe from spores from the rusts of the Russian steppes and from the downwind breeding grounds of such swarming insects as locusts. See F. S. Bodenheimer, *Materialien zur Geschichte der Entomologie bis Linné* (Berlin: 1928); K. Starr Chester, *The Nature and Prevention of the Cereal Rusts as Exemplified in the Leaf Rust of Wheat* (Waltham, Mass.: 1946), pp. 156–162; and Ernst Lehman, Hans Kummer, and Hans Danneman, *Der Schwarzerost* (Berlin: 1937). For a clear account of the ecology of parasites and their hosts, see Macfarlane Burnet and David O. White, *The Natural History of Infectious Diseases*, 4th ed. (Cambridge: 1972).

12. John Curtis, ''Observations on the Natural History of the Insects Affecting Turnip Crops,'' *Journal of the Royal Agricultural Society* 4(1843): pp. 101–102; ''Observations on the Natural History and Economy of the Insects called Wireworms,'' Ibid., 5(1844): pp. 180–237; and J.-B. Boisduval, *Essai sur l'entomologie horticole* (Paris: 1867), pp. 210–213.

13. I have attempted to articulate an economic account of this kind of organization in ''Science and Its Transactions Costs: The Evolution of an Implicit Contract,'' McGill University Department of Economics Working Paper (May 1983).

14. The following account of the history of Mockern is based on material in Gustav Kuhn, ''Geschichtliches über die landwirthschaftliche Versuchs-Station Mockern,'' in the Festschrift commemorating the 25th anniversary of the founding of Mockern appearing in *Die landwirthchaftlichen Versuchs-Stationen* Vol. 22 (1877); Karl Kohlsdorf, *Geschichte der Leipziger Okonomischen Sozietät* (Leipzig, 1913); and Theodor Reuning, *Die Entwicklung der Sachsischen Landwirtschaft in den Jahren 1845–1854* (Dresden: 1856).

15. A. M. H. *Matthews, Fifty Years of Agricultural Politics* (London: 1915); and E. A. Atwood,

"The Origins of State Support for British Agriculture," *Manchester School of Economics and Social Studies* 31(May 1963), pp. 129–148; *Journal of Royal Agricultural Society, England* 97(1936): 54–80.

16. Heinrich Wilhelm Crusius (b. 1790) is representative of Saxony's enlightened aristocracy. He was active in Saxon politics and economics. In 1824 he organized the first hail mutual insurance company. He was one of the founders of the Leipzig–Dresden railway in 1835. In 1837 he helped found the All-German Congress of Agricultural Societies, to which body he was elected president for the gathering at Altenburg in 1843. He was director of the Leipzig Economic Society from 1831 and guided its transformation into a purely agricultural association. His estate at Sahlis was a standard stop for visiting agriculturists and in 1846 he established a small chemical experiment station there. In politics he was a deputy for the Knight's *Stande* in 1848, entering the first Saxon Assembly serving as a minister for the Leipzig Kreisverein. According to the historian of the Leipzig Economic Society, it was through his influence that Reuning obtained the directorship of the *landeskulturrat* (Kohlsdorf, *Gesch*, p. 43). His estate at Sahlis is described by the French agricultural inspector in C. E. Boyer, *L'Agriculture Allemande, ses écoles, son organisation, ses moeurs et ses pratiques les plus récentes* (Paris: 1847), pp. 461–472. See the entries for Crusius in the *Allgemeine Deutsche Biographie* and the *Neue Deutsche Biographie*.

17. Reuning appears to have been a deep student of von Thunen and was a firm supporter of free trade. He believed that Saxony's industrialization was pushing Saxon agriculture toward more intensive forms in which livestock husbandry would predominate. He advocated government intervention to ease and guide this transformation which, he asserted, "can only really develop strongly by rooting itself securely and deeply in intellectual effort." Reuning, *Entwicklung*, pp. 13, 42–43.

18. See Stockhardt's obituary by Nobbe in *Die Landwirtschaftlichen Versuchs-Stationen* 33(1887): 424–433. His role in stimulating interest in agricultural chemistry is described in Kuhn, "Geschichtliches . . . Mockern," pp. 1–12. With the exception of Julius Kuhn, who founded and expanded the great institute at Halle, nearly all the first generation of German agricultural scientists came out of the lower middle classes of clergy, pharmacists, and doctors. Given the early importance of chemistry and the social sources of recruitment to the chemical professions, this is perhaps not surprising. See Gunter Franz, *Grosse Landwirte* (Frankfurt/Main: 1970); and R. Theile, *Erster Bericht über die Arbeiten der Landwirtschaftlichen Versuchs-station zu Jena* (Jena: 1866), pp. 2–4.

19. *Die organische Chemie in ihrer Anwending auf Agricultur und Physiologie* (Braunschweig: 1840).

20. According to Margaret Rossiter, it is not clear how Liebig happened on this topic. I have followed her speculations. See *The Emergence of Agricultural Science, Justus Liebig and the Americans, 1840–1880* (New Haven, Conn.: 1975), pp. 27–28.

21. Cited in Wolfgang Krohn and Wolf Schafer, "The Origins and Structure of Agricultural Chemistry," in Gerard Lemaine et al., *Perspectives on the Emergence of Scientific Disciplines* (Paris: 1976), p. 31.

22. The above account is drawn from the unpublished doctoral dissertation of Gerrylyn K. Roberts, *The Royal College of Chemistry (1845–1853): A Social History of Chemistry in Early-Victorian England*. The Johns Hopkins University, Baltimore, 1973.

23. J. Eduard Heiden, *Lehrbuch der Dungerlehre*, 2nd ed. (Hannover: 1887); and Josef Pawlowski, *Beitrage zur geschichtlichen Entwicklung des Umganges und der Art der Anwendung von Handelsdunger*, (Jena: 1896), p. 20. Evidently tests carried out on guano in the 1820s and 1830s failed to detect its remarkable fertilizing powers, which is surprising but may reflect poor experimental design. In 1841 seven ships sailed to the Chincha Islands. The next year 41 ships returned to England from the guano grounds. Charles L. Bartlett, *Guano: A Treatise on the History, Economy as a Manure, and Modes of Applying Peruvian Guano* (Boston: 1860), p. 4. See also W. M. Mathew, "Peru and the British Guano Market 1840–1870," *Economic History Review* 2nd ser., 23(1970): 112–125.

24. Peruvian guano's nitrogen content varied naturally from 12 to 19 percent, and sometimes

was as low as 4 percent, which made fraud difficult to detect. See France, Commission des Engrais, *Enquête sur les engrais industriels,* Vol. 2 (Paris: 1865–66), pp. 52, 226.

25. Improvements in organic chemistry lowering the cost of performing analyses of organic substances to a level that made the multiple determinations needed for agricultural work feasible occurred in 1831, with Liebig's new method for determining carbon and Dumas volumetric technique for measuring nitrogen. Liebig claimed his technique reduced the time required by twentyfold. See J. R. Partington, *A History of Chemistry,* Vol. 3 (London: 1964), pp. 237–239; Sieghardt Neufeldt, *Chronologie Chemie,* 1800–1870 (New York: 1977), p. 22. New fertilizers became available only in the 1820s, as can be seen from the descriptions in George Fussell, *Crop Nutrition: Science and Practice Before Liebig* (London: 1972). Most of them were due either to geographical discovery, such as the Chilean nitrates and guano, or were by-products of new industrial products such as ammonia, charred bones, and later phosphoric slag. The first of these were the spent charcoal of bones used from around 1815 as a filter and clarifying agent in sugar refineries. See Ralf Schaumann, *Technik und technischer Fortschritt im Industrialisierungsprozess* (Bonn: 1977), pp. 61, 66–67, 87.

26. Richard Woge, *Einfluss des Zuckerrubenbaues auf die Landwirtschaft* (Leipzig: 1892), p. 46; Saxony (Province), Landwirtschaftskammer, *Die Landwirtschafts Kammer für die Provinz Sachsen zu Halle a. s. und Ihre Institute* (Berlin: 1901), pp. 167–168; and Pawlowski, *Beitrage,* pp. 28–29. At the French hearings into fertilizer frauds a farmer declared that he could not grow sugar beets without guano. *Enquête sur les engrais,* Vol. 1 (Paris: 1865–66), p. 533.

27. The Peruvian government held a monopoly on guano so that prices actually rose in the 1850s. According to Liebig, who argued that plants took their nitrogen from the ammonia in the atmosphere, the nitrates in guano were superfluous, and since there were other sources of phosphates, guano itself was not necessary. See Richard Aulie, "The Mineral Theory," *Agricultural History* (July 1974): 369–382. Mathew, "Peru and the British Guano Market," p. 212. Credit sales of fertilizers to peasants are extensively described in *Enquête sur les engrais.*

28. See Henry Handly, "Account of the Meeting of German Landowners in 1841," JRASE 3(1841), pp. 217–233; and Eduard Pelz, *Die neueste Versammlung Deutscher Land und Forstwirthe in Breslau* (Breslau, 1845), p. 17.

29. Reuning, *Entwicklung,* pp. 52–53. The role of the agricultural *vereine* in the political economy of nineteenth-century Germany has yet to be analyzed. As noted below they were not pressure groups, which would have implied an unacceptable pluralism in pre-1870 Germany. The standard account of their activities is R. Stadelmann, *Das landwirtschaftliches Vereinswesen in Preussen* (Halle: 1874). Their importance in regard to the creation of research institutions for agriculture can be seen in the fact that of 24 experiment stations in Prussia in 1900, 21 had been called into being by the *vereine.*

30. To the bureaucrats controlling the Prussian state the key problem of post-Jena organization was to secure the allegiance and active support of the propertied classes in restoring the nation without relinquishing any authority. The land reforms and the establishment of the *vereine* were part of this attempt. A similar process can be seen in the industrial regions of the Rheinland, where the French invaders co-opted local businessmen onto committees, giving them some very limited powers of self-administration. These institutions, in the rougher modes of Prussian bureaucracy, were adapted to tasks of securing cooperation after the region was handed over to Prussia. See Jeffrey M. Diefendorf, *Businessmen and Politics in the Rhineland, 1789–1834* (Princeton: 1980).

31. 14 September 1811. Both the acts regulating serfdom and lordship and establishing the *vereine,* were drafted by Thaer and were part of the same program to raise productivity by liberating the soil from feudal constraints. Stadelmann, *Das vereinswesen,* pp. 10–11. The best account of these changes is still Theodor von der Goltz, *Geschichte der Deutschen Landwirtschaft* Vol. II, (Stuttgart: 1903).

32. Stadelmann, *Das Vereinswesen,* p. 318.

33. Between 1820, when there were still less than a dozen, and 1840, 108 new *vereine* were follow a similar pattern. In the kingdom of Saxony, the number rose from a half dozen in the early

1830s to 55 in 1844, and 137 in 1854. See Stadelmann, *Das Vereinswesen,* pp. 298–299; Reuning, *Entwicklung sachsischen Landwirtschaft,* pp. 52–55; and Heinz Haushofer, *Die deutsche Landwirtschaft im technischen Zeitalter* (Stuttgart: 1972), pp. 74–76.

34.   In Saxony, a government official sat as general secretary of the chief district *vereine* as well as heading the advisory council. In Prussia the equivalent body was the Landes-Kollegium, which was composed predominantly of government appointees, including as in Saxony, a sprinkling of natural scientists.

35.   Wolfram Fischer, "Government Activity and Industrialization in Germany, 1815–1870," in W. W. Rostow (ed.), *The Economics of Take-off into Sustained Growth* (London: 1963), p. 90.

36.   See for the United States, Charles E. Rosenberg, "Science, Technology, and Economic Growth: The Case of the Agricultural Experiment Station Scientist, 1875–1914," *Agricultural History* 45(1971): 1–20.

37.   Felix Ponteil, *Les Institutions de la France de 1814 à 1870* (Paris: 1966), pp. 88, 312–313.

38.   *Journal d'agriculture pratique* 2(1861): 639. The Société Centrale d'Agriculture in Paris included scientists of the highest stature. A sample of the level of discussion can be found in excerpts of Boussingault's interventions. In the course of one of them in the early 1870s, Pasteur remarks that bacteria might be responsible for the fixation of atmospheric nitrogen. M. Lenglen, *Un aspect peu connu de l'oeuvre de J. B. Boussingault* (Beauvais: 1937), pp. 24–25.

39.   In the absence of a careful study of the *comices* any discussion of their role in encouraging agricultural science is speculative. One suspects that political considerations, which led to nonparticipation or exclusion of many local gentry from government-sponsored organizations limited their effectiveness. The predominance of purely political considerations in public decisions in France can be seen in Napoleon III's dismantling of the Institute Agronomique at Versailles in 1852 on the grounds that it was a Republican institution. See Albert Demolon, *L'Evolution scientifique et l'agriculture française* (Paris: 1946), p. 39.

40.   France, Assemblée Nationale Constituante, 1848–1849. Séance 21 août 1848.

41.   Terence de Vere White, *The Story of the Dublin Society* (Tralee: 1955), pp. 13–16. Kenneth Hudson, *Patriotism and Profit: British Agricultural Societies in the 18th and 19th Centuries* (London: 1972), pp. 3–5.

42.   G. E. Fussell, "John Wynn Baker: An 'Improver' in Eighteenth Century Ireland," *Agricultural History* 5(1931): 151–161. On the inadequacy of experimental techniques between 1750 and 1840, see E. M. Crowther, "The Technique of Modern Farm Experiments," *Journal of the Royal Agricultural Society* 97(1936), and G. E. Fussell, "The Techniques of Early Field Experiments," ibid. 96(1935): 78–88.

43.   The Royal Institution's commissioning Humphrey Davy to conduct experiments on agricultural chemistry and lecture on the subject to its members is a good early example. The Institution, whose membership overlapped considerably with that of the Board of Agriculture, demanded in addition that Davy analyze soils for its subscribers. For his part Davy seems to have persuaded the aristocrats that agricultural chemistry was "founded upon very simple *principles* which may be *easily acquired* and which are almost independent of the more abstruse and more complicated parts of the Science." The dissipation of effort and lack of real criticism this environment provided is perhaps one of the reasons Davy's contributions to agricultural chemistry were so slight, at a time when Theodore de Saussure was successfully distinguishing between the atmospheric and mineral sources of the elements found in plants. See Morris Bermann, *Social Science and Scientific Organization. The Royal Institution, 1799–1834* (Ithaca: 1978), pp. 41–42, 49, 55–67. For a judgment on Davy's contributions to agricultural chemistry see Charles A. Browne, *A Source Book of Agricultural Chemistry* (Waltham, Mass.: 1944).

44.   J. A. Scott Watson, *The History of the Royal Agricultural Society of England, 1839–1939* (London: 1939).

45.   John Le Couteur, *On the Varieties, Properties and Classification of Wheat* (Jersey: 1836).

46.   Hermann Aubin and Wolfgang Zorn (eds.), *Handbuch der Deutschen Wirtschafts-und*

Sozialgeschichte, Vol. 2 (Stuttgart: 1976), pp. 28–33; and Mack Walker, *Germany and the Emigration (1816–1885)* (Cambridge, Mass.: 1964).

47. See Ulrich Troitzsch, *Ansatze technologischen Denkens bei den Kameralisten des 17. und 18. Jahrhunderts* (Berlin: 1966); and Albion Woodbury Small, *The Cameralists* (Chicago: 1909).

48. Maurice Crosland, *The Society of Arcueil* (Cambridge: 1967), p. 105.

49. A University degree was required to enter the Prussian bureaucracy from the early 1770s. Wolfram Fischer and Peter Lundgreen, "The Recruitment and Training of Administrative and Technical Personnel," in Charles Tilly (ed.), *The Formation of National States in Western Europe* (Princeton: 1975), pp. 515–519. Bureaucrats continued to receive their university education in cameralism down to the 1840s, when the subject was displaced by the study of law. See "Kameralwissenschaften," in J. Conrad et al., *Handworterbuch der Staatswissenschaften* (Jena: 1900).

50. Troitzsch, *Ansatze,* pp. 151–155. The first generation of higher instruction in agriculture grew out of courses taught by professors of cameralism, and the foundation of the first agricultural academies for imparting higher learning in agriculture was strongly tinged with cameralistic concerns to diffuse new techniques more rapidly. Advancing knowledge through research was not a primary aim before the 1840s in these schools. See Goltz, *Geschichte deutschen Landwirtschaft,* Vol. 2, p. 86; and Gunter Franz, *Universitat Hohenheim, Landwirtschaftliche Hochschule, 1818–1968* (Stuttgart: 1968).

51. The importance of scientifically informed bureaucrats can be seen in the establishment of the National Agricultural School at Grignon by August Bella. Bella was an officer in Napoleon's army stationed at Celle in Hannover, where he studied with Thaer. While recovering from wounds at his family's estate in Savoie, he met the departmental engineer Polonceau. In the 1820s Bella was landowner and mayor of his town in Lorraine, when he once again met Polonceau, now chief engineer for Ponts et Chaussées in the Parisian department of Seine-et-Oise and very close to the king's ministers. Polonceau and Bella visited Mathieu de Dombasle's model farm and school at Roville and decided to establish a larger and better financed school near Paris. Through Polonceau's efforts the estate at Grignon was purchased by the king and ceded to the French Royal Agricultural Society, which had formed a joint stock company for the purpose of establishing the farm, which was to be main nursery of France's agronomists before 1870. In the 1830s and 1840s the government subsidized the station by giving fellowships to its students. See Rene Cercler, *Mathieu de Dombasle* (Paris: 1946), pp. 124–128; and Leouzon, *Agronomes et eleveurs,* pp. 246–253.

52. The dates are Celle (1790s), Weihenstephan (Bavaria, 1803), Moglin (1806), Hohenheim (1818), Roville (1822), Grignon (1828), Schleissheim (1822), Jena (1826), Eldena Griefswald, (1835). There were also a few professorial chairs of agriculture at Berlin (1810), Edinburgh (1790), the Jardin des Plantes (1785), Conservatoire des Arts et Métiers (1836), and the Royal Institution (1801–1812) where professors lectured and conducted simple experiments. Liebig criticized these institutions severely for their amateurism, and it appears that teaching loads and the lack of preparation of students limited their capacity to support profound research. Nevertheless, some of the basic work establishing the mineral theory of nutrition was carried out in the early 1830s by Karl Sprengel at Eldena and Jena, and in presenting a "system" of agriculture based on crudely estimated input–output tables for crops, animals, and manures, the professors provided the framework and agenda for the comprehensive program of research enunciated by Liebig in the 1840s.

53. For a suggestive, though not statistically supported, argument along these lines, see Lenore O'Boyle, "The Problem of an Excess of Educated Men in Western Europe, 1800–1850," *Journal of Modern History* 42(1970): 471–495. Friederic Moreau in Flaubert's *L'Education sentimental* is the classic portrait.

54. Friedrich Paulsen, *The German Universities: Their Character and Development* (New York: 1895), p. 202.

55. Antoine Prost, *L'Enseignement en France, 1800–1967* (Paris: 1968); and L. Liard, *L'Enseignement superieure en France, 1789–1893,* 2 vols. (1888–1894).

56. D. S. L. Cardwell, *The Organisation of Science in England* (Melbourne: 1957).

57. Paulsen, *German Universities*, p. 43. With a few exceptions the German universities, like the French and the English, had become moribund or plagued with religious niggling in the eighteenth century. In the early nineteenth century it was still a question whether they would be preserved in Prussia, or whether special technical schools would be established along the lines of France's Ecoles Polytechnique and the other engineering schools to provide the necessary trained personnel. See Charles E. McClelland, *State, Society, and University in Germany, 1700–1914*, (Cambridge: 1980), pp. 29–30, 78–79.

58. See Kenneth Arrow, ''Higher Education as a Filter,'' *Journal of Public Economics* 2(July 1973), pp. 193–216, and Joseph E. Stiglitz, ''The Theory of 'Screening', Education and the Distribution of Income,'' *AER* 65(June 1975): 285–300. A priori analysis does not predict an unambiguous excess demand for screening, since sorting does in general raise productivity. However, in the context of the largely literary training of early 19th-century secondary and post-secondary educational institutions, it would appear that the sharp rise in examination standards imposed in Prussia in the 1830s made no additional direct contribution to productivity. Its main effect was to raise the age of entering students and also their level of preparation, making it possible to give much more advanced training to students who desired it.

59. See the massive study by Paul Gerbod, *La Condition universitaire en France au XIXe siecle* (Paris: 1965).

60. Ludwig Haber, *The Chemical Industry in the Nineteenth Century* (Oxford: 1958), pp. 188–190. Beginning salaries for chemists at the experiment station at Hohenheim were 1200 to 1600 marks down to the end of the century. Wurttemberg, Finanz-Ministerium, *Haupfinanzetat des Konigsreich Wurttemberg* (Stuttgart: 1878). Baden Finanzministerium Voranschlag des Ausgehen und Einnahmen der allgemeinen Staatsverwaltung (1892–1909). Way's retainer from the Royal Agricultural Society of 200 pounds plus the 300 pounds he earned from special analyses for its members was equal to 10,000 marks. Watson, *History of Royal Agricultural Society*, p. 119. These figures are of course only suggestive. Proof would require a full-scale investigation into the supplies and demands of trained scientists in the nineteenth century.

MID-NINETEENTH-CENTURY CROP YIELDS AND LABOR PRODUCTIVITY GROWTH IN AMERICAN AGRICULTURE:

A NEW LOOK AT PARKER AND KLEIN

Jeremy Atack and Fred Bateman

I. OVERVIEW

In a pioneer work of the emerging "new economic history" entitled "Productivity Growth in Grain Production in the United States, 1840–60 and 1900–10," William Parker and Judith L. V. Klein presented new estimates of labor productivity growth in wheat, corn, and oats for the second half of the nineteenth century.[1] Practitioners of the new methodology had not previously shown any

Technique, Spirit, and Form in the Making of the Modern Economies:
Essays in Honor of William N. Parker
Research in Economic History, Suppl. 3, pages 215–242
ISBN: 0-89232-414-7

substantial interest in northern American agriculture despite the fundamental importance of the sector; rather, their interest had centered on more colorful topics such as slavery or railroads. Even in Vol. 30 of the National Bureau's *Studies in Income and Wealth,* where this work appeared and whose authors branched out into new areas of cliometric interest such as mining, manufacturing, and power sources, the Parker–Klein work stood alone in its focus upon the single most important economic activity among Americans throughout most of the nineteenth century. Since then, the paper has become a widely quoted standard reference work.[2]

Parker and Klein had two major goals. First, they sought to estimate labor productivity growth between 1840–1860 and 1900–1910 by combining crop yield estimates with the labor inputs at the respective dates. Second, they wanted to isolate and measure the individual contributions of technological change, scientific improvement, and westward expansion to that productivity growth. The decomposition procedure that they used became a model for other subsequent studies.[3]

Parker was also in the vanguard of cliometricians gathering large-scale samples from the manuscripts of the federal censuses. The Parker–Gallman sample of southern farms from major cotton-producing counties, collected in collaboration with Robert Gallman, has been the fundamental resource for much of the subsequent work on slavery. Moreover, it inspired other scholars to collect complementary samples for other areas of southern agriculture, other sectors of the economy, and other regions. With support primarily from the National Science Foundation, most of the available nineteenth-century federal census manuscripts eventually were sampled and subjected to some quantitative analysis.[4] These form the foundation of much contemporary cliometric research.

Unavoidably the Parker–Klein productivity study suffered from the methodological and data constraints of its time. Some of these have since relaxed. We examine below the implications for the labor productivity growth estimates of new evidence of mid-nineteenth-century crop yields in the northern and Midwestern states derived from a sample of farms from the 1860 federal census manuscripts. This sample, itself, was inspired by the Parker–Gallman initiative. We shall also consider the effects of the revisions on the relative importance of mechanization, land yields, and the westward movement as sources of productivity expansion.

The central results of Parker and Klein were first, the enormous growth of labor productivity in corn, wheat, and oats (in the neighborhood of 400 percent between 1840–1860 and 1900–1910) and second, the overwhelming dominance of mechanization in accounting for these gains. As presented, the Parker–Klein figures appear to be upper-bound estimates, but we find, to the contrary, that if anything they understate the case for labor productivity growth over the period. Whereas their numbers translate into average annual productivity growth rates of 2.06 percent in wheat and 1.86 percent in corn and oats, we find that the new

1859 crop yield data imply annual percentage growth rates of 2.46 in wheat, 2.28 in oats, and 2.23 in corn. Our revisions also affect the relative importance of mechanization, improved land yields, and the westward expansion of the totals, substantially raising the significance of increased yields. Ironically, these results seem more consistent than the originals with Parker's conception of the American family farm as experimental and adaptive to new methods and seed varieties as well as responsive to the developmental efforts of such agencies as the Commissioner of Patents, the U.S. Department of Agriculture (USDA), various state and county agricultural societies, and the agricultural press.

II. CONTEMPORARY YIELD ESTIMATES

Yield estimates are central to the productivity index. The data for the base period, 1840–1860, which Parker and Klein used, were from scattered sources and often of questionable accuracy. Figures for the terminal period were both more numerous and, presumably, more reliable. We propose no alterations in their 1900–1910 data.

Parker and Klein were aware of the shortcomings of the early data but were unable to offer any satisfactory alternatives. Instead they had to be content with the following caveat:[5]

> The most dubious use of data lies in the combination of the estimates of land yields by state based on the USDA revised estimates, with an average of labor inputs per acre derived from a sample of contemporary evidence which . . . is drawn largely from the most productive farms. . . . There is reason, however, to argue that labor inputs on such farms are less biased than a similar sample of yields would be. For one thing, if bias exists, it is not certain which way it would run. . . . Furthermore, in wheat and oats, the case is particularly strong since high yields are obtained by superior seed, soil, and skill rather than by labor-intensive operations of weeding and cultivating.

They used the average USDA revised yield estimates for 1866–1875 as proxies for the yields that a farmer might realize in 1839 or expect on average over the period 1840–1860.[6] No correction was made for trend. As justification for this choice, they offered an extensive survey of contemporary yield estimates for the earlier period, which they summarized in Appendix B of their work. Those contemporary yield estimates appeared in letters to the Commissioner of Patents such as:

> raised this season from one bushel's sowing, 29 bushels [of wheat]; said one bushel was sown upon 157 square rods [= 0.98 acre, or a yield of 29.6 bu/acre]. . . . The average product from an acre [of corn] is about 35 bushels, although in some instances the product has trebled it . . . ;[7]
>
> Since I have grown the flint-wheat, my average has been about 25 bushels per acre. . . .
> Oats—Average crop per acre, about 50 bushel. . . ;[8]
>
> Wheat—There are three kinds in use—the bald, which averages about 25 bushels per acre;

Black Sea average 25 to 30 bushels, and red-chaff, average 20 bushels per acre. . . . Corn—
Varieties, yellow and white; average crop, 50 bushels per acre . . . ; Oats, average yield per
acre, 40 bushels . . . ;[9]

Average product per acre [of wheat] for 1850, about 19 bushels . . . [corn], Fifty bushels . . . Oats—average yield, 36 bushels . . . ;[10]

The variety of wheat sown now is principally the Black Sea wheat, the red-bearded wheat and
the bald white, for spring sowing; and the average product per acre (unhurt by rust or weevil)
is, or rather has been, about 8 to 10 bushels . . . winter wheat . . . has yielded well, some as
high as from 35 to 40 bushels to the acre. . . . An average crop [of corn] . . . may be reduced
not far from 40 bushels per acre. . . . Oats yield very small . . . formerly 20 to 50 per acre,
now 6 to 25. . . .[11]

From their analysis of these and similar reports from 1843 to 1855, Parker and
Klein determined that "[E]xcept in the frontier states, where acreages are small
in any case and yields high for a few years, the median of the 1843–5 county
reports, by state, taken without regard to year, fall surprisingly close to the
1866–75 USDA state averages."[12] Nonetheless, one might question the representativeness of the experience of farmers who reported their yields in letters
which might be published.

Although one might expect an upward bias in the yields reported to the
Commissioner of Patents, these pale in comparison with those which appeared in
the popular press and in books, especially those directed at potential immigrants.
For example, in its sales literature for Illinois land, the Illinois Central Railroad
reprinted the following testimonials:

Our average crop of corn, say a field of eighty acres, did not vary much from fifty bushels per
acre. Winter wheat . . . upon a field of thirty acres, varied in different years from nineteen to
twenty-three bushels per acre . . . oats varied from forty to sixty bushels per acre,"[13]

and

I raised over twenty-five bushels per acre of the best wheat last year, on corn ground, without
ploughing, and sixty bushels of oats.[14]

Their sales brochure even quoted the editor of the *Prairie Farmer's* estimate of
Illinois yields from 18 years of experience:

With ordinary culture:

Winter Wheat	15 to 25 bushels
Spring Wheat	10 to 20 bushels
Indian Corn	40 to 70 bushels
Oats	40 to 80 bushels
Potatoes	100 to 200 bushels
Grass (timothy and clover)	1½ to 3 tons[15]

Such extravagant claims can perhaps be dismissed out of hand because of the obvious self-interest of the railroad in inflating productivity to raise the sale price of its land grants, but it is harder to ignore the (supposedly) more disinterested claims such as those cited by Frederick Gerhard in his book *Illinois as It Is*. They may be summarized as in the accompanying tabulations.[16]

| | Yield (bu/acre) | | |
County	Wheat	Corn	Oats
Cass	18–25	50–70	40–45
Jo Daviess	15–40	30–100	45
McLean	20–30	45–70	40–50
St. Clair	15–30	30–100	30–60
Marshall		50–70	
Pike	20–40	50–70	40–50
Adams	20–40	60–70	
Peoria	15–25	30–60	
Will		50	

Gerhard concluded: "according to these observations which were made in nine different countries of the State, throughout her longitudinal extension . . . we receive the following average numbers, per acre: —Indian corn, 56 bushels; wheat, 24; oats, 44 . . ."[17] For Illinois, Parker and Klein used yields of 30.6 bushels for corn, 11.3 bushels for wheat, and 30.5 bushels for oats.[18]

There are similar contemporary quotations for the other Midwestern states. For example, Nathan Parker offered possible immigrants to Iowa the following examples of that state's fertile soil:

[A] field of corn . . . produced the extraordinary yield of *one hundred and sixty-eight bushels to an acre!* Jerome Parsons of Jefferson County exhibited specimens of *Red-Chaff Bearded Wheat* from an almost unprecedented yield of *fifty-seven bushels to the acre.* . . .[19]

And the Minnesota Commissioner of Statistics quoted wheat yields in the range of 10–35 bushels per acre, corn yields of 23–70 bushels and average oat yields of 35 bushels.[20]

There is no dearth of crop yield estimates for the period 1840–1860; missing, however, is any consensus about central tendencies. Yet, the size of crop yields is important to the productivity index. The lower the base period yield, ceteris paribus, the higher will be the rate of productivity growth. Parker and Klein, by relying upon the average USDA revised estimates for 1866–1875 because of their presumed lack of bias, appear to inflate their productivity index since the USDA yields were lower than many of the contemporary accounts. Consequently, Parker and Klein provided an alternative set of estimates based upon higher median yields derived from the letters to the Commissioner of Patents for the western states. These reduced the overall index for each crop. A one-third increase in oat yields between the USDA figures and the median estimate in the Commissioner of Patents's letters, for example, reduced the index to 352 from 363, or to an annual rate of 1.81 percent. An approximately 20 percent increase in corn and wheat yields between these two sources lowered those indexes by 28 and 4 percent, respectively.[21] Those alterations also changed the conclusions to be drawn from an examination of the partitioned indexes of the sources of productivity change.

Because the alternative yield estimates used by Parker and Klein were still much lower than the upper bounds suggested by contemporaries, there remained the possibility that the Parker–Klein productivity growth index overstates the pace of productivity growth in American agriculture. Our results, however, suggest that their productivity growth estimates may, in fact, be unduly low, because even the USDA yields were too high.

III.   A SAMPLE OF NORTHERN FARMS

Most of the data for our study are taken from a sample of quantitative information from the manuscripts of the federal censuses of agriculture and population for 1860.[22] This sample, drawn from 20 northern states, contains data for 21,118 rural households, of which 11,943 operated farms (253 of these farms had fewer than 3 improved acres or reported no meaningful data). The agricultural data include: improved and unimproved acreage, the value of the farm and implements, holdings of individual types of livestock and their aggregate value, the type and quantities (or in the case of market garden, or orchard produce, their value) of crops produced, the value of home manufactures, and the value of livestock slaughtered. The farms were cross-matched with the population schedules using the name of the farm operator and in addition all data for the nonfarm households in each sample townships were also collected. These population data, however, are not used in this particular study.

The sample contains the information for all the farms (and households) in one randomly selected *nonurban* township from each of 29 randomly chosen counties in the eastern states and 73 in the western ones. By chance, no counties in Delaware, Maine, Massachusetts, or Rhode Island were chosen. Despite this, the sample is representative of the 20 northern states and subgroupings of the Midwest and the Northeast. The individual states are also generally representative of their respective parent populations. An extended discussion of sample tests is given elsewhere.[23]

IV. ESTIMATING YIELDS FROM CENSUS CROP DATA

By confining the selection of farms to specific townships, interfarm yield variations because of differences in soil type and local weather within any sampling unit are minimized. If such influences were the only source of yield variations in a township, the degrees of freedom would be seriously limited and the results might not be relevant beyond the confines of the townships. There is, however, sufficient interfarm variability due to such factors as differences in farming ability and agricultural practice within each township to identify our yield equations.

The census enumerators reported production of the following field crops:

1.	Wheat	6.	Tobacco	11.	Barley	16.	Hops
2.	Rye	7.	Cotton	12.	Buckwheat	17.	Hemp
3.	Corn	8.	Peas and beans	13.	Hay	18.	Flax
4.	Oats	9.	Irish potatoes	14.	Clover seed	19.	Flaxseed
5.	Rice	10.	Sweet potatoes	15.	Grass seed		

In addition they reported upon wool production, the value of orchard products and market garden produce, wine production, butter and cheese production, silk cocoons, cane and maple sugar and molasses, sorghum molasses, and beeswax and honey. Although the production of these latter outputs involved the use of land, the transformation from land to dollars of apples, pounds of butter, or gallons of molasses is not clear. Consequently we confine our attention to the field crops whose output is given in physical units.

Unfortunately crop yields cannot be estimated directly from the identity:

$$Y_i \equiv \frac{Q_i}{A_i}$$

for each crop, $i = 1, \ldots, 19$, where Y is yield per acre, Q is output, and A is acreage because the census enumerators did not collect data on the acreage devoted to each crop.

Consider, however, the following version of the yield identity:

$$A_i = \frac{Q_i}{Y_i}.$$

For all crops $i = 1, \ldots, 19$ we may write:

$$\sum_i A_i = \sum_i \left(\frac{Q_i}{Y_i}\right).$$

We can use this equation to estimate yields from the data given in the census. Acreage is measured by improved acres, which were defined by the census as "cleared land used for grazing, grass, or tillage, or which is now fallow, connected with or belonging to the farms . . . [B]y *improved* land is meant all pasture, meadow, and arable land which has been reclaimed from a state of nature, and which continues to be reclaimed and used for purposes of production."[24] It therefore includes all acreage harvested. Substituting improved acres for acreage harvested and allowing yields to vary because of differences in farm practice, farming ability, and "Acts of God," we have the equation:

$$\text{Improved acres} = \text{constant} + b_1 \cdot Q_1 + \ldots + b_{19} \cdot Q_{19} + u$$
$$= \hat{a} + \sum_i \hat{b}_i Q_i,$$

where $\hat{b}_i$ is the vector of yield reciprocals, $1/Y_i$. The constant term measures the acreage devoted to excluded crops such as orchards, market garden, or viticulture, as well as that given over to livestock grazing and to fallow. This equation was estimated by ordinary least squares for each state in the sample and for the western and eastern subregions as well as for the entire sample of northern farms.[25]

Not all farms produced all crops. Most farmers cultivated corn and wheat, but relatively few grew barley, rye, buckwheat, or other minor crops. The production of hay, oats, and potatoes varied greatly from farm to farm and region to region. We only report the yield estimates for wheat, corn, and oats. The other crops, however, were included in the estimating equations.[26] The regression coefficients for many of the unreported crops were often not significantly different from zero. In a few instances, negative coefficients were estimated. Never significantly different from zero, the negative coefficients were for infrequently cultivated crops. They were dropped from the equations in which they appeared, and the equations were reestimated without them.

The form of the regression equation forced upon us by the data that were available causes some econometric problems. First, the inference that a regression coefficient is not statistically different from zero implies that the yield (its reciprocal) is infinite. A more plausible interpretation, however, is simply that acreage devoted to a crop for which an insignificant coefficient was estimated is negligible. Second, negative regression coefficients are clearly nonsensical. Therefore crops whose coefficients were originally estimated to be negative were dropped from the equation. Third, even when a t-statistic was significant at better than the 95 percent level, the interval about the reciprocal of the coefficient could be very large. Consider, for example, the regression coefficient for potatoes for the entire northern sample (see below). The value, 0.0244, is significantly different from zero at better than the 99.9 percent level (t = 3.50), yet the interval for the yield is from a low of 26.3 bushels per acre (the reciprocal of the upper-bound limit of the 95 percent confidence interval about the regression coefficient) to as much as 93.5 bushels per acre (for the reciprocal of the lower bound of the confidence interval). Finally, it should also be noted that the interval defined by the confidence interval about the regression coefficient is not symmetric about the mean estimate of the yield, and statistical theory tells us nothing about the relationship between yields, $1/b$, and the vector $\hat{b}$.[27]

Bias may also enter our model via omitted variables. Suppose that large farmers had superior land, farmed more intensively, or were more highly mechanized; in that case, failure to correct for such quality differences would bias the slope of the regression plane downward and yields ($= 1/\text{slope}$) upward. The addition of variables to capture these phenomena (value of farm per acre as a measure of land quality, the number of adult equivalents in the farm family per acre as a measure of intensity of cultivation, and the value of implements per acre as a measure of the extent of mechanization), however, had no significant effect upon the crop yields in Table 1 (see Section V). Yields remained within 1–2 percent of the values as given without these variables included.

The potential presence of these and other biases which are less analytically tractible, however, force us to defend our estimates in later sections with various tests for plausibility, internal consistency, and agreement with independent estimates. We find little reason to doubt our yield estimates for 1859.

V. 1859 CROP YIELD ESTIMATES AND THEIR INTERPRETATION

The equation for the entire sample of rural northern townships is shown below:

Improved acres $= 27.9770 + 0.0334 \cdot \text{Corn} + 0.0370 \cdot \text{Oats}$
(t-statistic)　　(36.99)　(41.20)　　　　(14.89)

$+ \ 0.0794 \cdot \text{Wheat} + 1.1308 \cdot \text{Hay} + 0.1617 \cdot \text{Barley}$
　(19.77)　　　　　(35.00)　　　　(11.28)

$+ \ 0.1377 \cdot \text{Buckwheat} + 0.1025 \cdot \text{Rye} + 0.3012 \cdot \text{Peas \& Beans}$
　(9.50)　　　　　　(8.24)　　　　(6.27)

$+ \ 0.3559 \cdot \text{Grass-seed} + 0.1940 \cdot \text{Sweet Potato} + 0.0045 \cdot \text{Hops}$
　(6.71)　　　　　　(4.12)　　　　　　(4.26)

$+ \ 0.1736 \cdot \text{Flax} + 0.0244 \cdot \text{Potato} + 0.0019 \cdot \text{Tobacco}$
　(4.08)　　　　　(3.50)　　　　　(2.56)

$+ \ 15.2019 \cdot \text{Hemp (water-rotted)} + 0.0393 \cdot \text{Rice}$
　(1.12)　　　　　　　　　　　(0.57)

+ 0.1130 · Hemp (other, prepared) + 0.3436 · Cotton
(0.46   (0.23)

+ 0.0108 · Flaxseed
(0.12)

$$n = 11,690 \qquad \bar{R}^2 = 0.368 \qquad F = 359.70.$$

Clover seed and dew-rotted hemp, both originally in the equation, were dropped after their coefficients were estimated to be negative but not significantly different from zero, with t-statistics of only −0.39 and −0.33, respectively. The only noticeable change resulting from dropping these two crops was an increase in the constant terms. The constant, it will be recalled, measures the number of acres devoted to crops and other land-using activities which were not included in the regression. The F-ratio also increased.

The coefficients for all included crops down through tobacco were significantly greater than zero at better than the 5 percent level. The regression coefficients, their reciprocals (the yield estimates), and the intervals around the yields that are implied by the 95 percent confidence interval about the regression coefficients are shown in Table 1. The "confidence" intervals for the three crops of interest, corn, oats, and wheat, were quite narrow. The regression coefficient for corn implies a yield per acre of 30 bushels in 1859, while the implied yields for oats and wheat were 27 and 12.6 bushels, respectively. Notice that prior to the introduction of hybrid corn the corn and oat yields were similar.

To the extent that the township data within states are similar to those for the state as a whole, the estimates in Table 2 show the yields of corn, wheat, and oats for the 16 sample states and the two subregions. The average USDA revised yield estimate for the period 1866–1875 used by Parker and Klein also are included in this table.

Corn was the most widely cultivated of all crops. Virtually all farms grew it. Wheat and oats, on the other hand, were produced by fewer farmers and not in every township. These production differences apparently affected the standard errors of the estimates.

The average 1866–1875 revised USDA yields were less than the lower bound of the interval implied by the 95 percent confidence interval about the regression coefficient in only three cases: corn and wheat in Kansas and oats in New York. And only 10 of our yield estimates were numerically greater than the corresponding USDA figures. On the other hand, 22 of the upper bounds on the range about the yield estimates were below the 1866–1875 USDA yields. Of these lower yields, 9 (mostly in the Northeast) were for corn, 8 were for wheat, and 5 for oats.

The regression coefficients for corn in Minnesota, wheat in Ohio, and oats in Iowa and Connecticut were not significantly different from zero. In six instances,

Table 1. Yields per Acre on Northern Farms, 1859 (units as shown)

Crop	Regression Coefficient	Yield[a] (bushels, unless otherwise noted)	95% Confidence Interval[b]	
			Lower Bound	Upper Bound
Corn	0.0334	30.0	28.6	31.5
Oats	0.0370	27.0	23.9	31.1
Wheat	0.0794	12.6	11.5	14.0
Hay	1.1308	0.9 (tons)	0.8	0.9
Barley	0.1617	6.2	5.3	7.5
Buckwheat	0.1377	7.3	6.0	9.2
Rye	0.1025	9.8	7.9	12.8
Peas and beans	0.3012	3.3	2.5	4.8
Grass-seed	0.3559	2.8	2.2	4.0
Sweet potatoes	0.1940	5.2	3.5	9.8
Hops	0.0045	222.2 (pounds)	151.5	408.2
Flax	0.1736	5.8	3.9	11.1
Potatoes	0.0244	41.0	26.3	93.5
Tobacco	0.0019	526.3 (pounds)	303.0	2293.6
Hemp (water)	15.2019	0.1 (tons)	not significant	
Rice	0.3931	2.5	not significant	
Hemp (other)	0.1130	8.8 (tons)	not significant	
Cotton	0.3436	2.9 (bales)	not significant	
Flaxseed	0.0108	92.6	not significant	

[a]Yield = 1 regression coefficent.
[b]Implicit confidence interval = $1/($regression coefficient $\pm t\alpha_{0.025})$.

negative coefficients were estimated for one or another of the three crops. These were dropped from the equations, and reestimated versions are shown. Consequently, we have no estimate for corn yields in Wisconsin; in New Jersey none of the three crops had a nonzero coefficient in the regression equation; and no wheat yield was estimated for Connecticut or Maryland.

VI. THE CONSISTENCY OF 1859 CROP YIELD ESTIMATES WITH CONTEMPORARY ACCOUNTS

Given the potential biases in our regression yield estimates, it is not inappropriate to ask why these figures should be preferred to the USDA data utilized by Parker and Klein. Although we cannot definitively answer this question, we can show the consistency of some of our yields with contemporary evidence. Moreover, when this same technique was applied to 1880 census data, it produced yield estimates similar to those actually collected by the 1880 census.

The Prairie Farmer said of the 1859 Illinois wheat crop: "The senior editor of this paper has travelled somewhat extensively through the wheat growing sec-

Table 2. Best Estimates of Corn, Oat and Wheat Yields by State and Region for the 1859 Crop Year and the Average 1866–1875 USDA Revised Estimate

(Range about the yield implied by the 95% confidence interval about the regression coefficient)

State/Region	Corn (bushels per acre)		Wheat (bushels per acre)		Oats (bushels per acre)	
	1859	1866–1875	1859	1866–1875	1859	1866–1875
IL	28.0 (24.1, 33.4)	30.6	7.5 (6.2, 9.3)	11.3*	18.1 (11.3, 44.6)	30.5
IN	34.4 (32.5, 36.5)	33.5	10.4 (9.3, 11.8)	12.2	12.1 (9.9, 15.7)	27.3*
IA	31.7 (25.3, 42.4)	37.3	14.9 (9.9, 30.6)	12.1	46.1 —†	34.4
KS	43.1 (36.0, 53.7)	29.4**	29.4 (16.6, 128.9)	15.0**	8.5 (5.7, 16.7)	30.9*
MI	25.6 (20.0, 35.5)	33.3	10.4 (9.0, 12.4)	14.6*	23.8 (15.6, 49.3)	32.0
MN	6.6 —†	31.0	14.3 (9.5, 29.1)	15.8	22.6 (14.4, 52.9)	34.0
MO	16.7 (15.0, 18.8)	29.2*	9.7 (5.6, 38.6)	12.4	20.0 (11.0, 111.0)	26.8
OH	22.5 (17.4, 31.7)	35.7*	18.8 —†	13.4	10.2 (7.1, 17.8)	29.8*
WI	—	32.7	9.3 (8.2, 10.7)	13.1*	22.1 (15.8, 36.4)	33.0

Midwest[a]	28.2 (27.0, 29.5)	32.7*	11.4 (10.4, 12.5)	13.0*	27.9 (21.9, 38.6)	29.3
CT	3.0 (2.1, 5.1)	33.7*	—	17.2	12.4 —[†]	28.8
MD	16.3 (12.9, 22.1)	22.8*	—	12.1	24.7 (16.2, 51.6)	18.6
NH	5.2 (3.2, 14.6)	37.6*	1.6 (1.1, 3.6)	16.1*	3.7 (2.6, 6.7)	31.1*
NJ	—	31.7	—	14.1	—	23.9
NY	13.3 (10.6, 17.7)	32.1*	5.9 (4.6, 8.1)	16.1*	42.9 (32.3, 63.8)	29.9**
PA	17.3 (13.4, 24.3)	34.7*	13.7 (9.1, 27.5)	13.2	11.6 (10.0, 13.9)	27.4*
VT	11.5 (6.1, 105.7)	37.4	1.2 (0.6, 20.9)	16.7	16.1 (10.4, 36.3)	33.4
Northeast[a]	19.4 (16.4, 23.6)	33.5*	8.4 (6.8, 10.9)	14.5*	35.1 (29.1, 44.3)	28.5
Northern states	30.0 (28.6, 31.5)	—	12.6 (11.5, 14.0)	—	27.0 (23.9, 31.1)	—

*1866–1875 USDA yield lies above the range.
**1866–1875 USDA yield lies below the range.
[†]Range includes zero.
[a]The 1866–1875 yields for the Midwest and Northeast are those calculated by Parker and Klein.

tions of this State, and from the information gained by observation and inquiry among farmers, he is satisfied that the average yield [of winter wheat] per acre is not more than five to six bushels.''[28] Our yield estimate for Illinois in Table 2 is 7.5 bushels per acre, with an interval from 6.2 bushels to 9.3 bushels.

Also for Illinois, Robert Ankli has used county assessors' returns of planted acreage in 1859 together with the published census crop data for 1859 to estimate countywide yields of corn and wheat for 1859.[29] His estimates for our sample counties and our estimate of the yields in the sample township from these counties are shown in Table 3. We include only those regression coefficients that were significantly different from zero. The results show no uniform bias. Our regression estimates are neither consistently higher nor lower than the assessor

Table 3. Corn and Wheat Yields (in Bushels per Acre) by Assessor Returns and Regression Estimates in Illinois, 1859

County[a]	Corn		Wheat	
	Assessor	Regression (Interval)[b]	Assessor	Regression (Interval)[b]
Adams	27.8	40.3 (23.8, 140.8)	19.6	n.c.[c]
Bureau	18.1	n.c.[c]	11.5	5.4 (3.7, 10.1)
Dewitt	34.3	48.7 (28.1, 185.2)	7.3	n.c.
Kendall	18.7	n.c.	11.2	4.1 (2.3, 18.0)
Livingston	20.3	n.c.	5.4	1.0 (0.7, 1.7)
McDonough	28.8	35.7 (25.8, 56.5)	5.2	6.7 (4.8, 10.9)
Macoupin	32.8	32.3 (18.2, 137.4)	7.7	10.2 (5.6, 54.6)
Whiteside	17.6	n.c.	13.8	12.9 (8.7, 25.8)
Williamson	27.9	26.0 (20.8, 34.5)	7.6	n.c.

[a]The regression estimates are for *one township* within this county (from sample data).
[b]Range about the yield implied by the 95% confidence interval about the regression coefficient.
[c]n.c. = No estimate possible from the sample data.
Source: Assessor Yields from Ankli, op. cit., pp. 245–247.

yields, and in only two cases does the interval about the regression-based yield fail to include the assessor yield.[30] In many instances, such as wheat in McDonough or Whiteside counties of Illinois or corn in Macoupin County, Illinois, the estimates are very close to each other. In other instances, the interval around the yield estimate is very wide.

The statistical abstract for the state of Ohio gave yield estimates for the state and at the county level for most crops from 1858 and for corn and wheat from 1850.[31] The estimates were made by county assessors and can be compared with our regression estimates for 1859 (see Table 4). The 1859 crop seems to have been poor-to-average for corn and oats, and poor for wheat. The statewide wheat yield was 7.3 bushels, the corn yield 29.5, and the oat yield 23 bushels. In contrast, our regression estimate for Ohio wheat yields was not significantly different from zero, while our oat yield was substantially lower at 10.2 bushels per acre. The corn yield estimate, while lower, was not particularly different from the county assessor's yield. It was, however, much less than the USDA revised average yield estimate for 1866–1875.[32]

The yield estimates for the state of Ohio can also be used to examine the annual variability of yields. There were wide year-to-year variations and, in any given year, there was considerable intercounty variation. They also permit us to say something about the revised USDA estimates for the decade following the Civil War. The Ohio revised USDA yield estimates from 1866 to 1875 for corn, oats, and wheat show a similar pattern of year-to-year yield fluctuations as the county assessor series for the same years, but are higher, sometimes by as much as 50 percent (in the case of wheat in 1867). On average, the USDA corn estimates for Ohio between 1866 and 1875 were only 1.5 percent higher than the assessor yields, but oat yields were 12.5 percent higher and wheat, 16.5 percent. To the extent that this pattern was repeated for other states, it reinforces our argument that use of the USDA yields may bias labor productivity growth downward.

An attempt was made after the seventh census had been completed to ascertain crop yields by state for the various crops. The results were published in the census compendium, but DeBow cautioned in his introduction that the data were for good crops only.[33] Some of the figures are closer to the revised USDA yield estimates than they are to ours, and in some cases, the reverse is true. The results, however, are consistent in two respects: they were higher than our estimates in almost every case, which we would expect if they indeed represent good crop yields, and at the same time they were often lower than the USDA revised yield estimates for 1866–1875, which is consistent with our maintained hypothesis that the USDA yields are too high.

Other indirect evidence relating to our methodology and yields estimates comes from a variety of sources. Ankli reports the results of a comparison between the 1880 census yields for Illinois and those estimated using a regression model of the type used here with county-by-county data from the 1880 census.

Table 4. Corn, Oat, and Wheat Yields by the Ohio Commissioner of Statistics and Regression for Ohio, 1859 (bushels per acre)

County[a]	Corn		Oats		Wheat	
	Commissioner	Regression (Range)	Commissioner	Regression (Range)	Commissioner	Regression (Range)
Harrison	26.1	n.c.[b]	14.4	7.0 (2.9, 32.9)	8.0	n.c.[b]
Licking	31.5	31.3 (16.4, 332.2)	7.4	n.c.[b]	9.9	n.c.
Morrow	26.7	30.9 (18.1, 106.4)	16.8	20.4 (11.0, 140.8)	13.1	n.c.
Noble	27.4	14.3 (10.9, 21.1)	8.2	5.7 (4 , 10.1)	4.7	n.c.

[a]The regression estimates are for one township within the county (from sample data).
[b]n.c. = not estimated.
Source: Third Annual Report of the Commissioner of Statistics, Columbus (1860).

230

The comparison, which was favorable, boosts our confidence in the technique we employed. The "best" estimates were obtained using the 1880 data on tilled acreage, a measure not available at earlier dates. Unfortunately Ankli's equations use only a subset of the crops cultivated (hay, corn, wheat, and oats), and the effect of excluding other crops on the regression coefficients is uncertain.[34]

How well our regression equation performs in estimating yields in the sample townships may be judged in other ways. Consider the magnitude of the constant term in the equations relative to the average number of improved areas per farm. Total improved acreage represents land under cultivation as well as that cleared for grazing or grass land and fallow. The sum of the products of crop outputs and regression coefficients represents an estimate of the acreage under cultivation; therefore, the constant term in each equation should be positive, reflecting fallow and grazing areas. Its magnitude and its size relative to total improved acreage are shown in Table 5. In general, between one-quarter and one-half of improved acres could not be accounted for by crop production. This does not appear unreasonable. For 1849/50, DeBow's calculations indicate that, on average, 26 improved acres per farm were not under cultivation, or about one-third of the improved acreage on each farm.[35] Pasture, grassland, and fallow in 1879 amounted to 41 percent of all improved acres, or about the same percentage we calculated for our sample of northern townships in 1859.[36]

Consider also the average head of livestock on the typical farm (Table 5). This is an additional means of gauging the reasonableness of the ratio of fallow and grazing land to total improved acreage. The measure, however, is imperfect because it takes no account of different fallow practices and perhaps more importantly ignores variations in the cultivation of animal feeds, particularly hay and oats. This may well account for the relatively large numbers of animals, particularly milk cows and beef cattle, per acre in Connecticut and Vermont.[38]

Yet another test of reasonableness for our yield estimates at the state and regional level involves using the published census gross production statistics for 1859 as given by the census for the three crops to compute the acreage devoted to each crop from the formula: $A = Q/Y$. The sum of those acreages can then be compared with the total land area under cultivation.[39] A more rigorous version of this test repeats the calculation for all the crops. This latter test is particularly stringent, as the comparison of our yield estimates with those made by the USDA for 1866–1875 (Table 2) suggests that ours might be low, and the lower the yield estimate, the greater will be the estimate of acreage under cultivation. Hence there is a greater probability that the estimated harvested acreage derived from our "low" yield estimates will exceed the total available acreage. The results of both "tests" are shown in Table 6.

In the northern states approximately one-third of the improved acres were cultivated in corn, oats, and wheat, while all field crops account for about 65 percent of the acres under cultivation, which again is consistent with the proportion of pasture, grassland, and fallow land in the 1880 census. Except for Mis-

Table 5. Land Not Under Cultivation and Livestock Inventories on Mean-Sized Farms in Sample Townships, 1859–1860

State/Region	Acres Not Under Cultivation	Improved Acres Not Cultivated (%)	Livestock Inventory						
			Horses	Mules	Oxen	Cows	Cattle	Sheep	Hogs
IL	29.6	31	3.6	0.3	0.7	3.5	5.5	3.7	14.1
IN	22.9	37	3.3	0.2	0.4	2.7	4.4	7.5	19.9
IA	16.4	30	2.6	0.1	0.9	2.7	4.9	4.2	13.4
KS	20.5	46	2.7	0.2	2.1	3.1	5.4	2.3	14.3
MI	10.4	32	1.5	0	0.9	2.7	3.8	7.6	5.5
MN	12.8	45	0.8	0.1	1.6	1.7	2.3	0.0	5.6
MO	21.6	28	4.5	1.1	1.4	3.5	7.4	12.8	22.9
OH	32.2	40	3.4	0.0	0.3	3.8	4.5	41.5	8.2
WI	10.3	20	2.1	0.0	1.5	3.4	4.9	4.2	4.9
Midwest	24.1	38	3.1	0.3	0.8	3.0	4.9	9.2	15.7
CT	7.8	11	1.1	0	2.6	3.4	4.5	2.8	2.4
MD	29.6	42	1.5	0.3	2.3	1.9	3.8	5.2	11.6
NH	22.5	25	1.2	0.0	1.8	3.4	3.5	15.6	1.2
NJ	22.9	37	2.5	0.2	0.4	3.5	1.7	1.9	4.0
NY	25.1	29	2.7	0.0	0.6	6.3	4.1	22.6	3.6
PA	28.7	43	2.8	0.0	0.4	4.3	4.8	10.3	6.4
VT	2.5	3	1.8	0	1.5	2.7	6.0	4.0	4.5
Northeast	28.3	36	2.4	0.0	0.8	4.9	4.2	15.8	4.7
Northern states	28.0	40	2.9	0.2	0.8	3.7	4.6	11.6	11.6

Table 6. Estimates of Acreage Devoted to Corn, Oats, and Wheat and All Crops, 1859[a]

State	Total Improved Acreage[a]	Corn, Oats, and Wheat		All Crops	
		Acreage[c]	% Total	Acreage[c]	% Total
IL	13,096,374	8,135,002	62	10,185,915	78
IN	8,242,183	4,137,813	50	5,148,908	62
IA	3,792,792	2,031,932	54	2,617,214	69
KS	405,468	159,768	39	171,282	42
MI	3,476,296	1,454,112	42	2,506,496	72
MN	556,250	293,945	53	390,477	70
MO	6,246,871	4,983,560	80	6,716,832	108
OH	12,625,394	5,583,368	44	11,309,443	90
WI	3,746,167	2,184,493	58	3,100,680	83
Midwest[d]	52,187,795	24,546,188	47	33,900,077	65
CT	1,830,807	818,996	45	2,095,917	114
MD	3,002,267	1,010,293	34	1,088,143	36
NH	2,367,034	777,913	33	2,301,890	97
NJ	1,944,441	n.a.	n.a.	1,389,723	71
NY	14,358,403	3,806,998	27	13,430,123	94
PA	10,463,296	4,939,388	47	6,977,642	67
VT	2,823,157	709,466	25	2,624,472	93
Northeast[e]	42,641,243	10,493,954	25	35,168,176	82
Northern states[f]	94,829,038	31,752,197	33	62,058,923	65

[a]Acreage measured as the sum of the product of gross production as reported by the census and the appropriate regression coefficients.
[b]From the published census. See U.S. Bureau of the Census, Agriculture . . . in 1860, p. 222.
[c]Implied by the yield estimate and the gross production of the various crops by state reported by the census. See U.S. Bureau of the Census, ibid., pp. 185–187.
[d]IL, IN, IA, KS, MI, MN, MO, OH, WI.
[e]CT, DE, ME, MD, MA, NH, NJ, NY, PA, RI, VT.
[f]CT, DE, IL, IN, IA, KS, ME, MD, MA, MI, MN, MO, NH, NJ, NY, OH, PA, RI, VT, WI.

souri, the acreage estimates for corn, oats, and wheat are plausbile.[40] The acreage estimates using all crops are also quite satisfactory in the midwestern states (except for Missouri and Ohio). The exaggerated estimate of acreage under cultivation in Ohio was due to the low yield estimates for hay and buckwheat, while for Missouri it is simply a repetition of the problem with corn, oats, and wheat. The estimates for the Northeast were uneven. Acreages under cultivation were almost certainly too high in Connecticut, New Hampshire, New York, and Vermont and too low in Maryland. In none of these cases, however, is the fault attributable to unrealistically low estimates of corn, oat, or wheat yields.[41] For the Northeast as a region, however, the results are plausible.

Applying this same methodology to the 1849 crop year production, as given in the seventh census, produced similar results.[42] Only in Missouri did the estimate of acreage under cultivation exceed total improved acreage. In the West the total improved acreage accounted for by our estimate of the area under cultivation was somewhat higher than for 1860, as was the proportion accounted for by corn, oats, and wheat. In the Northeast, results were much the same as for 1860.[43] Using DeBow's figures for 1849 of the improved acreage devoted to various crops nationwide, we find 43 percent of acreage in corn, oats, and wheat and 67 percent given over to all crops.[44]

VII. THE 1859 CROP YEAR IN PERSPECTIVE

Despite the general plausibility of the results, the crop yields estimated from the manuscript census data suffer from one insuperable drawback: they may not be typical of the yields experienced over the entire period 1839–1859. One effort to verify this was the application of the 1859 yield estimates to 1849. Another check comes from contemporary accounts of the 1859 crop year. Although farm journals and Commissioner of Patents reports carry frequent mention of weather conditions and the ravages of disease and insects, it is virtually impossible to assimilate the frequently contradictory reports for quite small geographic areas into an overview of the way such factors affected yields at the regional, or even state, level.

Views about weather and crop prospects changed rapidly. *The Prairie Farmer,* for example, which reported in February 1859 that "the uniform opinion is that at least half of the wheat saved last fall is totally winter killed," by early March was reporting "fields that looked dead a week ago are now getting green, and bid fair to make a good crop."[45] Experiences within a state at the same time also varied. Charles Gilbert of Knox County, Illinois, for example, reported in the April 21 issue of *The Chester Democrat* that "we are having a gloomy spring, wet and cold. Spring grain, wheat in particular, is rotting," while the same paper reported from Clinton County, Illinois, that "wheat looks as promising as I have seen it during the last twenty years."[46] Furthermore, it is never clear whether opinions regarding yields and weather stemmed from overly sanguine expectations. *The Illinois Farmer,* for example, noted: "Our farmers have been much disappointed in the yield of their wheat.—Fields where it was confidently expected the yield would prove to be thirty-five bushels per acre, not more than twelve bushels were obtained."[47]

The picture is further complicated because weather that was bad for one crop was not necessarily so for all crops. The quotations above refer to wheat; those for corn ofttimes contradicted the views for wheat. For example, Charles Gilbert, who reported to the *Chester Democrat* that wheat was rotting, still expected a good corn crop.[48]

There is some agreement in the weather accounts that the late frosts of June 4 and 5 badly damaged the wheat crop and hurt the other small grains to a lesser extent.[49] The Chicago Board of Trade opined, "The new crop had realized our expectations, and although the yield had not been large for the area of ground sowed, the quality of our spring wheat was superior to any which has been raised for several years. The winter wheat, too, was of fair quality, although the yield was small."[50] For corn, however, the picture was quite different: "[T]he yield of grain per acre in 1859 was large, the crop was generally good, and secured in good condition."[51]

Perceptions of the 1859 crop year were thus quite varied depending upon when and where the crops were viewed and how they compared with expectations. Ex post, however, the crop traded on the Chicago Board of Trade was probably about average for oats and wheat and better than average for corn. Nonetheless, our yields are below those of the Commissioner of Patents and the revised USDA figures, reinforcing our belief that use of the latter figures biases the labor productivity growth downward.

VIII. IMPLICATIONS FOR THE PARKER–KLEIN INDEX

We hesitate to put too much confidence in our single-year point-estimates of crop yields, especially in those yields where the confidence interval around the regression coefficient was such that the range of possible yields was wide or where the coefficient was estimated to be not significantly different from zero. Nevertheless, the overall implication of the results seems clear: the average 1866–1875 revised USDA yields are upper-bound, at least with respect to our 1859 yield estimates, and probably represent an upper limit for the entire period. Conversely, our yields do not appear to be historically low. Our estimates can therefore be used to generate reasonable labor productivity growth estimates for American agriculture between 1840 and 1910. The Parker–Klein figures then delineate what we believe to be the lower bound.

The Parker–Klein productivity index is derived from the weighted average labor input per bushel of grain (corn, oats, or wheat) and is defined by

$$\sum_{R_1}^{R_3} \left(\frac{a + b}{y} + c \right) v,$$

where R represents the regions (Northeast, South, and West); a is preharvest labor per acre; b is harvest labor per acre; y is yield per acre; c is postharvest labor per bushel; and v is the weight (measured as regional production as a proportion of total production for each grain). Dividing a and b by yield per acre converts the labor inputs to labor per bushel. Parker and Klein took observations for a, b, c, y, and v for each region for 1840–1860 and 1900–1910 and computed the index of labor productivity as the ratio of the 1840–1860 labor input per bushel to the 1900–1910 labor input per bushel for each crop.

Changing the yield estimates alters the labor input per bushel for preharvest and harvest labor. We have recomputed labor productivity by substituting our 1859 yield figures for the average 1866–1875 USDA revised yields used by Parker and Klein. Our results are compared with theirs in Table 7. Where a regression coefficient for corn, oats, or wheat was not significantly different from zero or where a crop was excluded from the regression because it originally entered with a negative coefficient, we substituted the average regional yield. For the southern states we have retained the USDA estimates. As the comparison in Table 7 shows, our revisions indicate a substantially greater increase in labor productivity for every crop than do the Parker–Klein estimates. Rather than the slightly more than fourfold increase in wheat, and less than fourfold advance in oat and corn indicated by their computations, our estimates show 5.5-fold expansion for wheat, almost a fivefold growth in oats, and slightly more than a 4.5-fold increase for corn.

Besides calculating labor productivity changes over this period, Parker and Klein's research had another purpose, that of isolating the individual contributions of mechanization, the westward movement, and yield improvement to the measured aggregate advance in labor productivity. Our revisions alter the conclusions of that analysis as well, as shown in Table 8 where we have reproduced their figures and ours for various combinations of these individual influences. The index i_2 in each calculation, for example, shows what would have happened to labor requirements and labor productivity between the two periods if only

Table 7. Labor Requirements and Labor Productivity
as Calculated Using 1860 Census Manuscript Data
and Using USDA 1866–1875 Yields

Period	Labor Requirements per Bushel (L/O)[a]			Labor Productivity [(i_1/i_n) × 100]		
	Wheat	*Oats*	*Corn*	*Wheat*	*Oats*	*Corn*
Calculated with manuscript census data:						
1840–1860	4.17	1.93	4.48	100	100	100
1900–1910	0.76	0.40	0.96	549	483	467
Calculated with USDA yields (Parker–Klein):[b]						
1840–1860	3.17	1.45	3.50	100	100	100
1900–1910	0.76	0.40	0.96	417	363	365

[a]Here $\sum\limits_{R_1}^{R_3}\left(\dfrac{a+b}{Y}+c\right)v$. See text.

[b]From Parker and Klein, op. cit., Table 2.

Table 8. Labor Requirements as Affected by Interregional Shifts, Regional Yields, and Regional Labor Inputs per Acre Comparing the USDA 1866–1875 Regional Yields with Those Obtained from 1860 Manuscript Census Data

	Period for Values of			*Labor Requirement per Bushel (L/O)*[a]			*Labor Productivity* $[(i_1/i_n) \times 100]$		
Index	v	y	a,b,c	*Wheat*	*Oats*	*Corn*	*Wheat*	*Oats*	*Corn*
Calculated with manuscript census data:									
i_1	1	1	1	4.17	1.93	4.48	100	100	100
i_2	1	2	1	2.68	1.37	2.94	156	141	152
i_3	1	1	2	1.70	0.96	2.00	245	201	224
i_4	2	1	1	3.48	2.09	3.43	120	92	131
i_5	1	2	2	1.05	0.72	1.32	397	268	339
i_6	2	1	2	1.01	0.67	1.36	413	288	329
i_7	2	2	1	2.69	1.23	2.45	155	157	183
i_8	2	2	2	0.76	0.40	0.96	549	483	467
Calculated with USDA yields (Parker–Klein)[b]									
i_1	1	1	1	3.17	1.45	3.50	100	100	100
i_2	1	2	1	2.68	1.37	2.94	118	106	119
i_3	1	1	2	1.29	0.78	1.54	246	186	227
i_4	2	1	1	2.90	1.18	2.70	109	123	130
i_5	1	2	2	1.05	0.72	1.32	302	201	265
i_6	2	1	2	0.84	0.39	1.06	377	372	330
i_7	2	2	1	2.69	1.23	2.45	118	118	143
i_8	2	2	2	0.76	0.40	0.96	417	363	365

[a]Here $\sum_{R_1}^{R_3}\left(\frac{a+b}{Y}+c\right)v$. See text for definition of variables.

[b]From Parker and Klein, op. cit., Table 2.

yields had changed in the absence of any westward movement and any advance in mechanization. The other indexes i_3 through i_7 similarly hold constant specific influences, and index i_8 shows the total effect (from Table 7).

Although every index is affected by the changes, the most substantial effect appears in those indexes that take account of the greater rise in yields between 1840 and 1910 that is implied by our 1859 yield estimates. This is seen most dramatically in index i_2. Whereas on the basis of the average USDA yields for 1866–1875, productivity in wheat would have risen 18 percent if only yields had been allowed to change, using the census data, we show a 56 percent increase. The effect is similar for corn, but the difference is especially dramatic for oats. If only yields had changed, oats output per man-hour in 1910 would have been 41 percent higher than in 1840, while using the USDA yields the increase would only have been 6 percent.

Indexes for wheat and oats which reflect our changes in yields were 32 and 33 percent higher, respectively, than the Parker–Klein estimates. The indexes for corn which use our lower corn yield estimates are 28 percent higher than the similar Parker–Klein versions.

The effects of mechanization, represented by index i_3 and captured by changes in a, b, and c, are virtually untouched by our revision of yields. The effect of our changes on index i_4 for oats is, however, quite dramatic. Whereas Parker and Klein estimated that the shift in regional weights alone (their proxy for the westward movement) would have increased labor productivity in oats production by 23 percent, we estimate that it resulted in an 8 percent decline, as cultivation shifted away from the relatively high-yielding oat fields of the Northeast to the less suitable climate of the Midwest. The Midwest, however, still had to grow oats to feed its livestock, especially horses.

In the original Parker–Klein estimates, the interaction between mechanization and the westward movement (index i_6) accounted for virtually all of the productivity gains; in our revision it only accounts for between two-thirds and three-quarters of the productivity advance. Moreover, the interaction between yields and mechanization (index i_5), such as the cultivation of crop strains that matured more uniformly and needed prompt harvesting, is almost as important and would have produced well over half of the total productivity gains during this period. Lastly, as might be expected from index i_2, the interaction between yields and the westward movement resulted in substantially higher rates of productivity increase than in the original estimates.

IX. CONCLUSION

Our estimates for 1859 suggest that improvements in yields during the nineteenth century may have been greater than commonly supposed. These gains derived from the dissemination of knowledge about improved seed varieties and farming practices through the popular agricultural press, educational organizations, and government agencies such as the Commissioner of Patents and the U.S. Department of Agriculture. To the extent that this knowledge derived from systematic observation and experimentation, it deserves to be called "scientific farming."

These changes may have been disguised by the very agents which produced them. The early USDA yield estimates were drawn from the same network of county reporters that served as sources for the Commissioner of Patents reports. Hence the consistency between the two sets of observations is only to be expected. These data were almost certainly from best-practice (or certainly better-than-average-practice) farms, and it was not until toward the end of the century that the USDA had a comprehensive reporting network that would justify confidence in the representativeness of their average yields. By then, average-practice farm yields may well have approximated those of the best-practice farms of 20 or 30 years earlier.

Our results, however, should reinforce faith in the Parker–Klein labor productivity calculations as reasonable mid- to lower-bound estimates of productivity growth in American grain production during the nineteenth century. At the same time, our estimates demonstrate that there is nothing sacrosanct about the partitioning of these productivity gains, which in the past may have led us to overemphasize farm mechanization and the westward movement to the detriment of a much less spectacular but nonetheless important change, the diffusion and acceptance of knowledge about best-practice farming methods and crops. Parker's interpretive essays have stressed the "scientific attitude" of American farmers, even in a prescientific agricultural era, and the robust character of the information-disseminating agencies of that day. It seems only right that the quantitative record should reflect these achievements as well.

ACKNOWLEDGMENTS

Earlier drafts of this paper have been presented to workshops at the University of Chicago, the University of Illinois and Indiana University. We wish to thank participants, especially Jan Brueckner, Larry Davidson, Robert Fogel, David Galenson, Larry Neal, and William Travis, for their helpful comments. They are not to be implicated in any remaining shortcomings in this paper.

NOTES

1. William N. Parker and Judith L. V. Klein, "Productivity Growth in Grain Production in the United States, 1840–60 and 1900–10," in *Output, Employment and Productivity in the United States After 1800*, Studies in Income and Wealth, Vol. 30 (New York: National Bureau of Economic Research, 1966), pp. 523–582.

2. See, for example, Fred Bateman, "Improvement in American Dairy Farming, 1850–1910: A Quantitative Analysis," *Journal of Economic History* 28(June 1968): 255–273; also "Labor Inputs and Productivity in American Dairy Agriculture, 1850–1910," *ibid.* 29(June 1969): 206–229; Franklin M. Fisher and Peter Temin, "Regional Specialization and the Supply of Wheat in the United States, 1867–1914," *The Review of Economics and Statistics* 52(May 1970): 134–149; Richard Pomfret, "The Mechanization of Reaping in Nineteenth-Century Ontario: A Case Study of the Pace and Causes of the Diffusion of Embodied Technical Change," *Journal of Economic History* 36(June 1976): 399–415; Harriet Friedman, "World Market, State, and Family Farm: Social Bases of Household Production in the Era of Wage Labor," *Comparative Studies in Society and History* 20(October 1978): 545–586; Trevor J. O. Dick, "Productivity Charge and Grain Farm Practice on the Canadian Prairie, 1900–1930," *Journal of Economic History* 40(March 1980): 105–110.

3. See, for example, Fred Bateman, "Improvement."

4. In addition to those listed by Robert Fogel and Stanley Engerman, *Time on the Cross* (Boston: 1974), Vol. II, pp. 22–25. There is also a sample from the 1820 Census of Manufacturers taken by Kenneth Sokoloff, the Philadelphia Social History Project data, and the Public Use sample from the 1900 Census of Population made by Samuel Preston and Robert Higgs.

5. Parker and Klein, "Productivity Growth," 533.

6. U.S. Department of Agriculture, *Crop Yields and Weather*, Miscellaneous Publication No. 471 (February 1942), especially pp. 106, 110, 112. The average yields for 1866–1875 for corn, oats, and wheat are shown in Table 2 (see Section V).

7. U.S. Congress, House of Representatives, *Report of the Commissioner of Patents for the Year 1850:* Pt. II, *Agriculture,* 31st Congress, 2d session, Executive Document No. 32, p. 186. For Cumberland County, Maine.

8. Ibid., pp. 208–209. For Canadaigua, New York.

9. Ibid., p. 212. For Westmoreland County, Pennsylvania.

10. Ibid., pp. 244–245. For Adams County, Illinois.

11. Ibid., p. 248. For Somerset County, Maine.

12. Parker and Klein, "Productivity Growth," 551.

13. Illinois Central Railroad Company, *The Illinois Central Railroad Company Offer for Sale over 2,400,000 Acres Selected Prairie, Farm and Woodland Tracts of Any Size . . . On Long Credits . . . Situated Each Side of their Railroad . . . From the Extreme North to the South of the State of Illinois* (New York: Amerman, 1855), p. 19.

14. Ibid., p. 23.

15. Ibid., p. 27.

16. Frederick Gerhard, *Illinois as It is* (Chicago: Keen & Lee; also Philadelphia: Desilver, 1857), pp. 290–291.

17. Ibid., p. 291.

18. Parker and Klein, "Productivity Growth," 548, Table A-1.

19. Nathan Parker, *The Iowa Handbook for 1856* (Boston: Jewett, 1856), p. 18 (emphasis in the original). It must be noted that at the back of the book Parker appears as a principal in a land company selling Iowa and Minnesota land. Consequently he would have a vested interest in extravagant claims for the land he was trying to sell.

20. Minnesota Commissioner of Statistics, *Minnesota: Its Place Among the States* (Hartford: Case, Lockwood, 1860), pp. 89–96.

21. Parker and Klein, "Productivity Growth," p. 554. The corn estimate also reflects a revision of the yield in the South.

22. Preliminary tests of this sample, entitled *Agricultural and Demographic Records of 21,118 Rural Households Selected from the 1860 Manuscript Censuses,* are reported in Fred Bateman and James D. Foust, "A Sample of Rural Households Selected from the 1860 Manuscript Census," *Agricultural History* 48(Jan. 1974): 75–93.

23. More recent tests, correcting for cluster sample bias, are as yet unpublished but are part of the authors' manuscript "Reconstructing A Rural Democracy: The Northern Agricultural Community Through the Eyes of the Eight Census."

24. Carroll D. Wright, *The History and Growth of the United States Census* (Washington, D.C.: 1900), see especially pp. 234–237. The quote is taken from U.S. Census Office, 8th Census, 1860. *Eighth Census, United States—1860. Act of Congress of Twenty-third May 1850. Instructions to U.S. Marshals—Instructions to Assistants* (Washington, D.C.: Bowman, 1860), p. 23. Wright mistakenly asserts that all copies of these instructions were lost. Copies are now to be found in the Library of Congress and the University of Illinois Library.

If all farmers followed a fixed crop rotation, then fallow would vary directly with some of the crops, resulting in a "constant" term that was correlated with crop yields. We assume that no such fixed crop rotation was followed.

25. Peter Passell, one of Parker's students, may have pioneered use of this equation, although he did not report any yield estimates derived from it, and indeed any he may have done appear to have been lost. See Peter Passell, *Essays in the Economics of Nineteenth Century Land Policy* (New York: 1975 [1970 Yale Ph.D. dissertation]), pp. 128–136. See also Robert Ankli, "Gross Farm Revenue in Pre–Civil War Illinois," unpublished Ph.D. dissertation, University of Illinois, 1968, pp. 68–76. Parker now notes that those original estimates have been lost. See William N. Parker, "Labor Productivity in Cotton Farming: The History of a Research," *Agricultural History* 53(January 1979), 232–233.

26. See, for example, Table 1 (in Section V).

27. In the one-crop case, it can be shown that yields are biased upwards. In the multicrop case, however, the direction of the bias cannot be specified a priori. One can argue too that our model lacks economic sense. The model which we have posited, A = a + bQ, asserts that farm size, A, is determined by the vector of crop outputs, Q, whereas the reverse is more likely true. If land were freely available, such that the farmer made his production decisions and then farmed sufficient acreage to realize those goals, the model as given would represent a reasonable economic model. However, even if not all potentially cultivable land were included in farms, the time and expense involved in transforming that land into improved acreage make it far from a free good. Interpreted as a causal relationship, our model violates the Gauss–Markov condition that the errors are uncorrelated with the independent variable. The vector b is therefore a biased estimate of b*. However, since the relationship in the model was suggested by an identity, a strong case can be made for the irrelevancy of objections to the model based upon causal relationship.

Passel, *Essays,* pp. 128–136, suggests an alternative logarithmic form for the model, but it offers no advantage over this basic model, and regardless of which model is used, and whether E(b) = b*, E(1/b) ≠ 1/b*.

28. *The Prairie Farmer* 20, No. 9 (September 1, 1859): 137.

29. Robert Ankli, "Gross Farm Revenue in Pre–Civil War Illinois," unpublished Ph.D. thesis, University of Illinois (1968), especially pp. 245–247.

30. See wheat yields in Bureau and Livingston counties, Illinois, in Table 3.

31. Ohio Commissioner of Statistics, *Annual Report to the Governor,* Columbus. First report, for 1857, published in 1858. Yields back to 1850 are given in the Third Report (for 1859): *Third Annual Report of the Commissioner of Statistics (of Ohio), 1859* (Columbus: 1860), especially pp. 111–114.

32. U.S. Department of Agriculture, *Crop Yields.*

33. U.S. Census Office, *Statistical View of the United States . . . Being a Compendium of the Seventh Census* (Washington, D.C.: Nicholson, 1854), pp. 176–178.

34. Ankli, "Gross Farm Revenues."

35. U.S. Census Office, *Statistical View . . .*

36. U.S. Department of the Interior, *Report on the Productions of Agriculture* (Washington, D.C.: 1883), pp. 3–10.

37. DeBow also tries to reconcile the good crop year yield estimates with acreage under cultivation at the Seventh Census. See U.S. Census Office, *Statistical View . . .*

38. For a discussion of regional variations in the feeding and treatment of dairy cattle, see Fred Bateman, "Improvement in American Dairy Farming, 1850–1910," *Journal of Economic History,* 28(June 1968): 255–273.

39. U.S. Bureau of the Census, *Agriculture of the United States in 1860* (Washington, D.C.: 1864), especially pp. 184–187.

40. A corn yield estimate of 16.7 bushels per acre in Missouri is largely to blame for this anomalous result. The total crop of over 72 million bushels of corn in 1859 accounts for almost 4.4 million of the 6.2 million improved acres in Missouri. Using the 1866–1875 USDA estimate of 29.2 bushels per acre would reduce the land area devoted to corn in Missouri to 2.5 million acres, a more plausible figure. Acreages devoted to corn, wheat, and oats in the Midwest represented a greater proportion of the land under cultivation than in the Northeast, and their comparative advantage vis-à-vis the latter region lay in such concentration.

41. In Connecticut, the problem is largely due to the low hay yield estimate, which also causes problems in New Hampshire, where it is compounded by a low yield on potatoes. These same two crops account for the large acreage under cultivation estimate for New York and Vermont. The difficulties with Maryland, where the acreage under cultivation is almost certainly too low, partly result from our sample township's not cultivating tobacco, which was the state's major crop, and many crops were also excluded from that equation.

42. See U.S. Bureau of the Census, *Agriculture . . . in 1860,* especially pp. 188–191.

43.   The problem with the Missouri estimate is attributable to the low corn and hay yields for 1859 relative to the high production rates in 1849. The three crops—corn, oats, and wheat—account for between 34 percent to 77 percent of the land under cultivation in the western states and 29 percent to 48 percent of the land under cultivation in the eastern states.

44.   U.S. Census Office, *Statistical View*. . . . Notice too that if our yield estimates for corn, oats, and wheat were *too low,* then the average devoted to these crops would be very high. In 1860, it is not.

45.   *The Prairie Farmer* 19, No. 8 (February 24, 1859): 120; No. 9 (March 3, 1859): 136.

46.   *The Prairie Farmer* (quoting the *Chester Democrat*), 19, No. 16 (April 21, 1859): 248.

47.   *The Illinois Farmer,* 4, No. 9: 329.

48.   *The Prairie Farmer,* 19, No. 16 (April 21, 1859): 248.

49.   See, for example, *The Prairie Farmer* 9(June 30, 1859): p. 406, or *Third Annual Report of the Commissioner of Statistics* (*of Ohio*),*1859* (Columbus: 1860), especially pp. 97–103.

50.   Chicago Board of Trade, *Annual Statement of Trade and Commerce of Chicago* (Chicago: 1859), p. 18.

51.   Ibid., 1860, p. vii.

THE ECO-TECHNIC PROCESS AND THE DEVELOPMENT OF THE SEWING MACHINE

Ross Thomson

I. INTRODUCTION

Technical change is a little like God. It is much discussed, worshipped by some, rejected by others, but little understood. Even though virtually every theorist of economic development since Marx takes it to be a central cause of the pace and direction of the evolution of the modern economy, its precise importance is still debated. Its own causes are still less clear. Is it accommodating enough to come forth when called by the requirements of capital accumulation or by relative factor scarcities (depending on one's theory)? Or is it a simply exogenous determinant of economic life? To the historian, the problem takes the form of birth and renewal: how did the ongoing process of technological change of modern capitalism emerge, and how is it sustained?

Technique, Spirit, and Form in the Making of the Modern Economies:
Essays in Honor of William N. Parker
Research in Economic History, Suppl. 3, pages 243–269
Copyright © 1984 by JAI Press Inc.
All rights of reproduction in any form reserved.
ISBN: 0-89232-414-7

In a series of articles written over the past two decades, William Parker has articulated an important conception of the consequences and causes of technical change. Of its importance he has no doubt; his contention that "The course of development of technology . . . has set a succession of problems for mankind, the adjustment to which constitutes the main path of modern economic history" is supported by analysis of the effect of technological change on the composition of demand, industrial location, the growth and concentration of firms, and the vulgarization and homogenization of mass culture.[1] Of the causes and origin of ongoing technological change in modern capitalism, with which this paper is primarily concerned, Parker argues for two propositions. First, such ongoing change is an eco-technic process, a socially structured process generating a continuing flow of inventions and innovations in which technology progresses at a pace and in a direction affected by both the end of socially conditioned interest and the internal logic of technology itself. Second, the eco-technic process was preceded historically by, and qualitatively broke with, a quite different, Smithian, kind of process generating changes in the production process. This paper will first examine these propositions at greater length and will then try to illustrate and advance Parker's conception by analyzing the process through which the sewing machine developed.[2]

II. THE ECO-TECHNIC PROCESS AND ITS BIRTH

Technical changes are created in a process of determinant form; Parker's conceptualization of technical change depends upon a certain understanding of the requirements of this process. His most important paper on technical change, "Technology, Resources, and Economic Change in the West," begins by examining Usher's notion of invention as a process creating technological knowledge conditioned by the perception of the need to alter existing techniques, the technical knowledge already possessed, and the possibility of developing appropriate new techniques. The problem, then, is to identify the technical and social factors involved in meeting these conditions.[3]

Whatever else it is, technical change is an evolution of the knowledge and application of principles both of power generation and transmission and of the qualities of materials and biological processes. Three propositions concerning the character of such principles inform Parker's analysis. First, technical change is possible; all known principles have not found all applications, and new principles remain to be known and applied. Second, as particular applications of universal principles, technological principles form a whole, in Marx's words, a "modern science of technology,"[4] in which the parts are interdependent, so that a change in one technique has relevance for changes in others. Third, technological principles are divided into types having differing degrees of connection with one another. This particularization derives in part from distinctions of the kinds of scientific ideas existing at any time, ideas, for example, of mechanics, chemistry, electromagnetism, biology, and subatomic physics. As emphasized by Marx and Rosenberg, it also derives from the variety of applications of scientific principles of any type. In Rosenberg's terms, a "technological convergence" exists among the instances of one type of technological principle but not with other techniques.[5]

From these propositions important conclusions for the content of the process of technical change follow. Technical change is a development within technological knowledge. Its pace and direction depend upon the state of technological knowledge, which forms the context within which technological problems are posed, limits the kinds of solutions which can be given to these problems, and contains solutions to problems which technologically converge with its principles. Changes will occur in a certain order: "Nature gives out her secrets *seriatim.*"[6] Changes supposing knowledge of certain technological principles will develop later than those simpler principles. Hence, it is argued, mechanical developments preceded electrical and chemical, and these preceded subatomic and biochemical. Finally, technical changes will develop discontinuously between and to a lesser extent within major types of technology; the realization of the potential of a new technological principle will involve a process different from those developing other new principles.

Technical change is also conditioned by the evolution of needs, the structure and growth of the economy, and the social organization of technology. Indeed, such social conditions are so decisive that only in modern capitalistic societies is there any ongoing dynamic to technology. Social conditions are of two types, those which organize inventive ability and those which provide an incentive, seen typically as an economic interest, to invent.

Social organization conditions the communication necessary for inventions, including communication of the value of inventing, of general technical knowledge, of the orientation to and knowledge of particular problems, and of knowledge of solutions advanced to these problems. While such communication can occur by movement of objects, it more typically occurs through the mobility of people and documents. Its extent is influenced by technical changes in transportation and communication. When it exists, this inventive communication can draw on technological knowledge elsewhere in society to pose and solve the series of technological problems needed to develop an invention to practicality and can afterward make the technological knowledge and personnel developed through this invention available to the rest of the economy.[7] Invention is also conditioned by investment needed to meet the cost of making, developing, and marketing inventions prior to the generation of funds flowing from their use.

Marx's conception of the capitalist economy may help specify the social organization generating new technology. Fully developed capitalist production for Marx is both a process creating value and surplus value and a mechanized process generating homogeneous use-values. The rate at which value expands varies with the kind of machinery used, and machinery evolves when the technological principles embodied in its mechanisms are altered.[8]

The embodiment of technology in machinery helps determine the social location of the process of technical change. Those possessing technological knowledge are principally those who maintain, produce, or design machines. They can initiate productivity increases in two ways. A first, modificatory type develops the ability to use existing machinery and can occur in the factory using these machines. A second, more basic type alters the machine as a product; since machines are purchased, such technical change occurs through a new product development process undertaken in the sector making machinery. It would follow, as Rosenberg emphasizes more than Marx, that the technological communication generating important changes would be concentrated in the sector producing capital goods. Such communication would be socially conditioned by the organization of this sector and the logic of the process of new product development and would therefore depend on more than just the size of the market for new machinery.[9] The social organization of this communication will be considered more thoroughly in the analysis of the development of the sewing machine.

Social factors affecting the incentive to invent also influence the pace and direction of technical change. Three factors are stressed by Parker. Invention is stimulated by the size of the potential market for that invention, and this size is in general larger when aggregate income is larger and more rapidly expanding, when needs are more homogeneous, and when levels of per capita consumption are more equal. Economic bottlenecks may stimulate invention to overcome them. Barriers to factor movement and equalization of wage and profit rates are considered endemic; demand changes in the presence of such barriers may spur invention needed to increase output. Finally, technical bottlenecks may direct invention. To increase the capacity of a machine or a system of machines, inventive effort is focused on altering the limiting part, operation, or machine.[10]

The sustained technological progress which can emerge out of a combination of these social and technical factors is called the eco-technic process.[11] It is an "invention industry," an institutionalized process generating both technical changes which are widely adopted and new technological knowledge out of which another round of change can come. Its social conditions have only recently been met. The peculiar combination of the extent, kind, and distribution of wealth needed to stimulate widespread technical change with the level, broad dissemination and ready communication of technical knowledge required to undertake that change has existed only in modern capitalism.

Within capitalism technological change can be ongoing when the conditions of widespread invention are regenerated by the operation of the system. In part this regeneration is a direct effect of technical change, for such change adds to the body of technological principles in a way which renews and advances inventive ability and therefore facilitates technologically convergent invention. It also removes technical bottlenecks and, as a result, focuses inventive attention on new limiting features; in Rosenberg's terms, "compulsive sequences" of inventions are initiated.[12] The unevenness of technical change, a result of the differential pursuit of and ease of making inventions, itself has important economic consequences, including the establishment of bottlenecks and changes in the composition of demand and the location of industry, which can spur further technical change.

Yet technical change cannot account for its own sustenance. It varies in direction and pace with the growth and distribution of income, the level of and opportunities for investing profits, and the evolution of needs. While technical change does influence such factors—and to the extent that it does, the causes and consequences of technical change are not separable—these factors also have other determinants. Moreover, technical change is conditioned by yet other factors. Some inventions involve such a break with existing technology that little incentive exists in the economy to develop the underlying scientific and technological principles. These inventions are conditioned by a science growing outside the economy.[13]

One further issue remains in this survey of Parker's analysis of technical change. If the eco-technic process exists only in modern capitalism, how did production develop previously and how did the eco-technic process originate? For Europe and America from the sixteenth century to the Industrial Revolution, Parker interprets production to have evolved according to a Smithian dynamic led by market growth. The expansion of the market overcame limits to the division of labor, allowing economies of scale, specialization, and increased output per worker. Production evolved through a specialization initiated within the enterprise rather than through the modification of technological principles applicable throughout the economy.[14]

The character of this Smithian dynamic can be further identified by considering Marx's concept of craft production. Such production is inherently subjective, in that the laborer must himself conceive the product and its fabrication and carry out this fabrication by his skill in using hand tools. Productivity growth occurs partly by changing tools but more basically by altering the conceptions and skills of the worker and by specializing craft operations between laborers. The productivity increase which can be generated within a craft system is limited by the necessity that workers must conceive and be able to implement any change, by the tie of the diffusion of such changes to the movement of craftsmen, and by the lack of consequences which changes in some techniques have for other crafts. Technical changes in mechanized production processes overcomes each of these limits.[15]

The eco-technic process did not originate directly out of this craft dynamic. It depended more on other factors attending or resulting from the expansion of trade, especially the growth of capitalist enterprise and acquisitiveness, the creation of a market of sufficient size and integration to make inventions profitable, the extension of the sphere over which regular contact allowed inventive activity to be diffused, and the barrier posed by the immobility of capital and labor to the expansion of output. A supply of craftsmen, holding the Renaissance values that the physical world was orderly and validly subject to theoretical and practical investigation and perhaps possessing nascent technological knowledge learned in making clocks, mills, water wheels, firearms, and scientific instruments, proved sufficient to initiate a process of industrialization. The dynamic centered on the birth of factory production in the textile industry, where techniques were simplest to mechanize, demand largest, and bottlenecks most acute. Facilitated by the invention of the steam engine and development of iron production, the dynamic was consolidated when a machinery sector was formed and machine tool inventions proliferated. The eco-technic process which would generate the ongoing mechanical inventions of the nineteenth century was in place.

One change was needed to give this process its full vitality. Scientific development, which had played little direct role in the Industrial Revolution, entered the eco-technic process in the person of the mechanical engineer and, more fundamentally, as the conceptual underpinning for the new chemical and electrical technologies of the late nineteenth century. Since then, science has played an ever more important role in technical change; it has become more closely integrated into the economy without losing its self-directing and self-validating logic. Its consequences have accelerated the pace of the eco-technic process by extending communication through inventions like the jet, telephone, and computer. For Parker, it also has a more ominous side, for it threatens both to eliminate technology's character as a means to given ends through the power that the images transmitted by radio and television have in creating needs and values, and through inventions in weaponry, to annihilate civilization together with its ongoing technical change. It is the very character of the eco-technic process embedded in modern societies that leads Parker to conclude that "the uncontrolled and evidently uncontrollable development of natural science, pure and applied, is the deepest problem of the modern world."[16]

III. THE DEVELOPMENT OF THE SEWING MACHINE

Properly understood, the eco-technic process, as conceived by Parker, Marx, or Rosenberg, is economywide; it unites technical changes of all types. Yet it is made up of many individual technical changes, and, to be useful, the concept of eco-technics must account for the individual invention by showing it to be a part of the eco-technic process. The sewing machine will be examined with this issue in mind.

Any particular invention can illustrate only some features of the overall process of technical change. However economically important it was, the invention of the sewing machine did not introduce any new, universally relevant technological principles, nor did it depend on any new scientific developments. Its technological continuity made it a more typical invention, and if its generation had technological and social determinants other than demand, then surely more basic changes in technology did also. Moreover, it was not a technical change stimulated by the scarcity of materials or by bottlenecks coming from the mechanization of complementary operations. Its relevance lies more in understanding the technological determinants and social organization of the process developing the mechanical technology of machine design and production in a time when that technology had not found widespread application.[17]

A. Development to Practicality

The invention of the sewing machine demonstrates the independence of technological development from the economic circumstances of any particular country. In the 60 years prior to Elias Howe's invention in 1846, 17 machines capable of mechanically forming a stitch were invented in the United States, Britain, France, Austria, and Germany. As evidenced by the fact that these machines were invented not only by machinists and professional inventors but also by cabinetmakers, tailors, hosiers, and storekeepers, the prior technological knowledge required to design a stitching mechanism was minimal. Sufficient demand existed; after the American Civil War, thousands of machines were sold annually in each of these countries, and, in any case, no inventor anticipated sales on anything like the scale achieved.

Since the inventors of stitching devices often had little technological knowledge, it might seem that the eco-technic thesis, which would tie technical changes in the present to those in the past, is either invalid or that the eco-technic process had not yet formed. But the design of a stitching mechanism is one thing; the widespread use of a practical sewing machine is quite another. None of the stitching mechanisms devised prior to Howe's developed into commercially successful sewing machines, and Howe was unaware of any of these earlier inventions. Whether this differential success has an eco-technic explanation remains to be seen.

Some of these early inventions failed because of the technological inferiority of their stitching mechanisms.[18] Many of these copied the stitching motion of the hand, which involved a series of mechanically complex operations, so that these machines did not attain the speed which mechanization made possible. Several machines overcame this limit by eliminating the hand conception of sewing. In place of a thread which penetrated the cloth in one place and returned in another, they substituted a thread which entered and exited the same hole and formed a stitch by either catching the thread and securing it to its next penetration or intertwining a second thread with the first.[19]

In part, such a technological conception was arrived at fortuitously, as in the case of Barthelemy Thimonnier, a French tailor who, in the 1820s observed the hand chain-stitching techniques used in embroidering on a tambour, noted that these techniques could also be used for forming a stitch, and designed a sewing machine which made this stitch. But the conception of machine stitching was also derived by those trained in technological principles, including Walter Hunt, a New York inventor, Elias Howe, a Massachusetts machinist, and John Fisher and James Gibbons, British inventors aware of the design and use of embroidering machinery.

Some machines with adequate stitching mechanisms failed for social reasons. Financing for patenting, producing, and marketing machines was a barrier to some, including Hunt's machine. Lack of contact with machinists who could construct a durable machine out of sufficiently precise metal parts was another barrier. Opposition by craftsmen slowed and perhaps even suppressed introduction of machines, as in Thimonnier's case. Other machines attained commercial success, but not as sewing machines. Three British inventions of the first half of the 1840s incorporated machine stitches on embroidery machines. Their inventors aimed at mechanizing embroidery; that embroidery was technologically similar to sewing was lost on them. Like the eighteenth-century French luxury trades, the embroidery trade in the second quarter of the nineteenth century developed techniques with great potential significance for other industries, but no mechanism existed to realize this potential. As in a craft system, invention in one industry was largely independent of that in others.

One last social context was decisive for the development of a practical sewing machine; Howe's machine, unlike the others, was born in an environment which undertook the critical revisions needed to develop it to practicality. Besides minor inadequacies of stitching mechanisms, all early machines, including Howe's, lacked both an adequate device to feed the material into the stitching mechanism and a power source which allowed the operative to use both hands to manipulate the material. The further technological development of the Howe machine had two underpinnings, the social organization of machinists and early attempts to sell the machine.

By the 1840s, machinists in New England and New York were organized and trained to be able to develop new technologies. Socially, machinists resembled a craft. Hand labor with the file was common, and the few machine tools in use typically required considerable skill to set up and use. Their products were generally built for local customers ordering one or a few machines of any type; consequently, much planning was required to execute the order. An apprenticeship system gave training and the transmission of technological knowledge a personal character.

The organization of machinists was central to technological diffusion and development. The technological knowledge of machinists was widely relevant and had already been applied to design and produce locomotives, enginework, and machinery to make textiles, woodwork, agricultural implements, firearms, clocks, scientific instruments, and other commodities. The diffusion of technology between these sectors occurred in part through machine sale and licensing, but more importantly through the movement of machinists. In a context in which independent invention was a means to advancement, machinists utilized their communication with other machinists and customers to pose technological problems and then used their knowledge to solve these problems. As a result, a technological dynamic deepening and spreading mechanization was well under way in the textile and general machine shops of eastern Massachusetts, Rhode Island, Philadelphia, and New York and, somewhat separately, in the interchangeable parts manufacturing shops of the Connecticut River valley.

The first of these two loci of machinery development was central to the birth of the practical sewing machine. Howe himself was a product of this dynamic. He was trained in a Lowell textile machine shop and then worked in shops in Cambridge and Boston making textile machinery and scientific instruments. Discussion in a Boston machine shop turned Howe's attention to the possibility of inventing a sewing machine, and his general technological knowledge undoubtedly helped identify the inadequacy of the hand stitch. His solution to the problem of machine stitching resembled and may have derived from weaving technology; his lockstitch, like woven cloth, was formed by the mutual constraints of two threads where one of the threads, as on the loom, was carried on a bobbin in a reciprocating shuttle. His training also led him to construct workable machines made of metal parts from the start.[20]

This context also generated critical improvements of the Howe machine. To mention only the most important, a mechanism to continuously feed material was developed by John Bachelder, a Boston machinery maker, in 1849. Bachelder's principle was independently discovered and given more adequate form by Allen Wilson, a cabinetmaker whose only training in machine design was as a child's hobby. After exposure to other machines, Wilson developed an adequate feeding device, the four-motion feed, which allowed the material to be fed continuously and at any angle without bunching. Two other revisions bear mention: a foot treadle and a stationary overhanging arm were developed by Isaac Singer, whose attention turned to sewing when exposed to the inadequacies of a sewing machine being repaired in the Boston machine shop in which he was trying to sell a printing machine he had invented.

The train of developments leading to the practical sewing machine would not have proceeded had inventors not attempted to sell their machines. At first they adopted the traditional local mode of machinery sale. Howe tried this route around Boston, but, in spite of demonstrations and races with seamstresses, he failed and, discouraged, left for England in 1849 to sell his machine there. But his efforts had not gone unnoticed; John Bradshaw improved the Howe machine, and Charles Morey and Joseph Johnson improved Bradshaw's. Both machines attained limited commercial use; at least 50 of the Morey and Johnson machines were constructed. Bachelder was familiar with both the Howe and the Morey and Johnson machines. The most commercially important early machine, the Blodgett and Lerow, was invented by a Boston tailor aware of the local ferment brought about by the sewing machine. This machine was the first to be marketed elsewhere in the East, including New York City and Worcester, and knowledge of its success and mechanical deficiencies stimulated the invention of one of the three major machines of the 1850s, the Singer, and probably a second of these machines, the Grover and Baker. Only the third of these major machines, the Wheeler and Wilson, came from outside Boston, and it had developed from Wilson's earlier machine under the influence of Boston machines being sold in New York. Within eight years after Howe left for England, the major technical weaknesses of his machine had been overcome, and the three companies which would dominate sales for the next 20 years had already emerged as the major firms of the industry.[21]

Was the emergence of the sewing machine an eco-technic process? The general technological principles of this machine had the requisite relatedness to the existing body of technology, and even the stitching operation had some similarity to operations on other machines. The distinctiveness of the sewing operation gave sewing technology a particularity which implied both that the sewing machine could not be a simple adaptation of existing techniques and that its technological development would acquire an autonomy which tied its further evolution more to the problems and limits of its current state than to the general evolution of mechanical technology. Finally, the direction of evolution of sewing technology had been determined in part by criteria of technological adequacy. Even though solutions to technological problems were not unique—different kinds of stitches and stitching mechanisms coexisted, for example—all machines adopted the machine stitch, continuous feed devices and were motivated by foot, hand, or steam power. The technological potential for an eco-technic process existed.

This potential was realized through the institutions of the machinists' craft. Through the interpersonal relations characteristic of this craft, including those of training in general technological principles, of work, of mobility, and of product sale, an orientation to the invention of sewing machines was communicated among those with knowledge of relevant technical principles and existing marketing methods. Inventions thereby acquired a social existence which redefined the technological context for others, so that new problems were posed and new solutions found. A dynamic internal to sewing technology and the distinctive relations of those participating in it was born; the eco-technic process had taken the form of ongoing new product development.

Yet such new product development was limited by its tie to the institutions of the machinists' craft. Widespread contributions to the dynamic of sewing technology were made difficult by the personal, mostly local contacts through which these technical changes occurred. That no organized mode of financing such developments existed formed a further limit. Howe, Singer, and Grover and Baker all used personal contacts to acquire even modest sums; only Wilson, by forming a partnership with Wheeler, applied the capital, plant, and marketing system of an existing manufacturing firm. The local character of machinery marketing imposed a still greater barrier to the dissemination of this new product.

The introduction of the sewing machine, as suggested by the eco-technic thesis, was effectively independent of relative factor prices; labor costs were so reduced that the level of the wage rate was irrelevant.[22] Its introduction did depend upon the potential market and the perception of and ability to reach this market. The wide potential of the sewing machine as a means of consumption, bought by families for their own use, was inherent in the level and distribution of income and the kinds of needs of families in the United States and much of Europe, but this potential was only discovered and actively fostered in the second half of the 1850s. The more immediately perceived limit was that of acquiring national sales in a context in which machinery was generally sold locally for custom order. Only when the sales of territorial rights was abandoned in favor of a system of company commission agents and then branch offices did sales multiply. The expansion of this system was self-sustaining; profits generated in some branches were invested to establish others. Sales then took off; from 1,500 machines in 1851, sales for the major three companies grew to 3,200 in 1855, and then surged to 42,500 in 1859. Thus it was through the formation of a unified national market organized through the agents and offices of major sewing machine firms that the sewing machine diffused and its potential market was discovered. The mode of diffusion of the machine shop was giving way to that of the modern firm.

The eco-technic process developing the sewing machine contrasted sharply with the prior evolution of craft production. Consider shoemaking. Both the putting-out system initiated in the late eighteenth century and the central shop system of the early nineteenth century spread through the mobility of trained craftsmen aiming to set up their own putting-out operations. Tied to those trained in a particular craft, these changes occurred independently between crafts. The two changes in hand shoemaking which were not so tied, the development of the pegged and the standardized shoe, were themselves early results of the eco-technic process, for both were spread by companies making means of production, pegs and standard lasts, and these companies utilized new machines to form their products, the peg-making machine and the lasting lathe. The development of these machines rested on an earlier development of technological knowledge; the peg-making machine was invented by a textile machinist who had invented a bark mill, and the lasting lathe was a simple application of Blanchard's gunstocking lathe. Through these changes, even the evolution of craft labor depended on the eco-technic process.[23]

B.   Further Sewing Machine Development

If the development of the sewing machine was an eco-technic process, one further result would follow; this development would alter the technological context in a way which would contribute to further technical change. What is not clear from either Parker's concept of eco-technics or Marx's analog is the variety of forms this contribution can take. Most directly, of course, the birth of the sewing machine originated a sewing technology relevant to further mechanization of sewing. Further, the evolution of such technology may have drawn on and contributed toward other kinds of technical changes. Less directly, the commercial success of the sewing machine may have altered the eco-technic process inside and outside the sewing machine industry, for this success altered not only the extent but also the social form of technological communication. Furthermore, it resulted in the growth of large firms and the size, organization, and growth imperatives of these firms could have affected the form and kind of technical change.

The principles embodied in the practical machine of the mid-1850s did indeed form the starting point from which mechanization spread to virtually all types of sewing operations by 1900. The most important limits, the restricted applicability and automaticity of the standard dry thread machine, were embodied in the design of stitching and feeding mechanisms and overcome by the redesign of these mechanisms.

The evolution of the sewing machine took four directions, corresponding to four types of technical problems.[24] First, the standard dry thread machine was refined. While improvements were devised, like an adequate single thread chain-stitch mechanism and different forms of shuttles, the basic mechanisms of the standard machine remained much the same. But these mechanisms were extended to new uses by the introduction of both attachments to embroider, hem, bind, cord, and buttonhole and specialized machines for cylindrical work, parallel seams, leather working, decorative stitching, glovemaking, and straw hat sewing. The technical problems were minor and, for the most part, easily solved.

More difficult technological problems faced those pursuing the second and third directions of sewing machine development, and distinct technological dynamics developed to solve these problems. Sewing buttonholes, carpets, and buttons posed problems of automaticity of feed. Over a quarter of a century, beginning in 1860, a series of inventions solved the problem of feeding the machine around the buttonhole as well as the connected problem of the appropriate form of the stitch. The carpet sewing machine utilized this over-edge stitch. Beginning in the 1870s, it took the carpet sewing machine about 20 years to achieve automaticity. The button sewing machine achieved its object in the 1880s by adapting a mechanism to feed eyelets used earlier in shoe production.

The third direction addressed the distinct problems associated with sewing with a waxed thread. The friction of the wax generated one problem since it clogged the eye of the needle; a hook to pull the thread through and a looper to put the thread in the hook solved this problem in the early 1850s. A second basic problem was to form the stitches required to bottom a shoe. A first solution, developed in the Civil War, formed a new kind of shoe by putting the looper on a rotating horn inside the shoe. A second solution, not fully perfected until the early 1890s, used curved needles to copy the stitches of the hand-sewed shoe.

Finally, limits to the durability, speed, and power source of the sewing machine became objects of invention after the practical sewing machine had emerged. These problems were not specific to sewing technology, and their solution depended more on innovation elsewhere in the economy. Durability increased through new modes of production of central parts, most importantly drop forging for shuttles. The replacement of springs and cams by cranks and eccentrics increased machine speed. But one problem was not overcome. Over the last third of the nineteenth century, attempts to replace the foot treadle by a motor which could be used on a small scale were common; some 75 such patents had been taken out before 1880. Yet, until the electric motor at the end of the century, all were in vain. This problem could not be solved within mechanical technologies; no matter what the potential demand, the invention of such a motor had to wait until a wholly new technology had emerged. The slowness of invention of a sewing machine motor illustrates Parker's claim that major technologies develop discontinuously.

The effect of the practical sewing machine of the mid-1850s on later development rested on the communication of sewing technology, and this communication was transformed by the commercial success of that machine. Technological knowledge spread nationally and internationally through the production, sales, servicing, and use of the machine, as well as through the communication of machinists and sale of journals like *Scientific American*. Hence, innovation lost the geographic localization which characterized the origin of the sewing machine. It also lost its direct connection to the general machinist. Sewing machine invention was increasingly undertaken by those with some professional contact with this machine and who, through this contact, had become aware of problems of sewing technology. Such technology had acquired a social autonomy to go along with its technological autonomy. Moreover, the communication of technological knowledge was tied to the firms which grew through the commercial success of the sewing machine. Inventors increasingly were educated through the media of such firms. Some, like James Morley, the inventor of the first successful button sewing machine, and John Reece, the inventor of the most advanced buttonhole machine of the 1880s, had been agents of sewing machine companies. Others were involved in producing sewing machines, like Duncan Campbell and Frank Merrick, who produced and then invented waxed thread machines, and Andrew Eppler, who did the same for shoe bottoming machines. Still others were trained in sewing machine agencies, including Lyman Blake, the inventor of the McKay sewing machine, the most important shoe bottoming machine until the late 1890s.[25]

Most basic sewing machine inventions after the mid-1850s took the same petty bourgeois form which characterized the sewing machine's origin. Mechanics attempted to develop and patent new types of machines and attachments and then

either founded new companies or sold their inventions to others who would do
so. The number of companies making sewing machines grew greatly in this way.
This form of invention was aided by the greater willingness of investors to buy
and develop patents after the extent of the market for sewing machines had been
demonstrated. While Howe had relied on personal contacts for modest financing
to invent his machine and in 1850 or 1851 had unsuccessfully tried to sell the
exclusive right to use his patent to Singer for $2,000, in 1859 Lyman Blake
found several financiers in competition for his patent and sold it for $70,000.
Over time petty bourgeois inventors found another source of demand for their
patents, the established sewing machine firm.

The invention and development of new machines within existing firms constituted a quite different social form of technological change. Dry thread firms
were early to adopt this form; the major companies each hired investors to adapt
their machines to light leather sewing in the early 1850s. Research and development developed rapidly thereafter, until by the 1870s even minor companies had
staffs for this purpose. This form removed the contingencies of petty bourgeois
invention by internalizing each aspect of development of a new product into the
firm. Inventive ability was purchased as a commodity, the labor of a research and
development staff, which guaranteed inventors the time and facilities in which to
undertake their task. The capital needed to develop and disseminate new machines was given by the profits generated from sales of existing machines. Once
practical, new machines could be produced in the firm's existing plants and sold
in their established marketing outlets. This form regularized new product development within the firm and also outside it, since firms formed a market for the
products of independent inventors and supplied the services needed to develop
and disseminate their products.

Existing firms had two rationales to undertake the technical development of
their products, the competitive purpose of protecting and extending their shares
of established markets and the aim of real new product development to extend
their markets, as well as the aggregate sewing machine market, by mechanizing
new kinds of sewing.

Different kinds of sewing machine development involved distinct combinations of petty bourgeois and capitalist forms of technical change as well as
different mixes of competitive and product-originating purposes. The standard
dry thread machine evolved through improvements which were largely competitive. Dozens of new firms entered the industry, many with new machines they
claimed to be technologically superior. Established firms likewise developed
their products. The ensuing improvement of the standard machine, the addition
of a host of attachments, and the introduction of specialized family and manufacturing machines may have somewhat extended the uses of and hence market for
sewing machines but primarily redistributed the existing market.[26]

Inventions of wholly new types of machines of course involved competitive
purposes to a smaller extent. The feed and automaticity inventions of the but-

tonhole, carpet, and button sewing machines were initiated by independent inventors originally to be used as attachments to standard sewing machines and later as distinct kinds of machines. Quickly these developments lost their petty bourgeois form; Singer and Wheeler and Wilson diversified to buy out and develop the principal inventions. But petty bourgeois invention was not finished; in a roundabout way, it was stimulated by large companies. A buttonhole operative invented and produced an automatic stop attachment which Singer adopted, and John Reece, a buttonhole company agent, successfully organized his own company and invaded the market for these machines with his own invention in the 1880s. Similarly, the button sewing machine was developed by an agent of the Florence Sewing Machine company who successfully formed his own company to produce and market it.

Likewise, waxed thread machines were initially developed by independent inventors to mechanize new kinds of sewing. Early leather sewing machines were generated out of a combination of the groups which developed Howe's machine and developed out of that machine—the nexus of eastern Massachusetts machinists and sewing machine plants and agencies. A Boston machinist undoubtedly familiar with the sewing machine, William Wickersham, invented the waxed thread machine in 1853; Elmer Townsend, a Boston shoe wholesaler, bought the patent and follow-up patents and employed a number of mechanics to develop the machine over the rest of the decade. By the time he invented his shoe bottom sewing machine, Lyman Blake had been a contractor and later partner in a South Abington, Massachusetts, shoe firm, had been trained by a Singer agent and had used Singer, Grover and Baker, and Townsend's New England machines in his shop. Unable to develop and market the machine, in 1859 Blake sold the patent to Gordon McKay, a long-time machinery producer who was the superintendent of the Lawrence Machine Works in 1858. By 1862, McKay brought out a practical machine. Finally, the second solution to bottom sewing, which copied the hand stitch, was patented by a New York mechanic, Auguste Destouy, in 1862; Charles Goodyear, Jr., the son of the inventor of vulcanization and president of American Shoe Tip Company, bought the patent and, over a 25-year period, developed it to adequacy. Unlike the dry thread sewing machine, waxed thread machines typically developed by the sale of patents to capitalists who could perfect, produce, and market these machines.

The rapid spread of waxed thread machines depended on the experience of sewing machine procedures for more than technology. Virtually from the beginning, waxed thread firms copied the marketing innovations of dry thread producers. Townsend developed an agency system, which McKay followed. But further innovations were needed; the higher capital cost of bottom sewing machines posed a barrier to their introduction which McKay overcame by leasing machines for an installation fee and a royalty per pair of shoes bottomed. Under this system, shoe machinery spread and its producers grew rapidly. Like the sewing machine a decade earlier, the introduction of the McKay machine was effectively independent of the wage rate; unit labor costs were much less than in hand-sewed shoes, and the product was of a higher quality and price than that of the pegging machine. Likewise, the Goodyear shoe had similar advantages in relation to hand sewing and other types of shoes, including the McKay.

Once adequate machines had been created, the rationale and form of technical change altered. Waxed thread machine producers tried to develop their own machines further in order to preempt competition, but without a great deal of success. New innovations came from independent inventors who had often been trained by the waxed thread companies and who were able to form new companies to market their machines. Heads of machinery production seemed particularly prone to bolt; three major inventors had headed production for waxed thread firms, Duncan Campbell for Townsend, Frank Merrick, who had worked for Townsend's successor, National Waxed Thread, and Andrew Eppler, Goodyear's superintendent.

Waxed thread producers also diversified. In part the rationale was technological. To be effective, bottom sewing machines required precision in other operations, which could be gained only by mechanization; recognizing this, firms developed and sold systems of technologically interdependent machines. The rationale was also to maintain rapid growth. Companies successfully developing new machines found that the financial expenditures were biased toward the early stages of product development but that revenues came later. Such revenues were often spent in developing other new products, particularly other leather-working machinery where firms could apply their technological knowledge and marketing systems. Townsend's movement into pegging and eyeletting machines and McKay's financing of Goodyear machines, machines which bottomed by screwing and nailing, heeling machines and lasting machines were cases in point. Finally, even diversification took a competitive purpose, to preempt others from entering the market for particular machines. Goodyear defined the commodity it sold to be use of a whole system of machines; it was propelled to broaden its system of machines to gain advantage over others, and others tried to extend their system beyond that of Goodyear to invade the lucrative Goodyear market. The direction of this diversification, grounded in the technological relatedness of leather-working machinery and the structure of shoe machinery marketing, divided bottom sewing machine and dry thread sewing machine producers into the principal firms of two industries, shoe machinery and sewing machinery.

The further development of the sewing machine, it can be concluded, was an eco-technic process. The technological principles of the machine of the mid-1850s formed the basis on which the more complex principles of later machines were built, and the limits of this machine, particularly its limited applicability, formed a number of problems which led sewing machine invention in quite different directions. The existence of the sewing machine as a commodity educated the individuals who grasped and solved these problems. It had consequences for the structure and growth of the firms making it which were relevant for further technical change. The marketing innovations to realize its potential market brought a new, vertically integrated firm structure, generated rapid growth, and spread technological knowledge. Its limited uses led to diversification of the firm through the organization of a new, capitalist social form of technical change quite different from the inherited petty bourgeois form. Moreover, the direction of new product development by firms making different kinds of sewing machines had the dynamic consequence of distinguishing the shoe and sewing machine industries. While the technology of the sewing machine, in the context of the kinds of needs existing or nascent in the United States and Europe, provided a potential for further technical change, the economic existence of that machine determined whether, in what form, and with what consequences that potential would be realized.

However profound the effects of the technology of the sewing machine were on the sewing industries, they had little direct importance for technological evolution elsewhere in the economy. Certain minor devices spread from sewing machine production, like the Goodyear rapid stitching and reverse drive mechanisms and the mechanisms for feeding small objects of the eyeletting and button sewing machines. Of course, the sewing machine industry added to the pool of machinists capable of generating other mechanical technologies. Yet the very particularity of sewing technology limited its importance for the rest of the economy.

In its impact on firm growth, the sewing machine had wider repercussions. Firms in other industries copied the innovations used to market the sewing machine, including the agency system, installment buying, internationalization, and the understanding of the possibility of selling new commodities to consumers. The profits of sewing machine firms also had a relevance, most importantly the investment of Singer in the expansion of Babcock and Wilcox. In the twentieth century such profits would finance the diversification of Singer and the successor to the McKay and Goodyear companies, United Shoe Machinery, into other industries. In its effect on firm growth, then, the sewing machine had an impact on further technical change outside the sewing and shoe industries quite independent of its direct technological consequences.

C. The Evolution of Production

The sewing machine had one further potential effect on technological change elsewhere in the economy. Its commercial success, concentrated as it was in a few firms, increased the scale of production well above anything previously experienced by machinery producers, and in the decade from 1855 to 1865 this increased scale was attended by the introduction of interchangeable parts manufacturing techniques widely applicable to other industries. If this increased scale caused the generation of new techniques and these were applied elsewhere, then the sewing machine would have had a further effect on technical change outside the sewing industries. Such techniques were in fact applied elsewhere, but whether the sewing machine caused their generation depends on the character of the process developing sewing machine production. Was it a direct response to increased scale, like Parker's Smithian dynamic? Or was it a result of a part of an eco-technic process, dependent upon prior technical change elsewhere, and, if so, did it have any impact on later technical changes?

Central parts of the answers to these questions come from the work of Nathan Rosenberg.[27] The limits coming from application of general machine shop practice to a mass production process were overcome by the diffusion of the methods of interchangeable parts metalworking from a technologically convergent industry, firearms. From it came knowledge of the principles of turret lathes, milling machines, and other mass production machine tools, of devices like gauges, jigs, and fixtures, and of factory organization. Sewing machine firms of 1865 indeed responded to increased scale, but by adapting techniques developed elsewhere rather than originating new techniques; it was an eco-technic rather than a Smithian process. Later, the sewing machine industry became a center of invention and diffusion of significant mass production technology in its own right, for, to solve its technological problems, such central inventions as the universal milling machine, the universal grinding machine, the automatic turret lathe, and dramatic improvements in drop forging techniques were made.

Technical relatedness was not by itself sufficient to account for the diffusion of techniques from the firearms to the sewing machine industry or from sewing machines elsewhere; the social mechanisms carrying this diffusion must be identified. As a mass-produced, partly iron-based mechanism, firearms had the greatest potential for altering sewing machine production, but other mechanisms and metal products produced or coming to be produced on a large scale, like clocks, locks, hardware and axes, were also technically related. Within the component parts of this mass production metalworking sector, a craftlike mode of technological change had a history by the 1850s a half-century long. Typically, machinists undertook inventions largely within the plant in which they worked, often as contractors, superintendents, and foremen, produced these inventions within the machine shop of that plant, and used them principally within that plant. Such new technologies diffused in part through the building of machinery for custom order but more commonly by the movement of machinists. The Blanchard lathe, milling machine, turret lathe, and drop forging techniques had all been invented and diffused in this way.

Prior to 1840, such diffusion had been slow and accidental, with the result that a great dispersion of techniques existed in firearms factories in 1840, and even more between industries. By the 1850s, communication was more regular, the pace of diffusion of new inventions quickened, its scope widened to include other industries, and consequently factory techniques became more general. This was particularly true within the Connecticut River valley. Alongside this mode of diffusion a second came into existence in the 1850s; the sale of standard designs of mass production machine tools and precision measuring devices was initiated, most notably the Lincoln miller from 1855 and Brown and Sharpe's vernier caliper in the early 1850s.

This movement of machinists from the clock, lock, and especially the firearms industries to the sewing machine industry was the principal mechanism which supplied the conception of interchangeable parts production and machine tools to implement that conception. William Perry, Joseph Alvord, and James Wilson, who between them had worked in the Ames Armory in Chicopee, the Springfield Armory, and the Hartford armories of Colt, Robbins and Lawrence, and Sharps, were the central figures in organizing and equipping the most advanced sewing machine plant, that of Wheeler and Wilson in Bridgeport. The drop forging techniques to make the central distinguishing part of the Wheeler and Wilson machine, the rotary hook replacing the shuttle of most lockstitch machines, were introduced in 1856 by another contractor, Albert Eames, who for a decade and a half had organized standardized firearms production and developed die-forging and specialized drilling machines for Ames Manufacturing and Remington. The factory of a new firm formed out of the wealth of a successful litigant of sewing machine patents, one Elias Howe, was designed and built by two of the foremost experts in precision mass production, Alfred Hobbs, who had achieved fame by picking the Bramah lock and technological knowledge from organizing standardized lock production, and Frederick Howe, who had superintended the Robbins and Lawrence plant and later the armory of the Providence Tool Company and had designed milling machines, profiling machines, and turret lathes.[28]

Other modes of diffusion also operated. In an astute move, Willcox and Gibbs, the company making Gibbs's single thread chain-stitch machine, contracted to have their machines built by Brown and Sharpe, which brought to sewing machine manufacturing the expertise of an originator of precision devices such as a gear cutting machine for clockmaking, the vernier caliper, and a turret lathe with a self-revolving head designed originally for firearms factory use. Also of importance was diffusion by means of commodity purchase. Sewing machine companies became major purchasers of the Lincoln miller from the late 1850s and of the turret lathes produced by Henry Stone, formerly of Robbins and Lawrence, by Brown and Sharpe, and by Pratt and Whitney from the early 1860s. Through both forms of diffusion, along with the adaptation of these techniques for sewing machine production, it took only a decade to apply the most advanced mass production metalworking techniques in the world to making the sewing machines of progressive firms, like Wheeler and Wilson, Willcox and Gibbs, and Weed. Yet because the mobility of machinists trained in mass production techniques was concentrated in southern New England, diffusion elsewhere was slow. Singer did not adopt these techniques in its Elizabethport plant until the late 1870s.

Sewing machine production continued to evolve after the new factories were constructed in the late 1850s and early 1860s, but in a different manner. Having contributed its technological principles, firearms production declined as a center of diffusion to the sewing machine industry. In certain instances, sewing machine production emulated the craft mode which had developed the fabrication of firearms—inventions by machinists for use in their own plants and diffused by the movement of machinists. Some important machines were so invented; Albert Eames's molding press was conceived and used in the Wheeler and Wilson plant in 1873, and Thomas White's multispindle automatic turret lathe originated in his own factory in 1895. Moreover, specialized machines were so invented, and many machines were improved within the factory. As evidenced by Brown and Sharpe's sales of only 200 machines to all sewing and shoe machine producers in the great expansion from 1865 through 1874 and by Singer's production within its Scottish plants of 9,800 of the 12,400 machines used in these plants from 1870 to 1914, sewing machine factories continued to produce most of their machinery, so invention within sewing machine plants must have remained substantial.[29]

But many major technical changes came instead as commodities developed and produced by technologically advanced firms. Brown and Sharpe's central inventions, the universal milling machine, formed miller, grinding lathe, and then universal grinding machine, micrometer caliper, and a host of minor inventions found their way into sewing machine factories through commodity sale. The major advances in drop forging made by Billings and Spencer were diffused through the sale of sewing machine parts, most importantly shuttles, and Spencer's automatic turret lathe was utilized to make and sell bobbins and one other widely used new commodity, the machine screw. Pratt and Whitney similarly developed a whole line of specialized machine tools embodying a flow of significant improvements. Even White's multispindle automatic turret lathe, while invented in his sewing machine factory, was soon produced in a separate firm. For the first time, mass production machine tools and other metalworking machinery were being developed outside the mass production industries in which they would be used.

These industries, and particularly the sewing machine industry, played a central role in the process developing this new machinery. On the one hand, sewing machine production was of a scale on which such machines could be used in considerable numbers; in 1870 U.S. production topped 400,000 sewing machines and would remain at or above that level for the remainder of the century. In the boom decade from 1865 through 1874, sewing and shoe machine producers purchased 40 percent of the machine tools shipped by Brown and Sharpe; with the stabilization of sewing machine output and the birth of other new mass production industries, this share fell to 24 percent from 1875 through 1884 and to 5 percent for the remainder of the century.[30] On the other hand, sewing machine production, unlike the sewing machine itself, faced basic technological problems common to virtually all precision and mass production metalworking and soluble within the principles of mechanical technology.

Barriers to automaticity formed the problems Spencer solved with the automatic turret lathe, which multiplied labor productivity in screwmaking some 8–20 times. The lack of durability of shuttles, particularly of the Weed machine he manufactured, led Billings to develop the board drop, which could precisely drop forge a shuttle out of a single piece of metal. The problem of imprecision led to the development of the universal milling and grinding machines by Brown and Sharpe. The slowness and inaccuracy of hand work in making the twist drills and spiral milling cutters used in producing the Willcox and Gibbs machine, together with Frederick Howe's recognition of the same limitation in rifle production, led Joseph Brown to develop the universal milling machine. The universal grinding machine gave accurate form to the hardened steel parts of the Willcox and Gibbs machine.

Since the sewing machine industry provided the opportunity and technological problems which stimulated invention, it can be said to have been both a center of invention and, because the new techniques were widely applicable and would widely diffuse, a center of diffusion. Yet it was not a center in the sense in which firearms had been, where inventions had originated in and emanated out of the industry itself. Rather, inventions were born in, or quickly led to, firms producing separate commodities, particularly machinery firms. This difference influenced the pace of invention and diffusion. The major machinery inventions were recognized to overcome widespread technical problems and therefore to have potential demand in many industries. The universal miller was a response made to problems in producing both firearms and sewing machines by a company which already sold precision devices widely, like the vernier caliper and gear cutting machines; it was designed to be used generally and soon discovered wider markets. The universal grinder was perfected in 1876, well after sales of the grinding lathe had illustrated the breadth of potential applications. Billings recognized the board drop was useful wherever drop forgings were needed, and Spencer was quick to develop his bobbin machine into a fully general automatic turret lathe.

Moreover, that inventions became commodities allowed them to diffuse independently of the movement of machinists. The pace of diffusion therefore quickened. Brown and Sharpe quickly came to sell its universal millers and self-revolving head turret lathes to several industries and later utilized their then-established marketing network to sell a series of new commodities, including the universal grinder, micrometer caliper, formed millers, and many other precision machine tools and devices to an ever growing number of industries. Billings and Spencer likewise sold their drop forging machines and dies to many industries, and Spencer's Hartford Machine Screw Company, Pratt and Whitney, and others diffused new techniques in the same way.

The eco-technic process had taken a new form, that of new product development undertaken by capital goods firms and those hoping to establish such firms. The sewing machine industry played a central part in the origin of this new form. The universal miller and grinder, the board drop forging process, and the multispindle automatic turret lathe were all developed by sewing machine producers and were used in their own factories. Yet each of these innovators recognized the potential importance of their inventions to companies in the sewing machine industry and in other industries, and in each case either the same firm or a new firm came to produce and sell the new machines themselves or some product of these machines.

Once in existence, this new form of the eco-technic process became self-sustaining. Firms producing these new products generated profits and technical and marketing knowledge which promoted further innovation; sequences of new products came out of major companies. Their sales also grew as a result of the more general eco-technic process; firms making typewriters, bicycles, cash registers, and other new products could, unlike earlier producers of firearms and sewing machines, begin as factory producers. This form also supported petty bourgeois new product development by spawning independent inventors from those they trained. Brown and Sharpe generated, to mention the most notable, Henry Leland, an important automobile inventor and president of Cadillac, and Charles Norton, the most significant contributor to the conversion of the grinding machine into a heavy-duty basic machine tool. Pratt and Whitney had a similar record; they trained mechanics who formed Warner and Swasey, manufacturers of machine tools and especially turret lathes, National-Acme Manufacturing Company, which invented and produced a multispindle automatic turret lathe, E. P. Bullard, which manufactured small boring machines, and Gardiner Machine, which developed a disc grinder. These firms not only spread mass production machine tools among light manufacturing industries but also adapted them to the quite different technological problems of heavy interchangeable parts production; the automobile industry and other twentieth-century centers of American development would not have been the same without them.

Thus, the sewing machine industry had widespread significance for technological change in other industries through both the spread of machinery generated to produce sewing machines and through its effect on developing a new social form of technical change, that of new product development. This form did not immediately displace either the invention of new machines for use internal to the innovating firm or the receipt of other kinds of revenues by machine tool producers; the value of machine tools made by Brown and Sharpe did not exceed the value of the Willcox and Gibbs sewing machines it manufactured until 1885 and did not surpass the value of all its other products combined until 1898. But the dynamic had been born, and, as the number of purchasers of machine tools expanded, it would come to dominate.

IV. THE ECO-TECHNIC LEGACY OF THE SEWING MACHINE

By the turn of the twentieth century, the period in which the sewing machine had formed a center of technological evolution was over. Neither the sewing machine nor its production developed in a way which stimulated significant technical change elsewhere. It had been replaced by other centers, heavy machinery, electricity, and chemicals. It had, however, left a legacy of importance for the technical change in the twentieth century.

Most directly, this legacy was technological. Sewing machines continued to evolve in the twentieth century by the refinement of their mechanical principles but more basically by the infusion of new technology, notably the introduction of the electric motor. The universal millers, automatic turret lathes, drop forging equipment, and grinding machines which had been developed to produce the sewing machine continued to spread among sectors and to evolve technologically, though now in response to the technological problems of other industries. Personnel trained in designing and making sewing machines also had a significant role in solving the technical problems of other sectors.

Less directly, the evolution of the sewing machine had economic consequences which spurred technical change in the new century. Such change was undertaken in part by sewing machine firms. The very success of the invention and sale of the sewing machine in fostering rapid growth created accumulations of capital which could not be readily invested in making sewing machines for existing markets. A deepening penetration of existing markets and a widening of international markets were two solutions followed by Singer and United Shoe Machinery; further new product development was another. Around 1905, United Shoe Machinery completed its system of bottoming machinery by developing the pulling-over machine. It also began its diversification into other producer goods, including leather-working machinery, heavy machine tools and capital equipment, industrial fastenings, and industrial chemicals. White Sewing Machine moved into multispindle automatic turret lathes and then into automobiles. While it failed at sewing machine production, Remington put technological skills acquired in making firearms and sewing machines together with an emulation of Singer's marketing techniques to successfully sell typewriters; in the early twentieth century it was a leader in the application of scientific management to factory organization.[31]

Sewing machine companies also fostered the growth of other firms which were technologically progressive in the twentieth century. Singer's profits financed the evolution of Babcock and Wilcox into one of the largest and most innovative firms in the machinery sector. The wide emulation of Singer's marketing techniques by firms making both producer and consumer goods facilitated the growth of many firms of importance for technical change in the twentieth century. Singer even influenced market growth by changing laws; its successful legal challenges in the 1870s and 1880s to laws limiting its ability to compete with local producers and sellers of sewing machines helped to establish a national market for goods of all kinds.[32] Finally, the sewing machine industry was instrumental in forming a mass production machine tool industry which grew greatly in the early twentieth century due to the expansion of mass production metalworking industries and the continued development of technologically advanced products by existing and new machine tool producers.

The eco-technic legacy of the sewing machine extended to stimulating the development of those industries which would emerge as technological leaders. Sewing machine firms and the individuals they trained helped develop the products of these emerging eco-technic centers; White's influence on automobile design, the invention by Phillip Diehl, a Singer employee, of an electric motor for sewing machines in the 1890s which was applied more generally in the twentieth century, and the part played by United Shoe Machinery in developing industrial fastenings and chemicals are important instances. The marketing practices of sewing machine firms extended the scale of these new industries. The sewing machine industry influenced the production of autos and electrical machinery in part by application of its own techniques but more centrally by the stimulus it had provided for the growth of machine tool firms which undertook innovations central to the mass production of heavy machinery, especially Norton in heavy grinding and Leland in automobiles.

To contribute to the formation of that combination of the modern firm and the heavy mechanical, chemical and electrical technologies which would give such vitality to the eco-technic dynamic of the twentieth century was surely among the most important and least intended consequences of the development of the sewing machine. Indeed, it is the very success of this dynamic in generating not only technical change but also new electronic, biochemical, and nuclear technologies, together with the social consequences of this evolution, which led Parker to claim that the uncontrolled development of science and technology is the central problem facing the modern world. Is this claim valid? And does this problem have a solution? These questions of course have no ready answer, nor can they be posed solely within economic theory. But they cannot be ignored in practice and cannot be answered without theory. If Parker is right, their answers, as well as solutions to more mundane problems of economic development, rest upon understanding modern technical change to be an eco-technic process.

ACKNOWLEDGMENTS

This article has benefited from the comments of Gavin Wright and Floria Thomson on an earlier draft.

NOTES

1.   "Technology, Resources, and Economic Change in the West," in A. J. Youngson, *Economic Development in the Long Run* (London: 1972), p. 70. Besides this article, Parker's major writings on technical change include "Economic Development in Historical Perspective," *Economic Development and Cultural Change* (October 1961): 1–7; "European History, 1500–1850, in Peter Burke, ed., *New Cambridge Modern History,* Vol. XIII (Cambridge, England: 1979), pp. 43–79; "European Development in Millenial Perspective," in Charles Kindleberger and Guido di Tella, *Econom-*

ics in the Long View: Essays in Honour of W. W. Rostow, Vol. II, pp. 1–24; "Communication Techniques and Social Organization in the World Economy," presented at the Eighth International Economic History Congress, Budapest, August 1982. Except for the first, these essays are all included in *Europe and the World Economy,* Volume I in Parker's *Europe, America, and the Wilder World* (Cambridge University Press, 1984).

2. This conception of technical change is not uniquely Parker's. His arguments resemble, and in part rest upon, those of A. P. Usher in *A History of Mechanical Inventions,* 2nd ed. (Cambridge, Mass.: 1954), Nathan Rosenberg in the essays grouped together in *Perspectives on Technology* (Cambridge, England: 1976) and *Inside the Black Box: Technology and Economics* (Cambridge, England: 1982), Paul Mantoux in *The Industrial Revolution in the Eighteenth Century* (New York: 1961), and Joseph Schumpeter in various works, to mention only the most important. In central ways, Parker's ideas also resemble those of the first major economist to conceive technical change to be an ongoing process within capitalism—Karl Marx. See especially *Capital* (New York: 1967), Vol. I, Chaps. 13–15, and Vol. III, Chap. 5, and *Grundrisse* (Harmondsworth, Middlesex, England: 1973), especially pp. 690–716. The exposition and illustration of Parker's ideas presented in this article will therefore also pertain to at least elements of similar ideas put forth by others. It is the character and usefulness of the conception advanced by Parker, and not its precise authorship, that interests us here.

3. The primary sources for this section are "Technology, Resources, and Economic Change in the West," "Economic Development in Historical Perspective," and "European Development in Millenial Perspective."

4. *Capital,* Vol. I, p. 486. Attempts made in the nineteenth century to theorize this science of technology can still be read with profit, most notably Franz Reuleaux, *The Kinematics of Machinery* (London: 1876).

5. *Perspectives on Technology,* pp. 15–18.

6. Parker, "Technology, Resources, and Economic Change in the West," p. 63.

7. The social organization of communication relevant to invention is not even listed as a determinant of invention by Habakkuk, as distinct from sociological influences or the volume of capital accumulation. H. J. Habakkuk, *American and British Technology in the 19th Century* (Cambridge, England: 1967), p. 1.

8. *Capital and Grundrisse.* Illuminating expositions of Marx's analysis of technical change are contained in Paul Sweezy, *Modern Capitalism and Other Essays* (New York: 1972), pp. 127–46, and in Nathan Rosenberg, "Karl Marx on the Economic Role of Science," *Perspectives on Technology,* pp. 126–138, and "Marx as a Student of Technology," *Monthly Review* (July/August 1976): 56–77, and reprinted in *Inside the Black Box.* Rosenberg has elaborated many of the same themes throughout his work.

9. Marx's emphasis on the machinery sector should be broadened to the producers goods sector more generally. As Marx notes and Parker stresses, technical change can alter materials; the knowledge of such alteration is concentrated outside the machinery sector but inside the producers goods industries. Parker's emphasis on the effect of technical change on the production of materials adds dimension to technical change beyond the Marxian emphasis on mechanization, a dimension which supports Marx's criticism of the Ricardian notion that the differential fertility of the soil, and the natural scarcity of materials more generally, generates a falling profit rate and a tendency toward a steady state.

10. As distinct from such bottlenecks, relative factor prices are accorded little role in determining the pace or direction of technological change in Parker's analysis. Both economic and technical bottlenecks are central determinants of the direction of technical change for Rosenberg, particularly in his "The Direction of Technological Change: Inducement Mechanisms and Focusing Devices," *Perspectives on Technology,* pp. 108–125. For Marx, technical bottlenecks and some economic bottlenecks, like labor militancy, give a direction to technical change. In addition, some have interpreted Marx to argue that the labor-saving direction to technological change, which for Marx

causes the rate of profit to tend to fall, results from the scarcity of labor. See *Capital*, Vol. I, Chap. 25, and Vol. III, Chap. 13; and Maurice Dobb, *Political Economy and Capitalism* (New York: 1937), pp. 94–129.

Paul David has recently applied a mode of argumentation similar to—though not necessarily entailed by—that of Parker to the classical case where high wages have been interpreted to induce labor-saving technical change in the nineteenth-century United States. Purely technological propositions were used to link resource abundance in the United States to the direction of technical change [*Technical Choice, Innovation and Economic Growth* (Cambridge, England: 1975), pp. 57–91]. It is interesting to note that the principles David introduces to effect this linkage depend to a considerable extent on the work of Rosenberg.

11.   The term *eco-technic process* is used by Parker in "European Industry," p. 73, and "European Development in Millenial Perspective," pp. 10, 13; I am taking the liberty to apply this term to describe Parker's conception of modern technical change as a whole. This term can also be applied to the similar conceptions of the ongoing technological change in modern capitalism put forth by Marx and Rosenberg.

12.   *Perspectives on Technology*, pp. 110–117.

13.   Parker and Marx both make technical change the central determinant of the evolution of the economy, including those factors which condition technical change. In "Economic Development in Historical Perspective," Parker explicitly subscribes to a technological determinism; in "Technology, Resources, and Economic Change in the West," economic history is simply the adjustment of mankind to problems created by technological development. To the extent that the tendency for the rate of profit to fall is determined by the direction of technological change, Marx also interprets technology to govern economic development. Yet such technological determinism is not entailed by the eco-technic conception of the process generating new techniques. For a subtle attempt to understand the place of technical change in a theory of capital accumulation, see David Levine, *Economic Theory*, Vol. II (London: 1981).

14.   The analysis of the Smithian dynamic is most explicit in "European Development in Millenial Perspective," and the investigation of the origin of the eco-technic process in this essay and in "European Industry."

15.   Like Parker, Marx associated the dynamic of craft production with a whole epoch in the birth of capitalism, called the stage of manufacturing, in which production was led by the expansion of trade. This notion in Marx was formed as early as *The German Ideology* and persisted through the writing of *Capital*, seen particularly in Vol. I, Chaps. 13–15, 30, and 31.

16.   "European Development in Millenial Perspective," p. 17.

17.   The following study is based on several chapters of my manuscript, *The Origin of Mechanized Production in the United States*. Notes will indicate only major sources this manuscript used.

18.   The best sources for the failure of early machines are Grace Rogers Cooper, *The Invention of the Sewing Machine*, Smithsonian Bulletin No. 254 (Washington, D.C.: 1968), and John Alexander, "On the Sewing Machine: Its History and Progress," *Journal of the Society of the Arts* (April 10, 1863): 358–370.

19.   However much hand-type machines were inadequate, the process of their development had diverse and at times serendipitous importance for the evolution of technology. Consider the example of the American inventor of one of these machines, George Corliss, who left his Greenwich, New York, general store to find someone to finance and produce his sewing machine. He went to Providence, where he contacted a machinery maker who, uninterested in his sewing machine, hired him to work in his steam engine shop. The Corliss steam engine followed. *Bulletin of the Business History Society* 4(January 1930): 4–5; William Ewers and H. W. Baylor, *Sincere's History of the Sewing Machine* (Phoenix, Ariz.: 1970), pp. 19–20; Cooper, *Invention of the Sewing Machine*, pp. 14–15.

20.   Howe's invention and its development to practicality are discussed in J. Parton, "History of the Sewing Machine," *Atlantic Monthly*, 19(May 1867): 527–541; George Gifford, *Application of*

Elias Howe, Jr. for an Extension of his Patent for Sewing Machines: Argument of George Gifford, Esq., in Favor of the Application (New York: 1860), and in Cooper, op. cit.

21. Discussion of the sale of sewing machines is given in Andrew B. Jack, "The Channels of Distribution for an Innovation: The Sewing Machine Industry in America 1860–1865, *Explorations in Entrepreneurial History* 9(1956): 113–141; Robert B. Davies, *Peacefully Working to Conquer the World* (New York: 1976), Chaps. 1–3; and various issues of *Scientific American*.

22. The labor time of sewing shirts by machine could be reduced to one-fifth or less of its former level; similar advantages existed in making coats and summer pants and greater advantages in hat binding and fitting the uppers of shoes. See Gifford, *Application; Eighty Years' Progress of the United States* (New York: 1864), pp. 426–427; Edwin Freedley, ed., *Leading Pursuits and Leading Men* (Philadelphia: 1856), pp. 146–147.

23. The evolution of craft shoemaking is examined in Blanche Hazard, *The Organization of the Boot and Shoe Industry in Massachusetts Before 1875* (Cambridge, Mass.: 1921), and in various issues of *Shoe and Leather Reporter*.

24. The technical development of the sewing machine is considered in various issues of *Scientific American*, international exhibitions and technical dictionaries of the last half of the nineteenth century, and Charles McDermott, *A History of the Shoe and Leather Industries of the United States* (Boston: 1918).

25. The social form of technical change is discussed in issues of the *Scientific American* and *Shoe and Leather Reporter* and in both Cooper and McDermott, op. cit.

26. Technical change in the production of the sewing machine differed in this regard; by reducing unit costs, it allowed the price of the sewing machine to fall without decreasing profit margins, and this decreased price, in turn, made it possible for sales of family machines, far the most important proportion of output after the Civil War, to be extended to lower levels of the income distribution.

27. See especially "Technological Change in the Machine Tool Industry, 1840–1910," *Perspectives on Technology*, pp. 9–31.

28. The best sources on sewing machine production are issues of the *Scientific American*; Rosenberg, "Technological Change in the Machine Tool Industry, 1840–1910"; Joseph Roe, *English and American Tool Builders* (New Haven, 1916); Charles Fitch, "Report on the Manufactures of Interchangeable Mechanism," *Report on the Manufactures of the United States at the Tenth Census: 1880* (Washington, 1883); Robert Woodbury, *Studies of the History of Machine Tools* (Cambridge, Mass.: 1972); David Hounshell, "The System: Theory and Practice," in Otto Mayr and Robert Post, eds., *Yankee Enterprise* (Washington, D.C., 1981), pp. 127–152.

29. S. B. Saul, "The Market and the Development of the Mechanical Engineering Industries in Britain, 1860–1914," *Economic History Review* (1967): 111–130; Duncan McDougall, "Machine Tool Output, 1861–1910," in *Output, Employment and Productivity in the United States After 1800: Studies in Income and Wealth*, Vol. 30 (New York: 1966), p. 505.

30. Brown and Sharpe data is taken from McDougall, "Machine Tool Output, 1861–1910," pp. 497, 505, 515.

31. Chandler, *The Visible Hand*, pp. 277, 308–309. Both White's inventions and the Remington typewriter came to be made and sold by newly formed firms.

32. Charles McCurdy, "American Law and the Marketing Structure of the Large Corporation, 1875–1890," *Journal of Economic History* 38, No. 3 (September 1978): 631–649.

RINGS AND MULES AROUND THE WORLD:
A COMPARATIVE STUDY IN TECHNOLOGICAL CHOICE

Gary Saxonhouse and Gavin Wright

I. INTRODUCTION

In his influential 1961 article "Economic Development in Historical Perspective," William Parker observes

> Nearly all the production and transport techniques developed between 1770 and 1870 promoted the geographical concentration of industry. Those developed since that time have, in contrast, favored deconcentration. At first sight it appears odd that the drift of technological change should have been so strongly in one direction in one period and the reverse in another. It suggests that some relatively simple principle may underlie the variety of changes in each period and that a fundamental shift occurred between say, 1870 and 1920, in the principle on

Technique, Spirit, and Form in the Making of the Modern Economies:
Essays in Honor of William N. Parker
Research in Economic History, Suppl. 3, pages 271–300
Copyright © 1984 by JAI Press Inc.
All rights of reproduction in any form reserved.
ISBN: 0-89232-414-7

which technology advanced. Our ignorance of the history of modern technology is so profound that it is not possible to work out the nature of this shift in detail from readily available
materials.[1]

It was the fate of the cotton spinning industry to be the first industry of the
Industrial Revolution whose technology followed its goods out of the proximity
of the North Atlantic to Eastern Europe and Russia, to Mexico and Brazil, to
India, and to Japan.[2] By 1900, even as an enormous international trade in cotton
goods continued, and even as the British industry remained dominant, major
textile industries existed at numerous locations on three continents.

Unhappily, the multinational comparative possibilities of this first major modern case of technological transfer have never been exploited. Where a frontal
assault might have been made on the global economic watershed first identified
by Parker, there have been only purely binational or bi-regional comparisons.
British and American, Japanese and Indian, the New England and the American
South's experience with cotton textile production have all been the subject of
extended bilateral comparison. Unfortunately, in the same way that a perfect
least squares fit with a single independent variable is always achieved with a
sample of size 2, strictly binational comparisons run the risk of yielding facile
but specious or even fallacious interpretations of complex phenomena. The historical laboratory, however, unlike the statistical services of the twentieth-century international institutions, does not serve up large samples easily, and the
economic historian is usually left with a choice between binational comparison or
no contemporaneous comparison at all. This is all the more reason why the
global experience of the cotton textile industry should be examined. In particular, this essay will study the global adoption pattern of the two famous competing
spinning processes during the 50 years after 1870. It is true that the choice
between ring and mule spinning during this period has already been subjected to
British–American and Indian–Japanese comparisons.[3] Using entirely new
sources of information, however, the British and Indian experiences will be
reevaluated and set within a global framework.

II. MULE AND RING TECHNOLOGY

Both mule and ring spinning are direct adaptions of and improvements on spinning processes which date from the earliest days of the Industrial Revolution.
The mule is based on the principle of intermittent spinning, the same principle
which underlies both the spinning wheel and the famous Hargreaves jenny. Mule
spindles rest on a carriage which travels on a track a distance of better than five
feet while drawing out and spinning the yarn. On the return trip as the carriage
moves back to its original position, the newly spun yarn is wound onto the
spindle to form a cone-shaped cop. The process of building up this cop is
regulated by a wire which moves up and down to guide the yarn. The mule, as its

name implies, is traditionally thought of as a hybrid machine. As the mule spindle travels on its carriage, the sliver which it spins is fed to it through rollers geared to revolve at different speeds to draw out the yarn. Such rollers were also a principle element of Arkwright's water frame, which was the early alternative to the spinning jenny.[4]

The late-nineteenth-century ring spinning machine also rested on better than 100 years of development of continuous spinning processes. The mule spindle does not spin while the yarn is being wound. By contrast, the ring, which is an immediate descendant of Arkwright's water frame, is spinning all the time. Again, unlike the mule, the frame on which ring spindles rotate is fixed in place. On each ring spindle is a little wire called a traveler, and around each spindle is also a steel ring. After the thread is drawn through rollers similar to those used by the mule, it passes through the traveler onto a wooden bobbin which has been placed on the spindle. As the spindle revolves, this traveler is drawn around the ring, receiving its impetus from the yarn. By revolving a little more slowly than the bobbin, twist is put into the yarn. At the same time, the yarn is wound on the bobbin, and, in order to secure uniformity in winding, the frame of rings moves up and down slowly.[5]

While both the late-nineteenth-century ring and the mule are clearly recognizable descendants of eighteenth-century machines, the pace of their development in the intervening 100 years was quite uneven. The original Hargreaves spinning jenny and Arkwright's water frame were produced within a year or two of one another in the late 1760s.[6] The yarn which the water frame produced was strong but rather coarse. By contrast the drawing-out feature of the jenny produced yarn which was weak and broke easily but which could be extremely fine. Yarn from the water frame was most suitable for warp, and yarn from the jenny was most suitable for weft. In consequence, these two early spinning machines proved to be complementary rather than competitive. The water frame, incorporating as it did hundreds of spindles at a time, made possible the factory production of cotton yarn at the same time that it first also enhanced cottage production of weft yarn.

As is well known, this complementarity between factory and cottage ended not long after the invention of mule spinning in 1779. While the first mules were made of wood and their small size made them suitable for use in cottages, by 1790 large mule spinning machines with metal rollers and wheels, fitted with hundreds of spindles and powered by waterwheels, were being used in large factories. Mule spinning meant the demise of Hargreaves' jenny, but it did not mean the end of spinning by continuous methods. The water frames, and later the throstle, by twisting and drawing the yarn simultaneously, could produce coarse yarn faster and cheaper than the mule, so continuous spinning retained a niche in this segment of the yarn market.

This cost advantage was threatened in the 1830s with the introduction of the self-acting mule. Until this new device appeared, a man's strength had been required for pushing the mule spindles back and forth on their carriage. The self-actor removed this requirement, allowing a potentially more diverse, if still highly skilled, labor force and greatly increasing the size of individual frames.[7]

Hardly had such dramatic improvements in mule spinning begun their diffusion when equally important improvements were made in continuous spinning. The development of cap spinning and ring spinning at this time allowed continuous spinning to achieve higher speeds than ever before. The key step was dispensing with the U-shaped ''flyer'' fixed at the top of the spindle. Cap spinning substituted a conical cap mounted over the spindle, to guide the yarn to the bobbin below. Ring spinning replaced the flyer with a ''c''-ring traveling at a high speed around a grooved circular raceway mounted on a plate, which in turn traveled up and down the spinning bobbin. These improvements meant dramatic increases in output per spindle, with less labor and no increase in energy required. By the 1850s average speeds on ring machines reached 5,500 rpm, and there were already reports at this time of successful ring spinning of coarse yarn at 9,000 rpm.[8] Because of this continuing increase in speed, ring spinning was never eclipsed by the self-acting mule in the United States. By the 1860s the American industry had almost as many ring as mule spindles.

Mule technology did not change radically during the remainder of the nineteenth century, but major improvements in ring spinning continued with the introduction of the Sawyer spindle in the early 1870s. This new spindle was reduced in weight, and its point of support was changed to an elevated holster. By these changes, the power cost was reduced, the speed increased, and the quality of work improved. The average speed of rings in operation reached 7,500 rpm by the mid-1870s. The late 1870s saw the development of the Rabbeth spindle, and within a few years average spindle speeds were as high as 10,000 rpm.

By the late nineteenth century, as machine-spinning was becoming truly global in location, the textile industry continued to face two competing spinning technologies, as it had since the Industrial Revolution. Mule spinning continued to require a large number of highly skilled if not exactly brawny operatives. By contrast, ring spinning remained a relatively unskilled task, and, because it required no complicated rolling carriage, it took up a third less space than did mules of comparable capacity. Despite these advantages, the very simplicity of ring spinning which spun and wound yarn in one motion placed special demands on the fiber being spun. In the absence of large inputs of labor in the preparatory stages, rings could successfully spin yarn for any given fineness from only a narrow range of cotton grades. These special strains on the yarn also made it difficult to spin extremely fine yarns on the ring machine. Other disadvantages could be more or less important in particular settings. While the ring had to wind its spun yarn onto wooden bobbins, the mule wound its yarn onto a paper tube called a cop. If the yarn must be transported a significant distance before being woven, this was an important advantage for mule-spun weft.[9] Also, since a cop holds more yarn than a wooden bobbin, mule spinning did not require as frequent labor-using removal of yarn from spindles as did ring spinning.

III. PREVIOUS INTERPRETATIONS OF RING SPINNING DIFFUSION

By the 1950s, some 80 years after the major improvements in the ring spinning machines, the ring had completely supplanted the mule worldwide. At what point and by what process did the century of coexistence between intermittent and continous spinning become a rout? Was the protracted and uneven diffusion of the ring a matter of imperfect information and entrepreneurial inertia, or is this another of Rosenberg's cases where a lag in diffusion is really the playing out of changing market circumstances in the presence of good knowledge of local circumstances?[10] Most of the bilateral or single-country studies have not pursued this question directly, but elements of an implicit interpretation do seem to be present in recent writing. D. W. Farnie writes of a "broad new division of the market" arising after the crisis of 1891–1893, "wherein Europe installed mules and Asia adopted the ring frame in the slow recapture of its great traditional industry."[11] Similarly, Sandberg divides the modern cotton industries of the world (outside the United States) into three broad groups, and asserts that ring spinning spread first to Asia, then to Continental Europe, last to England (1969, p. 25). Since Sandberg argues that the ring was adopted rapidly in England for lower-count yarns, the suggestion seems to be that mules remained predominant only in conjunction with specialization in high-quality products. This specialization would in turn be attributable to the highly skilled character of the English labor force, as elaborated in C. K. Harley's 1974 article on "Skilled Labor and the Choice of Technique in Edwardian Industry." From this we infer that the global diffusion of ring spinning is seen as determined by the relative price of skilled labor and as progressing in association with a division of the product market according to yarn count.

The Sandberg–Harley interpretation of the English situation has been challenged by William Lazonick, who finds (on the basis of major corrections in the cost assumptions) that mules were only "rational" because of the extreme degree of vertical specialization which prevailed there. Not only did the high cost of shipping wooden bobbins absorb the gains from ring spinning, but the fragmented decision-making structure blocked efforts at a coordinated modernization program.[12] This interpretation suggests a somewhat different international scenario (in which industrial organization patterns and timing effects are determining). But from a global perspective, both interpretations appear to agree that the mule remained a major technology into the twentieth century primarily because England remained a holdout against trends under way elsewhere, and England bulked extremely large in total world production (see Table 1).

Table 1. Spindles in Place, 1907

United Kingdom	43,154,713	United States	23,200,000
Germany	9,191,540	Russia	7,562,478
France	6,609,105	India	5,279,595
Austria	3,584,434	Italy	2,867,862
Spain	1,800,000	Japan	1,483,497
Brazil	1,000,000	Belgium	1,000,000
Canada	893,761	China	755,938
Mexico	693,843		

Source: United Kingdom, United States, Italy, France, Germany, Russia, and Austria—
M. T. Copeland, "Technical Development in Cotton Manufacturing since
1860," *Quarterly Journal of Economics* 24 (1909–1910): 109–159. Japan—Dai
nihon bōseki rengōkai, *Menshi bōseki jijō sankoshō meiji yon-jūnen*; Spain,
Brazil, Belgium, Canada, Mexico—U.S. Department of Commerce Special
Agent Series; China—A. S. Pearse, *Japan & China: Cotton Industry Report*
Manchester, England: International Federation of Master Cotton Spinners' and
Manufacturers' Association, 1931).

The empirical basis for international comparisons of ring diffusion has been
highly uneven. It is reasonably well established that, following the American
improvements of the 1870s, diffusion in America was rapid in the late nineteenth
century. Even prior to the development of the Sawyer–Rabbeth spindle, census
returns indicate that the ring was preferred (Table 2). In the southern branch of
the industry, rising from the 1870s with an unskilled labor force producing low-
count yarns in integrated mills, the choice of the ring was clear. But because all
variables pointed in the same direction, the southern case does not help us to
separate decisive from incidental factors. Even in New England, however, new
mule installations had virtually ceased by 1890.

Japan is another famous example of rapid ring diffusion, with somewhat
different initial circumstances (Table 3). With the exception of two minor instances, the Japanese cotton spinning industry's early mills (including the highly
successful Osaka Spinning Mill) all used mules.[13] But the Japanese mule experience proved short-lived. By the mid-1880s, the first ring spinning machines were

Table 2. Spindleage in the United States (millions)

	1870	1880	1890	1900	1905	1910	1915	1920
Ring	3.7	—	8.9	13.4	17.9	22.7	27.1	30.6
Mule	3.4	—	5.4	5.6	5.2	4.7	3.7	3.1
Total	7.1	10.6	14.3	19.0	23.2	27.4	30.8	33.7

Source: M. T. Copeland, "Technical Development in Cotton Manufacturing Since
1860," *Quarterly Journal of Economics* 24, No. 1 (November 1909): 128.
Fourteenth U.S. Census (1920), Vol. X, p. 176.

Table 3. Spindle Investments in Japan

	(1) New Mules	(2) Mules Scrapped	(3) Total Mules	(4) New Rings[a]	(5) Total Rings
1866	1824	—	1824	—	—
1871	2000	—	3824	—	—
1873	—	—	3824	720	720
1875	2000	—	5824	—	720
1880	4080	—	9904	—	720
1881	10000	—	19904	—	720
1882	6000	—	25904	—	720
1883	14500	—	40404	1152	1872
1884	6000	—	46404	—	1872
1885	24800	—	71204	4020	5892
1887	—	—	71204	5164	11056
1888	13500	2000	82704	36272	47328
1889	29224	—	111928	108744	186072
1890	11664	—	123592	94953	251025
1891	—	5902	117690	51032	302057
1892	—	4560	113130	6872	308929
1893	—	31300	81830	97960	406889
1894	2000	4000	79830	156742	563631
1895	4000	13028	66802	76844	640476
1896	46140	16820	96122	265180	905656
1897	17020	14000	99142	226884	1132540
1898	11620	9800	100962	83000	1215540
1899	1616	—	102578	61908	1277448
1900	—	2000	100578	−1796	1275652

[a]Note: column 4 is net ring investment.

Source: Nōshōmushō, *Nihon menshi bōseki kijū* (Tokyo: 1901). In addition to rings and mules, some throstles were used in the early days of the Japanese cotton spinning industry. In 1866 the first spinning mill in Japan used 1800 throstle spindles as well 1824 mule spindles. Another mill erected in 1880 included 448 throstles in addition to its 2080 mule spindles.

purchased as an experiment, and by the end of the decade new orders for mules had stopped almost entirely. In Japanese eyes the ring now came so to dominate the mule that virtually all the mule spinning machines which had been in use in 1889 were scrapped within the next few years.[14] A few new mule machines were purchased in the late 1890s, but, whereas the scrapped mules were designed to spin coarse 10s, 12s, or 14s, the large mules purchased in 1896–1898 were designed to manufacture fine yarns in the 80s.[15]

It is widely assumed that India followed the American and Japanese examples, and indeed that is the contention of many Indian economists and industrial historians.[16] Following experiments in the mills in Bombay controlled by J. N. Tata after 1882, the ring was reportedly the universal choice by promoters of new mills in India. Supporting evidence may be found in data originating in Bombay

Table 4.   Indian Spindleage (millions)

	1884	1894	1905	1914	1923	1929	1939
Mules	2.0	2.2	2.0	1.6	1.1	0.9	0.5
Rings	—	1.2	3.2	5.2	6.8	7.9	9.6
Total	2.0	3.4	5.2	6.8	7.9	8.8	10.1

Source: Bombay Millowners Association data as cited in Y. Kiyokawa, ''Indo men-
kōgyō ni okeru gijutsu to shiba no keisei ni tsuite,'' *Keizai kenkyū* (July 1976);
Arno S. Pearse, *The Cotton Industry of India* (Manchester, England: 1980); and
N. Takamura, *Nihon bōsekigyō shi jōsetsu* (Tokyo: 1969).

Millowners Association series. Table 4 looks much like the Japanese and American series. Anecdotal accounts, in fact, suggest that Indian entrepreneurs may
even have pioneered in the early improvement of ring technology. Consider the
following authorized description of the initial introduction of the ring into Bombay by Tata:

> [Tata's] readiness to give an immediate trial to any new machinery quickly placed him at an
> advantage. In America, where the spindle was invented, the trials had not given sufficiently
> successful results to justify extensive use of the machine. While experiments in Lancashire
> were still at a tentative stage, and nothing had been done upon a large scale, two frames at the
> Empress Mill were in daily use. For Mr. Tata persevered, and insisted that the machines
> should run to their full capacity. The normal speed of 6000 rpm was soon exceeded; at the
> Empress Mills 9000 rpm was considered a fair average but 12,000 rpm were frequently
> obtained. . . . On account of this improvement, the output of the machines was so satisfacto-
> ry that Mr. Tata scrapped every other type. At first, his statistical results were received with
> incredulity even by the best English firms and he had great difficulty persuading Messrs. Platt
> Bros. of Oldham to take up the manufacture of the necessary plant. Their conservatism was at
> length broken down and in later years they supplied Mr. Tata with several ring frames (Harris,
> 1925, p. 31).

Unfortunately, this account of Tata's struggles is filled with major errors. In
1875, almost 10 years before these experiments in Bombay took place, millions
of American ring spindles were operating at an average speed of 7,500 rpm, and
in the mid-1880s speeds closer to 10,000 rpm were the average (Copeland, 1909,
p. 122). Similarly, while English machinery manufactures were undoubtedly
conservative, orders for at least hundreds of thousands of ring spinning machines
were taken by British manufacturers such as Howard & Bulloughs, Asa Lees,
Dobson & Barlow, Brooks & Doxey, J. Hetherington, and even Platt Bros.
between 1880 and 1885. Indeed, prior to the onset of Platt's reputed refusal of
Tata's request for rings, at least 13 orders for ring spinning machines for Indian
manufacturers were booked by Platt's (Table 5). These inconsistencies suggest
that further examination of the quantitative evidence may also be called for.
  Another data source, which appears to offer promise of a check on the Indian

Table 5.   Platt Bros. Orders for Ring Spinning Machines for Indian
Manufacturers

Date of Order	Location	Mill Name	Frames	Spindles per Frame
2/1881	Cawnpore	Muir Mills Co.	5	304
2/1881	Cawnpore	Muir Mills Co.	5	416
1/1882	Bombay	Manockjee Petit	52	280
1/1882	Bombay	Manockjee Petit	58	280
1/1882	Bombay	Manockjee Petit	50	248
5/1882	Cawnpore	Muir Mills Co.	2	304
5/1882	Cawnpore	Muir Mills Co.	6	416
10/1882	Bombay	Southern Makratta	7	304
11/1882	India	Gaiewer of Baroda	8	304
11/1882	India	Gaiewer of Baroda	4	80
12/1882	Bombay	Vandresh Spinning and Weaving	12	304
1/1883	Ahmedabad	Ahmedabad Cotton Mill	5	248
1/1883	Ahmedabad	Ahmedabad Calico Printing	14	280

Source: Platt Bros. Records.

series in comparison with figures for many other countries, is the international survey of the Master Cotton Spinners and Manufacturers Association. These surveys appear to be the original basis for many prevailing impressions about ring mule diffusion, though we know of no published discussion of the data. Unfortunately, they cannot help with the late-nineteenth-century episodes, because the surveys only began after 1903, and they did not distinguish ring from mule spindles until 1908. Between 1908 and 1913, the surveys do provide a semiannual series of stock estimates, which can be augmented with two additional surveys taken in 1920. The data, in excerpted form and expressed as percentages, are presented in Table 6. They show a remarkable dispersion of national cases, both in composition and rates of change. Belgium, for example, was moving rapidly toward the ring before the war, whereas France, Spain, and Canada were changing much more gradually. Broadly speaking, however, the data seem to confirm both the uniqueness of Great Britain and the early commitment of India to the ring.

Even for this late and short period, the spinners' association figures may be misleading. By the associations's own estimates, the returns covered between 85 and 90 percent of the world's spindles; more seriously, the undercount was not uniform by country. In the case of India, the estimated coverage was only 23 percent in 1908 and fluctuated between 50 and 75 percent in later years. But even these percentages are based on the association's figures for total spindles, which are themselves estimates. Lazonick's count of English rings and mules in Worrall's Directory for 1913 located an additional 2.7 million mule spindles and 1.0

Table 6.   Ring and Mule Distribution by Country,
According to Spinners Association Returns, 1908–1920

	1908		*1910*		*1913*		*1920*	
	%Mule	*%Ring*	*%Mule*	*%Ring*	*%Mule*	*%Ring*	*%Mule*	*%Ring*
Great Britain	83.6	16.4	83.4	16.6	81.3	18.7	78.7	21.3
United States	17.7	82.3	17.6	82.4	13.1	86.9	9.2	80.8
Germany	55.8	44.2	52.9	47.1	45.8	54.2	44.4	55.6
Russia	50.2	49.8	48.4	51.6	41.3	58.7	N.A.	N.A.
France	60.0	40.0	58.5	41.5	54.3	45.7	47.3	52.7
India	28.0	72.0	30.0	70.0	27.5	72.5	18.6	81.4
Austria	61.0	39.0	57.0	43.0	51.0	49.0	N.A.	N.A.
Italy	26.6	73.4	33.5	66.5	24.7	75.3	24.7	75.3
Spain	40.0	60.0	41.1	58.9	40.0	60.0	38.9	41.1
Japan	3.3	96.7	1.5	88.5	2.3	97.7	1.2	98.8
Brazil	3.0	97.0	N.A.	N.A.	N.A.	N.A.	0.3	99.7
Belgium	51.5	48.5	41.6	58.4	33.2	66.8	28.8	71.2
Canada	46.0	54.0	48.3	51.7	45.2	54.8	30.5	69.5
Mexico	4.0	96.0	N.A.	N.A.	N.A.	N.A.	4.4	95.6
World	55.8	44.2	54.4	45.1	49.5	50.5	44.6	55.4

Source: Master Cotton Spinners Manufacturers' Association, Official Reports of the International Congress, 1908–1920.

million ring spindles, as compared to Sandberg's figures, which originated in the spinners' association estimates.[17] That correction was substantial enough to have a bearing on the Sandberg–Lazonick debate over the allocation of investment between 1907 and 1913. In a country like India, potential biases are much larger, perhaps for many reasons but in particular because the sample comes exclusively from firms affiliated with an international association. Our new data sources suggest that the Indian story is in need of substantial revision.

IV.   NEW DATA SOURCES

Full discussion of the worldwide diffusion of ring technology has been hampered by lack of appropriate data. Beyond the four countries discussed above, there has been very little evidence on the timing of ring adoption. Indeed, even for these countries, in only the Japanese case has accurate and comprehensive data been previously available. We are now able to improve upon this situation. Unusually complete data on the worldwide shipment of ring and mule spinning machines between 1880 and 1920 have been obtained from six British textile machinery companies. These companies include Platt Brothers, Dobson & Barlow, Howard & Bulloughs, Asa Lees, Tweedales & Smalley, and Taylor & Lang. With the exception of the German, the American, and to a much lesser extent the French markets, the six English machinery manufacturers accounted for most worldwide machinery sales. It is possible to obtain from these records not only the amount of each piece of machinery sold in each national market but also the identity of each customer, the count of yarn to be spun, and grade of raw cotton to be used with each piece of machinery sold. The remainder of this article constitutes a preliminary report on our efforts to exploit this data source. At this stage in the research, we have concentrated on a handful of cases where the data are most directly informative, those countries for whom England was the major supplier of textile machinery.

Table 7 presents annual figures on ring and mule purchases by English firms from 1878 through 1920, summarized by time period in Table 8. The tables provide ample testimony to the persistent strength of the mule, not as hardy relics of the past but as the overwhelming preference in new investments up to World War I. Though the percentage of rings in new installations steadily rose by time period, this was more the incursion at the margin of a minority technique than the diffusion of a new and better method. The figures are not of course a complete census of spindle investments, but the missing observations include both ring and mule producing firms.[18] The ring series does sum to a smaller percentage of the reported 1913 stocks than does the mule series, so it is possible that there is some relative bias toward mules in the coverage. But since the six firms account for nearly 80 percent of employment in the textile machinery industry in 1913, and since there are omissions of both types, it is most unlikely that the basic picture of relative preference is far off. The extraordinarily large *absolute* new investment in mules between 1899 and 1914 is undeniable.

These data represent gross investment and cannot be directly compared to the net investment figures discussed by Sandberg and Lazonick. It is clear, however, that Sandberg's assumed scrapping rate of 2.5 percent per year is much too high. That rate would imply that mule investments even larger than those displayed in Table 7 would have been required just to maintain the stock; yet we know the stock of mules increased between 1907 and 1913. The replacement rate which would reconcile our gross series with Lazonick's estimate of net mule investment between these dates would be approximately 1.4 percent, which would imply that about 45 percent of the investment was for replacement purposes. This figure may be too low for the particular period under discussion, since 1907–1909 and 1910–1912 were identified as "peak replacement periods" for both rings and mules in a 1930 study of the age of textile machinery.[19]

As useful as it would be to have a definitive division of the totals, it is gross investment that matters for a study of technological diffusion. Spinning machines, especially mules, were among the most long-lived of investments; a decision to replace an old mule with a new one was in no sense routine. With a life expectancy conservatively put at 60–75 years, a replacement mule was just as much a vote of confidence in the future of the technology as an expansion mule. (Indeed, the very records we are now studying remained in active use for

Table 7.   Mules and Rings Ordered by
British Firms, Annually (spindles)

Year	Mules	Rings
1878	49,252	0
1879	208,994	0
1880	808,513	20,060
1881	847,352	46,474
1882	920,527	45,741
1883	1,396,242	39,656
1884	2,076,166	211,216
1885	1,325,271	130,193
1886	916,529	63,436
1887	752,958	37,366
1888	834,970	58,160
1889	940,346	90,986
1890	1,373,350	48,922
1891	880,097	80,554
1892	1,161,972	65,326
1893	828,200	90,650
1894	666,612	8,442
1895	604,712	55,726
1896	391,483	145,347
1897	288,304	271,582
1898	993,063	141,964
1899	1,341,650	171,570
1900	1,041,153	98,182
1901	1,955,587	163,580
1902	1,540,914	115,502
1903	1,503,762	203,072
1904	840,299	417,311
1905	2,509,469	702,831
1906	2,927,001	800,580
1907	1,963,587	393,005
1908	1,379,288	279,427
1909	1,064,115	352,006
1910	686,205	333,099
1911	1,137,158	351,636
1912	1,680,093	667,668
1913	933,421	495,918
1914	1,211,716	392,237
1915	261,490	314,902
1916	281,164	152,538
1917	21,523	59,537
1918	191,620	159,711
1919	161,512	496,434
1920	419,136	411,284

Source: See Table 8.

Table 8. Cotton Spinning Orders by British Firms, 1878–
1920 (spindles)

Period	Mules	%	Rings	%	Total
1878–1883	3,468,280	96	151,931	4	3,620,211
1884–1890	8,219,590	93	640,279	7	8,859,869
1891–1898	5,813,819	87	860,215	13	6,674,034
1899–1906	13,659,835	84	2,670,776	16	16,330,611
1907–1914	10,055,583	75	3,264,996	25	13,320,579
1915–1920	1,336,445	46	1,594,406	54	2,930,851

Source: Compiled from company records of Platt Bros., Dobson & Barlow, Howard and
Bullough, Asa Lees and Co., Tweedales and Smalley, and Taylor Lang and Co.

replacement-part orders into the 1950s!) What the gross investment figures suggest, much more strongly than the net figures, is that the pre–World War I ring-mule question in England was not a matter of sunk costs and refusal to write off old equipment; if it were, the occasion of scrapping would be the logical time to switch methods, but the British were not doing so in most cases. The mule was by no means being phased out before 1920.

It was not even being phased out on low-count yarns, as Table 9 shows. It does appear that Sandberg was correct in suggesting that the spread of the ring was concentrated in yarn counts below 40; 88 percent of ring installations in the 1880s were for sub-40 counts, and this figure had only fallen to 85 percent during 1910–1920. But the mule remained the distinctly preferred choice at counts below 40 as well, at least until 1910. During the decade after 1910 the evidence roughly confirms Lazonick's contention that about one-half of new sub-40 capacity consisted of mules, and suggests that if anything he was conservative for the earlier years.[20]

The Indian evidence is equally surprising. Table 4 had indicated that between 1884 and 1894 the Indian stock of spindles experienced an increase of 1.4 million, of which .2 million was the net increase in mule spindles and 1.2 million was the net increase in ring spindles. The new data show a gross investment of 2.3 million spindles during these 10 years, divided between 1.3 million mule spindles and 1.0 million ring spindles. Between 1884 and 1914, Table 4 indicates a .4 million decline in mule spindles, yet the English evidence lists more than 2.1 million mule spindles shipped to India during this period. With major mule orders coming into England from India throughout the period 1900–1914, it is hard to imagine the widespread scrapping implicit in the Indian historians' data. It is similarly hard to imagine the scrapping which would make Table 4 consistent with Table 10. More likely, the firms from which the older data were drawn were unrepresentative. On the basis of the new data, we can say that Indian spinning history differs substantially from both the Japanese and

Table 9. Distribution of British Purchases by Yarn Count, 1878–1920

Count Interval	Mules	%	Rings	%
1878–1890				
1–20	457,750	3.7	170,350	21.5
21–30	755,850	6.0	325,600	41.1
31–40	4,321,600	34.7	202,000	25.5
41–60	5,225,450	42.0	83,950	10.6
60+	1,689,600	13.6	9,500	1.2
	12,450,250	100.0	791,400	100.0
1891–1900				
1–20	811,550	9.9	228,150	20.2
21–30	1,032,850	12.6	377,200	33.4
31–40	2,336,200	28.5	285,700	25.3
41–60	2,434,600	29.7	176,200	15.6
60+	1,582,050	19.3	62,100	5.5
	8,197,250	100.0	1,129,350	100.0
1901–1910				
1–20	965,850	5.9	533,700	14.2
21–30	949,450	5.8	1,135,100	30.2
31–40	3,405,000	20.8	1,447,050	38.5
41–60	5,353,050	32.7	466,050	12.4
60+	5,696,850	34.8	176,650	4.7
	12,370,200	100.0	3,758,550	100.0
1911–1920				
1–20	535,400	8.5	420,200	12.0
21–30	541,700	8.6	742,400	21.2
31–40	1,719,600	27.3	1,810,450	51.7
41–60	1,933,750	30.7	259,150	7.4
60+	1,568,400	24.9	273,150	7.8
	6,298,850	100.0	2,837,150	100.0

Notes: Compiled from six-company sales records. The spindle figures are inflated proportionately, to match the totals in Table 7. Approximately 80% of the entries report the yarn count for which the machine was intended.

American cases, on the one hand, and the British case, on the other. In India, mule spinning remained important long after the early and very substantial adoption of ring spinning by some segments of the industry. The industry as a whole ordered as many mule spindles after 1884 as it did before. These mules were predominantly used to spin *low-count yarn*. Indeed, the median count yarn for which new mule spinning machinery was purchased was also lower than for ring

Table 10.   Indian Orders of Mule and Ring Spinning Machines 1880–1920

	Mule Machines	Median Spindles per Machine	Ring Machines	Median Spindles per Machine	Percentage of Spindles	
					Mule	Ring
1880–1890	1615	733	3209	286	56	44
1891–1900	1914	747	3877	322	53	47
1901–1910	468	739	5159	339	16	84
1911–1920	510	719	4322	331	20	80

	Median Counts for Which Machines Rated	
	Mules	Rings
1880–1890	18	19
1891–1900	14	18
1901–1910	17	20
1911–1920	13	20

spinning machines throughout the period 1880–1920. Despite the concentration on coarse yarns, it was only after 1900 that the ring was seen as the dominant spinning machine in India.

The records of the British textile machinery manufacturers also shed light on cases of ring-mule competition where little evidence had previously been available and consequently little discussion has taken place. An example is the Russian experience. At the turn of the century the Russian spinning industry was the fourth-largest in the world. In common with the revised view of the English and Indian cases, the Russian industry also shows a surprising and persistent commitment to mule spinning technology. Although rings began to outweigh mules about 60-to-40 after 1890, unlike all the other major spinning industries, preference for mules does not diminish decade by decade thereafter (Table 11). The median count differential between mules and rings is in this case in the expected direction, but it is remarkably small; in fact, it is statistically insignificant before 1910. It is noteworthy that India and Russia display a common stubbornness with respect to mules, despite the wide differences in typical yarn counts in the two cases.

In the three cases just described, the new archival material places more emphasis on the persistence of the mule than had been conventional. There are other newly discovered cases, however, which follow closely the Japanese pattern of rapid diffusion and almost exclusive use of the ring. Brazil is such a case. A substantial Brazilian industry developed in the 1880s which used rings almost

Table 11. Russian Orders of Mule and Ring Spinning Machines 1880–1916

	Mules Machines	Median Spindles per Machine	Ring Machines	Median Spindles per Machine	Percentage of Spindles	
					Mule	Ring
1880–1890	1625	1031	1826	317	74	26
1891–1900	1207	1056	4910	337	44	56
1901–1910	472	1112	1923	376	42	58
1911–1916	334	1159	1523	386	40	60

	Median Counts for Which Machines Rated	
	Mules	Rings
1880–1890	34	32
1891–1900	35	34
1901–1910	35	34
1911–1916	38	34

exclusively (Table 12). The Brazilian industry's commitment to rings was complemented by a heavy concentration on relatively coarse yarns. Note that all the ring spinning machines used in Brazil from 1881 onward came from the reputedly conservative and mule-oriented Platt Bros. of Oldham.

Lest it be thought that a Western Hemisphere consensus on ring spinning prevailed, the interesting though smaller case of Canada's industry provides a counterexample (Table 13). Prior to 1910 the Canadians nearly matched the British in their preference for the mule. The differential in median yarn counts for that period also resembles the British pattern, though the overall median was of course lower. Unlike Britain, however, Canada moved decisively toward rings after 1910, providing us with yet another diffusion scenario.

V. INTERPRETATION

The earlier described simple interpretation of the global pattern of spinning technology diffusion between 1870 and 1920 must now give way to new data which this simple interpretation cannot explain. The slow global diffusion of the ring is not simply an English adjustment to their own worldwide dominance in high-quality yarns. Indeed, the notion of a monotonic association between quality of yarn and choice between the ring and the mule is refuted on both an

Table 12. Brazilian Machinery Orders 1880–1920
(Number of machines)

	Number Mules	Number Rings	Percentage Mules	Percentage Rings
1880–1890	1	257	0.4	99.4
1891–1900	1	374	0.3	99.7
1901–1910	5	683	0.7	99.3
1911–1920	6	664	1.0	99.0

Distribution of Ring Machines by Count

Count Interval	Number of Machines 1880–1890	Percentage
1–20	101	43
21–25	29	12
26–30	26	11
31–35	1	1
36–40	75	32
41–60	—	—
60+	2	1

Table 13. Canadian Orders of Mule and Ring Spinning Machines 1880–1920

	Mules Machines	Median Spindles per Machine	Ring Machines	Median Spindles per Machine	Percentage of Spindles	
					Mule	Ring
1880–1890	28	900	2	325	98	2
1891–1900	66	817	110	302	62	38
1901–1910	87	1050	162	331	60	40
1911–1920	19	922	525	422	8	92

	Median Counts for Which Machines Rated	
	Mules	Rings
1880–1890	21	16.5
1891–1900	48	15.5
1901–1910	40	24
1911–1920	36	36

intranational and international basis. The English used the mule to spin both high-count and low-count yarn. By contrast the Japanese attempted to spin almost the whole quality spectrum using the ring. Many Indian manufacturers used the mule to spin coarser yarns while reserving the ring for relatively better-quality work. The actual magnitude of the mule's persistence generally and in particular with respect to low-count yarns is only now appreciated.

If quality of yarn demand or position in the global yarn market by itself cannot provide a satisfactory explanation of the global pattern of ring and mule use, what other variables might have greater explanatory power? The earlier review of spinning technology suggested that, in addition to quality of yarn demand (count of yarn), considerations such as quality of labor supply (skilled–unskilled, male–female), quality of raw material used (short staple–long stable), industrial organization (integrated spinning–weaving or separate), managerial quality (presence or absence of trained engineers, British advisers), import barriers (output and/or input protection), market institutions (presence or absence of spot markets in output and inputs), and character of local power supply (availability of water) might be important. There is considerable variation in each of these variables across the available national cases, so much so that no single variable can possibly be brought up to the pedestal from which quality of yarn demand has been toppled. For example, England with abundant high-quality mule spinners and India with male labor cheap relative to female labor long persisted with mule machines, but Russia whose Czarist labor force was extremely unskilled (according to Gerschenkron and Rosovsky) also chose to use skill-intensive machines.[21] England's nonintegrated spinners by and large used mules while Japan's nonintegrated spinners used rings, and Canada's integrated mills chose mules. India, with British spinners in many positions of technological leadership, persisted in its use of the mule. Brazil, which for many years also had many British spinners among its founding fathers, used rings.

If the degree of ring diffusion is not easily subject to single variate explanation, it is hardly alone in this among economic processes! In this instance, given the character of both the dependent and independent variables, the risk of specification error and the lack of full quantitative information, we proceed by examining how closely each country case stands in relationship to an implicitly derived multiple regression plane. There are enough variables to ensure that every case can be explained, but it should be recognized that subtly many of the degrees of freedom added by using a large cross-country sample for comparative analysis are being used up. This is tantamount to violating classical statistical canons by adding higher-order terms after observing the output of a multiple regression. Too much like the straight-line regression between two points which was earlier derided, the fit may be excellent but without statistical significance! We acknowledge this risk but believe that certain plausible patterns come through. The reader will have to judge.

A.   United States

Turning first to the American case, it should be recalled that with the cut in energy costs associated with using the Sawyer–Rabbeth spindle and the substantial increases in productivity made possible by its higher speeds, the 1870s and 1880s saw a dramatic increase in the proportion of mills using rings. The typical American mill had weaving and spinning under one roof and sold only cloth, so it did not suffer from the expensive-to-ship wooden bobbins associated with the ring. Furthermore, the local availability and cost advantage of high-quality raw cotton meant that American spinners had relatively less need for the mule, one of whose great virtues was its ability to make use of very short staple cotton. Well before the spindle revolution of the 1870s, American preference for throstles was attributed not to low yarn counts but to the relative cheapness and high quality of American raw cotton, "much finer than that in general use in England."[22] Finally, notwithstanding many decades of mule experience, American mule spinners remained relatively scarce. The more rapid adoption of the ring removed an important labor constraint on textile manufacturing in the United States.[23] Since the Southern industry had integrated mills, cheaper cotton, unskilled labor, and produced coarse yarn, the mule never had a place there.

B.   Japan

By contrast with the American case, how can Japan's early exclusive reliance on mules followed by a dramatic and complete shift to rings be explained? The initial Japanese mills had been distributed around cotton-producing regions with the expectation that they would provide a market for Japan's cotton growers who had been hard hit by the collapse of hand-spinning in the face of competition from Indian cotton yarns. As Japanese cotton is coarse and extremely short-stapled, it is not surprising that the English engineers on whom the Ministry of Agriculture and Commerce and the late Yamabe Takeo, the celebrated president of the Osaka Spinning Mill, advised the use of mules. That the intended buyers of such yarn were geographically dispersed hand-loom weavers, that water power was thought to be readily available, and that male labor was available may also have influenced the English advisers' thinking. Having turned to English machinery manufacturers for advice in the 1870s and 1880s, it was highly probable that mules would be recommended. England was the home of the mule and the English manufacturers were the preeminent producers of such machinery. By contrast, the great developments in ring spinning technology in the 1870s were all American both in origin and development.

The switch from the virtually exclusive use of mules to the virtually exclusive use of rings in the space of four or five years went hand in hand with a number of other major adjustments in Japanese spinning. Whereas during the 1880s the

Japanese cotton spinning industry relied primarily on poor-quality, short-stapled Japanese raw cotton, the switch to rings was accompanied by a large increase in the use of higher-quality Chinese cotton and the significant use by the industry for the first time of still higher quality raw cotton imported from East India. The shift from domestic to imported raw cotton from China and East India, which was almost as complete and dramatic as the shift from rings to mules, was also facilitated by the removal of the 5 percent import duty on such cotton (Table 14).

The change in the type of machine and in the character of raw material was also accompanied by a change in the use of labor. Where the highly profitable, mule-using Osaka Spinning Mill operated in 1884 with an equivalent number of male and female operatives, the largely ring-using industry by 1891 had a labor force which was better than 80 percent female.[24] If the substitution of rings for mules required a higher-quality imported raw material, it did also give the industry opportunity to rely for its labor force primarily on very young girls who required very little training and who were not expected to remain for an extended period in the mills.[25] The opportunity to substitute cheaper unskilled female for potentially skilled male labor made it possible to significantly decrease the number of spindles a spinner might tend. The Japanese industry, while improving the quality of raw cotton which it was spinning, was still spinning with rings a quality of cotton which even mule spinners in England and the United States rarely used. Japanese ring spinning with such cotton made for many more breaks than would have occurred had mules been used. By assigning an unprecedentedly small number of spindles for each spinner to tend and by emphasizing labor-intensive cotton-mixing methods which improved the quality of predominantly short-staple raw cotton by judicious blending of small amounts of longer-stapled cotton, even while it permitted Japanese trading companies latitude in seeking low-cost solutions to the spinners' raw cotton needs,[26] it was possible to operate ring spindles at a very fast speed of 10,000 rpm without having frequent yarn breakages totally undermine efficiency. The increasing use of labor in the preparatory stages, in ring spinning and in reeling the yarn off the wooden bobbin prior to shipment, resulted in a near-doubling of total staffings in Japanese mills relative to the amount of machinery between the late 1880s and 1890s.[27]

Table 14. Japanese Cotton Industry Use of Domestic and Imported Raw Cotton (percentage)

	1883	1884	1887	1892	1893	1894	1895	1896	1897	1898
Domestic	94.3	87.6	86.5	29.1	25.9	23.3	14.8	9.1	6.8	6.0
Imported	5.7	12.4	13.5	70.1	74.1	76.7	85.2	90.9	93.2	94.0

Source: Nōshomushō, *Nihon menshi bōseki kijū* (Tokyo, 1901).

C. India

In understanding the newly discovered persistence of mule purchases by Indian manufacturers it is instructive to view Indian criticism of contrary Japanese practice. In June 1892, a lengthy translation of an article published in the respected *Indian Textile Journal* appears in the Japanese industry journal *Bōren geppō*. Note the following:

> The use of the ring or so many ring spinning machines is one reason for the lack of success of the Japanese spinning industry. The Japanese industry *uses many kinds of cotton and the managers of the new companies are very inexperienced.* When asked why they use the ring they reply that they are operated with success in the United States, England and India and with such reasoning it is no wonder they have met with little success.

The article then goes on to list seven factors which must be considered when deciding between the ring and the mule: (1) What raw materials are being used? (2) What is the technical skill of the workers? (3) What count yarn should be produced? (4) What is the climate? (5) When the yarn is not woven at the same mill, where will it be marketed? (6) What is the availability of repairs and new machines? (7) Is there available water?

In fact, the persistence of mules in India can be explained by most of the same factors which caused the Japanese to initially opt for mules. The relatively poor quality of the local cotton, and the far-flung network of hand-loom weavers to which the machine-made yarn would be shipped, doubtless made English textile machinery manufacturers urge on the Indians as they did the Japanese the adoption of the mule. Having adopted the mule, the Indians, unlike the Japanese, continued to make new purchases even after a ring section developed, in part because male mule spinners in India, unlike Japan, were relatively cheap and because the Indian industry quickly developed major yarn markets at home and abroad which could not be cheaply serviced by wooden bobbin-using rings. Even more important than either of these considerations was India's difficulty in emulating Japanese cotton-mixing practices. Depending on country and count, raw cotton is from 75 percent to 85 percent of the cost of cotton yarn. It was only sophisticated cotton mixing which could undercut the mule's ability to spin a better-quality yarn for a given quality of raw cotton. Because of the natural protection afforded locally grown cotton, the Indians found it relatively difficult to spend resources on efficiently improving the quality of input as a substitute for improving the quality of the machinery. As India came to lose its overseas yarn markets and as power looms improved to the point where more effective competition against the protected domestic hand-loom weavers was possible, interest in the ring greatly increased. Nonetheless, it was well into the first decade of the twentieth century before the Indian industry accepted the superiority of the ring spinning machine for most of the yarn counts spun in India.[28]

D. Russia

The Russian case combines elements of the Japanese and Indian cases plus government intervention, which produced the remarkable persistence for the mule. In its early days the industry faced a large hand-loom industry and a relatively short-staple Russian cotton. Behind a barrier of high effective tariff protection, a large cotton industry had developed as early as the 1840s, using mules and staffed by British engineers. This was true despite the relatively poor quality of Russian labor. Like the Indian case, the relative availability of male labor to some extent compensated for this. The improvements in rings in the 1870s and the successful large-scale importation of American cotton, together with continuing problems in training mule spinners, created the first substantial interest in ring spinning. This interest was reflected in the increase in ring spindleage in the 1880s and 1890s. Following a shift in Czarist policy toward aggressively encouraging Russian cotton growing, a stiff tariff was placed on imported raw cotton at the turn of the century. In 1895 no more than one-quarter of the raw cotton used by the industry was short-staple Russian cotton. Just 15 years later this cotton had largely supplanted the now higher-cost, longer-staple American varieties. The increased cost and deteriorating quality of raw cotton induced the Russian mills to work up their waste cotton, a task for which the mule was virtually required. At the same time a tariff on fine cotton yarns closed off much of the domestic market from outside competition. The combination of low-quality raw material and relatively high median yarn count created a premium on getting the most out of the raw material. The incentives all pointed to a continuing strong role for the mule, even in factories that integrated spinning and weaving.[29]

E. Brazil

In its exclusive use of ring spinning, the Brazilian spinning industry seems close to Japan, but there the similarity ends. In the first instance, as late as 1910 most Brazilian room bosses and mill managers were displaced Lancashiremen. Given their technologically conservative reputation, it may seem surprising that such a group ran an industry which relied entirely on rings. Furthermore, as in Russia, both domestic raw cotton and cotton goods were heavily protected. The major difference is that Brazilian cottons were long-staple arboreal varieties.[30] The same rule of thumb that insisted short-staple cotton should be spun on mules also allowed that, for coarse and medium yarns, high-quality raw cotton could be spun more cheaply on rings. If the British were conservative, it was not a universal preference for mules but a view that the choice of technique was dictated by raw material quality in relation to yarn count.

F. England

The English spinning industry's continuing commitment to mules appears in many ways less anomalous when viewed in this multinational setting. The uneven pace of diffusion of machine spinning and machine weaving created large overseas markets for English yarn. Much as in the Indian case, the survival of the hand-loom weavers supported specialized mule spinners, for whom the heavy wooden ring bobbin would have been a costly burden. The long-distance yarn market was one aspect of the English tradition of vertical specialization, which inclined them against rings. And like both India and Russia, the early start for the industry, in particular the growth during the ascendancy of the self-actor, created a class of skilled and experienced mule spinners. In England, their role had been institutionalized for decades. Finally, though we have criticized Sandberg's assertions about mules and low-count yarns, there is nonetheless a basic element of truth in his observation that the English worldwide supremacy in high-count spinning was a key element in the persistence of mule technology.

Yet all this does not seem to be enough. As the data show, the English commitment to mules continued right up to World War I, though the overseas yarn market had been a declining share of the total for years. High-count yarns cannot explain the preference for mules at low counts as well. And the accumulated experience of mule spinners does not explain the continuing net *expansion* of mule spindles. Other countries with a mule tradition still made some sort of a swing toward rings on new installations before World War I (including the most English-influenced cases, India and Canada). Even the fact of vertical specialization, emphasized by Lazonick, now seems less decisive. On the one hand, there are many international exceptions to this rule (Japan in one direction, Russia in the other). On the other, this explanatory variable itself requires explanation.

Before invoking the now unfashionable concept of "entrepreneurial failure," can we find other elements unique to England which might help to explain the unique aspects of the English preference for mules? In many of our examples, the key was cotton supply, either as an initial determinant (India, Brazil) or as an object of choice with simultaneous implications for the ring–mule decision (Japan, Russia). England, of course, had no local cotton and hence had an initial raw material cost disadvantage vis-à-vis virtually all competitors. What Lancashire did have was Liverpool, which offered "an established market for more different growths of cotton than has any other market in the world" (Cox, 1928, p. 84). Copeland's classic account pointed to the ready availability of short-staple cottons as a factor distinguishing England from the United States:

> In spinning the lower counts more short staple cotton is used in England than in this country. The English purchase more short staple, and they rework more of the waste from the card and comber, thus economising in raw material. This shorter staple would not stand the strain of the ring frame as well; the ends would break more frequently. (1909, p. 129)

By using the mule, the English spinners made use of a machine which unlike the ring could use a great variety of cotton to spin a given count of yarn. By virtue of their technology they sought low-cost solutions on extremely short notice for better than 75 percent of their input cost! This flexibility in raw cotton use, which was compatible with the intermittent character of mule spinning, allowed the British to respond not just to demands for commercial yarns and high-quality fabrics, but numerous other nonstandardized and variegated products. One of the unique aspects of the English position, as viewed by the same special agents who reported on Japan, India, Russia, and numerous other countries, was the presence of foreign merchants with offices in Manchester. Reportedly there was no parallel to this in any other textile manufacturing center (Hause, 1912, p. 6).

It was not just organizational inertia that perpetuated vertical specialization but the presence of highly developed markets in raw cotton (and relatively well developed markets in yarn), which removed much of the incentive toward vertical integration, allowing highly distinct managerial talents to find niches and pass market survival tests in spinning and weaving separately.[31] If the degree of vertical specialization was the structural feature that constrained the switch to rings, this was not a constraint that English manufacturers were trying very hard to break down. As an example of a possible alternative, the machinery manufacturers had struggled for years to adapt the lightweight paper tube to the ring spindle, as an alternative to the heavy wooden bobbin. By the early 1900s, they had had considerable success, selling an increasing number of ring machines equipped with paper tubes (see Table 15). But almost all of these buyers were on the Continent; the English spinners themselves showed almost no interest. It appears to us that the English attachment to the mule was distinctly positive, and not best attributed to constraints, rigidities, and inertia.

Finally, no account of ring-mule competition would be complete if it did not recognize that there were honest differences of opinion, persisting into the 1920s, about the relative advantages and the ultimate outcome of the ring–mule struggle. How else can we explain the Canadian preference for mules, and the fault-finding comments of the American visitors concerning the "English idea . . . that filling yarn should be spun on mules, and also that 'feel' is preferable to strength in cloth."[32] The English approached the matter with the knowledge that both basic techniques had coexisted and evolved for better than a century, and during that time many claims had proved unfounded. As a writer for the *Cotton Factory Times* commented in 1886:

> Fifty years ago throstle frames were going to supercede mules for yarn spinning, but after a short spell of popularity they went down. Then it was the ring frame that was going to revolutionize the trade, but still mules went on being erected. . . . Many mills are even now being filled by the much maligned mules, and many more will be filled which have not yet been started. As soon as ring frame makers prove that their machines can produce better and cheaper yarn than the mule they will get the trade. Until they do this no amount of puffing and letter writing will get their frame on the market. (April 23, 1886, p. 1)

Table 15. Orders of Ring Spinning
Machines with Paper Tubes, Platt Bros
and Dobson–Barlow 1890–1914

	Twist	Weft	Not Specified	Total
1890			23	23
1891	13		29	42
1892			61	61
1893	9	16	38	63
1894	5	43	56	104
1895	56	39	70	165
1896	43	4	82	129
1897	12	1	127	140
1898	10	12	48	70
1899	5	25	47	77
1900	41	9	59	109
1901	92	40	132	264
1902	100	38	81	219
1903	122	56	150	328
1904	59	53	56	168
1905	154	41	254	449
1906	121	30	133	284
1907	102	36	394	532
1908	179	77	215	471
1909	69	51	191	311
1910	121	36	305	462
1911	151	25	345	521
1912	117	33	279	429
1913	135	21	293	449
1914	60	5	50	115

The English may well be considered ''complacent'' in not recognizing that the
mule's underpinnings were shaky, but it was a well-educated complacency.

VI. CONCLUSION: THE BIG PICTURE

It is no coincidence that the central themes that emerge from our multinational
survey are similar to the themes of the Parker article with which we opened, and
its sequel, ''Technology, Resources and Economic Change in the West.'' Nineteenth-century technologies chiefly involved mechanical processing of natural
materials, constrained by nature's vagaries in material composition and fuel.
Though the ring offered great improvements in processing speed and therefore
effective labor productivity, there was a cost in terms of material handling and
flexibility. Within the limits of nineteenth-century science, the diffusion of the

ring was constrained initially by the locational geography of high-quality cotton and subsequently by ingenuity in devising alternatives like cotton mixing. Ring technology made steady progress, but so long as the cotton itself remained inviolate, there was a sizable market niche for the mule, a quintessential nineteenth-century machine in its respect for the cotton fibers. Ironically from an economist's perspective (but there are many other historical analogies), where markets were most highly developed to accommodate variety in cottons and give it appropriate valuation, the incentives to innovate along material-productivity lines were weakest. Twentieth-century science has transformed the entire process by creating synthetic fibers with uniform staple length, nullifying the advantage of a machine whose forte was getting quality yarn out of short or irregular staples. But even before the artificial-fiber revolution, the high degree of fiber control achieved under the Casablancas or "high draft" system virtually removed the underlying advantage of intermittent spinning. The system involved elastic bands or "aprons" which effected a minute sorting of the individual fibers prior to spinning. The conventional date for Casablancas is 1913, but the system was only perfected for commercial use in the mid-1920s, after which installation of new mules virtually ceased worldwide.

Overlaid on this struggle of man over nature are the variety of national industry histories, which serve to illustrate the second theme of the Parker articles, the extremely limited character of the nineteenth-century diffusion of industrial culture. Most of the world's great spinning industries seem to have behaved sensibly, adhering to rules of thumb pointed out by contemporary American and British observers and advisers (though we cannot establish with our data that these decisions were efficient in any rigorous sense). Only Japan moved to escape these dicta decisively, combining relatively short-staple cotton with an exclusive reliance on ring spinning technology. When long-drafting and other improvements made ring spinning the dominant technology in the 1920s, Japan was well positioned to take charge of large segments of the world textile market.

NOTES

1.   William N. Parker, "Economic Development in Historical Perspective," *Economic Development and Cultural Change* 10(October 1961): 5.

2.   In speculating on reasons for widening technological transfer after 1870, Parker emphasizes the relative decline in purely mechanical inventions and a redirection of invention into chemistry and subatomic physics. Cotton textiles, which was relatively uninfluenced by such redirections in inventive activity, was the only industry to achieve global status between 1870 and 1920.

3.   The British–American cases are analyzed in Lars Sandberg, "American Rings and English Mules," *Quarterly Journal of Economics* 83(February 1969), and William Lazonick, "Factor Costs and the Diffusion of Ring Spinning in Britain Prior to World War I," *Quarterly Journal of Economics* 96(February 1981). On India and Japan, see S. D. Mehta, *The Cotton Mills of India, 1854–1954* (Bombay: 1954); N. Takamura, *Nihon bōsekigyō shi josetsu* (Tokyo: 1969); and Y. Kiyokawa, "Indo menkōgyō ni okeru gijutsu to shijō no keisei ni tsuite," *Keizai kenkyū* (July 1976).

4.   Mule spinning technology is described in M. T. Copeland, *Cotton Manufacturing Industry of the United States* (Cambridge, Mass.: 1912), and W. Scott Taggart, *Cotton Spinning* (London: 1920).

5.   Ring spinning technology is described in Copeland, *Cotton Manufacturing;* Taggart, *Cotton Spinning;* and David Jeremy, "Innovation in American Textile Technology during the Early Nineteenth Century," *Technology and Culture* 14(1973).

6.   The classic account of the eighteenth-century inventions is Paul Mantoux, *The Industrial Revolution in the Eighteenth Century* (London: 1928), Chap. II.

7.   For a recent study stressing the prolonged diffusion of the self-actor, see William Lazonick, "Industrial Relations and Technical Change," *Cambridge Journal of Economics* 3(September 1979).

8.   M. T. Copeland, "Technical Development in Cotton Manufacturing Since 1860," *Quarterly Journal of Economics* 24(November 1909): 122. On the complementarity between self-actor and throstle in England, see G. N. von Tunzelman, *Steam Power and British Industrialization to 1860* (New York: 1978), pp. 185–192.

9.   Warp yarn, unlike weft yarn, needs to be rewound before weaving. If a ring mill did its own warping before shipping the yarn to a weaving mill, the initial spinning on bobbins was inconsequential. See Copeland, "Technical Developments," and Lazonick, "Factor Costs."

10.   Nathan Rosenberg, "Factors Affecting the Diffusion of Technology," *Explorations in Economic History* 10(Fall 1972).

11.   D. W. Farnie, "Platt Bros. & Co., Ltd. of Oldham," *Business History* 23(1981): 84–85. Farnie presents a time series of ring and mule shipments for Platt Bros. alone, separating the export market from the home market. Another recent study which uses the textile machinery company records for different purposes is Robert Kirk and Colin Simmons, "Engineering and the First World War," *World Development* 9(August 1981).

12.   Lazonick, "Factor Costs," pp. 100 and 104–107. A more general discussion of the organizational shortcomings of the British industry may be found in Lazonick, "Competition, Specialization, and Industrial Decline," *Journal of Economic History* 41 (March 1981).

13.   T. Kinugawa, *Hompō menshi bōseki shi* (Osaka: 1937), vol. 2.

14.   Spectacular fires of suspicious origin in the two largest Japanese mule mills contributed to this process. See Saxonhouse, "A Tale of Technological Diffusion in the Meiji Period," *Journal of Economic History* 34(March 1974).

15.   *Dai nippon bōseki rengōkai geppō* (June 1901).

16.   For examples, see Mehta, *The Cotton Mills of India;* Frank Harris, *Jin Tata: A Chronicle of His Life* (London: 1925); D. E. Wacha, *The Life and Work of J. N. Tata* (Madras: 1915); and N. Takamura, *Nihon bōsekigyo shi jōsetsu* (Tokyo: 1969). Virtually all of the errors documented here are repeated in the most recent study, by Dwijendra Tripathi, "Innovations in the Indian Textile Industry: The Formative Years," in Akio Okochi and Shin-Ichi Yonekawa (eds), *The Textile Industry and Its Business Climate* (Tokyo: 1982), pp. 176–77.

17.   The figures for rings and mules were based on a pro-rata extrapolation to the estimated total spindles, and came by way of R. Robson, *The Cotton Industry in Britain* (London: 1957), p. 355. See Lazonick, "Factor Costs," p. 96, note 6.

18.   Of the companies employing more than 500 in 1913, only two are missing from the sample. Of these, Brooks and Doxey was an early ring pioneer, but Hetherington is known to have been a major producer of mules. From Hetherington catalogs we are able to document more than 900,000 mule spindles constructed between 1908 and 1920, so that our totals for investment in new mules are undoubtedly understated. The employment figures may be found in Kirk and Simmons, "Engineering and the First World War," p. 775.

19.   John Ryan, "Machinery Replacement in the Cotton Trade," *Economic Journal* 40(December 1930): 576. Ryan's article has major shortcomings as a study of replacement patterns, which may arise from the author's affiliation with the Lancashire Cotton Corporation, a government effort to

consolidate and rationalize the industry. While the sample may not be representative, Ryan's reported age profile for machinery (in comparison with the age profile of our investment series) implies that 75 percent of mules installed in the 1880s were still operating in 1930.

20. Note that we do not follow the Sandberg–Lazonick practice of adjusting the ring figures upward by a factor of 1.3, converting them into "mule equivalent spindles" (m.e.s.). It is true that ring spindles were faster and hence produced more yarn in a given time period; but it is equally true that mules added more value of yarn to a given value of raw cotton, creating a downward bias in mule totals, especially at lower counts. Though there is no "true" measure of capacity, we prefer to keep the compilation of the raw data as separate as possible from the debate over efficiency and profitability.

21. A. Gerschenkron, "Economic Backwardness in Historical Perspective," in B. Hoselitz (ed.), *The Progress of Underdeveloped Countries* (Chicago: 1952); H. Rosovsky, *Capital Formation in Japan* (New York: 1961).

22. David Jeremy, *Transatlantic Industrial Revolution* (Cambridge, Mass.: 1981), pp. 65–66, 192, and 249.

23. A closely related discussion of the role of labor and choice of technique in American cotton spinning is contained in William Lazonick, "Production Relations, Labor Productivity and Choice of Technique: British and U.S. Cotton Spinning," *Journal of Economic History* 41(September 1981). The role of rings in blocking incipient organization by mule spinners is acknowledged in Sandberg, *Lancashire in Decline*, pp. 63–64.

24. Kinugawa, vol. 2, p. 193; *Dai nippon bōseki rengōkai geppō* (August 1891).

25. Saxonhouse, "A Tale of Technological Diffusion in the Meiji Period," *Journal of Economics History* 39(March 1974); and Saxonhouse and Wright, "Two Forms of Cheap Labor in Textile History," in this volume.

26. *Nichimen nanajūnenshi* (Osaka, 1957).

27. *Dai nippon bōseki rengōkai geppō* (August 1891).

28. In W. A. Graham Clark, *Cotton Fabrics in British India* (1907), it is observed that in 1906 mules were preferred on Indian cotton for spinning yarns above 26s and on most of the coarser counts. The preference for mules for counts above 26 continued to be reported in Ralph Odell, *Cotton Goods in British India* (1917).

29. Ralph Odell, *Cotton Goods in Russia* (1913); S. J. Chapman, *The Cotton Industry and Trade* (London: 1905), pp. 125–127.

30. Stanley Stein, *Brazilian Cotton Manufacture* (Cambridge, Mass.: 1957), pp. 45–49; W. A. Graham Clark, *Cotton Goods in Latin America* (1910), pp. 28–29 and 38.

31. See particularly S. J. Chapman, *The Cotton Industry and Trade*, pp. 44–45; J. M. Hause, *English Methods of Dyeing, Finishing, and Marketing Cotton Goods* (1912), pp. 8–9. Uncertainty in raw material supply as a motive for vertical integration is stressed in Alfred Chandler, *The Visible Hand* (Cambridge, Mass.: 1977).

32. W. A. Graham Clark, *Cotton Goods in Canada* (1913), p. 34.

REFERENCES

Barnshaw, Charles (1930). *High Drafting in Spinning*. London.

Catling, Harold (1970). *The Spinning Mule*. Great Britain: David & Charles.

Chandler, Alfred D. (1977). *The Visible Hand*. Cambridge, Mass.: Harvard University Press (Belknap).

Chapman, Sidney J. (1905). *The Cotton Industry and Trade*. London.

Clark, W. A. Graham (1907). *Cotton Fabrics in British India and the Phillipines*. U.S. Department of Commerce and Labor, Bureau of Manufactures, Special Agents Report No. 13.

———— (1910). *Cotton Goods in Latin America, Pt II.* U.S. Department of Commerce and Labor, Bureau of Manufactures, Special Agents Report No. 36.

———— (1913). *Cotton Goods in Canada.* U.S. Department of Commerce and Labor, Bureau of Foreign and Domestic Commerce, Special Agents Report No. 69.

Copeland, Melvin T. (1909). "Technical Development in Cotton Manufacturing Since 1860," *Quarterly Journal of Economics* 24(November).

———— (1912). *The Cotton Manufacturing Industry of the United States.* Cambridge, Mass.: Harvard University Press.

Cox, Alonzo B. (1928). "Marketing American Cotton in England." U.S. Dept. of Agriculture Technical Bulletin 69.

Farnie, D. A. (1981). "Platt Bros. & Co., Ltd. of Oldham, Machine-Makers to Lancashire and the World: An Index of Production of Cotton Spinning Spindles, 1880–1914." *Business History* 23.

Gerschenkron, Alexander (1952). "Economic Backwardness in Historical Perspective," in B. Hoselitz (ed.), *The Progress of Underdeveloped Countries.* Chicago: University of Chicago Press.

Harley, C. K. (1974). "Skilled Labour and the Choice of Technique in Edwardian Industry." *Explorations in Economic History* 11(Summer):391–414.

Harris, Frank (1925). *Jin Tata: A Chronicle of His Life.* London.

Hause, J. M. (1912). *English Methods of Dyeing, Finishing, and Marketing Cotton Goods.* U.S. Department of Commerce and Labor, Bureau of Manufactures, Special Agents Report No. 56.

Jeremy, David (1973). "Innovation in American Textile Technology During the Early Nineteenth Century." *Technology and Culture* 14.

———— (1981). *Transatlantic Industrial Revolution.* Cambridge, Mass.: MIT Press.

Kinugawa, T. (1937). *Hompō menshi bōseki shi.* Osaka.

Kirk, Robert, and Colin Simmons (1981). "Engineering and the First World War." *World Development* 9(August).

Kiyokawa, Y. (1976). "Indo menkōgyō ni okeru gijutsu to shijō no keisei ni tsuite." *Keizai kenkyū* (July).

Lazonick, William (1979). "Industrial Relations and Technical Change: The Case of the Self-Acting Mule." *Cambridge Journal of Economics* 3(September).

———— (1981a). "Factor Costs and the Diffusion of Ring Spinning in Britain Prior to World War I." *Quarterly Journal of Economics* 96(February).

———— (1981b). "Competition, Specialization and Industrial Decline." *Journal of Economic History* 41(March).

———— (1981c). "Production Relations, Labor Productivity, and Choice of Technique: British and U.S. Cotton Spinning." *Journal of Economic History* 41(September).

Mantoux, Paul (1928). *The Industrial Revolution in the Eighteenth Century.* London. [Original French edition, 1906.]

Mehta, S. D. (1954). *The Cotton Mills of India, 1854–1954.* Bombay.

Noguera, J. (1937). *Modern Drafting in Cotton Spinning.* Leeds: Pickersgill, 1937.

Odell, Ralph M. (1913). *Cotton Goods in Russia.* U.S. Department of Commerce and Labor, Bureau of Manufactures, Special Agents Report No. 51.

———— (1916–1918). *Cotton Goods in British India.* U.S. Department of Commerce, Bureau of Foreign and Domestic Commerce, Special Agents Report Nos. 124, 127, 138, 149, and 157.

Parker, William N. (1961). "Economic Development in Historical Perspective." *Economic Development and Cultural Change* 10(October).

———— (1973). "Technology, Resources and Economic Change in the West," in A. J. Youngson (ed.), *Economic Development in the Long Run.* New York: St. Martin's Press.

Pearse, Arno S. (1930). *The Cotton Industry of India.* Manchester, England.

Robson, R. (1957). *The Cotton Industry in Britain.* London: Macmillan.

Rosenberg, Nathan (1972). "Factors Affecting the Diffusion of Technology." *Explorations in Economic History* 10(Fall).

Rosovsky, Henry (1961). *Capital Formation in Japan*. New York: Free Press.

Ryan, John (1930). "Machinery Replacement in the Cotton Trade." *Economic Journal* 40(December).

Sandberg, Lars (1969). "American Rings and English Mules: The Role of Economic Rationality." *Quarterly Journal of Economics* 83(February).

———— (1974). *Lancashire in Decline*. Columbus: Ohio State University Press.

Saxonhouse, Gary (1974). "A Tale of Technological Diffusion in the Meiji Period." *Journal of Economic History* 39(March).

Stein, Stanley (1957). *Brazilian Cotton Manufacture*. Cambridge, Mass.: Harvard University Press.

Taggart, W. Scott (1920). *Cotton Spinning*. London.

Takamura, N. (1969). *Nihon bōsekigyō shi jōsetsu*. Tokyo.

Tippett, L. H. C. (1969). *A Portrait of the Lancashire Textile Industry*. New York: Oxford University Press.

von Tunzelman, G. N. (1978). *Steam Power and British Industrialization to 1860*. New York: Oxford University Press (Clarendon).

Wacha, D. E. (1915). *The Life and Work of J. N. Tata*. Madras: Granach.

Research in Economic History
Edited by Paul Uselding
Chairman, Department of Economics
University of Illinois

This annual series is devoted to the dissemination on original research in the field of economic history. Editorial selection places stress upon original interpretations of the economic past and work that adds to the body of empirical knowledge of the field. There are no limitations with respect to time period or national orientation. Contributions are selected from scholars who are recognized experts in their specialization, and individual volumes represent the best available work in the profession in a particular year. The individual essays are comparable in quality to those appearing in established journals, although frequently they will be of greater length thereby permitting in depth coverage of a particular topic that is frequently essential in the field of economic history. Editorial philosophy does not adhere to a particular time period, restricted set of topics or methodology. The point of view expressed is that economic history is an intellectually vigorous field and the series seeks to portray the breadth and vitality of that discipline.

Volume 1, 1976,
ISBN 0-89232-001-X

REVIEWS: "... the appearance of an important new outlet is cause for rejoicing ... a major publication offering work of the highest quality. He is off to a good start."
—Journal of Economic History

"Without exception, the papers are of good quality and deal with questions that should interest social as well as economic historians ..."
— Journal of American History

"... Volume 1 includes work not only in economic history but in institutional and modern social history as well ... Volume 1 is very good..."
—Business History Review

"... One can only hope the quality of articles remains as high as this initial offering."
—Agricultural History

CONTENTS: Foreword, *Paul Uselding.* **Manufacturing in the Antebellum South,** Fred Bateman, *Indiana University and Thomas Weiss, University of Kansas.* **Transference and Development of Institutional Constraints Upon Economic Activity,** J.R.T. Hughes, *Northwestern University.* **Three Centuries of American Inequality,** Peter H. Lindert and Jeffrey G. Williamson, *University of Wisconsin.* **English Open Fields as Behavior Towards Risk,** Donald N. McCloskey, *University of Chicago.* **The Business Advisory Council of the Department of Commerce, 1933-1961: A Study in Corporate/ Government Relations,** Kim McQuaid, *Northwestern University.* **Stagflation in Historical Perspective: The Napoleonic Wars Revisited,** Joel Mokyr, *Northwestern University and N. Eugene Savin, University of British Columbia and Cambridge University.* **Cross-Spectral Analysis of Long Swings in Atlantic Migration,** Larry Neal, *University of Illinois.* **Socio-Economic Patterns of Migration from the Netherlands in the Nineteenth Century,** Robert P. Swierenga, *Kent State University and Harry S. Stout, University of Connecticut.* **In Dispraise of the Muckrakers: United States Occupational Mortality, 1890-1910,** Paul Uselding.

Volume 2, 1977,
ISBN 0-89232-036-2

REVIEWS: "This volume contains an unusal variety of papers, several of which are refreshingly different from the usual run of journal articles ... Most of the papers ... diverge in length or approach..." *—Journal of Economic History*

"...The various authors...exemplify the sophistication and competence, as well as the occasional over-commitment to particular techniques, which British historians cannot yet match. They also exemplify the sort of 'relevance' at which the best economic historian has always aimed."
—The Economist

CONTENTS: Foreword. *Paul Uselding.* **A Bicentenary Contribution to the History of the Cost of Living in America,** Paul A. David and Peter Solar, *Stanford University.* **Depletion and Diplomacy: The North Pacific Seal Hunt, 1886-1910,** D.G. Paterson and J. Wilen, *University of British Columbia.* **Imperialism and Economic Development: England, The United States and India in the Nineteenth Century,** Harold D. Woodman, *Purdue University.* **The Growth of the Great Lakes as a Major Transportation Resource, 1870-1911,** Samuel H. Williamson, *University of Iowa.* **Land and Money in the Spartan Economy - A Hypothesis,** John Buckler, *University of Illinois.* **High Fertility in Mid-Nineteenth Century France: A Multivariate Analysis of Fertility Patterns in the Arrondissement of Lille,** Paul G. Spagnoli, *Boston College.* **An Economic History of Urban Location and Sanitation,** Louis P. Cain, *University of British Columbia and Loyola University-Chicago.*

Supplement 1 - Recent Developments in the Study of Economic and Business History Essays in Memory of Herman E. Krooss
Edited by **Robert E. Gallman,** *University of North Carolina*

1977
ISBN 0-89232-035-4

REVIEW: "... Given the quality of the essays, with their general success in meeting the initial assignment of surveying and extending recent research and providing bibliographic aid, the volume makes an excellent reference work for scholars as well as for graduate students."
—Journal of Economic History

CONTENTS: Preface, *Robert E. Gallman.* **Recollections of Herman Krooss,** Thomas C. Cochran, *University of Pennsylvania.* **Krooss on Executive Opinion,** J.R.T. Hughes, *Northwestern University.* **Business History: A Bibliographical Essay,** Ralph W. Hidy, *Harvard University.* **Twentieth Century Railroad Managerial Practices: The Case of the Pennsylvania Railroad,** Stephen M. Salsbury, *University of Delaware.* **Financial Intermediaries in Economic History: Quantitative Research on the Seminal Hypotheses of Lance Davis and Alexander Gerschenkron,** Richard Sylla, *North Carolina State University.* **Issues in Monetary Economics and Their Impact on Research in Economic History,** Michael D. Bordo, *Carleton*

University and Anna J. Schwartz, National Bureau of Economic Research. **Population Issues in American Economic History: A Survey and Critique,** Richard A. Easterlin, University of Pennsylvania. **Studies of Technology in Economic History,** Paul Uselding, University of Illinois. **Recent Research in Japanese Economic History, 1600-1945,** Kozo Yamamura, University of Washington. **Some Recent Developments in the Study of Economic and Business History in Western Germany,** Wolfram Fischer, Free University of Berlin. **Comparative Economic History,** Rondo Cameron, Emory University.

Volume 3, 1978,
ISBN 0-89232-056-7

REVIEWS: "...consistently excellent selection of articles. There is none of the uneven quality that often characterizes eclectic collections."
—*Business History Review*

CONTENTS: Foreword, Paul Uselding. **The Rhythm of Growth in the Atlantic Economy of the Eighteenth Century,** Brinley Thomas, University of California - Berkeley. **Growth Rates at Different Levels of Income and Stage of Growth: Reflections on Why the Poor Get Richer and the Rich Clow Down,** W.W. Rostow with the Assistance of Frederick E. Fordyce, The University of Texas -Austin. **Public Finance in the Jewish Economy in Interwar Palestine,** Nachum T. Gross and Jacob Metzer, The Hebrew University of Jerusalem and the Falk Institute. **Urban Growth and Economic Structure in Antebellum America,** Diane Lindstrom and John Sharpless, University of Wisconsin. **Discrimination and Exploitation in Antebellum American Cotton Textile Manufacturing,** Richard K. Vedder, Lowell E. Gallaway and David Klingaman, Ohio University. **Social Savings Due to Western River Steamboats,** Erik F. Haites, University of Western Ontario and James Mak, University of Hawaii. **Productivity in the Antebellum South: The Western Tobacco Region,** Donald F. Schaefer, North Carolina A & T State University. **An Appraisal of Some Recent Developments in the History of Economic Institutions in America,** Louis Galambos and Steven Sass, The Johns Hopkins University. **Entrepreneurship and the American Economy-A Sketch,** J. R.T. Hughes, Northwestern University. **Cliometrics versus Institutional History,** Peter D. McClelland, Cornell University.

Volume 4, 1979,
ISBN 0-89232-080-X

REVIEWS: "...a stimulating collection which is justifiably held by its editor to be 'a representative sampling of the most interesting new work'...The papers all relate to major topics in mainstream British or American economic history."
—*Economic History Review*

"Paul Uselding has performed yet another valuable service to the profession in editing this fine volume. —*Agricultural History*

CONTENTS: Foreword, Paul Uselding. **A Simple Model of the Kondratieff Cycle,** W.W. Rostow and Michael Kennedy, University of Texas. **Schumpeterian Waves of Innovation and Infrastructure Development in Great Britain and the United States: The Kondratieff Cycle Revisited,** Raymond S. Hartman and David R. Wheller, Boston University and Massachusetts Institute of Technology. **The Profitability of Northern Agriculture in 1860,** Fred Bateman, Indiana University and Jeremy

Atack, University of Illinois. **The Farm Enterprise: The Northern United States, 1820-1860s,** Clarence H. Danhof, Sangamon State University. **Urban Improvement and the English Economy in the Seventeeth and Eighteenth Centuries,** E.L. Jones, LaTrobe University and M.E. Falkus, London School of Economics and LaTrobe University. **Occupational Structure, Dissent and Educational Commitment: Lancashire, 1841,** Alexander James Field, Stanford University. **Industrial Work and the Family Life Cycle, 1889-1890,** Michael R. Haines, Cornell University.

Volume 5, 1980,
ISBN 0-89232-117-2

REVIEW: "Volume 5 of this annual compilation of research attest to the continuing vitality and diversity of the field. This fine collection of extended essays virtually encompasses the world and exhibits a variety of approaches. No common thread ties these contributions together, yet they suggest direction of research in the postcliometric era."
—*Technology & Culture*

CONTENTS: Foreword, Paul Uselding. **Patterns of Industrialization in the Nineteenth and Early Twentieth Centuries: A Cross-Sectional Quantitative Study,** Irma Adelman, University of California-Berkeley and Cynthia Taft Morris, American University. **The Agriculture and Commercial Revolution in Japan,** Kozo Yamamura, University of Washington. **The Tobacco Industry in the Chesapeake Colonies, 1617-1730: An Interpretation,** Russell R. Menard, University of Minnesota. **Emigration from the British Isles to the New World, 1630-1700: Inferences from Colonial Population,** Henry A. Gemery, Colby College. **Growth of the U.S. Social Welfare System in the Post WW II Era: The U.M.W., Rehabilitation, and the Federal Government,** Edward Berkowitz, University of Massachusetts-Boston. **Subsistence Crises and Political Economy in France at the End of the Ancien Regime,** John W. Rogers, Jr., Stanhome International, Inc.

Volume 6, 1981,
ISBN 0-89232-119-9

CONTENTS: Foreword, Paul Uselding. **Climate Change in European Economic History,** John L. Anderson, LaTrobe University. **The Tonnage of Ships Engaged in British Colonial Trade during the Eighteenth Century,** John J. McCusker, University of Maryland. **The U.K. Money Supply, 1870-1914,** Michael David Bordo, Carleton University. **The Development of Steamboats on the Volga River and its Tributaries, 1817-1865,** Richard Mowbray Haywood, Purdue University. **Entrepreneurship and Technical Progress in the Northeast Coast Pig Iron Industry: 1850-1913,** Robert C. Allen, University of British Columbia. **Rent Movements and the English Tenant Farmer, 1700-1839,** J.R. Wordie, University of Reading. **Bank Deposit Currency Before 1700 A.D.,** Morris A. Copeland, Cornell University (emeritus).

Volume 7, 1982, 372 pp. Institutions: $47.50
ISBN 0-89232-198-9 Individuals: $23.75

CONTENTS: **The Structure of Pay in Britain, 1710-1911,** Jeffrey G. Williamson, University of Wisconsin. **Legally Induced Technical Regress in the Washington Salmon Fishery,** Robert Higgs, University of Washington. **Fiscal Incidence and Resource Transfer Between Jews and Arabs in Mandatory Palestine,** Jacob Metzer, Hebrew University of Jerusalem. **Regional Exports to**

Foreign Countries: United States, 1870-1914, William Hutchinson, Miami University. The Fertility of American Slaves, Richard Steckel, Ohio State University. A Gerneral Equilibrium Model of the 18th Century Atlantic Slave Trade: A Least-Likely Test for the Caribbean School, William A. Darity, Jr. University of Maryland, University of Texas, and National Urban League Research Department. Melanesian Labor and the Development of the Queensland Sugar Industry, 1863-1906, Ralph Shlomowitz, The Finders University of South Australia.

Supplement 2 · Variations in Business and Economic History Essays in Honor of Donald L. Kemmerer
Edited by **Bruce R. Dalgaard**, Director, Center for Economic Education, University of Minnesota

1982,
ISBN 0-89232-262-4

CONTENTS: Preface. Bruce R. Dalgaard, Foreword, Albro Martin, Harvard University. The Canadian Newsprint Industry, 1900-1940, Robert Ankli, Associate Professor of Economics, University of Guelph. E.W. Kemmerer: The Origins and Impact of the "Money Doctor's" Monetary Economics, Bruce R. Dalgaard, Director, Center of Economic Education, University of Minnesota Government and Business in Early Eighteenth Century England: Anticombination Acts and the Stability of the Newcastle Coal Cartel, 1700-1750, William J. Hausman, Associate Professor of Economics, University of North Carolina, Greensboro. Regulations Without Historical Justification: The Case of Household Moving, Dana Hewins, Associate Professor of Economics, Ohio University. Labor Absorption: Conventional Wisdom and Additional Data for Latin America, John M. Hunter, Professor of Economics and Director, Latin American Studies Center, Michigan State University. African Entrepreneurs: A Case Study of Nigerian Industrialists, 1964-1965, E. Wayne Nafziger, Professor of Economics, Kansas State University. The Civilian Conservation Corps: A Work Fare Solution, Robert F. Severson, Jr., Professor of Economics, Central Michigan University. U.S. Teacher Organizations and the Salary Issue, 1900-1960, Robert J. Thornton, Associate Professor of Economics, Lehigh University. A New Look at the Gold Standard: Is Donald Kemmerer Right?, Richard K. Vedder, Professor of Economics, Ohio University. Some Monetary Standard of Value Concepts of the Latter Nineteenth Century, Richard Winkleman, Associate Professor of Economics, Arizona State University. The New Economic History and Capitalist Growth: The Moral Perspective, Stephen T. Worland, Professor of Economics, University of Notre Dame.

Volume 8,   1983,
ISBN 0-89232-261-6

CONTENTS: U.S. Economic Growth, 1783-1860, Stanley L. Engerman, University of Rochester and Robert E. Gallman, University of North Carolina-Chapel Hill. The Development of the Russian Petroleum Industry, 1872-1900, John P. McKay, University of Illinois, Urbana-Champaign. Causal Theories About The Origins of Agriculture, Frederic L. Pryor, Swarthmore College. Railroad Cartels Before 1887: The Effectiveness of Private Enforcement of Collusion, Thomas S. Ulen, University of Illinois, Urbana-Champaign. Asset Markets and Investment Fluctuations in Late Victorian Britain, Barry J. Eichengreen, Harvard University.

Creating Coordination in the Modern Petroleum Industry: The American Petroleum Institute and the Emergence of Secondary Organizations in Oil, Joseph A. Pratt, Texas A&M University. Regional Preferences and Migrant Settlement: On the Avoidance of the South by Nineteenth Century Immigrants, James A. Dunlevy, Miami University. The Telegraph and the Structure of Markets in the United States, 1845-1890, Richard B. Du Boff, Bryn Mawr College. British Rearmament and Industrial Growth, 1935-1939, A.J. Robertson, University of Manchester.

Volume 9,
ISBN 0-89232-415-5

CONTENTS: The Performance of the British Cotton Industry, 1870-1913, William Lazonick, Harvard University and William Mass, University of Massachusetts/Boston. Agricultural Output and Efficiency in Lower Canada, 1851, Frank D. Lewis, Queen's University, Canada and R. Marvin McInnis, Queen's University, Canada. A Cross-Section Study of Legitimate Fertility in England and Wales in 1911, N. F. R. Crafts, University College, Oxford. Notes on Economic Efficiecny in Historical Perspective: The Case of Britain, 1870-1914, William P. Kennedy, London School of Economics. The Economic Policy of the Mandatory Government in Palestine, Nachum T. Gross, The Hebrew University of Jerusalem and The Falk Institute. Bank Deposits and the Quantity of Money in the U.K., 1870-1921, Forrest Capie, The City University, London and Alan Webber, The City University, London. Energy Sources for the Dutch Golden Age: Peat, Wind and Coal, Richard W. Unger, University of British Columbia.

DATE DUE
